lonely pl

D0440521

15786

# Karakoram Highway

## John King
## Bradley Mayhew

**Karakoram Highway**

**3rd edition**

**Published by**
**Lonely Planet Publications**
Head Office: PO Box 617, Hawthorn, Vic 3122, Australia
Branches: 155 Filbert St, Suite 251, Oakland, CA 94607, USA
10a Spring Place, London NW5 3BH, UK
71 bis rue du Cardinal Lemoine, 75005 Paris, France

**Printed by**
SNP Pte Ltd, Singapore

**Photographs by**

| | |
|---|---|
| Greg Caire | Bradley Mayhew |
| Richard I'Anson | John Mock |
| John King | Bernard Napthine |
| Robert Matzinger | Julia Wilkinson |

Front cover: Man crossing suspension bridge, Hunza, Pakistan (Jonathan Blair)
Opposite page 9: KKH Memorial plaque, Pattan, Kohistan (Bradley Mayhew)

**First Published**
August 1989

**This Edition**
March 1998

GV
199.44
.K37
K56
1998
C.2

**Although the authors and publisher have tried to make the information as accurate as possible, they accept no responsibility for any loss, injury or inconvenience sustained by any person using this book.**

National Library of Australia Cataloguing in Publication Data

King, John (John S.).
Karakoram Highway.

3rd ed.
Includes index.
ISBN 0 86442 531 7.

1. Karakoram Highway (China and Pakistan) - Guidebooks. I.
Mayhew, Bradley. II Title.

915.491

text & maps © Lonely Planet 1998
photos © photographers as indicated 1998
climate charts of Gilgit compiled from information supplied by Patrick J Tyson, © Patrick J Tyson, 1998

### John King

John King grew up in the USA, destined for the academic life (in past incarnations he was a university physics teacher and an environmental consultant), but in a rash moment in 1984 he headed off to China to have a look around. Since then he has eked out a living as a travel writer, encouraged by his wife, Julia, who is also one. Together with their two children they split their time at 'home' between south-west England and remoter parts of Hong Kong. John has spent nine months as a traveller in Pakistan and fourteen months as an English teacher and traveller in China.

He is also co-author of Lonely Planet's *Pakistan, Central Asia, Russia, Ukraine & Belarus, Portugal* and *Czech & Slovak Republics* travel survival kits and of the *Prague* city guide.

### Bradley Mayhew

Bradley started travelling in south-west China, Tibet and northern Pakistan while studying Chinese at Oxford University. Upon graduation he fled to Central America for six months to forget his Chinese and then worked in Beijing in a futile attempt to get it back. Since then he has spent two months in the Silk Road cities of Bukhara and Khiva, two months trekking in Kyrgyzstan and has enjoyed extended trips to Iran, Eastern Turkey and Ladakh. He has been to Pakistan five times and is the co-author of Lonely Planet's *Pakistan*.

Bradley has also lectured on Central Asia at the Royal Geographical Society. He splits his time between Sevenoaks in south-east England and Las Vegas, Nevada.

---

## From the Authors

**John King** We're very grateful to Kim O'Neil and John Mock for advice, updates, corrections and contacts, and to John for last-minute research in Gilgit. Thanks to Dan Prior for help with Central Asian history.

For the cyclists' notes and other text, we are indebted to James Davies. Thanks also to Gavin Fox, Paul Cook and David Pindar, and Sue Hall of the Cyclists' Touring Club in the UK.

Expanded regional histories owe much to discussions with Karimullah Khan (Morkhun), who also provided a fine introduction to the Boiber Valley; Ejazullah Baig, Baltit Fort librarian, who shared documents and images; and the Balti scholar SM Abbas Kazmi, who helped with the Balti language. Others who helped with language info are Ablimit Ghopor (Kashgar) and Mohammad Jaffar (Gulmit).

For further work on their excellent Geology section we thank Dr Michael Searle of Oxford University and Dr Peter J Treloar of Kingston University. For an update on AKRSP work in the Northern Areas I am grateful to Sajjad Hussain in Gilgit. Thanks also to Katherine Hinckley, Director of Communications at the Aga Khan Foundation, for reviewing text.

For his monograph on Xinjiang's Turkic opposition, thanks to Dr Michael Dillon at the University of Durham. James Seymour at Columbia University provided information on homosexuality in Xinjiang.

Thanks to staff at WWF-Pakistan (especially Basit Khan and Qammer Naveed) and at IUCN-Pakistan (especially Richard Garstang in Islamabad, Saquib Hanif in Karachi and Amjad Tahir Virk in Gilgit) for good help with information, images and publications.

For hospitality and much help, thanks to Latif Anwar and Ali Anwar of Chalt, Abdul Bari Rana of Chorit and Ghulam Raza of Bagrot. Others who helped are Akbar Abdirakhman and John Hu (Kashgar), Niyatullah Baig (Tashkurgan), Manzoor Hussain (Karimabad), Ikram Beg and Abbas Ali (Gilgit) and Mohammad Iqbal (Skardu). Special thanks to Zang Bing of CITS Ürümqi.

For fine hospitality, thanks to Mohammad Yaqoob and to Mitch and Carol Ryan (Gilgit), Jehangir (Punial) and Sher Nabi (Gakuch).

Finally, love and thanks to Julia Wilkinson, Kit and Lia, for putting up with me and frequently making do without me.

**Bradley Mayhew** Thanks to Anwar Sajid and Saeed Anwar of PTL; SN Malik of Adventure Travel Islamabad; Mr Zulfiqar, manager of Pine Park in Shogram; and Tayhib in Naran. Best wishes to Michael Thetmacher and Fita Muhammed in Madyan and many thanks for their expert info on Swat. Several PTDC officials were unusually helpful: Khalid Khan (Abbottabad), Fazl-e-Rahim (Saidu Sharif), Shaheristan Khan (Besham), and Muhammed Nazeer Qureshi (Islamabad). Many thanks to Richard Garstang and Minna Pyhälä of IUCN Islamambad for detailed information on national parks and endangered species, and to Ms Aban Marker Kabraji of IUCN Karachi for additional information. Above all, thanks to John King for answering a thousand tiny questions on just about everything – that's the price you pay when two obsessive compulsives get together.

## This Edition

This 3rd edition of *Karakoram Highway* includes improved cyclists' notes in each chapter, an extension of the Geology section to Xinjiang, information on Pakistan's national parks, updates of Pakistan's Byzantine visa procedures, a section on online services, information for gay/lesbian and disabled travellers, an enlarged section on food in Xinjiang and northern Pakistan, expanded language notes, and more detailed regional histories.

Research for updating the introductory chapters was by BM and JK, with JK at the keyboard. On the ground, JK concentrated on Xinjiang and the Northern Areas, and BM on Indus Kohistan, Hazara and Rawalpindi-Islamabad.

## This Book

John King has toiled over this book since its inception, writing all three editions. The first two editions were solo efforts and Bradley Mayhew helped revise and expand this one.

## From the Publisher

This edition was edited by Martin Hughes of Lonely Planet's Melbourne office with distraction from Russell Kerr. Linda Suttie played grown-up and proofed the final product.

Between them, Lonely Planet's Bill 'n' Ben (aka Paul Piaia and Mark Germanchis) contrived to put the book together through mapping, design and layout. The cover design is down to Adam McCrow, and thanks to Trudi Canavan for additional illustrations. Thanks finally to David Andrew for the feathered touch and to Carolyn Papworth for suggesting that Martin take notice of the production manual.

## Thanks

Many thanks to the travellers who used the last edition and wrote to us with helpful hints, useful advice and interesting anecdotes. Your names appear on page 278.

## Warning & Request

Tourism continues to grow along the KKH. Hotels and restaurants are sprouting; prices are climbing; and jeep roads pushed into remote valleys. At the time of writing, inflation was on the order of 10% in China and Pakistan, so prices in this book will go out of date quickly. If you find the book isn't quite right any more, please write to Lonely Planet and help us make the next edition better.

We value all of the feedback we receive from travellers. Julie Young coordinates a small team who read and acknowledge every letter, postcard and email, and ensure that every morsel of information finds its way to the appropriate authors, editors and publishers.

Everyone who writes to us will find their name in the next edition of the appropriate guide and will also receive a free subscription to our quarterly newsletter, *Planet Talk*. The very best contributions will be rewarded with a free Lonely Planet guide.

Excerpts from your correspondence may appear in new editions of this guide; in *Planet Talk*; or in updates on our Web site - so please let us know if you don't want your letter published or your name acknowledged.

# Contents

# Map Legend

## BOUNDARIES

............... International Boundary

.......... State/Provincial Boundary

.................. Disputed Boundary

## ROUTES

........ Karakoram Highway (KKH)

.................................. Highway

...................... Secondary Road

.............................. Jeep Track

.............................. Town Road

.............................. Town Street

.............................. Town Lane

.......... Train Route, with Station

.......... Metro Route, with Station

........................... Walking Track

................. Cable Car or Chairlift

## AREA FEATURES

.................................... Building

.................................. Cemetery

...................................... Glacier

...................................... Market

.......................... Park, Gardens

........................................ Rock

.............................. Urban Area

## HYDROGRAPHIC FEATURES

........................................ Canal

.................................. Coastline

.............................. Creek, River

.............. Lake, Intermittent Lake

.................... Rapids, Waterfalls

...................................... Salt Lake

...................................... Swamp

## SYMBOLS

○ **CAPITAL** ......... National Capital

◉ **CAPITAL** ....... Provincial Capital

● **CITY** .......................... City

● **Town** ...................... Town

● Village ...................... Village

■ .............. Place to Stay

Å ....... Camping Ground

⛊ ........... Caravan Park

⌂ ............. Hut or Chalet

▼ .............. Place to Eat

🍺 ............... Pub or Bar

✈ ...................... Airport

... Ancient or City Wall

❸ ...................... Bank

🐦 ........... Bird Sanctuary

🏖 ...................... Beach

⌒ ...................... Cave

✝ .................. Church

⌒⌒⌒ .... Cliff or Escarpment

☯ .................. Embassy

🏯 ......................... Fort

⛳ .............. Golf Course

卍 ........... Hindu Temple

✚ .................. Hospital

※ .................. Lookout

⚱ ................. Monument

☪ .................. Mosque

▲ ...... Mountain or Peak

🏛 .................... Museum

← .......... One Way Street

🅿 ................... Parking

)( ...................... Pass

⛽ ........... Petrol Station

★ ........... Police Station

✉ ............... Post Office

∴ ...................... Ruins

🕍 ............ Sikh Temple

◎ ...................... Spring

🏛 ........... Stately Home

☎ ............... Telephone

🛕 .................. Temple

▣ ...................... Tomb

❶ .... Tourist Information

⊖ ............... Transport

🐘 ........................ Zoo

*Note: not all symbols displayed above appear in this book*

**SIGNAL COMPANY**

SOMETIME IN THE FUTURE WHEN OTHERS WILL PLY THE
KKH, LITTLE WILL THEY REALISE THE AMOUNT OF SWEAT
COURAGE, DEDICATION, ENDURANCE AND HUMAN SACRIFICE
THAT HAS GONE INTO THE MAKING OF THIS ROAD, BUT AS
YOU DRIVE ALONG, TARRY A LITTLE, TO SAY A SHORT
PRAYER FOR THOSE SILENT BRAVE MEN OF THE
PAKISTAN ARMY, WHO GAVE THEIR LIVES TO REALISE A
DREAM, NOW KNOWN AS

**THE KARAKORAM HIGHWAY**

# Introduction

Between the Central Asian desert and the plains of Pakistan is a geographical vortex that is rich with history, natural beauty and cultural diversity. In this 'collision zone' of the Indian and Asian continents, the Pamir, Kunlun, Hindukush, Karakoram and Great Himalaya ranges are knotted together and China, Tajikistan, Afghanistan, Pakistan and India all come within 250km of each other.

In the 1960s and 1970s, Pakistan and China jointly cut a road across these mountains, following a branch of the ancient network of trade routes called the Silk Road. In 1986 their mutual border was opened to travellers, completing an Asian 'high road' loop taking in Pakistan, China, Tibet, Nepal and north India.

The Karakoram Highway (KKH) connects the Silk Road oasis of Kashgar with Rawalpindi and Islamabad, Pakistan's capital, via the 4730m Khunjerab Pass, the semi-mythical Hunza Valley and the trading post of Gilgit. Despite half a dozen languages, the region crossed by the Highway has an identity of its own, defined by religion (almost everyone is Muslim), commerce (from the Silk Road era to present-day Kashgar-Gilgit barter trade), a demanding environment and a sense of alienation from greater China or Pakistan.

Within reach of the KKH is some of the most mind-bending mountain scenery anywhere and, in the Karakoram, the highest concentration of lofty peaks and long glaciers in the world, some virtually at the edge of the road. As the 20th-century scholar-traveller John Staley wrote: 'This is terrain in which even birds in flight are seen against a background of mountains.'

9

**Note to Visitors**
Many westerners have exaggerated fears of travel in Central Asia, and of Islamic fundamentalism. In fact Xinjiang and the KKH are among Asia's safest destinations, and the Muslim peoples along the KKH are likely to offer you only unfeigned hospitality. What *can* cause ill-will, however, are insults to Islamic sensibilities, in particular about dress. Clothes revealing the shape of the body or significant flesh beyond face, hands and feet, especially on women, are offensive to most Pakistanis. On the KKH, only in Islamabad will you find substantial acceptance of western dress or western attitudes.

The other urge likely to anger Pakistanis is photographing women without permission, even in liberal-minded communities like the Ismailis. The Muslims of Xinjiang are less vocal about these matters. ■

The region is also dense with history and artefacts, from the campaigns of Alexander the Great to the 19th-century rivalry between the British and Russian empires. It was through here that Buddhism first reached China and Tibet. In a sense, history is still alive in the camel caravans of Xinjiang and the tribal traditions of Indus Kohistan. Some of that history is disappearing before our eyes, in part because of the KKH itself.

Travel is cheap; going overland from one end to the other can cost less than US$45. Theoretically you could make the 1300km trip in 48 hours, but you might go crazy trying to do it in less than two or three weeks. Tourist development is accelerating but still mercifully modest outside Gilgit and Karimabad. And – at least for men and mixed couples – the Islamic tradition of hospitality can make visiting northern Pakistan a pleasure.

One thing KKH travel doesn't have is predictability. You may experience first-hand the fickleness of the Karakoram: steep and loose to begin with, shattered by KKH construction, always trying to bury the road. Rockfalls, floods and mud introduce unplanned delays. This is a frustrating place to be on a fixed schedule.

In Pakistan the Highway can sometimes feel like a tunnel of ragged roadside bazaars, slapped together to take advantage of the money coming through, and not at all typical of what may lie half a km away. The best of the KKH is usually off the road.

This book describes what you can find within a few days' village-hopping from the Highway. It goes from north to south because that direction prolongs the good weather in the best travelling season, September-October.

# Facts about the Region

## HISTORY

Although it straddles some of the highest mountains in the world, the KKH region is held together by several historical currents. These are the Silk Road and the spread of Buddhism; the arrival of Islam; imperial struggles, particularly the 'Great Game' between Britain and Russia; and of course the Highway itself.

On the other hand, the mountains have so hindered communication and movement that local histories are quite distinct. Each regional chapter, therefore, also has its own historical introduction.

### Early History

Over 4000 years ago a rich farming and trading culture flourished in the Indus Valley as far north as Gandhara (the historical name for the Peshawar Valley), but collapsed under an influx of Central Asian tribes which historians call Indo-Aryans, starting about 1700 BC. Under the Indo-Aryans and the Persian Achaemenian Empire (approximately 6th century BC to 4th century AD), Hinduism was born in the south.

After defeating the Achaemenians in 330 BC, Alexander of Macedonia (Alexander the Great) crossed the Hindukush, resting in the spring of 326 BC at Taxila, capital of Gandhara, not long before a mutiny of his troops ended his expansion.

This short visit resonates in the legends of northern Pakistan. Some tribes claim descent from Alexander or his stay-behind generals. Some people of the Northern Areas do have arrestingly Mediterranean features. Anthropologists are doubtful, though the visitors may well have enlivened local gene pools.

### Silk Road & the Flowering of Buddhism

A local king, Chandragupta, founded India's first empire, the Mauryan dynasty, which at its peak covered most of the subcontinent. The most famous (and last) Mauryan king was Ashoka (272-235 BC), a patron of the new philosophy of Buddhism, who developed Taxila as a centre for religious study.

After Ashoka's death, Hindu backlash and invasions by Bactrian Greeks, Central Asian Scythians (or Sakas) and Persian Parthians dragged Gandhara through 250 years of chaos.

Meanwhile, in China the Han dynasty was pushing its frontiers west and south over a growing network of trade routes that later came to be called the Silk Road. From the early Han capital of Chang'an (now Xian), a line of oases skirted north and south around the Takla Makan Desert to Kashgar. From there, tracks ran west across the Pamir and Turkestan (Central Asia) to Persia (Iran), Iraq and the Mediterranean, and south across the Karakoram to Kashmir. Caravans went west with porcelain, silk, tea, spices and seeds of peach, orange and other trees, and brought back wool, gold, ivory, jewels and European delicacies such as figs and walnuts – as well as new ideas.

Bandits from Mongolia, Tibet and the little Karakoram state of Hunza made these expeditions dangerous, often impossible, and Han emperors spent vast resources policing the road. Most powerful of these outlaws was the nomadic Mongolian alliance known as Xiong-nu (ancestors of the Huns who later terrified India and Europe).

Among the tribes driven south by the Han and the Xiong-nu, the Yüeh-chih (or Kushans) made the most of it and, by the 1st century AD, controlled an empire spanning Kashgar, most of the Karakoram, the Hindukush and northern India. Under the Kushan dynasty, finally centred in Gandhara, Buddhism experienced an artistic and intellectual flowering and spread up the Indus into Central Asia, China and Tibet. The Silk Road became as much a cultural artery as a commercial one.

In Gandhara, Buddhism found expression in an extraordinary fusion of Indian and Greek artistic styles. In monasteries across the Tarim Basin, wealthy merchants and pilgrims commissioned works in another fusion of styles – Chinese and Indian – which reached its height during the Tang dynasty from the 7th to 9th centuries.

The Kushans had fallen to the Persian Sassanians by the end of the 3rd century, and Taxila was destroyed by the Hephthalites (or White Huns) in the 5th century. But pilgrims continued to travel overland to Gandhara and India, providing the only detailed accounts of the Karakoram at that time. The best known of these travellers is the Chinese monk Fa Hsien, who, on a 15 year journey across Turkestan and the Karakoram to India, found Buddhism still dominant in early 5th century Gandhara. Hsuan Tsang, another monk traveller in the 7th century, found Buddhism fading, carried on by monks who no longer seemed to understand their own scriptures.

Nourished by Kushan patronage and fertile soil along the Silk Road, Buddhism left an extraordinary record in western China and northern Pakistan, from the cave frescoes of Dunhuang (Gansu) and Bezeklik (near Turfan in present-day Xinjiang) to the petroglyphs at Ganesh and Chilas, the bas-relief Buddha figures near Gilgit and Skardu, and the fabulous trove of sculpture at Taxila.

After the 8th century, a Hindu revival under the Shahi dynasty probably pushed Hinduism as far north as Gilgit.

## Historical Summary, KKH Region

| | |
|---|---|
| 2300-1700 BC | Harappa or Indus Valley Civilisation |
| 1500-1000 BC | Aryan invasions; birth of Hinduism |
| 563-483 BC | Life of Buddha |
| 560-330 BC | Persian Achaemenian Dynasty |
| 336-323 BC | Hellenic Empire of Alexander the Great |
| 321-185 BC | Mauryan Empire; patronage of Buddhism under Ashoka |
| 206 BC-220 AD | Chinese Han Dynasty; growth of Silk Road |
| 70 -240 | Kushan Empire; spread of Buddhism on Silk Road |
| 399-414 | Fa Hsien's journey from China to India |
| 570-632 | Life of Muhammad, founder of Islam & the Arab Empire |
| 618-907 | Chinese Tang Dynasty; Silk Road flourishes |
| 629-633 | Hsuan Tsang's journey from China to India |
| 711 | Arab naval expedition to the mouth of the Indus |
| 714 | Arab expeditions visit Tarim Basin & Indus Valley |
| 752 | Tang Dynasty displaced from Tarim Basin by Turks |
| 870-1001 | Hindu Shahi Dynasty; Hindu resurgence in Indus Valley |
| 977-1186 | Ghaznavid Dynasty in Afghanistan & north-west India |
| 999-1211 | Qarakhan Dynasty, Tarim Basin; appearance of Islam there |
| 1206-27 | Campaigns of Genghis Khan; start of Mongol Empire |
| 1369-1405 | Campaigns of Timur (Tamerlane) |
| 1526 | Babar takes Delhi; founding of Moghul Empire |
| 1600 | Charter granted to British East India Company |
| 1755 | Tarim Basin falls to Qing (Manchu) Dynasty |
| 1757 | Battle of Plassey (Bengal); beginning of Moghul decline |
| 1799 | Ranjit Singh founds Sikh Empire from Lahore |
| 1838-42 | First Anglo-Afghan War |
| 1846 | First Anglo-Sikh War; creation of Kashmir state |
| 1849 | Second Anglo-Sikh War |
| 1857-58 | Great Mutiny (Sepoy Rebellion); British Raj begins |
| 1862-75 | Muslim rebellions in China |
| 1867-77 | Yaqub Beg's rule over Kashgaria |
| 1877, 1889 | British Agency at Gilgit opened, re-opened |

## Advent of Islam, Decline of the Silk Road

An Arab navy reached the coast of what is now Pakistan in 711 and Arab armies from Persia visited Kashgar and Gilgit at about the same time, but it wasn't until the 11th century that Islam began to establish itself in this region.

Muslim Turkic raiders from Afghanistan, led by the warlord Mahmud of Ghazni, battered the Indus Valley in the early 11th century. Ultimately, the Persian-influenced Ghaznavid Empire spanned Afghanistan and the north-west of the subcontinent, destroying the Hindu kingdoms of the Indus Valley and paving the way for a series of Turkic-Afghan sultanates that ruled from Delhi from the 13th to 15th centuries. Conversion to Islam was widespread, for pragmatic as well as spiritual reasons.

In Turkestan the Silk Road was fading along with the Tang dynasty. The Tarim Basin fell to the Turks in the 8th century and then to a series of Turkic and Mongol kingdoms, among them the Qarakhan in the 9th to 12th centuries. The earliest appearance of Islam in Turkestan was under the Qarakhan.

In the early 13th century, the Mongol armies of Genghis Khan had subdued Central Asia and began raiding south into the

| | |
|---|---|
| 1878 | Xinjiang Province created under Qing Dynasty |
| 1878-80 | Second Anglo-Afghan War |
| 1882, 1890 | Russia, then Britain, open Kashgar consulates |
| 1897, 1907 | Anglo-Russian agreements on Pamir boundaries |
| 10 October 1911 | Chinese Revolution; end of Chinese dynasties |
| 7 November 1917 | Russian Bolshevik Revolution |
| 1931-34 | Muslim uprisings in Xinjiang |
| March 1940 | Muslim League demands a separate Pakistan |
| 1944-49 | Xinjiang independence as Republic of East Turkestan |
| 14 August 1947 | Partition; independence of Pakistan & India |
| 1 November 1947 | Gilgit Uprising against the Maharajah of Kashmir |
| 1947-48 | India-Pakistan War; UN ceasefire January 1949 |
| 1 October 1949 | Founding of People's Republic of China |
| October 1958 to March 1969 | Martial law in Pakistan under Ayub Khan |
| 1960 | Pakistan starts Indus Valley Road, Swat-Gilgit |
| September 1965 | India-Pakistan War |
| 1966 | Start of work on the Karakoram Highway |
| March 1969 to January 1972 | Martial law in Pakistan under Yahya Khan |
| December 1971 | India-Pakistan War; secession of Bangladesh |
| January 1972 to July 1977 | Zulfikar Ali Bhutto, civilian president of Pakistan |
| 1974 | Bhutto ends autonomy of Northern Areas princely states |
| July 1977 to August 1988 | Martial law under General Zia ul-Haq |
| 4 April 1979 | Bhutto hanged |
| December 1979 | Karakoram Highway finished in Pakistan |
| August 1982 | Khunjerab Pass opens to official traffic & trade |
| 1 May 1986 | Khunjerab Pass opens to tourism |
| November 1988 | Benazir Bhutto becomes prime minister, dismissed August 1990 |
| October 1990 | Nawaz Sharif becomes prime minister, dismissed April 1993 |
| 25 December 1991 | USSR dissolves into constituent republics |
| October 1993 | Benazir Bhutto again becomes prime minister, dismissed November 1996 |
| February 1997 | Nawaz Sharif again becomes prime minister |
| February 1997 | Riots in Yining, bomb explosions in Ürümqi and Korla |
| 1997 | Peace talks between Pakistan and India |

subcontinent. With the largest contiguous land empire in history cleared by the Mongols of bandits and boundaries, the Silk Road enjoyed a last burst of activity into the 14th century. Europeans, now forced to take note of Asian power, also took an interest in Asia itself; Marco Polo made (or made up) his epic journeys during this time. The subsequent eclipse of the Silk Road has been variously attributed to the arrival of Islam, the collapse of the Mongols, and the drying up of oasis streams.

Of the Muslim invaders from Central Asia the cruelest was Timur (known in the west as Tamerlane), a Turkic warlord from the western Pamir, who at the end of the 14th century savaged the Islamic cultural centres of Asia – including Kashgar and Delhi – in the name of 'purification'. Paradoxically, his capital city of Samarkand was one of the most splendid and cultured in Asia, full of his spoils.

The final nail in the Silk Road's coffin was the discovery in 1497 of a sea route from Europe around Africa to India by the Portuguese navigator Vasco da Gama. By this time the entire region now spanned by the KKH was Muslim, but it was in total disarray, fractured by quarrelling remnants of the Mongol Empire in the north, petty chieftains in the mountains and Timur's successors and Pathan (Pashtun) tribes in the south. A traveller wouldn't have stood a chance on any long-distance roads.

In 1526 Zahiruddin Babur, ruler of Kabul, displaced king of Ferghana and Samarkand, and descendant of both Timur and Genghis Khan, marched into Delhi to found a line of Persian-speaking Turkic Muslim emperors of India known as the Moghuls (a corruption of 'Mongol', local parlance for anybody from Central Asia). For six generations, often harassed by Pathans west of the Indus, they presided over a 'Golden Age' of Islamic art, architecture, literature and music, across what is now Pakistan and north India.

### Britain, Russia & the 'Great Game'

In 1600 Queen Elizabeth granted monopoly trading rights in Asia to a small merchant group, the East India Company. Starting with one-off expeditions to the Bay of Bengal for cotton and spices, within 50 years they had established a permanent presence on the subcontinent, trading under Moghul grants, gaining territory and influence by cunning and keeping it by force, gradually edging out French, Dutch and Portuguese competition.

The defeat of a Moghul viceroy in 1757 at the Battle of Plassey in Bengal demonstrated the strength of 'the Company' at the expense of the Moghuls, and trade began to give way to plain old imperialism. A century later, a mutiny in the Bengal army set off a two year rebellion against the British. After it was put down, the crown in 1858 took control of Company territory, bringing the Moghul Empire to a formal end. The 'Raj' (Britain's Indian Empire) by then covered most of present-day India, through alliance or direct control. (The East India Company later distinguished itself by introducing opium to China, in exchange for tea.)

Meanwhile, in Turkestan, a Manchu army marched into Kashgar in 1755 and the Tarim Basin fell within China's Qing (Manchu) dynasty for a century. A series of Muslim rebellions in the 1860s weakened its grip, but in 1878 Qing authority was tightened and a formal province, Xinjiang ('New Dominions'), was created.

To the west, Russian expansionism had triggered the Crimean War in 1853. Within 15 years, Russia was to take an area the size of Europe between the Caspian Sea and the Pamir, and to start eyeing Xinjiang and Afghanistan.

The British, anxious about this (and ever eager to trade) set out to pacify their insecure north-west frontier. In 1839 their installation of a hand-picked ruler in Afghanistan led to an uprising, a death-march from Kabul by the British garrison and a vengeful 'First Afghan War'. By the end, Britain's puppet was murdered and his predecessor back on the throne. This failure to control or befriend the headstrong Afghans was repeated in an equally ill-fated 1878 invasion.

Pathans from west of the Indus, in the course of tormenting the Moghuls, gave control of Lahore to an aggressive 19-year-old

Sikh chief named Ranjit Singh in 1799. Over the next three decades he carved out his own little military state across the Punjab, the Kashmir Valley, Ladakh, Baltistan, Gilgit, Hazara and the Peshawar Valley, and pushed the Pathans back to the Khyber Pass.

A treaty barring expansion into 'Company' India was violated by Ranjit's successors, and in 1846 the British fought the first of two short, bloody wars with the Sikhs and annexed Kashmir, Ladakh, Baltistan and Gilgit. Renaming the whole package as 'the State of Jammu and Kashmir', they sold it for £750,000 to a sycophantic Hindu prince named Gulab Singh, declaring him the first maharajah of Kashmir and thereby creating a friendly buffer state on the Russian flank. A second Sikh War brought an end to the Sikh state, and Britain took the Punjab and the Peshawar Valley.

With a grip now on the 'Northern Areas,' Britain began a cat-and-mouse game with Russia across the vaguely mapped Pamir and Hindukush. Agents posing as scholars, explorers, merchants and even Muslim preachers crisscrossed the mountains, mapping them, spying on each other, courting local rulers and staking subtle claims like dogs in a vacant lot. The British nicknamed it the 'Great Game'; the Russians , the 'Tournament of Shadows'.

In 1882 Russia established a consulate in Kashgar. A British Agency at Gilgit, opened briefly in 1877, was urgently reopened after the Mir (ruler) of Hunza entertained a party of Russians at Baltit Fort in 1888. Britain set up its own Kashgar office in 1890.

In advanced stages of the Game the British tried to persuade reluctant Afghan and Chinese authorities to assert a common border in the Pamir, sealing Russia's southward moves. In 1890 Francis Younghusband (later to head a British incursion into Tibet) was sent to do some politicking with Chinese officials in Kashgar. On his way back through the Pamir he found the range crawling with Russian troops, and was told to get out or face arrest.

This electrified the British, who raised hell with the Russian government and invaded Hunza the following year; at the same time Russian troops skirmished in north-east

Francis Younghusband was a notable 19th century explorer of the Karakoram region.

Afghanistan. After a burst of diplomatic manoeuvring, Anglo-Russian boundary agreements in 1897 and 1907 gave Russia most of the Pamir and established the Wakhan Corridor, the awkward tongue of Afghan territory that stretches across to meet Xinjiang.

The Pamir settlement merely shifted the focus of the Great Game toward Kashgar, where the two powers went on conniving over Turkestan (see the History section in the Kashgar to Tashkurgan chapter).

### 'Autonomous' Xinjiang

On both sides of the Karakoram the idea of a separate state appealed to Muslims living under non-Muslim rule. In the 1930s a fierce anti-Chinese insurrection raged across Xinjiang, contained only with the covert help of Stalin's USSR. An independent Republic of East Turkestan, declared at the end of WWII, foundered when the People's Republic of China was declared in 1949.

Despite the 1955 declaration of Xinjiang as an 'Autonomous Region', a cycle of anti-Chinese violence and government crackdowns has continued (see History in the Kashgar to

Tashkurgan chapter). While little more than a pinprick in china's political hide, unrest in this region threatens not only China's human rights image and relations with its Central Asian neighbours, but investors' interest in the Tarim Basin's natural resources: a quarter of China's natural gas reserves and 15% of its oil reserves are there.

## Muslim Pakistan

In India, as pressure for independence grew after WWI, Muslim-Hindu disagreement over how to achieve it was echoed in communal violence in the 1920s and 1930s. The idea of a Muslim state was first proposed by the philosopher-poet Alama Mohammed Iqbal in 1930 and adopted in 1940 as a platform of the All-India Muslim League.

In the end, Britain was forced to grant separate independence to a Muslim-majority Pakistan and a Hindu-majority India. Following the public announcement of the borders between the two countries, a few days after the formal Partition date of 14 August 1947, Muslims fled westward and Hindus and Sikhs eastward, some six million in each direction, probably the biggest mass population transfer in history. In riots and hideous massacres on both sides, between 200,000 and a million people were killed.

As 14 August came and went, Maharajah Hari Singh delayed his decision on whether Kashmir should accede to India or Pakistan, in hopes of remaining free of both. In October a band of Pathan tribesmen invaded Kashmir, having been told the maharajah was about to join India. This he promptly did. India flew troops into Kashmir and Pakistan moved in its own, and the two countries went to war. The Kashmiri governor was arrested at Gilgit and Muslim militiamen and soldiers there demanded to join Pakistan. A United Nations ceasefire in January 1949 gave each country a piece of Kashmir to administer, a 'temporary' arrangement that after half a century is looking rather permanent, though neither side will say so.

India and Pakistan again fought over Kashmir in 1965 and 1971. The latter war was followed by the secession of East Pakistan,

which became Bangladesh. In 1984 Indian and Pakistani troops moved up into the region of the Siachen Glacier, where the UN ceasefire line was vaguely drawn; intermittent hostilities ever since then have been called 'the world's highest war'.

At the end of 1989 the Indian army moved heavily into Kashmir to suppress a growing Muslim 'intifada', which India accuses Pakistan of bankrolling, and 1990 saw another war scare. To make matters more complex, a growing movement among Kashmiri militants supports an independent Kashmir.

In 1997 the election of new governments in both Pakistan and India, plus the crippling pressure of defence expenditures in Pakistan (over one-quarter of its annual budget), led to new peace talks and a surge of optimism that the Kashmir issue might be nearing a resolution. For further background on the political scene in the Northern Areas, see the History section in the Gilgit Region chapter.

## The Karakoram Highway

China, following its invasion of Tibet in 1950, occupied parts of Ladakh, Baltistan and the upper Shimshal Valley in the mid-

### Why a Road?

The KKH is a great travel opportunity, but what's it for? At such a cost in lives and displaced production – especially for the Chinese at the height of the Cultural Revolution – it was obviously more than a joust with nature. The mountain crossing gives both countries a back door for mutual aid, but the road is too fragile to be a strategic asset. Cross-border trade remains minimal.

The original Indus Valley Road from Swat to Gilgit was the Northern Areas' first-ever all-weather connection to the outside world, and the Pakistan government presumably hoped development would bind the north closer to the rest of the country. In fact this seems the most plausible reason for the KKH as a whole. In the 1980s and 1990s both Pakistan and China have consolidated their grips on independent-minded outer regions, particularly through control of communications and transport.

Both countries continue to improve the KKH into an all-weather road, and China is at work on a railway line from Ürümqi to Kashgar. ■

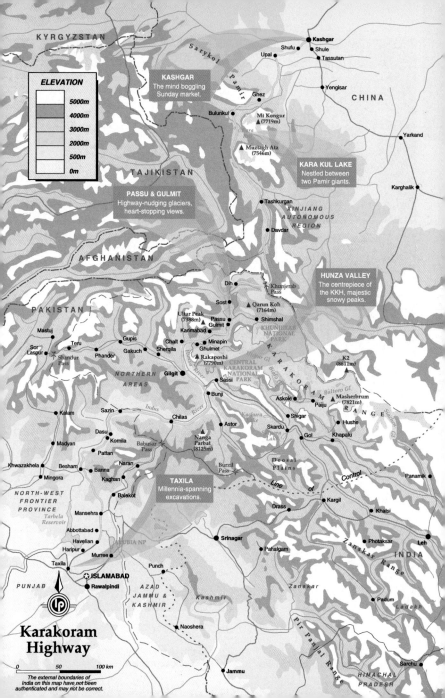

KYRGYZSTAN

Sarykol Pamir

Shufu · Shule · **Kashgar**
Upal · · Tassutan

Ghez · · Yengisar     CHINA

Bulunkul · · Mt Kongur
         ▲ (7719m)

**KASHGAR**
The mind boggling
Sunday market.

Yarkand

▲ Muztagh Ata
   (7546m)

TAJIKISTAN

Karghalik

**KARA KUL LAKE**
Nestled between
two Pamir giants.

· Tashkurgan   XINJIANG
               AUTONOMOUS
· Davdar        REGION

**PASSU & GULMIT**
Highway-nudging glaciers,
heart-stopping views.

AFGHANISTAN

Dih ·   Khunjerab
        ✝ Pass

**HUNZA VALLEY**
The centrepiece of
the KKH, majestic
snowy peaks.

PAKISTAN

Sost ·   ▲ Qarun Koh
            (7164m)

Ultar Peak ·   · Shimshal
(7388m)  Passu
         Gulmit
Mastuj ·  Karimabad   KHUNJERAB
                      NATIONAL
Chalt ·   · Minapin    PARK
Sor    Teru · Gupis  Sherqila · Ghulmet
Laspur ·  · Phander  Gakuch · **Rakaposhi**
  Shandur              (7790m)                K2
  Pass                                        (8611m)
        NORTHERN      · **Gilgit**    CENTRAL
         AREAS                       KARAKORAM
                      · Sassi       NATIONAL         ▲ Masherbrum
                                     PARK    Askole ·  (7821m)
                      · Bunji              Paiju ·   R A N G E
Kalam ·   Sazin ·                   Askole ·
                      · Chilas   Kachura    · Shigar   · Hushe
Dasu ·              Lake      Skardu ·  Gol   · Khapalu
Madyan ·  Komila ·    · Astor                · Hushe
      Pattan          ▲ Nanga
Khwazakhela · Besham   Parfat    Burzil
              Banna    (8125m)   Pass        Deosai
Mingora ·  Naran ·                           Plains       Panamik ·
  NORTH-WEST  Kaghan ·          Burzil              Line  of  Control
  FRONTIER    Balakot ·         Pass                        Kargil ·
  PROVINCE                                Drass ·            Khatsi ·
     Tarbela   Mansehra ·                                        Photaksar ·
     Reservoir                                                        Leh ·
        Abbottabad ·                                    Zanskar
        Havelian ·     **Srinagar**                       Range    INDIA
   Haripur ·  Murree ·        · Pahalgam
Taxila ·                Punch ·              Zanskar
  **ISLAMABAD**                                        Padum ·  Ladakh
PUNJAB  **Rawalpindi**    AZAD
                         JAMMU &    Kashmir
         **TAXILA**      KASHMIR              Pir Panjal Range
         Millennia-spanning
         excavations.      · Naoshera              HIMACHAL    Sarchu ·
                                                   PRADESH

· Jammu

**Karakoram
Highway**

0        50        100 km

The external boundaries of
India on this map have not been
authenticated and may not be correct.

ELEVATION
5000m
4000m
3000m
2000m
500m
0m

RICHARD I'ANSON

JOHN KING

RICHARD I'ANSON

ROBERT MATZINGER

JOHN KING

Left Panel: Men of Kashgar.
Top Right: All smiles, Bagrot Valley.

Right: Uyghur boy taking care of business,
Sunday market.

### Cross-Border Trade

Caravans are once again crossing between Gilgit and Kashgar, though diesel lorries have replaced yaks and camels. From Pakistan, the government-sponsored Northern Areas Traders Cooperative (NATC) annually sends several truck 'caravans' bearing cigarettes, dried fruit, medicinal herbs, razor blades, copper pots, woollens, bedsheets and nylon cloth. From China, the Kashgar office of the Ministry of Foreign Trade sends back bicycles, quilts, cotton cloth, crockery, tea, farm tools, diesel generators, hydroelectric turbines – and of course silk.

All the government-sponsored business is barter trade. In its first year, 1963, the NATC did about US$10,000 worth of business. By 1996 that had grown to US$5 million. There are freelance Pakistani traders too, though they suffer high import taxes, and can only hire government vehicles.

In 1994 Pakistan, China, Kyrgyzstan and Kazakhstan signed an agreement to upgrade the roads linking them. In October 1996 a government truck convoy loaded with Pakistani goods went from Karachi, via Gilgit and Kashgar – where China added a few trucks of its own – over the Torugart Pass to Bishkek and Almaty. No trade agreements have yet been signed between Pakistan and the Central Asian republics, but they're under consideration.

The present route via Kashgar has the handicap of a Chinese stranglehold on transport: the symbolic 1996 convoy aside, all goods between Kashgar and the Torugart Pass (and more northerly crossings) must go in Chinese trucks. In hopes of sidestepping this, Pakistan is studying more direct routes into Central Asia, including from the Northern Areas via the Ishkoman Valley or the Chapursan Valley, across Afghanistan's relatively peaceful Wakhan corridor to Tajikistan. At the time of research, Chinese road crews were in fact upgrading sections of the road west from Gilgit towards Ishkoman and the Shandur Pass into Chitral. ∎

---

1950s. All traffic across the border stopped. While the Chinese border with Indian-held Kashmir is still in dispute today, a thaw in China-Pakistan relations in 1964 led to a border agreement, China's return of 2000 sq km of territory, and talk of linking the two countries by road – a staggering idea, considering the terrain.

In 1966 the two countries embarked on one of the biggest engineering projects since the Pyramids: a two lane, 1200km road across some of the highest mountains in the world – the Pamir and the Karakoram – from Kashgar in China to Havelian in Pakistan. Much of this 'Karakoram Highway' (KKH) would be in terrain which until then had barely allowed a donkey track. It was to be 20 years before it was fully open.

Pakistan had already started a road of its own in 1960, the 400km Indus Valley Road between Swat and Gilgit, built by the Frontier Works Organisation (FWO), a wing of the Pakistan army. This and a road north from Havelian were completed in 1968 and linked by a bridge at Thakot. Between then and 1973, Pakistani crews worked north from the Indus, while the Chinese cut a road over the Khunjerab Pass to Gulmit, as well

as north from the Khunjerab to Kashgar. In 1974 Pakistan asked the Chinese back for more work south of Gulmit. All of the nearly 100 bridges from the Khunjerab to Thakot were originally Chinese-built.

Chinese workers departed in early 1979, and later that year the KKH was declared complete in Pakistan. In August 1982 the highway was formally inaugurated, the Northern Areas were opened to tourism as far as Passu, and the Khunjerab Pass was opened to official traffic and cross-border trade. On 1 May 1986 the Khunjerab and the entire road to Kashgar were opened to tourism, although work on bridges, Ghez canyon road-cuts and paving on the Chinese side went on until 1989.

The workforce in Pakistan at any one time was about 15,000 Pakistani soldiers and between 9000 and 20,000 Chinese, working separately. Landslides, savage summer and winter conditions, and accidents claimed 400 to 500 lives on the Pakistani side of the border, roughly one for every 1.5km of roadway (though some claim the Chinese took away many more dead than they admitted). The highest toll was in Indus Kohistan.

Few statistics are available about work on

the Chinese side. Crews there were a mixture of soldiers, convicts and well-paid volunteers with nothing but picks and shovels, hauling rocks and dirt on shoulder-poles, sunburned and half-crazy.

Maintenance is a huge and endless job for the khaki-suited FWO. The mountains continually try to reclaim the road, assisted by earthquakes, encroaching glaciers and the Karakoram's typical crumbling slopes – and by the KKH itself: blasting so shattered the mountainsides that they are still settling. Rockfalls, mud and floods are routine, and travel is inherently unpredictable.

## GEOGRAPHY

The KKH threads its way through a 'knot' of five great mountain ranges: the Pamir, the Kunlun, the Karakoram, the Hindukush and the Himalaya, all of them part of the vast collision zone between the Asian continent and the Indian subcontinent. Here the ground rises higher, over a greater area, than anywhere else on the planet.

The Pamir is a range of rounded, 5000m to 7000m mountains stretching 800km across Tajikistan. With very broad, flat valleys nearly as high as the lower peaks, the Pamir might be better described as a plateau. The valleys are treeless, grassy (*pamir* roughly means 'pasture' in local dialects), sometimes swampy with meandering rivers. The KKH crosses the eastern limb of the Pamir, called the Sarykol or Taghdumbash Pamir.

The Karakoram arches for 500km along the border between China and Pakistan-held Kashmir, parallel to the Himalaya and cleanly separated from it by the trough of the upper Indus River. To a geographer the Karakoram reaches west to the Ishkoman Valley (beyond which it becomes the Hindukush) and south-east into Ladakh in Indian-administered Kashmir. It's characterised by closely packed, steep, jagged high peaks and deep gorges; immense glaciers (the longest outside the subpolar regions); and lush high valleys. The world's second highest mountain, K2 (or Mt Godwin-Austen) is in Baltistan.

The 'Great Karakoram' is the range's high

---

**Lofty Statistics**

The highest peaks near the KKH – all in the Karakoram except as noted – are: Nanga Parbat (Himalaya, 8125m), Rakaposhi (7790m), Batura (7785m), Kongur (Pamir, 7719m), unnamed (at the head of the Passu Glacier, 7611m), Muztagh Ata (Pamir, 7546m), Malubiting (7450m), Haramosh (7400m) and Ultar II (7388m). In the Northern Areas alone there are about three dozen peaks over 7000m.

The Karakoram has at least five glaciers over 50km long: the Batura, Hispar, Baltoro, Biafo and Siachen. The Batura comes right down to the KKH at Passu. ■

---

backbone, grouped in clusters called *muztagh* (Uyghur for 'ice mountain') from which the biggest glaciers descend. In northern Hunza is the Batura Muztagh, source of the Batura, Passu and Ultar glaciers; south-east is the Hispar Muztagh, from which Nagar's glaciers flow; in Baltistan is the mighty Baltoro Muztagh, home of K2. This crest zone is broken at only one point, by the Hunza River (accompanied by the KKH) in southern Gojal.

South of Gilgit, the Indus River divides the Himalaya from the Hindukush, which extends over 800km into central Afghanistan. The western anchor of the Himalaya is 8125m Nanga Parbat. Under the force of the collision that gave birth to the Himalaya, Nanga Parbat continues to rise at almost 7mm per year.

## GEOLOGY

A trip along the KKH reveals one of the world's greatest geological exhibits. The mountain chain comprising the Himalaya, Karakoram and Hindukush ranges was born 50 million years ago in a stupendous collision between India and Asia, a collision that is still going on today. The highway climbs right over the 'wreckage'.

According to the theory of plate tectonics, the earth's crust is made up of continent-sized slabs of rock (plates), afloat on a more fluid layer (mantle). As a result of currents and upwellings from below, the plates move around, bump into each other, break up and reform, all in hyper-slow motion.

About 130 million years ago, when dinosaurs still roamed the earth, the 'Indian Plate' broke away from a primordial super-continent that geologists call Gondwanaland (the ancestor of Africa, Australia and Antarctica) and drifted north toward another landmass called Laurasia, the 'Asian Plate'. Between the converging continents lay a wide, shallow sea called Tethys, and off the shore of Laurasia was a chain of volcanic islands, similar to present-day Indonesia or Japan.

Following a collision, the Indian Plate buried its edge under the Asian Plate, lifting it up. Both plates compressed and piled up against each other. Trapped in the middle, the small oceanic plate supporting the offshore island chain was flipped almost on end, and the Sea of Tethys was swallowed up.

Continents are not easily slowed down. India continues to plough northward (at about 5cm per year), and the mountains are still rising, in some cases faster than erosion can wear them down. Frequent earthquakes reveal the strains underneath.

From Kashgar to Islamabad, the KKH crosses the entire collision zone – the Asian Plate, the remnants of the offshore volcanic islands, and the Indian Plate. Evidence of this ongoing encounter is easy to see, both on the grand scale – in the size and sequence of the mountains – and up close, in the colours and patterns of roadside rocks and minerals.

**The Asian Plate**

From Kashgar all the way to Chalt, in Nagar, the road crosses old Laurasia, with Laurasia's

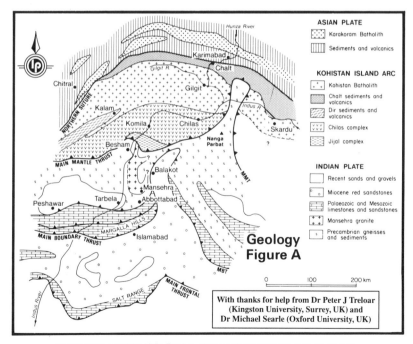

Geological map of the KKH Region, showing the major rock units and thrust zones in the three 'plates' crossed by the KKH.

former southern shore now heaved up into the Karakoram Range itself.

The most dramatic geological 'monuments' on the Xinjiang side are two mountain massifs, Kongur and Muztagh Ata, consisting of metamorphic rocks and granites which have been squeezed up from deep in the earth's crust, and then exposed in the last 5 million years by a combination of weathering and enormous vertical faulting. ('Metamorphic' refers to rocks reformed from older ones deep in the earth's crust under high temperatures and pressures; 'faulting' is the sliding of blocks of crust against one another.)

These two massifs are sandwiched between the two main strike-slip faults of the Tibetan Plateau: the Altyn Tagh fault running west to east through the Kunlun range, and the Karakoram fault running north-west to south-east through the northern Pamir and the Tashkurgan Valley. (On a 'strike-slip' fault, adjacent blocks move horizontally in opposite directions.)

The geology from Khunjerab to Passu is dominated by dark and light-coloured shale and limestone, seen prominently in the saw-tooth peaks around Passu. From Passu to Karimabad, the high spine of the Karakoram is composed mostly of 50-million to 100-million-year-old granite (the Karakoram Batholith in the diagrams), part of a vast body extending eastward for 2500km along the India-Asia boundary to Lhasa and beyond.

There is a variety of metamorphic rocks in the Hunza Valley itself, with large red garnets very common. White marble bands are conspicuous around Karimabad. The famous ruby mines of Hunza are in the hills north of the river, between Karimabad and Hassanabad (although the 'rubies' offered to you by the urchins of Baltit are probably garnets).

The edge of the Asian Plate (called the Northern Suture or NS on the diagrams) is exposed near Chalt, in a multicoloured jumble of sedimentary rocks, volcanic material, talc and greenish serpentine. Southward, the road crosses onto the eroded remains of the small oceanic plate that was pinned between India and Asia.

Vertical section in the vicinity of the KKH, showing major rock units and thrust zones in the Asian, Kohistan and Indian 'plates'. The diagram is schematic only.

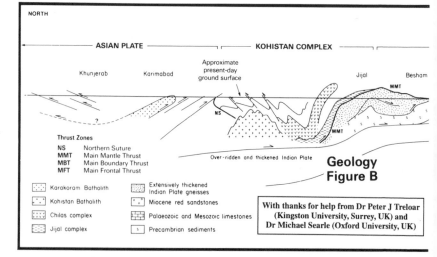

## The Kohistan Complex

In the course of the continental collision, the plate bearing the old volcanic island chain was effectively upended, with the shallower ocean sediments and volcanic materials tilted to the north and its very deep parts exposed in the south. Consequently, the northern part of this so-called Kohistan Complex, from Chalt to Raikhot Bridge (east of Chilas), is a mass of sedimentary and volcanic rocks. Dark patches are remnants of ocean-floor crust upon which the island chain was built. The area around Gilgit and the confluence of the Gilgit and Indus rivers was invaded at a later stage by granites from a deep molten reservoir (the Kohistan Batholith in the diagram). At the confluence especially, hundreds of small intrusive granite sheets cross-cut one another.

By contrast, the southern part of this unit reveals rocks formed under conditions of extreme heat and pressure deep in the earth, ie beneath the old oceanic plate. Examples include the black-banded pinkish rocks seen just east of Chilas (the Chilas Complex on the diagrams), and garnet-rich outcrops between Pattan and Jijal that include some dark red, nearly pure garnetites (Jijal Complex).

Just west of the Shangla Pass, on the Besham-Swat road, are outcrops of the rare rock blueschist, which laboratory studies indicate can form only at depths of at least 25km.

At Jijal, the KKH crosses the boundary from the volcanic island complex to the Indian Plate. The green rocks at Jijal belong to Kohistan, and the contorted white and grey gneisses, 100m south, belong to the Indian Plate.

## The Indian Plate

As it drove into and under Asia, the top of the Indian Plate was compressed and bull-dozed back, most severely along the leading edge. Under the resulting compression the crust became fractured and sliced. Along certain fronts or 'thrusts', individual slices, some up to 10km thick, slid southwards and upwards over originally higher rocks. The effect was to throw up great piles of material, some still visible as hill or mountain ranges.

The direct contact between Kohistan and the Indian Plate (called the Main Mantle Thrust or MMT in the diagrams) is not marked by a distinct chain of hills but does pass through the rugged terrain from Babusar Pass via Besham into the Swat Valley. The emerald deposits at Mingora, in Swat, are within this zone.

To the south, major thrusts are associated with escarpments (mountain fronts), eg the steep terrain between Abbottabad and Havelian (the Panjal Thrust in the diagram), the Margalla and Murree hills along Islamabad's northern side (the Main Boundary Thrust or MBT in the diagrams) and the Salt Range, 100 to 150km south of Islamabad (the Main Frontal Thrust or MFT in the diagrams).

The severest compression, right at the northern edge of the plate, tended to push up the oldest and deepest material, subsequently exposed by erosion. Thus, as you go southward the exposed surface gets younger. Material from deep in the plate's crust, where temperatures are high and rock is slightly plastic, tended to fold and deform, and the geology south as far as Mansehra is dominated by contorted and streaky metamorphic rocks from the plate's Precambrian 'basement' (more than 600 million years old). Precambrian slate outcrops are visible along the road between Mansehra and Abbottabad.

From here, south through the Taxila Valley to the Margalla Pass, the road crosses 160-million to 600-million-year-old Palaeozoic and Mesozoic limestones. At the road-cut through the Margalla Pass, the thrusting of these limestone strata, southward up and over younger rock, is well exposed. South of Margalla, red rock outcrops indicate Miocene Age (about 20 million years old) sandstones, originally eroded from the embryonic Himalaya chain.

## Nanga Parbat

An unmistakable feature of the region is massive Nanga Parbat, 8125m high and rising by 7mm every year, faster than almost any other part of the Himalaya chain. The sharpest elevation differences found anywhere on earth are here: 6.5 vertical km from the summit into the adjacent Indus gorge, and the mountain's sheer, unbroken 4000m south wall (the Rupal Face).

Nanga Parbat sits atop a mass of ancient Indian Plate rocks, sticking oddly northward into the volcanic-island material of the Kohistan Complex. Its unusual position and growth are still matters of active research; explanations involve the dynamics of the entire Himalayan system.

At the Liachar Valley, about 4km upstream from the Raikhot Bridge over the Indus (between Gilgit and Chilas), across from the KKH, you can see the grey Precambrian granite of the Indian Plate, hundreds of millions of years old, pushed over on top of river sediments less than 100,000 years old. This reversal is part of the continuing disruption as Nanga Parbat rises.

This geological instability, coupled with an earthquake, caused a colossal landslide near Liachar in 1841, which dammed up the Indus and created a lake stretching nearly to Gilgit. The remnants of the slide can be seen in a steep-sided, 2km-long ridge on the river's east bank, below Liachar. When the dam broke, the wall of water thundering down the canyon and out onto the plains of the Punjab washed away scores of towns and villages and drowned thousands of people, including an entire Sikh army battalion camped at Attock.

At another side valley just above Raikhot Bridge, the boundary between the Kohistan Complex and the Indian Plate is visible. Across the river from the highway, a 100m stretch of jeep track passes from grey Indian Plate granite, southward through a layer of brown garnet-bearing schists that formed a sedimentary cover to the granite, and into the greenish rocks of Kohistan.

## Other Evidence of Geological Activity

Insistent reminders of the stresses within the earth are the earthquakes that constantly jar the Karakoram and Pamir.

The worst in recent times struck near the Indus River village of Pattan, north of Besham, in December 1974. Pattan and many smaller villages virtually disappeared under collapsing hillsides. Between 5000 and 8000 people died, and tens of thousands were injured. Pattan was entirely rebuilt with government and international relief money but, like many towns along the KKH, it continues to be at the mercy of its tormented surroundings.

In the same year, earthquakes probably triggered a mud and rock slide that thundered out of the Shishkat Valley in Gojal (Upper Hunza) and dammed the Hunza River. The resulting lake, extending to well above Passu, lasted so long before the river cut its way through again that the once deep and fertile valley filled with silt and gravel and is now a shallow, flat-bottomed wasteland. A section of the KKH, including a major bridge, was permanently buried, and had to be rerouted and rebuilt.

Another fault that has made life miserable for many people in Xinjiang is the Karakoram fault (see The Asian Plate earlier in this chapter), one of the most active in Asia and indeed anywhere in the world. Although the Pamir is an older range than the Karakoram, the India-Asia collision put new stresses on it, giving rise to frequent tremors. In 1996 and 1997, a string of at least four powerful earthquakes (6.0 or more on the Richter scale) rocked the region around

Jiashi, just east of Kashgar, killing scores of people and rendering thousands homeless. These jolted Kashgar and much of the KKH on the China side as well.

A happier consequence of geological activity is the high frequency of hot springs along the KKH. Relatively recent 'faults' or fractures permit easy upward movement of underground water that has been in contact with hot rock deep in the crust.

## CLIMATE
July and August get uncomfortably hot along most of the KKH, except in high-altitude trekking zones. The most pleasant temperatures for KKH travel are in May to June and September to October. From Kashgar to Gilgit, winter is long and cold (often well below

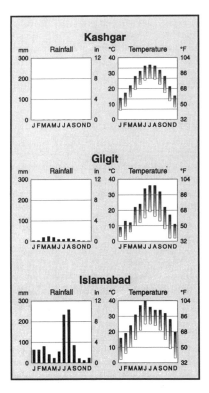

freezing, especially in January to February), and snow closes many high passes. Snow has in the past closed the Khunjerab Pass from November to April, though Pakistan and China are discussing ways to keep it and the KKH open all winter.

Large variations between day and night temperatures are common in the north, especially at higher elevations, where much of the warmth of the day is radiant heat, and sunset (or a rest in the shade) brings a sudden plunge in temperature.

In northern Pakistan the wettest months are during the monsoon, from late July to early September, with random summer storms from Hunza southward, and steady rain and high humidity from Kohistan and the Kaghan Valley southward. These monsoony regions are also sporadically drizzly from December to March. The driest months are May to June and mid-September to November, with the most cloud-free skies in autumn. Xinjiang remains extremely arid all year long, with a trace of rain in summer.

For more about when to go, see Planning in the Facts for the Visitor chapter.

## ECOLOGY & ENVIRONMENT
'Ecology' makes many westerners think of plants and animals, but the ecology of the Karakoram is a tight interweaving of human and natural patterns, established over centuries. Following are examples of these ancient links, and threats to them.

• Most farmed land is on steep alluvial slopes, supporting subsistence crops on small, carefully tended patches, irrigated with water often brought many km in intricately constructed stone channels. There are very few options for the creation of new farmland. According to traditional inheritance patterns, land is shared out among male offspring, so each generation gets a decreasing per capita share. As a result, subsistence farming is no longer viable for many people along the KKH, who are turning instead to cash crops, or giving up farming in favour of trade or tourism-related activities.

- Perhaps the Northern Areas' most precious long-term resource is its landscapes, combining compact human habitations and magnificent scenery. But as succeeding generations inherit less space per person, more people abandon clustered villages and build new houses in the middle of prime farmland. This not only displaces agricultural production but degrades the views upon which future generations may depend for tourism-related income.

- Even in the remotest areas, land is used by people and their domesticated animals as well as by wild animals. Traditional husbandry requires families and often entire villages to relocate several times a year, and often to range very far, in search of pasture. And herders need not only to graze their animals, but to protect them and to hunt their own food, so habitats and populations of certain wild animals are under severe pressure. Merely closing certain areas to grazing (as was done in the early days of the Khunjerab National Park) deprives local people of their livelihood.

- Trophy hunting has pushed certain animal species – eg the snow leopard, Kashmir markhor and Marco Polo sheep – close to extinction in the Karakoram. Until recently the 'trophy trade' was administered from (and fees paid to) Islamabad, with local people left to look on as these animal populations dwindled.

- Unregulated private logging in some of the Northern Areas' most beautiful upper valleys, eg around Nanga Parbat and above Chalt, has led to slope instability, water pollution and landscape degradation, and few profits (apart from the sale of their land) have accrued to local people.

- A big issue across the border in Xinjiang is scarce water supplies, with fierce competition, overuse and degradation as Han Chinese immigrants arrive and state farms and labour camps are annexed to the Tarim Basin's small, mainly Uyghur oasis settlements. There is little visible evidence of solutions yet.

## Impact of Tourism

The arrival of large numbers of down-country and foreign visitors since the opening of the KKH has put stress on the Northern Areas and western Xinjiang in a number of ways.

Local sources of accommodation, food, transport, fuel and other supplies and services have come under pressure. In many cases the new needs are met by hoteliers, shopkeepers and travel and trekking agencies from outside the area, so capital flows away just when it's needed locally. Visitors and agencies pay over the odds, driving up prices for local people.

Infrastructure for clean water, waste treatment, electricity and other services has been strained, with government agencies responding slowly in the Northern Areas. Only in recent years have most tourist areas of the far north seen the arrival of hydroelectric power; before that, valleys filled in the evenings with the roar of diesel generators.

Trekking and mountaineering parties often leave behind gear and litter, and deposit human waste in the wrong places. Popular areas are being stripped of forest cover for firewood by trekking groups' porters. While the number of mountaineering expeditions has levelled off, trekking is growing fast; the Baltoro Glacier, for example, now has some 30,000 visitors a year. In 1994 almost three-quarters of all treks in the Northern Areas went up the Baltoro to Concordia and K2 base camp.

Tourism draws local people away from farming and other traditional occupations, and traditional ways of life. On a more subtle level, pride in the area's resources, achievements and traditions often shrinks in the face of the superficial wealth of visitors.

Not everyone sees tourism as wholly destructive, however. It has provided solutions as well as problems – eg alternative work for herders forced out of work by the establishment of protected areas. Competent local

## Responsible Tourism

Following are some ways to pass through the KKH region with minimal cultural and environmental impact.

- Try to patronise hotels and shops run by local people. Buy trekking food in local markets rather than bringing it from home (but try to be self-sufficient in remote villages, where there is often little enough to go round).
- Patronise local tour operators where possible, and tell them why. Otherwise, deal with down-country or overseas agencies with a demonstrated commitment to responsible tourism.
- If you want a guide or porter, hire one from the valley you're exploring. Learn in advance what the going wage is; paying over the odds and giving huge tips only creates local inflation, for locals and future visitors alike.
- Dress conservatively (see the Society & Conduct section in this chapter for tips) as a sign of respect for local sensibilities. Public hand-holding or kissing between men and women is viewed by locals more or less as you might view public copulation back home.
- Try to give local people an honest perspective on life in the west. Note that you're 'rich' only because you happen to be here; income and expenses still balance out in Hoboken just as they do in Haramosh. Praise aspects of local culture that you appreciate, whatever they are – lifestyle, strong family ties, low crime, low pollution etc.
- If you're lucky enough to see wild animals, keep your distance and make an early retreat to minimise your disturbance. If anyone offers you wild game to eat, remind them that you're here to look at the animals, not eat them.
- On a hike, carry your rubbish out; if it's a long trek, burn the burnables and bury organic (eg cooking) wastes. In town, pocket it till you see a bin; many towns and villages have now organised public bins and small recycling facilities.
- On a hike where there are no pit toilets, dig a latrine at least half a metre deep and 50m from all open water sources. On the move, dig a small hole away from water sources and from the trail, burn the paper and cover everything with clean soil. Encourage fellow hikers, as well as porters and other local companions, to do the same.
- Concentrate your impact. Pitch your tent only in established camp sites. Prepare your meals where others have done so. Stay on trails when walking to limit erosion.
- Use your own fuel, not local trees, for cooking fires. Carry enough clothes to eliminate the need for purely warming fires.
- Come equipped to treat and/or filter local water, rather than buying bottled water and clogging up the environment with plastic bottles.
- Resist the temptation to leave your signature on rocks or trees.

For more tips on special conditions for trekkers, see the section on Ecotourism in Lonely Planet's *Trekking in the Karakoram & Hindukush*. ■

entrepreneurs are gradually turning the flow of capital inward. And, at least in Hunza, exposure from tourism has generated increased interest in the region on the part of development agencies.

### Conservation

After some false steps, and despite continuing problems of underfunding and understaffing, northern Pakistan is the stage for some pioneering efforts to create conservation zones without threatening traditional lifestyles.

An Environmental Protection Council within the Pakistan government's Ministry of Environment, Local Government & Rural Development has, in consultation with nongovernment bodies, created a National Conservation Strategy (NCS), with parallel provincial strategies in preparation in the North-West Frontier Province (NWFP), the Northern Areas and other provinces. The strategies are in fact part of a global effort, first proposed in 1980 by the World Conservation Union (IUCN), the

World Wide Fund for Nature (WWF) and the UN Environmental Programme, to help governments strike a balance between economic development and the conservation and use of their natural resources.

At the heart of Pakistan's NCS is the devolution of responsibility to local 'custodian' community organisations and nongovernmental organisations (NGOs). This wisdom was acquired the hard way in the early days of the Khunjerab National Park. After vast areas of land were unilaterally declared off limits to grazing in 1975, resentful local people refused to co-operate, continuing to graze their yaks and to hunt, rendering the whole idea of a national park meaningless

there. The government and its consultants are still trying to regain their trust, and even now the government remains wary of giving away any of its prerogatives to local communities.

Proposed management plans for this and other national parks now include provisions for local involvement in policy and administrative decisions, for the return of entry and other fees to communities in and around the parks, and for retraining and hiring people displaced from traditional occupations. Many of the new jobs would be in wildlife management and protection.

In a related move aimed at the sustainable use of wildlife resources – in particular the Himalayan ibex, on the way to being hunted

## Endangered Species

Little is actually known about the current status of most wildlife in the Karakoram and adjacent Hindukush ranges. Some species, such as the Himalayan brown bear *(Ursus arctos isabellinus)* and the Bharal or blue sheep *(Pseudois nayaur)*, appear endangered, although globally they are not. IUCN, the World Conservation Union, attempts to track the status of species worldwide and classifies the following species as endangered:

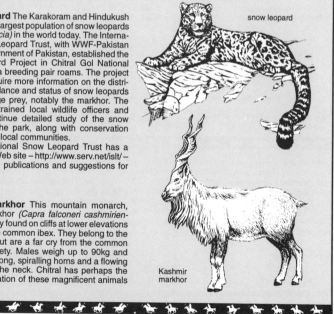

snow leopard

**Snow Leopard** The Karakoram and Hindukush may hold the largest population of snow leopards *(Panthera uncia)* in the world today. The International Snow Leopard Trust, with WWF-Pakistan and the government of Pakistan, established the Snow Leopard Project in Chitral Gol National Park, where a breeding pair roams. The project seeks to acquire more information on the distribution, abundance and status of snow leopards and their large prey, notably the markhor. The project has trained local wildlife officers and plans to continue detailed study of the snow leopards in the park, along with conservation education for local communities.

The International Snow Leopard Trust has a World Wide Web site – http://www.serv.net/islt/ – offering facts, publications and suggestions for public action.

**Kashmir Markhor** This mountain monarch, Kashmir markhor *(Capra falconeri cashmiriensis)*, is typically found on cliffs at lower elevations than the more common ibex. They belong to the goat family, but are a far cry from the common domestic variety. Males weigh up to 90kg and have unique long, spiralling horns and a flowing white ruff at the neck. Chitral has perhaps the largest population of these magnificent animals on the planet.

Kashmir markhor

out of existence – Prime Minister Benazir Bhutto in 1994 granted accredited community organisations the right to collect the substantial fees set for trophy hunting in their respective valleys and keep 75% for themselves. In turn locals have stopped their own hunting and now survey wildlife and keep track of visiting hunters, and villages are applying this income to their own social development projects.

Similar efforts are under way for the management of other wildlife resources, eg migratory bird stopovers like Borit Lake in Gojal. Local organisations have also taken it upon themselves to regulate private (and even government) logging.

The organisations advising government and local organisations on implementation of these policies in the Northern Areas and NWFP are the Pakistan branches of IUCN and WWF. Most commonly they and the government work at local level through the network of Village Organisations, established since 1982 under the Aga Khan Rural Support Programme (see Economy later in this chapter).

**IUCN (World Conservation Union)** IUCN, founded in 1948, is the world's largest partnership of governmental and nongovernmental conservation groups. IUCN-Pakistan, founded in 1976, is the force behind the national and provincial conservation strategies, and the

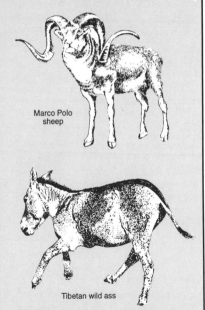

**Marco Polo Sheep** As recently as 1968, hundreds of Marco Polo sheep *(Ovis ammon polii),* with their enormous curly horns, could be seen on the Khunjerab Pass. But during the construction of the KKH they were slaughtered to feed workers and soldiers, and hunted by visiting bigwigs. This magnificent species is now strictly protected. They can still be found in remote Khunjerab valleys, now closed to foreigners.

**Tibetan Wild Ass** The Tibetan wild ass *(Equus hemionus kyiang),* or kyiang, is found in China, adjacent to the Khunjerab National Park and Central Karakoram National Park. Its presence in the Khunjerab Pass area has not been confirmed but is probable.

**Other Endangered Species** Other Karakoram species identified by IUCN as endangered are the woolly flying squirrel *(Eupetaurus cinereus)* and the urial or red sheep *(Ovis orientalis).* Punjab urial are found in the NWFP while others, perhaps Ladakhi urial, were once known in eastern Baltistan, although their current distribution is not known. The largest known population of the threatened western tragopan, a kind of pheasant, is in Indus Kohistan's upper Bar Palas Valley.

Marco Polo sheep

Tibetan wild ass

**John Mock & Kimberley O'Neil**

Mock & O'Neil are co-authors of Lonely Planet's *Trekking in the Karakoram & Hindukush* and have their own World Wide Web site – http://www.monitor.net/jmko/karakoram/ – with papers and some good links on biodiversity, ecotourism and protected areas in the Karakoram and Hindukush ■

government's main consultant on the Central Karakoram National Park. It also publishes a good quarterly magazine, *The Way Ahead*, for US$15/year.

IUCN-Pakistan headquarters (☎ (021) 586 1540/1/2; fax (021) 587 0287; email jrc@iucn1.khi.sdnpk.undp.org) are at 1 Bath Island Rd, Karachi 75530. IUCN-Pakistan branches along the KKH include those in Islamabad (House 26, St 87, G-6/3; ☎ (051) 270 686/7; fax (051) 270 688; email mail@ iucn-isb.sdnpk.undp.org) and Gilgit (Babar Rd, PO Box 525, Gilgit 15100; ☎ & fax (0572) 2679; email mail@iucn-glt.sdnpk. undp.org).

**WWF (World Wide Fund for Nature)** WWF is the largest conservation and wildlife management NGO in Pakistan. Among its projects near the KKH are the management of ibex trophy hunting in several watersheds above Chalt in Nagar; the Himalayan Jungle Project, to preserve primeval habitat in the upper Palas Valley in Indus Kohistan; surveys of the brown bear on the Deosai Plains and of fish in the Northern Areas; and research on migratory bird patterns in Chitral. WWF-Pakistan is the government's chief consultant on the ticklish management of Khunjerab National Park.

WWF-Pakistan's head office is on Ferozepur Rd, PO Box 5180, Lahore 54600 (☎ (042) 586 2359, 686 9429; fax (042) 586 2358; email anwar@wwf.edunet.sdnpk. undp.org). Other offices near the KKH are at 543-A Shahrah-i-Quaid-i-Azam, Khomer, Gilgit 15100 (☎ & fax (0572) 4127); and 90 Razia Sharaf Plaza, Blue Area (G-7), Islamabad (☎ & fax (051) 829456).

### FLORA & FAUNA

A detailed and helpful introduction to the plants and animals of the Karakoram, and how to get a look at them, is Dan Blumstein's *An Ecotourist's Guide to Khunjerab National Park*, published by WWF-Pakistan and sold at least at WWF's Lahore and Gilgit offices (see WWF earlier) for US$5.

### Flora

One of the delights of the Karakoram is its unexpectedly lush, glacier-watered pastures, hidden in high valleys. The few alpine trees there are mainly dwarf juniper, with some willow and birch. Pastures are carpeted with tiny wildflowers during the short summer. Lower down are pine, spruce, juniper, deodar (Indian cedar), birch and willow; shrubs including wild sage, tamarisk and viburnum; and violets, poppies, columbine, forget-me-nots, mallow, geranium and other wildflowers in spring.

Parts of the lower Hindukush and Himalaya are heavily forested with pine, fir and cedar, especially where the monsoon reaches. The forests of Hazara include oak, chestnut and eucalyptus, plus acacia and other plantations for fodder and erosion control.

Domestic crops include wheat, maize and – nowadays in Hunza and Gojal – potatoes; orchards bulging with apricots, peaches, plums, pears, apples, mulberries, cherries and other fruit, as well as walnuts; and poplars for fodder, firewood, timber and erosion control.

### Fauna

**Mammals** The variety of wild animals is surprisingly rich in the High Karakoram, though some species are unlikely to show themselves to you down on the KKH. These include the snow leopard; the Himalayan ibex and the Kashmir markhor (wild goats that also figure in the region's oldest legends); the wild sheep, including the muscular Marco Polo sheep with its huge, curling horns, and the bharal, or blue sheep; the tiny musk deer; and the wolf, deeply hated and relentlessly hunted by farmers and herders. Another rare species is the kiang, or Tibetan wild ass, found mainly across the border in China.

One creature you're sure to see if you cross the Khunjerab Pass, the Deosai Plains or the Subash Plateau in Xinjiang in warmer weather is the golden marmot, sunning itself near its burrow, whistling in alarm when you get close. Others you might see while trekking are the Tibetan red fox, the ermine, the

The brown bear *(Ursus arctos)* usually lives above the treeline and during summer may prey on livestock grazing in the high pastures.

alpine weasel, the cape hare, the mouse-hare (or pika), the field mouse and the high mountain vole. Bigger, shyer residents include the black bear and the brown bear (but stay away from them), the Himalayan lynx, the marten, the ermine and the Ladakhi urial, or red sheep.

The woolly flying squirrel, thought to be extinct for 70 years, was recently rediscovered in Sai Nala, just south of Gilgit. Wild animals in Pakistan's lower mountain forests include black and brown bears, wild cats, wild boars, jackals, foxes, hares, monkeys, porcupines, small rodents, reptiles and bats.

On the Chinese side of the border, rabbits and marmots were spotted at Kara Kul. Sparsely populated regions of Xinjiang provide a habitat for magnificent creatures

The sandy-grey Himalayan lynx *(Felis lynx isabellina)* is found in the southern part of the Karakoram, between 2745m and 3355m altitude in summer.

including snow leopards, argali sheep and wild yaks.

The main domesticated animals in the High Karakoram are yaks and a cow-yak hybrid called *dzu* or *dzo*. In the more temperate mountains to the south, some cattle are kept, and goats and sheep are driven into high valleys in summer.

## National Parks

Pakistan's protected areas were set up mainly to protect particular endangered wildlife species. In 1966-67, at the request of the government of Pakistan, the WWF did a series of surveys which revealed a steady decline in the populations of dozens of species, especially mammals. A high-profile government committee then recommended the establishment of three categories of protected areas:

- National Park: accessible to the public, but with a total ban on hunting, trapping or capture of wild animals, on disturbing or felling plants or trees, on clearing land for cultivation or mining, on pollution of water flowing into or through the park, and on structures except those necessary for park operation.

- Wildlife Sanctuary: mostly former princely hunting grounds, now to be off limits to the public, with similar prohibitions as for a national park, plus a ban on the introduction of exotic species and of domestic animals.

- Game Reserve: also mostly former royal hunting grounds, similar to wildlife sanctuaries except that special hunting permits are available, for specific species, dates and areas.

But for years all this 'protection' remained fairly theoretical, with little money for either surveys or management, and insufficient legal provision for the control of land use. Where action was taken, eg in the Khunjerab National Park, it failed to take account of the traditional interests and livelihoods of local

# Away with the Birds

The KKH traverses many habitats at various altitudes, from broad, cultivated river valleys to frigid glaciers and mighty peaks. Although they may not be immediately apparent and not always in great numbers, a good variety of birds can be found in nearly all these habitats. Unlike larger wildlife, which has been hunted for centuries, birds are able to take advantage of the most difficult terrain and the most elusive medium of all – the sky – and thus have survived in far greater number and variety than mammals. While they may not be so apparent from a moving vehicle or in the dusty towns along the way, as soon as you get off the track you should see some.

The higher regions are subject to extremes of temperature and precipitation, and consequently support fewer species than lowland areas. Nonetheless, in the all too short spring when alpine meadows are in bloom, birds of many varieties ascend to higher elevations to court and nest.

Larger species include the majestic lammergeier (or bearded vulture), a huge bird of prey with a wingspan of nearly 3m. Like other vultures the lammergeier feeds on dead animals, but unlike other species (griffon and black vultures are two that may also be seen along the route) it feeds almost exclusively on bones, which it swallows whole. The lammergeier is particularly fond of leg bones, and those that are too big it drops repeatedly from a great height onto rocks, thus shattering the bone and making it easy to swallow.

Other birds of prey which may be encountered in the heights are the golden eagle and falcons such as the peregrine. Falcons are often trapped in northern Chitral and sold to falconers in Peshawar. They are keenly sought by wealthy Arabs and Indians, who use them to hunt the Houbara bustard, an endangered game bird. Falconry is an ancient sport, but it puts undue pressure on wild populations of both falcons and their quarry.

The group known as game birds includes pheasants and partridges. Central Asia has several species, of which the Himalayan monal is without doubt the most spectacular. This beautiful, iridescent pheasant is still common in many parts of its range. Other game birds include the Himalayan snowcock, at higher altitudes, and the more common rock partridge or Chukar.

The high-flying swifts are aerial specialists that spend most of their lives on the wing – even sleeping in flight. They are superficially similar to swallows, but have long, slender backswept wings and nearly all species are drably coloured. Choughs nest among the rocky crags and may be seen wheeling in flocks far up a mountainside. Choughs are members of the crow family and are all black; the red-billed chough has a red bill and legs, while the similar alpine chough has a yellow bill. The mighty raven is the largest of the crows and can be identified by its black bulk and raucous, far-carrying call.

Many types of smaller birds make their homes in the valleys between the great peaks, where both cultivated and natural vegetation provide shelter. They include various types of thrushes, accentors, buntings and finches. The thrush family includes the wheatears, redstarts and rock thrushes. The various wheatears are usually boldly patterned in black, white and browns. Other small birds include wrens, tits, the beautiful golden oriole and the dipper, an extraordinary little bird that feeds by walking underwater in fast-flowing streams.

Right: The plumage of the male Himalayan monal is a shimmering array of iridescent green, gold, blue and purple.

Migration is one of the wonders of the bird world. Millions of birds of many species undertake vast journeys during spring and autumn to or from their breeding grounds. The mechanisms whereby birds

*Left: Mammals such as marmots and rabbits form much of the prey of the majestic golden eagle.*

*Below: Despite its bold markings, the Chukar can be surprisingly well camouflaged among the mountains' rubble.*

navigate across hostile terrain in all kinds of weather and at night are poorly understood, but a visitor may be lucky enough to witness a 'fall' of small birds that literally drop from the sky to rest on their long journey. V-shaped formations of geese and ducks are another form of visible migration.

The river valleys and associated marshes and lakes support the greatest concentration of birds along the way, both in numbers and variety. The Indus and Hunza river valleys and flyways support at least 10 species of ducks and geese that migrate from as far away as Siberia; about 200,000 of these waterfowl migrate through Chitral from September to April. Waterfowl have been hunted for centuries and today this pressure continues; significant waterways deserve protection but, in reality, it is difficult to stop traditional hunting habits.

The larger bodies of water provide food, shelter and nesting resources for many varieties of ducks, geese, the long-legged wading birds such as storks, herons, and the smaller terns, gulls and shorebirds. East Lake in Kashgar is easily reached and could provide a few hours' birdwatching. Look

for warblers and other songbirds in the willows that line the banks; a flash of blue over the water could be a kingfisher, darting from perch to perch as it looks for small fish and tadpoles; wagtails strut around open spaces, wagging their tails up and down as they search for insects; and water-loving birds may include terns, the diving grebes and the grey heron.

Even human habitation can be of service to birds; in fact a few, such as the ubiquitous sparrows and crows, are rarely found far from human activity. Swallows and their cousins, the house martins, can be seen darting between buildings, equally at home nesting on walls, banks or cliffs. Crow and vultures are scavengers that may frequent rubbish tips.

If you want to read more about the birds of the region, TJ Roberts' two-volume *The Birds of Pakistan* describes their life histories in some detail. *The Field Guide to the Birds of the USSR*, by VE Flint, is more compact and since parts of the former USSR abut the Karakoram region, this portable volume is probably more useful for travellers.

people and ran up against fierce opposition. The government has since engaged the help of a number of wildlife conservation organisations, especially WWF and IUCN, to assist with further surveys, public input and management plans.

There are currently 14 national parks, about 100 wildlife sanctuaries and 95 game reserves in Pakistan, administered by the government's Division of Forestry. Major responsibility for their development rests with the National Council for the Conservation of Wildlife, within the Ministry of Food, Agriculture & Cooperatives.

Following are those parks closest to the KKH; at the time of research, none of these was far enough along to have formal public offices, maps or other information sources.

**Khunjerab National Park (KNP)** This park comprises about 2270 sq km in northern Gojal, on both sides of the KKH from Sost to the Khunjerab Pass, and along the China border. It was founded in April 1975 to protect the region's few remaining Marco Polo sheep. Its early years saw unkept promises of compensation for lost livelihood, a unilateral ban on grazing, a court order obtained by local people reversing the ban, eviction of herders, and now deep local mistrust which is only slowly thawing. Since then WWF-Pakistan has been the government's main interlocutor and 'midwife'. For information, contact WWF-Pakistan (see WWF in the Conservation section earlier) or the KNP Directorate, Jutial, Gilgit (☎ (0572) 55061). Across the border, China has established the Tashkurgan Nature Reserve. For more information on the KNP, see the Khunjerab Pass & Gojal chapter.

**Central Karakoram National Park (CKNP)** At 9738 sq km, this is by far Pakistan's biggest national park, taking in many of the world's loftiest peaks (including K2) and longest glaciers (the Braldu, Hispar, Biafo and Baltoro) in the highest reaches of the Karakoram. It's mostly in Baltistan, south of the KNP and east of the KKH and the Gilgit-Skardu road. It was designated in 1993 in response to severe ecological pressure on the Baltoro Glacier region as a result of both trekking and military activities. In 1996 the park was formally nominated for UNESCO World Heritage Status; if approved, this will be the first natural area in Pakistan with such a listing.

IUCN-Pakistan has been the government's primary consultant on the CKNP. For information contact IUCN-Pakistan (see the Conservation section earlier). For more on the CKNP, see the Gilgit Region chapter.

**Deosai Plains National Park (DPNP)** This national park, about 3630 sq km in size, was declared by the chief secretary of the Northern Areas in 1993, in response to the impact of increasing tourism on the Deosai's subalpine scrub, alpine meadows and a vulnerable population of Himalayan brown bears. It's about 50km south-west of Skardu on the popular jeep-trek route to and from the Astor Valley. See Baltistan in the Gilgit Region chapter.

**Shandur-Hundrup National Park (SHNP)** This 518 sq km park, in the region of the Shandur Pass on the Gilgit to Chitral road, was also declared in 1993 in response to the damage on the area from the annual Shandur polo tournament. Also see the Gilgit Region chapter.

**Wildlife Sanctuaries & Game Reserves** In the Northern Areas there are five wildlife sanctuaries, ranging from 272 to 443 sq km, in Naltar Valley, Kargah Nala, lower Astor Valley, south of the Gilgit to Skardu road and around Satpara Lake in Baltistan. While hunting is restricted, few of the sanctuaries' other legal restrictions are enforced.

There are at least nine game reserves, ranging from 75 to 650 sq km, though the lack of legal provisions to control land use means that so far they receive minimal protection.

## GOVERNMENT
### The Northern Areas
As the fate of the Northern Areas is linked to that of Kashmir, it is not yet constitutionally

part of Pakistan (for more on Kashmir, see the History sections of this chapter and of the Gilgit Region chapter). It is run directly from Islamabad by the Ministry of Kashmir Affairs & Northern Areas (KANA). Communications and infrastructure are largely managed by the army. While the government is generous with development money, and levies no direct taxes, Northern Areas people cannot, for example, vote in national elections. Nevertheless, by fits and starts the region has acquired many of the political features of a province.

From Rawalpindi (and later Islamabad) the joint secretary of KANA initially wielded complete administrative and judicial power over the region. In the 1950s came the post of chief secretary, based in Gilgit. Reporting to the chief secretary were deputy commissioners for each of the Northern Areas districts, today five in number: Gilgit (including Hunza, Nagar and Gojal), Diamar (including Astor and Chilas), Ghizar (the upper Gilgit River watershed), Skardu and Ghanche (these last two including Baltistan). Each of these is served by subdivisional assistant commissioners.

By the 1970s there were separate Northern Areas departments for power and works, health, education, rural development, agriculture, planning and revenue. Since the 1980s responsibility for identifying and approving government development schemes has been handed to a network of elected local councils, topped by a Northern Areas Council. Judicial power has been shifted to a sessions court, with right of appeal to the Pakistan Supreme Court.

In 1994 the system was further reformed, with a boost in the size of the Northern Areas Council from 16 to 24, including two appointive seats for women. The joint secretary for KANA is now called the chief executive of the Northern Areas – still appointive, still in Islamabad, still the ultimate administrative power, now with the financial reins as well, though divested of judicial power. But the Northern Areas Council elects the deputy chief executive, with the rank of a minister of state in Pakistan. On his/her advice the

chief executive appoints four advisers with the rank of provincial ministers.

Perhaps most interestingly, council elections can now be run on the basis of political party affiliation. This seems to have galvanised many people into voting, with a number of religious radicals elected to comfortable positions where they are a noticeably smaller threat to public order.

For all the pomp and ceremony, however, the Northern Areas remains in political limbo, hostage to the Kashmir issue.

### Xinjiang

Under China's 1982 constitution, supreme power is invested in the National People's Congress (NPC), with deputies elected from all of the country's regions for five-year terms. The NPC meets once a year, to congratulate itself and make plans for the future; for the rest of the year a permanent NPC standing committee does the legwork. The NPC elects the head of state, the president of the People's Republic of China, as well as the State Council – including the premier and various vice-premiers, state councillors, ministers and agency heads – which runs the country's day-to-day affairs.

This system is exactly mirrored in each tier of government, right down to the local level. China has 23 provinces, three municipalities and five autonomous regions, one of which is Xinjiang; all report directly to the State Council. Below this level come prefectures, municipalities, counties, cities and, in rural areas, townships and villages. At the bottom of the heap, nearly every individual Chinese person belongs to a work unit *(danwei)*, the state's main unit of social control.

But the real power lies with the Chinese Communist Party (CCP), with its own structure that parallels and controls government from top to bottom, as well as parallel structures in the army, industry and universities. Nobody gets anywhere without the blessing of the Party. The NPC is in fact only a rubber stamp for decisions of the CCP's 25 member Politburo and subsidiary 210 member Central Committee; its members depend for election on the Central Committee's recommendation.

## ECONOMY

Most people living near the KKH are subsistence farmers or herders. For their maize, wheat, millet, barley, abundant fruit and (in Xinjiang) cotton, farmers depend heavily on irrigation from wells and isolated streams around Kashgar and from channelled glacial melt-water in the Northern Areas. Plots are tiny and harvests meagre (though yields per hectare are well above those in down-country Pakistan). Herders, especially in Kohistan and the Northern Areas, make long migrations to pastures only accessible in summer.

Little except fruit and (in Hunza and Gojal) seed potatoes, plus timber (mainly from Hazara), is exported from the region. Annual per capita income is estimated at about US$150 in Xinjiang and US$300 in the Northern Areas – in each case about two-thirds of the respective country average.

Into this setting the KKH has brought government and overseas grants, down-country developers, tens of thousands of tourists annually and a kind of wealth, but it has also tended to unravel old traditions, social structures and community self-reliance. A social redevelopment effort initially funded by the private Aga Khan Foundation has had striking results in the Northern Areas.

### The Aga Khan Foundation (AKF)

This foundation was started by the Aga Khan, spiritual head of Ismaili Muslims, to provide grants for health, education and rural development projects in certain low-income areas of Asia and Africa. Ismailis actually make up only a fraction of its current beneficiaries, although it's obvious in northern Pakistan that the Ismaili community provided the initial enthusiasm and energy necessary to get many AKF-funded programmes off the ground.

Major recipients of AKF (and now other) money in northern Pakistan include the Aga Khan Rural Support Programme, Aga Khan Educational Services Pakistan and Aga Khan Health Services Pakistan.

### The Aga Khan Rural Support Programme (AKRSP)

When General Yahya Khan ended the semi-autonomy of Hunza, Nagar and other princely states in 1969 (and especially after Prime Minister ZA Bhutto withdrew their subsidies in 1974), the local rulers' traditional power to initiate collective works also ended.

The central government's own public-works projects tended to be vast in scale and run from Islamabad. At the same time population growth was exceeding the capacity of the land under cultivation and forcing people into the towns for work. Village productivity and collective confidence seemed to be fading away.

The AKRSP was formed in 1982 to encourage a homegrown solution in the form of self-sustaining village bodies that could carry out their own development projects. It offered starter loans, technical resources and management advice to any village that would form its own decision-making body (Village Organisation or VO), name its projects and commit itself to acquiring the necessary skills and saving its own money. AKRSP's role was to act as a catalyst only until the projects were self-managing.

The effects have been dramatic. As of early 1997 there were 2065 villages with VOs, covering over 80% of all rural households in the AKRSP project area – the Northern Areas districts of Gilgit (including Hunza, Nagar and Gojal), Diamar (mainly the Astor Valley), Ghizar (the Gilgit River basin up to the Shandur Pass), Skardu and Ghanche (comprising Baltistan), and Chitral district in the NWFP. All had self-help projects under way or completed, and most had several further projects, undertaken with their own funds.

Early projects tended to be irrigation schemes and link roads; AKRSP signs sprouted weekly by the highway, announcing new works. Some impressive ones near the KKH include a 400m irrigation tunnel above Sost, a 45km road being pushed up the Shimshal Valley, and the Karimabad to Aliabad link road. Later projects have included flood control, afforestation, seed improvement, pest control, livestock management, commercial development and marketing. Projects embracing several VOs at a time, eg more extensive irrigation channels, are relatively new. Just under half of the villages with VOs have also started separate Women's Organisations (WOs), with their own projects.

A new area for AKRSP involvement is the provision of seed money and expertise to encourage other NGOs to undertake their own AKRSP-style programmes. An example is the Naunehal Development Organisation, founded by 16 VOs in Nagar, with their own education and health projects. An NGO at Kachura in Baltistan has started a resource centre for rural development. There is a growing trend in the region towards such wide-scale initiatives, often oriented towards environmental or wildlife conservation issues as well as social development, and often interacting directly with the government, other agencies and the private sector.

Nowadays, significant AKRSP money comes not only from the AKF but from EU, German, Dutch, Norwegian, Canadian, US and British overseas aid agencies, the World Bank, and the Pakistan government.

Those with an interest in AKRSP or local projects can contact the General Manager (☎ (0572) 2480; fax (0572) 2779), AKRSP, PO Box 506, Babar Rd, Gilgit. The Aga Khan Foundation is at Avenue de la Paix 1-3, 1202 Geneva (postal address PO Box 2369, 1211 Geneva 2), Switzerland.

**Other Programmes** Aga Khan-initiated programmes have the highest profile in the Northern Areas and northern Chitral, although an increasing number of local NGOs are getting into the picture and filling some gaps.

Aga Khan Health Services Pakistan (AKHSP), established in 1964, is the major nongovernmental provider of health services in the Northern Areas. It operates a network of local health centres and dispensaries whose main emphasis is on maternity and child health. AKHSP also runs an expanding primary health-care programme for villages and rural areas, and a modern medical centre with western-trained staff at Singhal in Punial.

The Naunehal Development Organisation (based at Jaffarabad in Nagar) has established health centres in Nagar. The Pakistan government's Social Action Programme (SAP) has founded a school of midwifery at Gilgit.

The major NGO providing educational services in the region is Aga Khan Educational Services Pakistan (AKESP), with several hundred schools in Gilgit and Ghizar districts (two prominent ones are the Aga Khan Academy, a residential high school for girls on the west side of Karimabad, and a middle and secondary school at Sherqila in Punial), and in Chitral in the NWFP. Most are for girls and provide the main access to education for women in the Northern Areas. AKESP programmes have trained thousands of government as well as AKESP teachers. AKESP's history goes back to 1946 when the previous Aga Khan founded the Diamond Jubilee Schools programme, which now encompasses 126 'DJ' schools in the Northern Areas.

Other private educational initiatives include a string of primary schools established by the Naunehal Development Organisation in Nagar, more by the Hunza Education Resource Project in Aliabad, and others started in individual villages. The private Fauji Foundation, managed by retired army officers, runs several urban schools and vocational training centres for women. Several such initiatives have also sprung up in Baltistan. The trend is to English-medium teaching, though SAP has also kicked off hundreds of Urdu-medium primary schools.

The comment is often made that Aga Khan-funded programmes serve Ismailis at the expense of other communities. In fact AKRSP efforts have always covered both Ismaili and non-Ismaili villages, and since 1987 non-Ismailis (especially in Chitral) have benefited significantly from AKHSP's primary health care project and AKESP's teacher training efforts. Other population-wide health efforts go back even further.

### Xinjiang

In 1993 China, for the first time, became a net importer of oil. Several offshore oil projects have fizzled, and the output of oilfields in Manchuria and Shandong is beginning to slacken. By the turn of the century the focus of economic development in China is very likely to have shifted towards resource-rich Xinjiang, with uranium deposits and huge oil and gas reserves thought to lie beneath the Tarim Basin. Beijing would also like to develop Xinjiang into the country's top producer of cotton and textiles.

The region's ethnic unrest (see the History section earlier in this chapter) is therefore doubly unwelcome to the authorities, who have clamped down hard. At the same time, the flow of Han Chinese settlers into Xinjiang is on the rise, in part to dilute the Uyghurs' demographic dominance in the Tarim Basin, and in part to provide a supply of labour for the building of roads and other new infrastructure. Xinjiang's inflation in 1996 was 10%, compared with a national average of 6%, and the gap in wealth between indigenous Uyghurs, Kazakhs, Tajiks and Kyrgyz and the army of Han immigrants is growing.

Among the most significant and telling projects for the Tarim Basin is a railway line being pushed out from Ürümqi to Kashgar.

## POPULATION & PEOPLE
### Population
There has been no census in Pakistan since 1981 (although at the time of research one had been announced for March 1998), so population data has been estimated using various assumed growth rates. The government's own estimate of the population of the Northern Areas in 1996 was about 1.6 million; other estimates are closer to 1.2 million. There is no reliable breakdown by district.

An estimated 18 million people live in Xinjiang Autonomous Region, of whom about six million (38%) are Han Chinese, 7.2 million (45%) Uyghurs, 1.1 million (7%) Kazakhs, and the rest other nationalities, including Tajiks and Kyrgyz. In the Tarim Basin around Kashgar, the proportion is more lopsided in favour of non-Chinese. That, however, is sure to change once the new Ürümqi-Kashgar railway line is completed. When the PRC was born in 1949 there were

only about 300,000 ethnic Chinese in Xinjiang; some estimates suggest Xinjiang will be majority-Han within a decade.

### People
The KKH region's invaders and traders have left behind the most kaleidoscopic array of peoples you might find in an equivalent space anywhere on the planet. But the mountains seem to have isolated them from one another just enough that many languages, customs and gene pools remain fairly distinct today. This huge variety in a relatively small space is one of the things that makes KKH travel so absorbing. Of course the KKH itself now contributes to this diversity.

Uyghurs are predominant from Kashgar to the Khunjerab, plus large rural populations of Tajiks, Kyrgyz and Kazakhs, each sharing ancestry, language and customs with communities in the Central Asian republics, Afghanistan, Iran and (in the case of Tajiks) Pakistan. In Kashgar you will see the occasional descendant of White Russians. And, of course, Han Chinese labourers and administrators are everywhere on the China side.

The people of Gojal are mainly Tajiks, originally from Afghanistan's Wakhan Corridor and speak Wakhi, a form of Persian. The Burusho of southern Gojal, the Hunza Valley and upper Nagar speak Burushashki, a language whose origins continue to mystify scholars. The people of lower Nagar have similar roots but speak mostly Shina, the language of Gilgit.

Up the watershed of the Gilgit and Ghizar rivers is a mixture of Burusho, Shina speakers and Pashto-speaking Pashtuns (Pathans). Some Chitralis are here too, and speak Khowar, an Indic language. In the other direction from Gilgit is Baltistan, whose mainly Tibetan people speak a classical form of Tibetan.

Gilgit itself, the region's historical trading hub, is a veritable soup of peoples and languages from all over central and south Asia. Its dominant language is Shina, also spoken around Nanga Parbat and down the Indus to Chilas and beyond.

Indus Kohistan is a melting pot of local dialects, with borrowings from Shina and the

### The Gujars

Gujars (pronounced 'GU-jr'), descended from the landless poor of lowland Pakistan and India, eke out an existence as nomadic herders. In May and June they drive their cows and other animals into the high meadows of the lower Northern Areas (roughly as far north as Gilgit) and southern NWFP, sell a few when they need to buy supplies and descend in September and October. They are a common sight at these times, moving beside the road in long files of animals and people, or camped outside towns. They winter on marginal land in the Northern Areas, NWFP or the Punjab, seldom associating with local people.

Though Sunni Muslims, they are considered low-caste by many, even in nominally caste-free Pakistan. They rarely marry non-Gujars. Gujar women do not observe purdah, and on the KKH south of Gilgit they may be the only women whose faces you ever get a glimpse of. Gujars near Gilgit speak Shina, while those closer to the Shandur Pass and in Chitral speak Khowar. ■

other major language here, Pashto. Pashtuns inhabit the KKH well down into Hazara, along with speakers of Hindko and other Punjabi dialects. And from Gilgit right down to the Punjab you will see the ubiquitous itinerant Gujars, driving their animals into the high valleys in spring and down again in autumn.

Nearly everybody is Muslim, but in an equally diverse patchwork of Sunni, Shia, Ismaili and Nurbakhshi variants (see Religion later in this chapter). Each of these peoples is examined further in the introductions to the various chapters. For more on the region's languages, see the Language chapter.

### EDUCATION

The main reliable data on literacy in the Northern Areas is from Pakistan's last census in 1981, which show literacy among those over 10 years old ranging from 11% in Diamar district to 18% in Gilgit district. But estimates based on surveys in 1995 show a major increase, eg to 41% in Gilgit district.

This, however, conceals huge differences between men and women. For example, even the 1995 estimates show literacy in Gilgit

district of 59% for men but 21% for women. It may be less than 1% for women in the Darel and Tangir valleys, near Chilas.

Estimates from 1994 of school enrolment among school-age children range from 75% in Gilgit subdivision to 13% in Nagar and, for girls only, from 61% in Hunza to 4% in Nagar. While this seems to suggest that Nagar is educationally backward, it would be more accurate to say that access to schools has been highest in Hunza's Ismaili community, thanks largely to AKESP's efforts dating back to 1946, with the inauguration of its Diamond Jubilee Schools program. In fact some of the most energetic educational initiatives in the Northern Areas at present are by the Naunehal Development Organisation in Nagar.

Typical monthly fees in Northern Areas schools range from zero at government schools to Rs 50-100 at AKESP's Diamond Jubilee schools, to Rs 200-400 at private schools.

Major educational developments in recent years include the opening of hundreds of new Urdu-medium primary schools, mainly for girls, under the government's SAP, and a big shift to English-medium teaching in AKESP schools and in most new private schools.

### SOCIETY & CONDUCT

### Family Structure & the Status of Women

The social chemistry of the KKH region (and the whole of Pakistan) takes place largely within the family. Family and clan are dominant factors in a range of social commitments – eg personal loyalties, whom to marry, where to live. The plain walls around a family compound reveal little of the passion and strength inside, and it's a lucky visitor who's invited in.

One of the most unnerving aspects of first-time KKH travel is the almost total absence of women on the streets of some towns (eg Gilgit and nearly everywhere in Kohistan and Hazara), or the sundry veils or other textiles thrown over them in public in other towns (eg Kashgar). Then, just as you're getting used to this, an unveiled woman passes by at the wheel of a car, or you arrive in

Hunza or Ishkoman or Khapalu to find all the women unveiled and unashamedly cheerful to visitors of either gender.

Islamic societies allot very different social space to men and to women. Women are seen as subordinate to men, and judged by their abilities as wives, mothers and housekeepers. At the same time they're the standard-bearers of the family's honour, to be shielded from disgrace at all costs. In orthodox communities, women past the age of puberty observe *purdah* (the word is Persian for 'curtain'), ie they're kept away from all men outside the inner family. To the extent that the family can afford not to have them employed outside, they're kept at home. When they must go out they're veiled, often covered from head to toe in the tent-like *burqah*.

Likewise, men are discouraged from associating with women outside the family. Foreign couples may find that *her* questions are being answered to *him*, and that she can't even get eye contact. In a sense, this is respect – in the traditional style.

When she marries, a woman joins her husband's family, and that may mean moving in with them – a major life change in terms of work and responsibility. Once all the daughters have married into other families, the inner household 'matures' as a hierarchy of mother and daughters-in-law. The older women are in charge, involved not only in routine household decisions but often in wider ones, eg about marriages and children's education. Under their surveillance, the younger women are responsible for child rearing, household chores and light farming work.

This world tends to be off limits to foreigners, and certainly to men, though foreign women may be invited into the core of a house. But thanks in Xinjiang to official atheism in the years after 1949, and in Pakistan to mould-breaking attitudes encouraged among Ismailis, the wall between inside and outside is lower in those places. There is no purdah among Ismailis, Baltistan's Nurbakhshi Shias nor Gujar nomads, and it's limited in Xinjiang – although women remain the homemakers.

**South Asian Women's Network**
The South Asian Women's Network (SAWNET) operates a World Wide Web site on South Asian women's issues, with articles, reviews, news and links: http://www.umiacs.umd.edu/users/sawweb/sawnet/index.html. ∎

In Ismaili and progressive Shia areas, education and even outside employment may be available to women, and can elevate a woman in the domestic hierarchy, even into the realm of traditionally male decisions, eg on farming or property. Nowadays this trend is accelerating as some men in the Northern Areas go down-country for months at a time in search of work. Higher education for women does not always meet with increased opportunities, except in certain spheres like local health and education.

In the area of community decisions, the rural development programme of the AKRSP (see the Economy section earlier in this chapter) has encouraged the formation of Women's Organisations (WOs) separate from the usual, often male-dominated, VOs.

### Hospitality

In Islam, a guest – Muslim or not – has a position of honour not understood in the west. If someone visits you and you don't have much to offer, as a Christian you are urged to share what you have; as a Muslim you're urged to give it all away. Traditionally in Hunza, guests are seated higher than the head of the household. In several places we've been the only ones eating in rooms full of hungry-looking spectators.

In the Northern Areas this is a constant source of pleasure, embarrassment and temptation. Most people have little to offer *but* their hospitality, and a casual guest could drain a host's resources and never hear a word about it. It's tactful to very politely refuse gifts or invitations once or twice before accepting them. Someone who doesn't persist with an offer after you decline probably can't afford it anyway. Pulling out your

## Clothing

Nowhere is it easier to offend and insult Muslims – and nowhere have more foreigners done so without thinking – than in the matter of dress. To a devout Muslim, clothes that reveal flesh or the shape of the body are roughly equivalent to walking around in your underwear in the west – ridiculous on men and scandalous on women. Shorts and halter tops are especially offensive. Stick with long, loose, nonrevealing garments. One option is the *shalwar qamiz*, worn by both men and women in Pakistan – amazingly comfortable, and cheap off the shelf or made by a tailor.

This sounds preachy but cannot be emphasised enough. It's not a matter of brownie-points for 'dressing native'. Muslims from everywhere, fundamentalist and liberal, beg to know why so many foreigners refuse this simple courtesy. ∎

own food or offering to pay someone for a kindness may well humiliate them. All you can do is enjoy it, and take yourself courteously out of the picture before you become a burden.

If you're invited to someone's house, always arrive with a small gift, like postcards from home or sweets for the kids. Don't be surprised if you aren't thanked for it: gifts are taken more as evidence of God's mercy than of your generosity. If you're going for a meal, something for the table might do (eg fruit from the market), but don't expect to see it again as some consider it bad form to offer guests food they have brought themselves.

Traditional homes are divided into women's quarters and guest quarters. Most visiting men will never see anything but guest rooms, while women may be coaxed further into the house.

You'll probably be showered with snacks. In this case a refusal would be rude, although meat for a vegetarian or a glass of water from an unknown source can be a problem. Try to present your excuses *before* it's put in front of you; a useful one for drinks is a bad stomach and doctor's orders to drink only hot tea.

If you are to be given food, especially in rural areas, you may first be offered an ewer of water with which to wash your hands before and after the meal; always accept.

In China, at least on the tourist trail, reflex generosity is rare. Uyghurs mainly ignore you in Kashgar. Han Chinese officials, attendants and drivers are generally beastly to everyone.

### Eating with Your Right Hand

The left hand is considered unclean, and handling food with it is disagreeable, if not revolting, to most Muslims. It's an acquired skill to break off bits of chapatti with only the right hand, and not everybody bothers, but few Muslims raise food to their mouth with the left hand. (Many westerners recoil at the thought of eating with *either* hand in some places along the KKH, though even the grottiest cafe usually has a wash stand somewhere.)

### Talking with Hands & Head

Between Pakistani men a handshake is as essential to conversation as eye contact in the west. See the boxed text Handshakes for more about the art of shaking hands.

A common – and oddly appealing – way Pakistanis say 'yes' is by a sideways tilt of the head; foreigners often mistake this for 'I don't care'. Pakistanis may say 'no' with a single *tsk* or *tut*, often with raised eyebrows or a slight backwards flick of the head. It's neither rude nor does it necessarily imply disapproval or surprise. A mere raising of the eyebrows has the same meaning: you may see taxi drivers and rickshaw-wallahs give it when refusing a fare.

A twist of the wrist with fingers outspread seems to be a generalised question, eg 'What's going on here?', 'Where are you going?'. The thumbs up and thumbs down gestures are either rude or likely to be misunderstood.

### Other Body Language

Public physical contact between men and women – holding hands or kissing, with fellow travellers or with local people – is a 'touchy' matter, very often offensive to locals. Holding hands in public is acceptable

**Handshakes**
A heartfelt handshake between older men is a gesture of great warmth and elegance. The hands are held close together and the right hand gently inserted between the other's hands, as he does the same. There is no grabbing or western-style firmness, just a light touch. They are then pulled back, and one hand may be placed over the heart. In Central Asia the hands may, following the handshake, be instead turned palms up and drawn down in front of the face as if washing (a gesture of completion and thanks called the *amin* which you may also see at the end of a meal).

An alternative to the handshake is an equally delicate hug. The hand-on-heart is also a way to convey warmth if you're greeting someone at a distance.

Don't be offended if someone offers you his wrist; he just considers his hand unclean at the moment, eg if he's been eating with it.

Offering a handshake to a Pakistani of the opposite sex may put them in an awkward position; let them make the first move. If you try to shake hands with someone in China, on the other hand, they may act as if you're trying to kiss them. ■

only between members of the same sex (and is not a sign of homosexuality).

Male tourists have been known to wink at local women or otherwise seek out eye contact, but this is as offensive (and potentially risky) as more overt approaches.

Never point the sole of your shoe or foot at a Muslim, step over any part of someone's body or walk in front of someone praying to Mecca.

**Inquiries**
Avoid phrasing questions for yes/no replies, because people will say anything just to avoid saying nothing. For example, ask not 'Is this the bus to Gilgit?', but rather 'Which bus goes to Gilgit?' – and don't believe the answer unless several more people give the same answer!

**RELIGION**
Although the Indus Valley saw the birth of Hinduism and an early flowering of Buddhism (see History earlier in this chapter), both traditions were swept aside by Islam. With the exception of small Christian and Hindu communities in Pakistan and scattered Buddhists in western China, nearly everyone from Turkestan to the Arabian Sea is Muslim, and a good deal of the flavour of KKH travel stems from this fact.

**Islam – History & Schisms**
In 612 AD the Prophet Muhammad, then a wealthy Arab of Mecca, began preaching a new religious philosophy, Islam, based on revelations from Allah (Islam's name for God). Islam incorporated elements of Judaism, Christianity and other faiths (eg heaven and hell, a creation story much like the Garden of Eden, myths like Noah's Ark) and treated their prophets simply as forerunners of the Prophet Muhammad. These revelations were eventually to be compiled into Islam's holy book, the Quran (or Koran).

In 622 Muhammad and his followers were forced to flee to Medina (the Islamic calendar counts its years from this flight or *Hejira*). There he built a political base and an army, taking Mecca in 630 and eventually overrunning Arabia. By the end of his life Muhammad ruled a rapidly growing religious and secular dynasty. The militant faith meshed nicely with a latent Arab nationalism and, within a century, the empire stretched from Spain to Central Asia.

Succession disputes after the Prophet's death soon split the community. When the fourth caliph (ruler), the Prophet's son-in-law Ali, was assassinated in 661, his followers and descendants became the founders of the Shia (or Shi'ite) sect. Others accepted as caliph the governor of Syria, a brother-in-law of the Prophet, and this line has become the modern day orthodox Sunni (or Sunnite) sect. In 680 a chance for reconciliation was lost when Ali's surviving son Hussain and most of his male relatives were killed at Karbala in Iraq

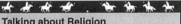

## Talking about Religion

It's not hard to get Muslims to talk about Islam, at least in Pakistan. While you'll probably get into trouble with broad criticisms of Islam, a genuine interest in it will bring an enthusiastic response. You'll probably be asked frequently about your own faith too. Muslims regard Jews and Christians as *ahl-i-kitab*, or 'people of the Book', whose prophets were forerunners to Islam (their name for Jesus is Hazrat Issah) – and therefore to be respected, although Zionism is a favourite bugbear. If you say you don't believe in anything or that you're an existentialist or something, your host may feel obliged to proselytise you.

It is polite to refer to the Prophet Muhammad as such, or as the Holy Prophet, rather than by his name alone. Whenever devout Muslims utter his name, they follow it with *sallallaho alaihe wasallam*, Arabic for 'peace be upon Him'. ∎

by Sunni partisans. Today over 90% of Muslims worldwide are Sunni.

Among Shia doctrines is that of the *imam*, or infallible leader, who continues to unfold the true meaning of the Quran and provides guidance in daily affairs. Most Shias recognise an hereditary line of 12 imams ending in the 9th century (though *imam* is still used, loosely, by modern Shias). These Shias are known as Ithnashari (Twelvers). This book refers to them simply as Shias.

An 8th century split among Shias gave rise to the Ismaili, or Maulai, sect, who disagreed on which son of the sixth imam should succeed him. For Ismaili Shias the line of imams continues into the present. Ismailis today number several million in pockets of Pakistan, India, East Africa, Iran and Syria, and their present leader (since 1957), Prince Karim Aga Khan, is considered to be imam No 49. Doctrines are more esoteric and practices less regimented than those of Ithnashari Shias or Sunnis. The style of prayer is a personal matter (eg there is no prostration), the mosque is replaced by a community hall called a *jamaat khana* and women are less secluded. The present Aga Khan has considerably modernised Ismaili life and set up institutions to bring social and political secu-

rity to the scattered Ismaili communities (see Economy in this chapter).

## Islam along the KKH

Although an Arab expedition reached Kashgar in the 8th century, the earliest conversions to Islam in the Tarim Basin were by rulers of the Qarakhan dynasty in the 12th century. Today most non-Chinese there are Sunni Muslims.

Almost simultaneously with the 8th century Central Asia explorations, an Arab naval force arrived at the mouth of the Indus, but likewise left little religious imprint.

Conversions to Sunnism under duress followed raids from Afghanistan by Mahmud of Ghazni in the 11th century, and later work by Pathan missionaries. Today, people as far north on the KKH as Chilas are all Sunnis, and more fervently so than their Kashgar counterparts.

Alternative doctrines appear to have come to the northern mountains much later. In the 16th century, Taj Mughal, ruler of Badakhshan in north-east Afghanistan, seized Chitral and Gilgit, and is credited with bringing Ismailism

### Sectarian Distribution along the KKH

Following is an approximate 'map' of Islam's variants near the KKH. Shia and Ismaili traditions show a strong Sufi influence.

| | |
|---|---|
| **Xinjiang:** | Sunni, with a small Ismaili Tajik minority near Kashgar, and a few Shia Uyghurs near Yarkand |
| **Gojal:** | all Ismaili |
| **Hunza:** | Ismaili, with a few Shia villages and some Sunnis |
| **Nagar:** | all Shia |
| **Gilgit:** | Shia, Sunni and Ismaili |
| **Ghizar (upper Gilgit River basin):** | Ismaili majority, Sunni minority, with some Shias in Yasin |
| **Chitral:** | mostly Ismaili in the north, Sunni in the south |
| **Baltistan:** | mostly Shia, with a significant minority of Nurbakhshi, and a few Sunni villages |
| **Diamar:** | Chilas, Darel and Tangir are Sunni; Astor about equally Shia and Sunni |
| **Hazara & Indus Kohistan:** | mostly Sunni |

to the region. From Kashmir, Shia Islam moved into Baltistan at perhaps the end of the 16th century, and from there into Bagrot, Haramosh and Hunza-Nagar in the 17th century. Hunza and Gojal, Shia at first, adopted Ismailism in the 19th century. Even today a few old carved Shia mosques can be seen there, a sharp contrast to the spanking green and white jamaat khanas.

A separate Shia sect, called Nurbakhshi, persists in Baltistan's upper valleys, with its own doctrinal variations. While generally conservative, they are noticeable (eg in Khapalu) because, like the Ismailis, the women are not veiled in public.

### Sectarian Violence around Gilgit
Gilgit is the only KKH town with sizeable proportions of Sunnis, Shias and Ismailis. In the past, during the Shias' gripping Ashura processions, Shias and Sunnis exchanged taunts and sometimes gunfire. The opening of local chapters of militant down-country religious parties in the late 1980s politicised this already edgy situation. In 1988, at the end of Ramadan, gun battles erupted in the valleys around Gilgit, leaving at least 100 dead. Many Gilgitis tell stories of armed zealots flooding in from outside the area. There were further killings in the following years.

In 1994 reforms to Northern Areas regulations allowed political parties to field candidates for election to local councils. A number of religious rabble-rousers were elected to comfortable positions, at which point the violence abruptly subsided. Recent years have seen a strenuous effort to heal Gilgit's sectarian wounds, in sharp contrast to the continuing bloodshed down-country.

Tensions remain, of course. Ismailis and Shias are uneasy about puritanical Wahhabi Sunni missionaries; Sunnis and Ismailis are uneasy about contacts between Shias in Baltistan and those in Iran; and Sunnis and Shias cannot always conceal their envy at Ismaili educational and other gains.

Perhaps hardest for Muslims along the KKH are the internal tensions between their traditions and the libertarian popular culture

imported by down-country Pakistanis and foreign tourists. These have undoubtedly pushed most locals into a more conservative religious posture than before.

### Practice
Islam translates loosely from Arabic as 'the peace that comes from total surrender to God'. God's will is articulated in the Quran. In addition to the creeds set out there, Muslims express their surrender in the form of daily prayers, alms giving, fasting and pilgrimage to Mecca. In its fullest sense Islam is an entire way of life, with guidelines for doing nearly everything. Among prohibitions honoured by the devout are those against eating pork and drinking alcohol.

In addition to midday congregations on the Friday day of rest, devout Muslims pray five times each day, in a mosque if possible (though generally women may not enter mosques). Sunnis pray at prescribed times: before sunrise, just after high noon, late afternoon, just after sunset and before retiring. For Shias there are three fixed times – before sunrise and twice in the evening – the other two being at one's discretion. Prayers are preceded if possible by washing, at least of hands, face and feet.

Just before fixed prayers a *muezzin* calls the Sunni and Shia faithful, traditionally from a minaret, nowadays often through a loudspeaker. The Arabic *azan*, or call to prayer, translates roughly as 'God is most great. There is no God but Allah. Muhammad is God's messenger. Come to prayer, come to security. God is most great'.

Islam has no ordained priesthood, but *maulvis* or *maulanas* (commonly called *mullahs)* are rather like priests, trained in theology, respected as interpreters of scripture, and very influential in rural areas. Many educated people in Pakistan despise them, not out of scorn for Islam but because some mullahs are corrupt and distort teachings for their own ends.

When visiting a mosque, always take your shoes off at the door, and make sure your feet or socks are clean. Often at larger mosques there is an attendant to look after your shoes, who may expect a small tip, say Rs 5.

## Sufism

The original Sufis were simply purists, seeking knowledge of God through direct personal experience, unhappy with the worldliness of the early caliphates. There never was a single Sufi movement, but numerous branches. For many of them music, dance or poetry about the search for God were routes to trance and revelation. This is the mystical side of Islam, just like similar traditions in other faiths.

Sufis were singularly successful as missionaries, perhaps because of their tolerance of other creeds. It was largely the Sufis, not Arab or other armies, who took Islam into Central Asia and the subcontinent. In some ways southern Pakistan is Sufism's 'home' now, abounding with colourful shrines to *pirs*, or Sufi holy men, and bursting into colourful celebration at their various *urs*, or death-dates.

## Ramadan

Ramadan (also called Ramazan in Pakistan) is the Muslim month of fasting, a sort of ritual cleansing of body and mind, with eating, drinking (even water) and smoking forbidden from sunrise to sunset. The devout take meals in the evening and just before sunrise; muezzin calls signal the end of each day's fasting. Ismailis don't take part.

Children, pregnant women, very old and/or ill people, travellers and non-Muslims are exempt, though they are expected not to eat or drink in front of those who are fasting. People on flights and shorter train journeys may continue to observe the fast.

Food and drink are hard to find during daylight hours, offices keep odd hours, tempers are short and very little serious business gets done. On the KKH, the best places for non-Muslims to find food are tourist hotels, bus stations, Ismaili neighbourhoods in Gilgit, or almost anywhere in Gojal or Hunza (but not Nagar).

Curiously, Pakistanis are said to eat *more* during Ramadan than at other times, putting away bigger than normal meals during the night. Food prices actually go up then. *Approximate* future dates for the beginning of Ramadan are 19 December 1998, 9 December 1999 and 27 November 2000.

# Facts for the Visitor

## PLANNING
### When to Go

**Weather** For clear skies and moderate temperatures, the best time to travel the KKH is September to October, and good weather stays with you longer on a southbound journey. Both mountain cold and lowland heat are quite bearable at this time. Mountain roads are in decent condition. Fresh vegetables and fruit are plentiful. Since most tourists have gone home, hotels may lower their rates. Next best is May to June, with good weather following you north-bound, though skies aren't as reliably clear as in the autumn.

Summer is ferociously hot and dry in Kashgar, pleasantly warm and occasionally stormy in Gojal and Hunza, very hot and rainy from Kohistan south. From Kashgar to Gilgit, winter is long and cold (often well below freezing), with snow common in the mountains. Kashgar can be unpleasant from mid-October, when wet cold can set in, to mid-November, when winter officially arrives and the heat is turned on.

**Crossing the Khunjerab Pass** The pass is formally open to travellers from 1 May, though on rare occasions it opens later on account of snow. When it closes depends on whom you ask. The Northern Areas Transportation Company (Natco) at Sost says 30 November, while immigration at Sost says it closes on 15 November for foreigners coming or going and for Pakistanis going to China, but remains open all the time for Pakistanis returning from China.

Snow often closes it by mid-November anyway. The closure decision is taken at the last possible moment, and only senior immigration or transportation officials at Sost or Tashkurgan really know what's going on.

The pass stays open year-round for traders, officials and postal service. Both governments would like to make the KKH an all-weather road, but haven't made plans yet for a winter crossing.

**Crowds** Two very popular areas – the Kaghan Valley and the Galis – get so crowded in summer that they're worth avoiding unless you

---

have a booking or a tent. Hotel prices sky-rocket then, but off season you can strike some fine bargains in these same places.

**Ramadan** The KKH from Gilgit south is difficult during Ramadan, the Muslim month of daytime fasting. People are irritable and food can be hard to find until sunset except in Ismaili areas (north of Gilgit) or at tourist hotels – though one traveller reported a strong atmosphere of camaraderie (shared suffering?) at this time. The dates change each year; see the Public Holidays & Special Events section later in this chapter.

### What Kind of Trip?
Just start at one end and go to the other, by cheap bus or minibus if you're hardy, or with a gorgeous air journey between Gilgit (or Skardu) and Islamabad if you can bag a seat. Alternatives are to go from Pakistan into China as far as Kashgar and return, or from China as far as Hunza or Gilgit and return – though you'll need a double-entry visa for the starting country.

It's possible to do the trip in relative comfort if you have the cash – in a hired Land Cruiser from Kashgar to Sost, minibus or Land Cruiser from Sost to Hunza and Gilgit, and a Gilgit to Islamabad flight. If you're northbound, however, Pakistani vehicles can only go to Tashkurgan, so there's little alternative to the bumpy Chinese bus from there to Kashgar.

### Maps
The maps described here are for village-hoppers and map freaks.

**Pakistan** Best is the US Army Map Service (AMS) multi-colour U-502 series at 1:250,000 scale. Last revised in 1958-64, they show the topography and most villages but not the KKH and many other roads. Pakistan sheets for the KKH region are: NJ 43-15 (Shimshal, covers the Khunjerab area), NJ 43-14 (Baltit, covers Gojal and Hunza), NI 43-2 (Gilgit), NI 43-3 (Mundik, covers Skardu) and NI 43-1 (Churrai, covers northern Indus Kohistan). These have an

up-to-date successor, a four colour series called JOG (Joint Operations Ground), but it's in use by the US military and unavailable to the general public.

The Swiss Foundation for Alpine Research has a pricey but precise two-sheet 1:250,000 scale trekking map of the Karakoram. A good but expensive four sheet Karakoram set at 1:200,000 scale is published by Leomann.

Finely detailed three-colour maps at 1:50,000 by Deutscher Alpenverein (DAV) – *Minapin* (north slopes of Rakaposhi) and *Nanga Parbat* – are top of the line for these peaks. DAV also publishes a 1:100,000 scale *Hunza-Karakorum* map of the Hunza Valley.

The coloured Operational Navigation Chart (ONC) aeronautical chart series at 1:1,000,000 scale by the US Defense Mapping Agency includes two of the KKH in Pakistan, G-6 and G-7. They make fine wall hangings, but precision is low, many place names are obsolete and they're expensive.

The Survey of Pakistan has coloured topographic maps at 1:1,000,000 and 1:500,000 scale. Another useful Survey map, low on precision but with historical, linguistic, ethnic and religious maps of the Northern Areas, is the 1:500,000 scale *Northern Area of Pakistan*.

You can find some or all of these in Gilgit bookshops, and in Rawalpindi at the Survey of Pakistan, the Book Centre in Saddar Bazaar or, at twice the price, in the Pearl Continental Hotel's bookshop.

IUCN-Pakistan, the Pakistan branch of The World Conservation Union, plans to publish a map of the Central Karakoram National Park (for addresses see Ecology & Environment in the Facts about the Region chapter).

**Xinjiang** The handsomest map for the region around Kongur and Muztagh Ata is the multi-colour 1:100,000 scale *Kongur Tag – Muztag Ata*, published by the Lanzhou Institute of Glaciology and Geocryology, and available from GeoCenter ILH (see the following Ordering Maps section).

ONC sheets covering the Tarim Basin in

Xinjiang are G-7, F-6 and F-7, though their use may be frowned upon in China. U-502 maps are not generally available for Xinjiang. The only other available maps of Xinjiang are the Russian Survey's 1:200,000 scale *Mir* series.

**Ordering Maps** Following are good mail-order sources.

Aree Greul, Am Goldsteinpark 28, D-60529 Frankfurt am Main, Germany (☎ /fax (069) 666 1817)

GeoCenter ILH, Schockenriedstrasse 44, Postfach 80 08 30, D-70508 Stuttgart, Germany (☎ (0711) 788 93 40; fax (0711) 788 93 54; email geocent erilh@t-online.de)

Libreria Alpina, Via C Coroned-Berti 4, 40137 Bologna, Zona 3705, Italy

Stanfords, 12-14 Long Acre, Covent Garden, London WC2E 9LP, UK (☎ (0171) 836 1321; fax (0171) 836 0189)

US Library of Congress, Geography & Map Division, 101 Independence Ave, Washington, DC 20540, USA (photocopies only; their post-1968 maps can be searched on their Web site)

**Regional & City Maps** Pakistan Tourist Development Corporation (PTDC) offices occasionally have brochures on the KKH & the Silk Road, Trekking, the Northern Areas, Hunza, the Gilgit Valley, Skardu, Swat, the Kaghan Valley and Taxila, though the tiny maps are no use for finding your way around. PTDC has two versions of a tourist map of Rawalpindi and Islamabad, for sale at tourist information centres in both cities; the better of them has Faisal Mosque on the cover. There's no PTDC map of Gilgit.

The Survey of Pakistan's *Islamabad & Rawalpindi Guide Map* at 1:30,000 is quite detailed, though many street names are out of date. It's available at bookshops in the capital area. A good 1996 Islamabad map from Pakistan Views and Tourism System, including an office-by-office guide to the commercial Blue Area, is unfortunately hard to find; they have been spotted at Islamabad's Friday Bazaar.

**Other Maps** The Capital Development Authority (CDA) in Islamabad has a map-brochure, *Trekking in the Margalla Hills,* showing walks and resthouses in the hills behind Islamabad. CDA is on Khayaban-i-Suhrawardy (south G-7, west of Aabpara).

**What to Bring**
Bring as little as you can. You can pick up many items in Kashgar, Gilgit or Rawalpindi. It's cheap to have clothes and sleeping sheets made in Pakistani bazaars; you can even get your western clothes copied. You can find toilet paper, candles, matches, second-rate batteries, laundry soap, toothbrushes, old-style razor blades, shampoo (including handy individual sachets), aspirin and instant coffee in shops.

For carrying it all, an internal-frame or soft pack is most manageable on buses; a 'convertible' (an internal-frame pack with a handle, and a flap to hide the straps) looks respectable when you want to.

**Clothing** For the range of KKH conditions and the potential for cold-weather exertion, many light layers work better than a few heavy ones. On the China-Pakistan bus you'll need warm clothing in any season. Rain can strike in Pakistan at any time but especially in July and August.

Comfortable, sturdy, water-resistant walking shoes are adequate for all but glacier walks and long or snowy treks, for which you'd need good boots. Non-trekkers might get away with trainers (gym shoes) except in the rainy season, although you tend to walk more than you expect. Sandals are a relief in warm, dry weather; high-tech trekking sandals are the rage in western shops. Local sandals *(chappal)* are cheap and common (though they're often hard to break in), as are shower flip-flops. Shoe repair is cheap and convenient.

Clothing has powerful social overtones in Islamic countries, and in no other way have westerners managed to offend Asians more than by the way they dress. To a devout Muslim, clothes that reveal flesh (other than face, hands and feet) or the shape of the body look silly on men and scandalous on women. Shorts, singlets and halter tops are especially offensive. For women visitors, avoiding these is not only an elementary courtesy but may also reduce hostility or harassment.

This doesn't mean you have to wear a choir robe – just long, loose, nonrevealing shirts, trousers or skirts (which are in any case the most comfortable in summer). Ideally your arms should be covered to the wrist, and your ankles should remain covered even when you're sitting cross-legged. For women a light scarf over the hair is appropriate when visiting homes. The local *shalwar qamiz* (shalwar is baggy trousers, qamiz is a long shirt) is very comfortable and can be made in the bazaar for Rs 350 and up. In big cities conservative western dress is common.

**Camping Gear** For one-off trips you can often find second-hand tents, pads and cooking equipment for sale in shops or for rent from local tour agencies in Gilgit and Skardu.

Sleeping bags are hard to find anywhere. You can find basic food for camping but you might want to bring favourite dried foods such as soup mixes.

**Trekking Equipment** Bring your own. Trekking equipment is not manufactured in Pakistan, and the most you can hire or buy are the bits left behind by expeditions. Guides, agencies and a few shops in Gilgit, Passu, Skardu, Hushe and Chitral have tents, sleeping pads, stoves and mountaineering gear. Note that down clothing is hard to find.

**Gifts** If you are invited to a private home, you should never arrive empty-handed. Some portable but well received gifts are badges, pins, key rings, sweets, postcards, cancelled stamps and flower seeds from home. Family photos always go down well. Drivers are especially keen on stickers (placed near the top of your pack, these may also deflect greedy customs officials from more expensive gadgets). For special friends, consider a picture book of the nearest big city to your home, a good fountain pen or music tapes.

**Other** Besides the usual take-alongs, good KKH ideas are eating utensils, water bottle, sunglasses, sunscreen, lip salve, sunhat, a light daypack, penknife, thermal long johns, shower flip-flops and a compass. A torch is welcome in places with dodgy or nonexistent electricity. A universal sink plug is very handy: Islamic custom favours washing in running water so lower-end hotels rarely have plugs. Hotels tend not to give you towels, either.

Other ideas are a length of cord as a washing line, stuff-sacks or plastic bags, and a small sewing kit. Ear plugs provide relief in noisy hotels. People love exchanging business or visiting cards.

Women should buy tampons before coming to Pakistan, though you can find them in upmarket shopping areas of Islamabad. Chinese department stores, including those in Kashgar, have sanitary towels.

Men who decide to leave blade and brush behind and get their shaves at public barbershops should give a thought to the risk of Hepatitis B or HIV transmission via shared razors.

Seasoned travellers will already have a secure passport-and-money belt. It's worth taking a good portable water filter. For a medical kit and photography gear, see the Health and Photography & Video sections later in this chapter.

## TOURIST OFFICES
### Local Tourist Offices – China
**China International Travel Service** (CITS-lüxingshe in Chinese) is the original state travel bureau for non-Chinese group tourists. Since CTS (see the following section) now competes for the same market, CITS's attitude to individual travellers has improved, but their prices – to book hotels, transport, tours and tickets – remain high. In Kashgar they serve mainly as a travel agency and are not a reliable source of local information.

CITS Beijing (Head Office; ☎ (010) 6601 1122; fax (010) 6601 2013), 103 Fuxing Mennei
CITS Ürümqi (☎ (0991) 282 1428 or 284 5707; fax (0991) 281 8691 or 281 0689; email citsxj@ public.wl.xj.cn), 51 Xinhua Beilu

CITS Kashgar (☎ (0998) 282 5390; fax (0998) 282 3087), 2nd floor, 93 Seman Lu (beside Chini Bagh Hotel)

CITS Hong Kong (☎ (852) 2732-5888; fax (852) 2721-7154), 12th floor, Tower A, New Mandarin Plaza, 14 Science Museum Rd, Tsimshatsui East, Kowloon

**China Travel Service** (CTS) originally looked after overseas Chinese 'compatriots' with cheaper hotels and lower fares than CITS, but since 1992 it's after the non-Chinese market too. Standards are more modest than at CITS but bookings on the whole are cheaper. Like CITS, the Kashgar office is mainly a travel agency.

CTS Beijing (☎ (010) 6461 2591; fax (010) 6461 2593), 2 Beisanhuan Donglu, 4th floor, CTS Tower

CTS Ürümqi (☎ (0991) 451 1403; fax (0991) 451 7401), 71 Youyi Nanlu

CTS Kashgar (☎ (0998) 283 2875; fax (0998) 282 2552), 4th floor, 93 Seman Lu (beside Chini Bagh Hotel)

CTS Hong Kong (☎ (852) 2853 3888; fax (852) 2541 9777), 4th floor, CTS House, 78-83 Connaught Rd, Central

**China Youth Travel Service** Little (CYTS) offers most of the same services as CTS, at similar prices, and they're no longer just for 'youth'. CYTS in Ürümqi (Jianshi Lu just east of the Holiday Inn, with branches at the Hongshan and other hotels) seems the best bet there for bookings to Kashgar. There is no Kashgar office.

## Local Tourist Offices – Pakistan
**Pakistan Tourism Development Corpora-tion** (PTDC), the promotional arm of the Tourism Division, Pakistan Ministry of Culture, Sports & Tourism, operates tourist information centres in major towns, a few of which are very helpful. However, PTDC's commitment in the Northern Areas can be gauged by a general lack of useful informa-tion for individuals (eg no map of Gilgit or other Northern Areas towns) and its huge motels that hog – and often spoil – the most popular of the region's panoramic views.

PTDC's group-tour affiliate is Pakistan Tours Ltd (PTL).

PTDC Head Office (☎ (051) 294790; fax (051) 294540), House 170, Street 36, F-10/1, Islam-abad

PTDC Motels Reservation Office (☎ (051) 920 3223; fax (051) 921 8233), Block 4-B, Bhitai Rd, F-7 Markaz, Islamabad

PTL, Flashman's Hotel, The Mall, Rawalpindi (☎ (051) 581480; fax (051) 565449)

Tourist information centres near the KKH include:

Abbottabad: Club Annexe, Jinnah Rd (☎ (0992) 34399)

Balakot: PTDC Motel (☎ (0985) 208)

Besham: PTDC Motel (☎ (0941) 92)

Gilgit: Chinar Inn, Babar Rd (☎ (0572) 2562)

Islamabad: 13-T/U College Rd, F-7/2 (☎ (051) 920 2766)

Rawalpindi: Flashman's Hotel, The Mall (☎ (051) 517073)

Saidu Sharif: PTDC Motel (☎ (0936) 711205)

Skardu: K2 Motel (☎ (0575) 2946)

Taxila: PTDC Motel, Museum Rd (☎ (0596) 2344)

**Tourism Development Corporation of the Punjab** (TDCP) has a few brochures and maps of the Punjab, and in Murree they're more helpful than PTDC. Tourist informa-tion offices near the KKH are:

Murree: Cart Rd (☎ (0593) 410729) and The Mall (☎ (0593) 410730)

Rawalpindi: 44 Mall Plaza, corner of The Mall and Kashmir Rd (☎ (051) 564824)

## Tourist Offices Abroad
**China International Travel Service** Over-seas, CITS is represented by the China National Tourist Office (CNTO). Offices include:

CITS Australia (☎ (02) 9299 4057; fax (02) 9290 1958), Level 19, 44 Market St, Sydney, NSW 2000

CITS France (☎ (01) 44 21 82 82; fax (01) 44 21 81 00), 116 Avenue des Champs-Elysées, 75008 Paris

CITS UK (☎ (0171) 935 9787; fax (0171) 487 5842), 4 Glentworth St, London NW1

The start of a long descent toward Kara Kul, Xinjiang, China.

JOHN KING

JOHN KING

JOHN KING

Top Left: Rama Lake and Nanga Parbat, Astor Valley.
Top Right: Muztagh Ata (7546m) looms over a Kyrgyz village.
Bottom: A Pakistani view of Khunjerab Pass.

CITS USA (☎ (212) 760-9700; fax (212) 760-8809), 350 Fifth Ave, Suite 6413, Empire State Bldg, New York, NY 10118

CITS USA (☎ (818) 545-7507; fax (818) 545-0666), 333 W Broadway, Suite 201, Glendale, CA 91204

**China Travel Service** Overseas CTS offices include:

CTS Australia (☎ (02) 9211 2633; fax (02) 9281 3595), 757-759 George St, Sydney, NSW 2000

CTS Canada (☎ (250) 872-8787; fax (250) 873-2823), 556 West Broadway, Vancouver, BC V5Z 1E9

CTS France (☎ (01) 44 51 55 66; fax (01) 44 51 55 60), 32 Rue Vignon, 75009 Paris

CTS UK (☎ (0171) 836 9911; fax (0171) 836 3121), CTS House, 7 Upper St Martin's Lane, London WC2H 9DL

CTS USA (☎ 800-332-2831 toll-free, or (415) 398-6627; fax (415) 398-6669), 575 Sutter St, 2nd floor, San Francisco, CA 94102

## VISAS & DOCUMENTS
### Passport
Check the expiry date of your passport, as you may have trouble getting a visa if it expires during or soon after your proposed visit. Domestic passport offices and many overseas embassies can provide you with a new one, or insert new pages in your present one, fairly quickly. However, some won't, so you should ensure that you have enough space in your passport *before* your trip.

### Visas
While there are many stories of visa-related hassles – mostly on arrival or departure – a few essential moves will keep you out of trouble. Get your visas *before* you arrive; you can't enter China without one, and getting one in advance for Pakistan avoids a stressful paper chase in Islamabad. Don't let them expire, even by a day: it's just an excuse for 'regulations' and 'fees' you can't verify. And if you're staying more than 30 days in Pakistan, register with the police.

You can almost always get China and Pakistan visas from the respective embassies in your home country. Some accept applications by post, though this takes longer. You'll need one or two passport-size photos. Some travel agents will get visas for you.

There are also visa services, eg Visa Services (☎ (202) 387-0300, or toll-free ☎ 800-222-VISA; fax (202) 387-5650), 1519 Connecticut Ave NW, Washington, DC 20036, USA; and Worldwide Visas (☎ (0171) 379 0419; fax (0171) 497 2590), 9 Adelaide St, London WC2 4HZ, UK.

**Travel to Hong Kong SAR**
With Hong Kong reverting to Chinese control from 1 July 1997, becoming the Hong Kong Special Administrative Region, what's changed for the traveller to Hong Kong? The situation may change, but the short answer is 'not much'. The long answer is this:

**Visas** British citizens do not need tourist visas to enter Hong Kong (for up to six months) but they are now required to apply for working visas. The visa requirements for Australians, Canadians and other Commonwealth nations ( generally three months visa-free stay), Americans (one month visa-free) and EU citizens (usually three months visa-free; Germans get one) do not change.

Note that some Hong Kong travel agencies, eg Phoenix Services and Shoestring Travel, and the Visa Office of the PRC Ministry of Foreign Affairs (see the China Visas section) will still arrange visas to mainland China.

The border between Hong Kong and mainland China will remain in place. Delays at the Hong Kong-Shenzen crossing have occurred; in September 1997 authorities began looking at streamlining it.

**Consulates** The British have opened a new consulate, while the Australian, Canadian and other Commonwealth-country commissions will become consulates. Other consulates remain as before.

**Currency** Hong Kong's currency (HK$) will not change. ■

**China Visas** Everyone needs a visa to enter the People's Republic of China (PRC), and you cannot get one at the border with Pakistan. A normal tourist ('L') visa allows you to enter China up to three months from the date of issue, and stay for 30 days from the date of entry. With it you can visit any open city or region, and while in China you can extend your visa and get travel permits for some restricted areas.

Visas are fairly easy to get from PRC embassies or consulates in western and other countries, including Pakistan. Fees depend on nationality and where you apply, eg at the time of research a single-entry, 30 day visa, available in about a week, was £25 for Britons in the UK, US$30 for Americans in the USA and A$30 for Australians in Oz (cash only).

One of the easiest places to get a China visa is Hong Kong, most cheaply from the Visa Office of the PRC Ministry of Foreign Affairs (☎ (852) 2585 1700), 5th floor, Low Block, China Resources Building, 26 Harbour Rd, Wanchai. A 30 day, single-entry visa, issued in one working day, is HK$100, plus a HK$160 surcharge for US passport holders; quicker service costs more.

Pricier multiple-entry and long-stay visas are available, most easily in Hong Kong. Two reliable Hong Kong travel agencies who can get these are Phoenix Services (☎ (852) 2722 7378), 6th floor, Milton Mansion, 96 Nathan Rd, Tsimshatsui, Kowloon; and Shoestring Travel (☎ (852) 2723 2306), 4th floor, Block A, Alpha House, 27 Peking Rd, Tsimshatsui, Kowloon.

In your application you must identify entry/exit points, itinerary and means of transport, though you can deviate from these as much as you like. Don't give your occupation as writer or journalist, and don't mention bicycles. For information on bringing a bicycle into China, see the Bicycle entry in the Getting There & Away chapter.

**Pakistan Visas** Just about everybody needs a visa to enter Pakistan. With a single-entry tourist visa you can normally enter up to six months from the date of issue, and stay for

up to three months from the date of entry. You can go almost anywhere except sensitive border areas and remote or high-elevation places where you'd need a trekking or mountaineering permit. Pakistan may refuse entry to nationals of Israel (except transit passengers and children under two years old).

It's clearly sensible to get a visa before you arrive. Travellers arriving in Pakistan without a visa may get a transit visa (also called a landing permit), but policies change as fast as the weather, and immigration officials can be a bit arbitrary. You may get as little as 72 hours. At the time of research travellers arriving from China at Sost were getting a week at most.

You can apply for one at most Pakistan embassies or consulates in western and other countries. Processing usually takes a few days. Costs vary wildly, depending on nationality and where you apply, eg Britons pay £40 in the UK, Americans pay US$20 in the USA, Australians pay A$40 in Oz (cash only).

From the embassy in your own country you're most likely to get the full three months, plus multiple-entry options. Visas from some consular offices, eg Hong Kong, are only valid for three months and good for a one month stay.

If you decide while in Pakistan to depart and then return (eg from Sost up to Kashgar and back) and don't already have a multiple-entry Pakistan visa, you can get a re-entry visa in Islamabad.

***Foreigners' Registration*** On arrival in Pakistan you complete an embark/disembark card and a health declaration, and immigration puts an entry stamp in your passport. If you stay for 30 days or less, no other formalities apply, and on departure immigration just puts an exit stamp in your passport.

But if you stay more than 30 days you become a 'resident', and before the 30 days are up you must register at a Foreigners' Registration Office (FRO) in the district where you're staying. Bring three or four passport-size photos, photocopies of the data pages of your passport and of your visa, and – if you happened to get one on entry to

Pakistan – the Temporary Certificate of Registration or Form C (see the boxed text). Fill out multiple copies of the Certificate of Registration (Form B). You will get a copy of Form B and a Residential Permit. There is no fee.

It might be wise to ask them to note your proposed point of exit on the Residential Permit, if it's different from your entry point. Some officials have chosen to hassle travellers who didn't have such a note, though we know of no legal requirement to have it.

If as a resident you go to a new district and stay for more than seven days, you're expected to transfer your registration by reporting to the FRO there within 24 hours of your arrival, with Form B and the Residential Permit. For example, if you registered in Rawalpindi and then head up the KKH with the intention of exiting to China, you should reregister at Gilgit, the closest FRO to the border; while if you merely visit Peshawar for four days, there's no need to reregister there. Other places in northern Pakistan to which you can shift your registration are Skardu, Khapalu, Chilas, Gakuch and Chitral.

When you're about to leave Pakistan, go to the FRO in the town where you're currently registered, surrender your Certificate of Registration and Residential Permit, and apply for a Travel Permit – essentially a permit to get from there to a specified border point, valid for seven days (although the Gilgit FRO officer told us 'one to two weeks'). Some FRO officers may insist that you return to your original place of registration, as opposed to the current one, but stand your ground. Be sure they get the right border point too. There is no fee. You then turn in the Travel Permit to immigration on departure.

What if you stay more than 30 days but don't register, or don't get a Travel Permit, or want to linger more than seven days en route to the border? You *might* have no problem if you're headed for China; Sost officials are pretty laid-back. But you may run into big problems or even a shakedown if you depart via Karachi airport. If you have quite accidentally stayed over 30 days without

**Whatever Happened to Form C?**
As if Pakistan's registration process isn't already Kafkaesque enough, arriving visitors are occasionally handed a Temporary Certificate of Registration (Form C), to be handed over if and when they register, although few if any FRO officers seem interested in it. Nevertheless, we travelled out of Pakistan at Sost with the first Georgian (from the Caucasus) they had ever seen, and on exit immigration officers asked him for Form C, even though he hadn't stayed for 30 days. You figure it out! ■

registering, you're expected to get a Certificate of No Objection from the Interior Ministry, in Block R of the Secretariat in Islamabad, and then register.

***Exemption from Registration?*** The 30 day registration requirement is claimed *not* to apply to certain nationalities, including Australians, Britons and citizens of the UAE. However, FRO officials at Gilgit told us that this exemption no longer applies. For current information on this, you'll have to ask at Islamabad.

**China & Pakistan Visa Extensions** With a China visa you can get at least one 15-day extension after arrival, at the Foreign Affairs section of any Public Security Bureau (PSB). In Kashgar, this office (called the Division of Aliens & Exit-Entry Administration) is on Shengli Lu. Price depends on nationality, eg in Kashgar at the time of research it was Y60 for Australians, Y65 for Britons and Y110 for Canadians.

Islamabad is the only place to extend a Pakistan visa. If you're somewhere else with time running out, local police might provide a letter of authorisation giving you a few extra days to get to Islamabad or to the border. The Civil Secretariat in provincial capitals can do the same, eg if you arrive from Iran and get 72 hours, Quetta's Civil Secretariat will give you an extra seven days to get to Islamabad.

For details of the paper chase in Islamabad, see the boxed text Visa Extension,

Replacement or Modification, in the Information section of the Rawalpindi & Islamabad chapter.

## Travel Permits

Besides the open areas accessible with just a visa, there are restricted areas in China you can visit with an Alien Travel Permit *tongxing zheng*, available from the Foreign Affairs section of any PSB for Y10. An example near Kashgar is Kara Kul lake (although lately nobody seems to be asking for this at Kara Kul). They're available from the police in Kashgar and Tashkurgan. For information on the need for permits for cyclists, see the boxed text Chinese Bicycle Permit? in the Getting There & Away chapter.

## Travellers Cheque Purchase Receipts

You'll need these to replace lost or stolen travellers cheques. Carry them in a separate place from the cheques. Some Pakistani banks may even ask to see the purchase receipts when you cash travellers cheques.

## Travel Insurance

However you're travelling, it's worth taking out travel insurance. A policy for theft, loss, flight cancellation and medical treatment overseas is a good idea. For an extended trip, insurance may seem an extravagance, but if you can't afford it, you can't afford a medical emergency overseas either. Many agencies like STA Travel, Trailfinders and Campus Travel offer cheaper policies with no baggage cover.

Check the small print. Some policies are not valid outside the country of issue. Some exclude 'dangerous activities', which can include white-water rafting or even trekking. If these are on your agenda, ask about an amendment to permit some of them (at a higher premium).

Few medical services along the KKH will accept your foreign insurance documents for payment; you'll have to pay on the spot, get receipts for everything, save all the paperwork and claim later.

## Hostel Card

Hostels run by the Pakistan Youth Hostels Association in the Kaghan Valley, Abbottabad, the Galis and Taxila are part of the Hostelling International (HI) network, and a HI card from your hostelling association at home entitles you to the standard cheap rates (see the Accommodation section in this chapter).

## Student & Youth Cards

Occasional discounts – eg for long-distance buses, and occasionally at hotels – are available to full-time students and may also be given to those under 26 years of age.

The International Student Identity Card (ISIC), specifically aimed at travel-related costs, is sold by youth-oriented travel agencies and directly by ISIC Mail Order, Bleaklow House, Howard Town Mills, Mill Street, Glossop SK13 8PT, UK, for about UK£5. The 'Under-26' youth card, offering more general discounts but fewer travel benefits, is available from youth-travel agencies and directly from Under 26 Mail Order, 52 Grosvenor Gardens, London SW1W 0AG, UK, for UK£6. Both cards are good for a year.

Student cards can often be left as a deposit (instead of your passport) when you rent a bicycle in China.

## Bicycle Details

If you're cycling on your own machine, seasoned bicycle tourists suggest carrying a written description and a photograph of it (to help police in case it's stolen), and proof of ownership.

## HIV & Other Health Certifications

At the time of research, visitors planning to staying in China longer than six months or in Pakistan longer than a year were required to give proof of a negative Human Immunodeficiency Virus (HIV) test when they apply for a visa.

Anyone required to take medication containing a narcotic drug should have a doctor's certificate.

## Currency-Exchange Receipts

At some Pakistani banks some travellers have been asked for exchange receipts when they sold back rupees on departure. The total of the receipts should be more than the amount you want to sell back. (See also the Changing Money section later in this chapter.)

## Export Permit

An export permit is necessary to *post* out of Pakistan any purchase whose declared value is over Rs 500. Getting one on your own is a headache, though PTDC or your hotel-wallah might help. To the export office in Islamabad or another big city you must bring purchase receipt, foreign exchange receipts to at least the value of the purchase, an explanatory letter from you to 'The Controller (Import & Export)', plus photocopies of these and of the data pages of your passport.

Many carpet shops will give you a receipt for a fraction of the true cost of the carpet to help you around this requirement.

## Photocopies

It's wise to carry photocopies of the data pages of your passport and of your visas, to ease paperwork headaches should they be lost or stolen. Other copies worth carrying are of your credit card and travellers cheque numbers (plus telephone numbers for cancelling or replacing them), airline tickets (easily mangled in a sweaty money belt) and travel insurance policy.

Carry these in a separate place from the originals. If you're travelling with someone, you could swap copies. To be doubly secure, leave copies with someone at home too.

## Other Documents

Half a dozen passport-size photos will save you some annoyance in the thick of bureaucratic paperwork, though it's possible to get them in any sizeable town. Important-looking cards and documents with seals, stamps, logos and plastic laminations may also impress people when the need arises.

## EMBASSIES

Embassies are usually open for visa formalities only during limited hours, and usually close on the national holidays of both their own and the host countries, so it's smart to call ahead before trekking out to one.

## People's Republic of China Embassies Abroad

Australia
　(☎ (06) 273 4780; fax (06) 273 4878), 15 Coronation Drive, Yarralumla, ACT 2600; there is also a consulate in Melbourne.
Canada
　(☎ (613) 234-2706), PO Box 8935, 515 St Patrick St, Ottawa, Ontario K1N 5H3; there are also consulates in Toronto and Vancouver.
France
　(☎ (01) 47 20 86 82), 21 Rue de l'Amiral Destaing, 75016 Paris
India
　(☎ (011) 600328), 50-D Shantipath, Chanakyapuri, New Delhi 110021
Kazakhstan
　(☎ (3272) 634966, 639291), Furmanov köshesi 137, Almaty
Kyrgyzstan
　(☎ (3312) 222423; fax (3312) 639372), Toktogul 196, Bishkek
Netherlands
　(☎ (070) 355 1515), Adriaan Goekooplaan 7, 2517 JX The Hague
New Zealand
　(☎ (04) 587 0407) 104A Korokoro Rd, Petone, Wellington
Pakistan
　(visa office; ☎ (051) 279600), Diplomatic Enclave, Islamabad
Switzerland
　(visa office; ☎ (031) 351 4593), Kalechewegg 10, 3006 Bern
Turkmenistan
　(☎ (3632) 473683), Ulitsa Sankt Pazina 2, Ashghabat
UK
　(☎ (0171) 631 1430; recorded visa information ☎ (0891) 880808), Consular Section, 31 Portland Place, London W1N 3AG; there is also a consulate in Manchester.
USA
　(☎ (202) 328-2500; visa section ☎ (202) 338-6688; fax (202) 588-9760), 2300 Connecticut Avenue NW, Washington, DC 20008; there are also consulates in Chicago, Houston, Los Angeles, New York, and San Francisco.

Uzbekistan
(☎ (3712) 333779, 338088), Gogol 79, Tashkent, but does not normally issue tourist visas.


## Pakistan Embassies Abroad

Australia
(☎ (06) 290 1676), 59 Franklin St, PO Box 198, Manuka, Canberra, ACT 2603; there is also a consulate in Sydney.

Canada
(☎ (613) 238-7881; fax (613) 238-7296), 151 Slater St, Suite 608, Ottawa K1P 5H3; there are also consulates in Montreal and Toronto.

China
(☎ (010) 532 2504), 1 Dongzhimenwai Dajie, Sanlitun Compound, Beijing; there is also a consulate in Hong Kong (☎ (852) 2827 0681) at Suite 3806, China Resources Building, 26 Harbour Rd, Wanchai.

India
(☎ (011) 600604), 2/50-G Shantipath, Chanakyapuri, New Delhi

Iran
(☎ (021) 934331), Kheyabun-e Doktor Fatemi, 1 Kheyabun-e Shahid Sarhang Ahmad E'temad Zade; there are also consulates in Zahedan and Mashhad.

Kazakstan
(☎ (3272) 333548, 331502), Tölebaev köshesi 25, Almaty

Tajikistan
(☎ (3772) 212227), Prospekt Rudaki 37a, Dushanbe

Turkmenistan
(☎ (3632) 512287, 512317), Ulitsa Kemine 92, Ashghabat

UK
(☎ (0171) 235 2044; recorded visa information ☎ (0891) 880880), 34 Lowndes Square, London SW1X 9JN; there are also consulates or vice-consulates in Bradford, Manchester, Birmingham and Glasgow.

USA
(☎ (202) 939-6200; fax (202)387-0484; consular section ☎ (202) 939-6295), 2315 Massachusetts Ave NW, Washington, DC 20008; there are also consulates in New York and Los Angeles; the embassy has a Web site, including visa information and forms.

Uzbekistan
(☎ (3712) 771003; fax (3712) 771442), Chilonzor 25, Tashkent


## CUSTOMS

Following is relevant information on China and Pakistan customs. For more on the over-

land China-Pakistan crossing, see the Khunjerab Pass & Gojal chapter.


## China

At entry customs, you fill out a form declaring money, cameras, radios and so on; you get a copy, which you must present on departure. Baggage inspection is usually cursory for foreigners, but not always – eg it is excruciatingly thorough at the Torugart Pass from Kyrgyztan.

Chinese authorities have occasionally seized documents they deem pornographic, political or intended for religious purposes. Magazines with photographs (including advertisements) that are commonplace in the west might be considered pornographic in China. Books, films, records or tapes might be temporarily seized in order to determine that they do not violate regulations.

At departure customs, you turn in the declaration you filled out when you entered, and they may want to see listed items again. You're not allowed to take out antiquities; a purchase receipt can save arguments over an item's status. Chinese airline staff will confiscate any souvenir Uyghur knives (or other knives) in your hand luggage.


## Pakistan

Pakistan airport customs now have red and green customs channels for arrivals. They might ask if you're bringing in liquor (you're not supposed to). Unless you're here to hunt, you can't bring in firearms either. There are no other significant restrictions.

Baggage inspection on departure is usually cursory for foreigners unless you have obvious items like furniture, in which case

**Beg Pardon, Madam?**
My favourite moment of exasperation was at the airport...At *outbound* customs a young woman who spoke little English was asked if she had narcotics. She said, 'yes, 250', thinking the officer had meant rupees. This was ignored with a shrug of the shoulder.
**Tony Eaude**

you may be asked for sales receipts and bank encashment receipts. Pakistani airport security staff are likely to confiscate batteries from cameras, walkmans etc, so put these in your checked baggage.

You may not export antiquities; if in doubt about something, ask a museum curator or top-end hotel shopkeeper who deals in it. Pakistani airline staff will also confiscate any souvenir Uyghur knives (or other knives) in your hand luggage.

### Photographic Equipment
You can bring any reasonable amount of equipment and film or casettes into both China and Pakistan, although customs officials may well want to ogle it. Registering your equipment with customs at home is not only proof against paying double duty there, but gives you a paper full of government stamps and serial numbers to wave around if trouble arises. It might even be worth asking for an endorsement in your passport on arrival, to avoid any questions about ownership on departure.

### MONEY
### Costs
With modest self-control you can spend three weeks on the KKH for under US$15 a day. This includes a total ground transport cost (Kashgar to Rawalpindi) of as little as US$45, daily per person accommodation (double rooms) of US$5 to US$7 and US$4 to US$5 each for food. This means staying in lower-cost hotels, eating local food and travelling by bus.

Of course you can do even better by

staying in dorms or a tent, self-catering and hitchhiking (though the latter isn't recommended; see the Hitching section in the Getting Around chapter). Rooms and food are cheaper in the north than around Rawalpindi and Islamabad. A student or under-26 card can get you 50% off on Natco's long-distance connections, eg Gilgit to Rawalpindi (but not on its deluxe buses).

At the time of research, Kashgar and Tashkurgan were still holding out against China's elimination of two tier pricing for ground transport, with long-distance bus fares for foreigners about three times the local prices. When they finally give in, foreigners' prices are likely to fall and local prices rise.

Overland travel between Kashgar and Hong Kong adds at least US$150, plus accommodation and food; or by air, about US$580. An overnight sleeper train between Rawalpindi and Karachi adds about US$17 (or 25% less with a tourist concession); or by air, US$55 to US$70, depending on the carrier and when you travel. See the Getting There & Away chapter for more on links with Kashgar and Islamabad.

### Credit Cards & International Transfers
Credit cards aren't widely accepted for purchases except at top-end hotels, restaurants and shops in Rawalpindi and Islamabad. But you can get cash with a major card at western banks in Rawalpindi and Islamabad and at Bank of China in Kashgar (and Ürümqi), usually in a few minutes. Facilities for validation in Pakistan seem better for Visa than for MasterCard.

American Express readily accepts their own cards for cash or travellers cheques; cardholders can also cash personal cheques. For cash from a Visa card in Rawalpindi, you pay a 2% commission at Bank of America, 3% at Citibank and Grindlays (minimum Rs 350 at Grindlays). Bank of China takes a 4% commission, and has a *lower* limit of Y1200 on cash advances, but no upper limit.

Failing that, banks suggest a telex or telegraphic transfer of funds from your home bank, which takes about a week – though it's

**Inflation**
Prices in this book were in effect at the time of research. Inflation drives them up year by year, and local hoteliers, restaurateurs and shopkeepers will almost certainly *not* be charging the same prices by the time you arrive. Treat prices here as a lower limit and useful mainly for comparisons. Don't lean on local people to accept the prices in the book. ∎

simpler to have someone post a bank draft by express registered mail to you at a reliable address, eg your embassy.

American citizens can have *emergency* money wired to them via the US embassy in Islamabad, and British or other citizens may have luck with their embassies. The process takes several business days. The sender in the USA should contact the State Department at ☎ (202) 647-5225 (☎ (202) 647-4000 after hours). The British Foreign Office number is ☎ (0171) 270 3000; the Australian Department of Foreign Affairs & Trade is ☎ (06) 261 9111.

### Chinese Currency

Generically, Chinese money is called *renminbi* (RMB) or 'people's money'. The formal unit is the yuan (Y), divided into 10 jiao or 100 fen. But when talking prices, Chinese use 'counting words': yuan is called *kuai* (Uyghurs say *koi*) and jiao is called *mao* (Uyghurs say *mo*); fen is still *fen*, pronounced 'fun'. Renminbi comes in paper notes of Y100, Y50, Y10, Y5 and Y2, and coins of five, two and one fen. Slowly disappearing are old, Monopoly-like fen notes: 5 fen (with a green boat), 2 fen (blue aeroplane) and 1 fen (yellow truck).

### Pakistani Currency

The unit of Pakistani money is the rupee (Re, but nearly always written in the plural, Rs), divided into 100 paisa. Paper notes come in denominations of Rs 1000, Rs 500, Rs 100, Rs 50, Rs 10, Rs 2 and Re 1, and there are one-rupee and half-rupee coins (25, 10 and 5 paisa coins are vanishing). Very worn or tattered notes may occasionally be refused. Rs 1000 and Rs 500 notes can be a headache in small towns where change is scarce, so ask for smaller ones when you buy your rupees.

### Currency Exchange

Approximate cash exchange rates at the time of writing were as follows (Chinese rates are the same everywhere; Pakistani rates aren't). Rates are a few per cent poorer for travellers cheques.

| | | | | | |
|---|---|---|---|---|---|
| US$1 | = | Y 8.19 | = | Rs 43.41 |
| UK£1 | = | Y 13.79 | = | Rs 71.74 |
| A$1 | = | Y 5.65 | = | Rs 30.55 |
| NZ$1 | = | Y 5.10 | = | Rs 27.03 |
| C$1 | = | Y 5.82 | = | Rs 30.84 |
| FF1 | = | Y 1.43 | = | Rs 7.40 |
| DM1 | = | Y 4.79 | = | Rs 24.82 |
| Y1 | = | | | Rs 5.30 |
| Rs 1 | = | Y 0.19 | | |

US dollar and pound Sterling cash and travellers cheques are the easiest to cash. National Bank in Gilgit also accepts cash and travellers cheques in deutschmarks, French francs and Canadian dollars, but not Australian or New Zealand dollars. Other Pakistani banks are shy of anything other than US dollars or Sterling. Bank of China in Kashgar accepts cash and travellers cheques in most major currencies.

Redesigned US$100 notes introduced in 1996 may eventually cause older versions to be rejected in Pakistan, though they remain legal tender. American Express cheques can, if lost, be replaced at their offices in Islamabad, Rawalpindi, Lahore, Faisalabad and Karachi.

At Tashkurgan's Bank of China you can directly exchange rupees and RMB.

### Travellers Cheques

Travellers cheques may not be as useful nor as safe here as elsewhere in the world. They draw poorer exchange rates than cash, and sometimes extra commission, eg 0.75% at Bank of China. Unless you're cashing *their* travellers cheques, foreign banks in Rawalpindi and Islamabad nail you with high commissions (Grindlays takes the booby prize at Rs 350 per transaction).

While National Bank of Pakistan accepts travellers cheques in major currencies, other Pakistani banks may not, or may ask to see purchase receipts for your cheques. Banks in the Northern Areas may refuse to accept any travellers cheques until late in the morning, when someone pulls his thumb out and telexes the head office for the day's rates.

Several travellers have had a miserable

time trying to recover lost or stolen cheques while in Pakistan.

## Changing Money

In China you must go to the Bank of China; there are branches in Kashgar and in the customs building at Tashkurgan. In Pakistan you can exchange at half a dozen domestic banking companies, the most competent being National Bank and United Bank (UBL).

New Pakistani regulations have also spawned authorised money changers, who are much quicker and give up to 5% more for cash. In Rawalpindi and Islamabad you can also go to top-end hotels and to foreign banks including Grindlays, Bank of America, Citibank and American Express.

Exchange receipts come in handy later, not only for reconversion (they are not always demanded) but, in Pakistan, for air ticket purchases, export permits etc. You may have to ask for one. To be of any use they must have the amounts in both currencies, the exchange rate, an official signature and the bank's stamp.

Outside the tourist season, many banks in the Northern Areas seem to shut down, though money changers and shopkeepers might accept limited amounts of US dollar cash. If you're headed north at this time, the best advice is probably to change money in Rawalpindi.

When you leave China you can sell your RMB back at the border, though you're expected to show exchange receipts. Unspent rupees can be reconverted by some Pakistani branch banks, including all those at customs, and by licensed money changers. Some banks may ask to see exchange receipts, although National Bank and Alam Money Changer at Sost don't.

If you're flying out of Pakistan from Karachi, reconvert before Immigration as there's no bank on the other side.

## Black Market

Kashgar's Uyghur black-marketeers buy western banknotes at rates not much different than the bank's. For tips on avoiding rip-offs, see the Money section under Kashgar.

The Pakistani rupee is now convertible and there's little difference between official and black-market rates.

## Tipping

Most upper-end hotels and restaurants automatically add a 5% or 10% service charge to your bill; a further 5% from you might be appropriate for especially fine service, but it's definitely optional.

Big-city taxi drivers in Pakistan expect about 10% of the fare, and railway porters charge an officially set Rs 7. Tips are appreciated in mid-range places in Rawalpindi, Abbottabad and Gilgit, but might even be returned in rural areas where it runs counter to the Islamic obligation to be hospitable. Hardly anyone in China seems to expect tips.

## Bargaining

Bargaining is appropriate in bazaars throughout Xinjiang and Pakistan; indeed, shopping without bargaining is like giving your money away. It's not as hard nor as competitive as you might think; as long as you do it with a smile and don't get fixated on driving a price into the ground, it's taken in a good spirit.

The minute you eye their goods, some shopkeepers will insist that you come in for a cup of tea. Start with a bit of small talk. Don't show too much interest in that item you're dying to have. Casually ask the seller's price for various things, including your favourite. Roll your eyes and offer half or two-thirds of that, perhaps pointing out this or that imperfection or the number of others offering the same goods. They'll roll their own eyes, make a lower offer, and you're on your way to a compromise and a handshake. Soon you'll be bargaining without even thinking about it.

For food, initial asking prices tend to be in a saner proportion to the expected outcome. Sellers will be genuinely surprised if you reply to their '50' with '10'; they're more likely expecting 40 or 45 in the end.

Of course many places have fixed prices, but these are usually posted, or shopkeepers will tell you so. Certain basic goods, such as oil, flour and fuel, are also sold at (officially)

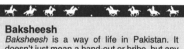

**Baksheesh**
*Baksheesh* is a way of life in Pakistan. It doesn't just mean a hand-out or bribe, but any gratuity for services rendered. Lower-echelon staff who depart even minutely from normal routine – opening a closed gate, getting a bigwig's signature, fixing a broken tap – may expect something for it, and five or 10 rupees here and there goes a long way when it's deserved.

Resist the temptation to see those who ask for it as beggars. It's part of the Islamic code that better-off people give part of their income to the less well-off. Pakistan has relatively few 'career' beggars. ∎

fixed prices. Transport is rarely negotiable, except with the untrustworthy donkey-cart drivers of Kashgar.

Surprisingly, lower-end hotels in Pakistan are often open to a bit of discounting, especially in the off season and especially if you say you're travelling on a budget.

### Taxes

For most services, including accommodation and restaurant food and drink, a 12.5% Central Excise Duty (CED) is supposed to be added to your bill; this is like VAT in the UK or sales tax in other countries. Many lower-end places don't charge it, and at others a discreet request to have it omitted may be rewarded (though the waiter or receptionist might then expect a further tip). If you need a proper receipt, CED must be included.

### POST & COMMUNICATIONS
#### Postal Rates

**China** Overseas air mail letters up to 10g are Y5.40 (except Y2 to Hong Kong). Air mail postcards are Y4.20. Parcels under 1kg can go at lower 'small packet' rates. Rates for parcels over 1kg depend on the country of destination. Registration is a few yuan extra.

**Pakistan** Overseas air mail letters up to 10g are Rs 15 to Europe and Rs 17 to North America and Australasia; air mail postcards

are Rs 11 and Rs 13. A 5kg parcel by ordinary international surface mail would cost Rs 700 to Rs 800 and about twice that for air mail. Registration is a few rupees extra, and a good idea for letters and parcels.

Couriers in Rawalpindi and Islamabad, including DHL and TNT, will send a 500g parcel to Europe or the USA for about US$40, with a delivery time of two or three days.

### Sending Mail

Outgoing international service is fairly reliable. Air mail letters and postcards from larger towns will probably take under 10 days; surface mail takes up to two months. Post office staff are usually happy to frank letters on the spot, eliminating the risk of stamp theft.

Except for printed matter, outgoing parcels must generally be sewn into cloth bags in both countries – tedious, but it probably helps them survive. All require customs declarations and an inspection, so leave the bag open when you take it to the post office and finish the job there.

Avoid posting out from Pakistan any purchase whose declared value is over Rs 500, as you'll need an export permit, which is a headache to get (see the Export Permit section earlier in this chapter).

### Receiving Mail

International service is slow but fairly dependable for letters to Kashgar, Gilgit, Rawalpindi and Islamabad. Parcels, especially books or magazines, are less likely to make it.

Big-town post offices will hold letters at poste restante for months, and the Kashgar post office has even returned unclaimed mail. Kashgar charges Y2.30 per letter collected. American Express card and travellers cheque holders can have letters (but not registered ones, nor parcels) held for up to a month at American Express offices in Islamabad or Rawalpindi.

In China, where family names come first – and even in Pakistan – check at poste restante under your given name too, and even under Mr or Ms! It is also worth having your surname written in caps and underlined.

## Telephone

The entire KKH region except Gojal now has International Direct Dialling (IDD), so international calls are quick from almost anywhere and charges are by the minute. You can also place calls more cheaply in the old, tedious way, by booking them through Islamabad or Beijing and waiting; in this case you must pay for a minimum of three minutes.

Calls can be made from Chinese and Pakistani government exchanges and, in Pakistan, from privately run public call offices (PCOs). A three minute overseas station call from an exchange is about Y20 from China and Rs 130 to Rs 260 from Pakistan. Calls from hotels and travel agencies are considerably more expensive (eg about 40% more from a Gilgit travel agency). Collect calls cannot be made from either country.

There are cardphones in bigger Pakistan cities, though none on the KKH beyond Rawalpindi (an attempt in Gilgit appears to have flopped). Cards are sold at newsagents and chemists (pharmacies). Unfortunately most cardphones are on street corners, so you can barely hear yourself speak.

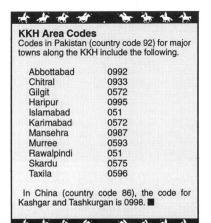

**KKH Area Codes**
Codes in Pakistan (country code 92) for major towns along the KKH include the following.

| | |
|---|---|
| Abbottabad | 0992 |
| Chitral | 0933 |
| Gilgit | 0572 |
| Haripur | 0995 |
| Islamabad | 051 |
| Karimabad | 0572 |
| Mansehra | 0987 |
| Murree | 0593 |
| Rawalpindi | 051 |
| Skardu | 0575 |
| Taxila | 0596 |

In China (country code 86), the code for Kashgar and Tashkurgan is 0998. ∎

See the boxed text for a list of area codes for major KKH towns.

To call in from abroad, dial your international access code, the country code for China (86) or Pakistan (92), the local code (minus the first zero) and the local number. For calling out, the international access code in both countries is 00.

## Fax, Telegraph & Email

**Fax** Thanks to improving telephone lines, domestic and international fax communication is increasingly feasible and common. Kashgar, Rawalpindi and Islamabad are the most reliable places on the KKH from which to send them. Faxes can be sent from main telephone exchanges and some travel agencies and top-end hotels. Many small-town fax lines only work for domestic connections.

On an IDD line, a one page overseas fax takes about a minute and costs considerably less than a three minute call. Normally you pay for a one minute minimum, plus 20-second increments after that. If you dial a joint fax/telephone number and someone picks up the phone, you must pay for that minute and try again. If the fax doesn't go through properly, you probably not be charged the first time but you probably will after that.

In Pakistan at the time of research, a one page fax to the UK was anywhere from Rs 85 to Rs 170, depending on its point of origin and whether it was government-run or private.

**Telegraph** The cheapest quick message remains the telegram, with overseas rates of Y2 to Y3 per word from China and Rs 5 to Rs 6 per word from Pakistan. Domestic and international telegrams can be sent from main telephone exchanges and some top-end hotels.

**Email** Improved telephone lines have also made email a feasible way to communicate with and within Pakistan, although connections are still unreliable. The main users appear to be travel agencies and overseas development agencies.

Public facilities remain scarce. At the time

of research you could send email from the business centre of Rawalpindi's Pearl Continental Hotel (for Rs 50 per message) or from the United Nations Development Project's Sustainable Development Networking Programme (SDNP; ☎ (051) 270684; fax (051) 216909; email root@sdnpk.undp.org), upstairs at House 26, Street 87, G-6/3, behind the Covered Market in Islamabad (or at PO Box 3099, Islamabad 44000). At SDNP you can open an email account with a Rs 500 deposit, which is applied in full to your first bill.

## BOOKS

If you can't find the following titles at home, many are available as reprints (often pirated) in Pakistan bookshops. Beware of pirated editions of LP's own guidebooks, which are often old editions with new-edition covers.

### Lonely Planet

Other good Lonely Planet guidebooks with information on the KKH region are *Pakistan*, *Trekking in the Karakoram & the Hindukush*, *China* and *Central Asia*.

### Travel

Dalrymple, William, *In Xanadu: A Quest*. Dalrymple tries to follow in the footsteps of Marco Polo from Jerusalem to Xanadu, Kublai Khan's fabled city on the Mongolian steppe. His trip turns out rather grittier than Polo's. By the time he gets to the KKH he's into his stride, observant and wry.

Danziger, Nick, *Danziger's Travels*. An incredible modern-day overland odyssey through Turkey, Iran, Afghanistan, Pakistan, China and Tibet – without much regard for visas, immigration posts, civil wars and the like. He's entitled to sound a bit self-important.

Denker, Debra, *Sisters on the Bridge of Fire*. Denker travelled solo through Baltistan, Hunza and Chitral, and shared the lives of local women.

Fa Hsien, *A Record of Buddhistic Kingdoms*. The Buddhist monk's own dry account of his 5th century pilgrimage through Xinjiang and the Karakoram, down the Indus to Gandhara and on to India. Excellent and more lively descriptions of this and the later journey of another pilgrim, Hsuan Tsang, are in *The Great Chinese Travelers*, edited by Jeannette Mirsky.

Jamie, Kathleen, *The Golden Peak: Travels in Northern Pakistan*. An insightful book about the Northern Areas, by a poet with an eye for the ironies of life for women, Muslims and travellers. Included are glimpses of private lives that male visitors will never see.

Knight, E F, *Where Three Empires Meet*. Travels of a Victorian journalist in Kashmir, Ladakh and the Northern Areas, including a thrilling but lopsidedly colonial version of the 1891 invasion of Hunza.

Macartney, Lady Catherine, *An English Lady in Chinese Turkestan*. In 1898 Catherine Borland married George Macartney and was immediately swept off to Kashgar, where he was head of the British mission keeping watch on the Russians. This is her own account of 17 years in Kashgar, where she turned 'Chini Bagh' into an improbable oasis of gardens and hospitality.

Maillart, Ella, *Forbidden Journey*. 'Kini' Maillart was an internationally known sportswoman, traveller and writer, who in the 1930s joined writer Peter Fleming in a tempestuous seven month journey across western China, out of which came this book, and Fleming's strikingly different version, *News from Tartary*.

Murphy, Dervla, *Full Tilt*. The first quest of the legendary eccentric Irish traveller: a solo bicycle journey from Ireland to India, including Pakistan. Hair-raising adventures recounted in a matter-of-fact, almost deadpan, tone.

Murphy, Dervla, *Where the Indus is Young*. The redoubtable Irishwoman's account of a winter in Baltistan, travelling on foot and horseback with her six-year-old daughter.

Schomberg, Colonel R C F, *Between the Oxus & the Indus*. Chronicles of late 19th century Gilgit and Hunza by an acidic British officer who found the landscapes nobler than the people.

Stein, Sir Aurel, *On Alexander's Track to the Indus*. Stein, a Hungarian-English archeologist famous for his ravaging of central Asian sites between 1900 and the 1940s, was the first westerner into parts of Indus Kohistan. He also retraced the routes of earlier travellers, including Alexander the Great and the monk Fa Hsien.

Teichman, Sir Eric, *Journey to Turkistan*. Beijing to Kashgar by car in 1935, by a British diplomat and his friends, at a time when Xinjiang was virtually in Russian hands.

Tilman, H W, *Two Mountains and a River*. Accounts of travels via Gilgit, Chalt and Rakaposhi to Tashkurgan.

### History, Culture & Politics

Fairley, Jean, *The Lion River: The Indus*. A detailed and elegant book about the Indus River and the people along it, from Tibet to the Arabian Sea.

Forbes, Andrew, *Warlords and Muslims in Chinese Central Asia*. A political history of pre-Communist Xinjiang.

Franck, Irene, and David Brownstone, *The Silk Road: A History*. Three hundred well mapped pages of history of the multi-stranded caravan routes that began crossing central Asia in the 2nd century BC.

French, Patrick, *Younghusband*. Sir Francis Younghusband is known to Asia scholars as the archetypal Great Gamester: crossing China solo, facing down Hunza bandits and Russian spies in the Karakoram, and leading the British invasion of Tibet. He was also a dyed-in-the-wool imperialist (some say racist), and at the end of his life a raging mystic. This excellent biography intertwines the lives of its subject and its author as he tracks the story down.

Hopkirk, Kathleen, *Central Asia: A Travellers Companion*. Handy historical background on central Asia, including the KKH; not as entertaining as her husband Peter's books, but a good companion for those keen to know more about the places they're seeing.

Hopkirk, Peter, *Foreign Devils on the Silk Road*. Tales of turn-of-the-century adventurers and archeologists who crisscrossed Xinjiang in search of Buddhist art treasures buried in its desert sands, and hauled them off by the tonne to western museums. Hopkirk steers carefully between calling them heroes (as many of their peers did) and plunderers (as the Chinese continue to do).

Hopkirk, Peter, *The Great Game*. A fast-paced, very readable history of the Great Game – the 19th century cold war between Britain and Russia – as it unfolded across Europe and Asia. It's carried along in Hopkirk's trademark style, in a series of personal stories – all men, all westerners, all resolute and square-jawed, with Victoria Crosses for everybody – melodramatic but essentially true.

Hopkirk, Peter, *Setting the East Ablaze*. Takes up where *The Great Game* stops: a cloak-and-dagger history of the murderous early years of Soviet power in Central Asia, including efforts to spread revolution to British India, and via Xinjiang to the rest of China.

Keay, John, *When Men & Mountains Meet*. Gripping and often hilarious stories of the Europeans who first penetrated the western Himalaya in the early 1800s.

Keay, John, *The Gilgit Game*. A very readable account of the explorers and oddballs who played in the Great Game, the imperial rivalry between Britain and Russia across the Pamirs, Hindukush and Karakoram in the late 19th century.

Skrine, C P & Pamela Nightingale, *Macartney at Kashgar*. The story of the career of one of Britain's most dedicated Great-Gamers, Sir George Macartney, who spent 28 years watching (and outflanking) the Russians as the unofficial, and later official, British representative in Kashgar.

Staley, John, *Words For My Brother*. Culture, politics, religious traditions and recent history of pre-KKH Chitral, Kohistan, Gilgit and Hunza. Staley and his wife studied and travelled here in the 1960s.

Waller, Derek, *The Pundits: British Exploration of Tibet & Central Asia*. An account of the heroic but unsung journeys of Indian scholars and soothsayers trained by the British to be undercover surveyors and spies across the Hindukush and Karakoram during the Great Game.

Wood, Frances, *Did Marco Polo go to China?* A provocative but excruciatingly well researched treatise that suggests that Marco Polo never did make his famous *Travels*, offering at the same time a good look at medieval European and Chinese history.

Younghusband, Sir Francis, *The Heart of a Continent*. The adventures in Kashgar and the Karakoram of one of Britain's foremost players in the Great Game.

## Natural History

Mason, Kenneth, *Abode of Snow*. Mason was a well known Himalayan explorer. Chapter 3 introduces the geography of the Karakoram.

Miller, Keith, ed, *Proceedings of the International Karakorum Project*. A surprisingly readable account of the Karakoram's geography and geology, and their overlap with disciplines as diverse as architecture and cultural anthropology; based on a 1980 expedition and later studies.

Polunin, Oleg, & Adam Stainton, *Concise Flowers of the Himalaya*. An easy-to-carry field guide, distilled from the authors' huge *Flowers of the Himalaya*.

Roberts, T J, *The Birds of Pakistan* and *The Mammals of Pakistan*. Standard references, the latter demonstrating how quickly large mammals disappear when modern roads appear.

Schaller, George, *Stones of Silence: Journeys in the Himalaya*. Low-key, sometimes tedious but still gripping accounts, by the misanthropic biologist who first photographed the snow leopard, of the author's researches on this and other creatures in the Hindukush, Karakoram and Himalaya.

## Petroglyphs

Dani, Dr Ahmad Hasan, *Human Records on Karakorum Highway*. A paperback guide to rock inscriptions along the KKH from the Khunjerab Pass to Mansehra, by a Pakistani researcher who has translated many of them; available in Pakistan bookshops.

Jettmar, Dr Karl, *Rockcarvings & Inscriptions in the Northern Areas of Pakistan*. By a German colleague of Dani, this is stuffy but illuminating; available in Pakistan bookshops.

## Ethnography & Arts

Kalter, Johannes, *The Arts and Crafts of Turkestan*. A detailed, beautifully illustrated historical guide to the nomadic dwellings, clothing, jewellery and other 'applied arts' of Central Asia.

## Islam

Ahmed, Akbar, *Living Islam*. A sensitive introduction to Islam by a Pakistani scholar who has dedicated himself to bridging the mutual ignorance and misunderstanding between the Muslim and non-Muslim worlds, based in part on a BBC television series.

Dillon, Michael, *China's Muslims*. The author, Lecturer in Modern Chinese History at the University of Durham, looks at the history, customs, languages and daily life of China's major Muslim groups, the particular character of Chinese Islam, and its relationship to the state. Dr Dillon is also author of a detailed University of Durham monograph called *Xinjiang: Ethnicity, Separatism and Control in Chinese Central Asia*.

Guillaume, Alfred, *Islam*. Dry as dust but dense with information on history, doctrine and practice.

## Fiction

Kipling, Rudyard, *Kim*. The master storyteller's classic epic of the Raj during the Great Game.

## ONLINE SERVICES & INTERNET

Several good World Wide Web sites make good starting points for general information on the KKH region. One of the best is the WWW Virtual Library, with a huge number of links to online information. The URL for Pakistan resources is http://www.clas.ufl.edu/users/gthursby/pak/. For Xinjiang, try http://yellow.ccs.uky.edu/rakhim/et.html.

Lonely Planet's web page (http:www.lonelyplanet.com) has advice, photographs, travel tales and general information on travelling through the region, with many links to other relevant sites. Visit Destination China or Destination Pakistan, or drop by the Thorntree for all the latest on the KKH.

Specific online resources are mentioned in appropriate sections of this book, including Flora & Fauna in the Facts about the Region chapter; Gay & Lesbian Travellers, and Disabled Travellers in the Facts for the Visitor chapter; and in the Getting There & Away and Getting Around chapters.

## RADIO & TV
### Radio

The state-run Pakistan Broadcasting Corporation plays its role in transmitting government viewpoints and promoting Islamic values. Private stations do broadcast from Islamabad, Rawalpindi and elsewhere, but they can only report news fed to them by the government-run Associated Press of Pakistan.

For English-language programming you'll need a shortwave radio to pick up BBC World Service, Voice of America (VOA) or Radio Australia. For current frequencies and schedules, contact the BBC at PO Box 76, Bush House, London WC2B 4PH, UK (fax  0171 257 8258; URL http://www.bbc.co.uk/world service/), VOA at Washington, DC 20547, USA (fax  (0202) 619 0916; URL http://www.voa.gov/) or Radio Australia at GPO Box 428G, Melbourne, Victoria 3001, Australia (fax  (03) 9626 1899; URL http://www.abc.net.au/ra/).

### Television

The Pakistan government runs all but one semiprivate television station, STN, which offers some CNN and BBC programs. CNN and BBC news content is rarely censored, though segments considered socially offensive may be. The deadly boring government-run Pakistan Television Network (PTV) disseminates the views of the party in power. Television now reaches over 80% of Pakistanis.

But now a major – and fairly depressing – revolution is taking place as more and more people tune in to uncensored satellite television, regardless of where they live or how wealthy they are. Even the grottiest of Gilgit's restaurants now have 'dishes', though you're more likely to be assaulted by Indian musicals than by BBC News. Other options include Star Sports, Star Movies and the VTV music channel.

All you can watch in Xinjiang is sleep-inducing Chinese state-controlled programming.

## PHOTOGRAPHY & VIDEO
### Film & Equipment
Western-brand colour print film (eg Kodak, Agfa, Fuji and Konica, most of it fairly fresh) and processing are available in Kashgar, Karimabad, Gilgit, Rawalpindi and Islamabad. In Rawalpindi at the time of writing a 36 frame roll of Kodak Gold 100 was around Rs 150, with developing and printing (including some one-hour services) about Rs 250 for 36 exposures. Prices rise and reliability drops as you go north. In Kashgar western colour print film is about 20% more expensive than in Rawalpindi; kiosks there also have cheap Chinese colour and black & white film, though processing is second-rate and dusty at best.

Western colour slide film (E6 only) is available in Rawalpindi at Rs 200 to Rs 300 for 36 frames, but only a few shops in Islamabad, Lahore or Karachi can process it. Prices for this in Kashgar are about double those in Rawalpindi. Kodachrome is rarely for sale and, in any case, cannot be processed in China or Pakistan.

Posting film from anywhere in China or Pakistan is asking for trouble; better to take it home for processing.

Equipment is a personal matter, but an SLR camera with a mid-range zoom, eg 35 to 135mm, covers a wide range of situations; a good second lens might be a 28mm for panoramas and indoors. 'Skylite' filters protect lenses and cut down on high-altitude UV glare. A squeeze bulb for blowing dust from inside the camera is also a good idea.

**Hazards** To avoid magenta-tinted memories, keep photographic film away from heat. If you line a stuff-sack with a patch cut from an aluminised mylar 'survival blanket', film will stay cool inside through fierce summer days. Be careful where you buy film; some shops proudly display their film in the window – which cooks it.

In very cold weather, avoid ruinous moisture on film and inside the camera by putting them in plastic bags *before* going indoors, and leaving them there till they're warm. Camera batteries get sluggish in down-jacket weather; keep the camera inside your coat and keep some spare batteries warm in your pocket.

### Video
Properly used, a video camera can produce a fine record of your trip, though you run the risk of forgetting to come out from behind it now and then.

As well as the obvious things – spectacular views and special events – remember to record ordinary everyday details, which will tell you much more about a place later. A good rule for beginners is to film in long takes, without moving the camera too much; too much panning may make your viewers seasick! Better video cameras have stabilisers, allowing you to shoot even while on the move.

Many video cameras have very sensitive microphones, which can be a problem when there's lots of ambient noise. Filming by a roadside might seem OK at the time but on viewing, your soundtrack may be just a deafening roar of traffic.

Bring the right charger, plugs and transformer for Pakistan or China (see the Electricity section) Video cartridges are sold in Rawalpindi and in Kashgar department stores, though it's safest to bring your own; both China and Pakistan use PAL format.

### Restrictions & Etiquette
In China it's forbidden to photograph or video military sites, factories, airports, railway stations and bridges, and often there are people nearby who'll collar you and take your film. You're not supposed to take pictures from aeroplanes but we've never seen an Air China hostess swoop down on anybody. The insides of museums and temples are often off-limits. Some older Chinese shy away from cameras but nearly everyone loves having their kids photographed.

Prohibited subjects in Pakistan are military sites, airports, KKH bridges and, above all, women. To Muslims, especially in rural areas, it's an insult to photograph any woman older than a child without permission, and if a husband or brother is nearby it's risky as well. This is true even if you're shooting a mountain and a woman happens to be in a field in the foreground, and even if she's too far away to be recognised.

Ismailis sometimes loosen up once they have gotten to know you. Women photographers may get lucky if they've established some rapport. Pakistani men, on the other hand, are irrepressible in front of a camera, and quick to ask you for a print. Of course, if you do offer to send a print, follow through!

If you're using a video camera, follow the same guidelines on etiquette as for still photography. If anything, having a video camera shoved in your face is more annoying than a still camera.

### Airport Security

One dose of airport x-rays for inspecting carry-on bags won't harm slow or medium-speed films, but the effects are cumulative and too much will fog your pictures. We don't trust the machines at most Chinese airports. Lead 'film-safe' pouches help but the best solution is hand inspection; having all your film in clear canisters inside clear plastic bags makes officials less grumpy about it.

### TIME

While all China officially runs on Beijing time (GMT plus eight hours), out in Kashgar and Tashkurgan, 3500km away, people set their clocks and watches on (unofficial) 'Xinjiang time', two hours earlier. But most Chinese bureaucrats think in Beijing time, and Xinjiang Airways runs on Beijing time, so you must keep track of both. Pakistan is covered by a single time zone (GMT plus five hours). Neither China nor Pakistan has Daylight Savings Time (DST).

When it's noon on a summer (winter) day in Islamabad or Gilgit, it's:

midnight (11 pm) the previous day in San Francisco
3 am (2 am) in New York and Toronto

8 am (7 am) in London
12.30 pm (12.30 pm) in Delhi
1 pm (noon) in Bishkek
1 pm (1 pm) in Xinjiang – unofficially
3 pm (3 pm) in Beijing
5 pm (6 pm) in Sydney
7 pm (8 pm) in Wellington

Note that countries outside the region do have DST, with each switching from 'summer' to 'winter' time on its own schedule.

### ELECTRICITY

Electricity in both China and Pakistan is 220 volt, 50 cycle AC; some hotels also have 110-volt shaver outlets. Most sockets are two round pins, though some hotels have a third (earth or ground) pin.

Kashgar and Tashkurgan are reliably electrified. Except for parts of Gojal and Nagar, most villages near the KKH in northern Pakistan now have hydroelectric ('hydel') power, though supplies are weather dependent. In dry periods, villages may have no power after dark on a rotating basis; when this happens in a touristed area the evening's peace is ruptured by the sound of hotels' diesel generators. Gilgit's power supply, subject to high demand but the same weather-related problems, is the KKH's flakiest.

'Load shedding' can even happen in major cities, so it's useful to pack a candle or two.

### WEIGHTS & MEASURES

Officially China and Pakistan are metric but some traditional units persist locally. Old Chinese units include the *chi* (0.33m), *li* (0.5km), *jin* (0.5kg) and *liang* (0.1 jin or 50g).

Imperial units linger in Pakistan. Short distances are often quoted in furlongs; one furlong is 1/8 mile or about 200m. Cloth

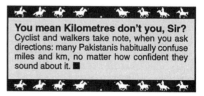

**You mean Kilometres don't you, Sir?**
Cyclist and walkers take note, when you ask directions: many Pakistanis habitually confuse miles and km, no matter how confident they sound about it. ■

merchants and tailors still use yards. Some traditional Pakistani weights still in use are the *tola* (about 11.7g), *pao* (250g) and *seer* (0.933kg).

## LAUNDRY

Staff at most hotels can wash and dry a load of laundry for a miniscule charge, though they might not iron it at lower-end places. Dry cleaners in Rawalpindi, Gilgit and Kashgar can usually do washing too; rates are normally per piece, eg Rs 10 to Rs 20 for a shalwar qamiz, Rs 10 for a t-shirt or Rs 30 for trousers.

Of course you can do it yourself; laundry soap is easy to find in department stores or markets of larger towns.

## HEALTH

Travel health depends on your predeparture preparations, your daily health care while travelling and how you handle any medical problem that does develop. While the potential dangers can seem quite frightening, in reality few travellers experience anything more than an upset stomach.

### Predeparture Planning

**Immunisations** For some countries no immunisations are necessary, but the further off the beaten track you go the more necessary it is to take precautions. Be aware that children have lower resistance to illness and there are often greater risks associated with disease in pregnancy.

Plan ahead for getting your vaccinations: some of them require more than one injection, while some vaccinations should not be given together. It is recommended you seek medical advice at least six weeks before travel.

Record all vaccinations on an International Health Certificate, available from your doctor or government health department.

The only vaccination required for entry to China or Pakistan is yellow fever if travellers are coming from infected or endemic areas. There is no risk of catching yellow fever in China or Pakistan.

Discuss your requirements with your doctor but vaccinations you should consider for this trip include:

- **Hepatitis A** This is the most common travel-acquired illness after diarrhoea; it can put you out of action for weeks. Havrix 1440 is a vaccination which provides long term immunity (possibly more than 10 years) after an initial injection and a booster at six to 12 months.
  Gamma globulin is ready-made antibody collected from blood donations. It should be given close to departure because, depending on the dose, it only protects for two to six months.
  A combined hepatitis A and hepatitis B vaccination, Twinrix, is also available. This combined vaccination is recommended for people wanting protection against both types of viral hepatitis. Three injections over a six-month period are required.
- **Typhoid** This is an important vaccination to have where hygiene is a problem. Available either as an injection or oral capsules.
- **Diphtheria & Tetanus** Diphtheria can be a fatal throat infection and tetanus can be a fatal wound infection. Everyone should have these vaccinations. After an initial course of three injections, boosters are necessary every 10 years.
- **Hepatitis B** This disease is spread by blood or by sexual activity. Travellers who should consider a hepatitis B vaccination include those visiting countries where there are known to be many carriers, where blood transfusions may not be adequately screened or where sexual contact is a possibility. It involves three injections, the quickest course being over three weeks with a booster at 12 months.
- **Polio** Polio is a serious, easily transmitted disease, still prevalent in many developing countries. Everyone should keep up to date with this vaccination. A booster every 10 years maintains immunity.
- **Rabies** Vaccination should be considered by those who will spend a month or longer in a country where rabies is common, especially if they are cycling, handling animals, caving, travelling to remote areas, or for children (who may not report a bite). Pretravel rabies vaccination involves having three injections over 21 to 28 days. If someone who has been vaccinated is bitten or scratched by an animal they will require two booster injections of vaccine; those not vaccinated require more.
- **Japanese B Encephalitis** This mosquito-borne disease is not common in travellers, but occurs in Asia. Consider the vaccination if spending a month or longer in a high risk area, making repeated trips to a risk area or visiting during an epidemic. It involves three injections over 30 days. The vaccine is expensive and has been associated with serious allergic reactions so the decision to have it should be balanced against the risk of contracting the illness.

**Medical Kit Check List**
Consider taking a basic medical kit including:

**Aspirin** or paracetamol (acetaminophen in the US) – for pain or fever.
**Antihistamine** (such as Benadryl) – useful as a decongestant for colds and allergies, to ease the itch from insect bites or stings, and to help prevent motion sickness. Antihistamines may cause sedation and interact with alcohol so care should be taken when using them; take one you know and have used before, if possible.
**Antibiotics** – useful if you're travelling well off the beaten track, but they must be prescribed; carry the prescription with you.
**Antifungal** cream or powder eg athlete's foot powder may be useful.
**Loperamide** (eg Imodium), Lomotil or a kaolin preparation (eg Pepto-Bismol) for diarrhoea; prochlorperazine (eg Stemetil) or metaclopramide (eg Maxalon) for nausea and vomiting.
**Rehydration** mixture – for treatment of severe diarrhoea; particularly important for travelling with children.
**Antiseptic** such as povidone-iodine (eg Betadine) – for cuts and grazes.
**Multivitamins** – especially for long trips when dietary vitamin intake may be inadequate.
**Calamine lotion** or **aluminium sulphate spray** (eg Stingose) – to ease irritation from bites or stings.
**Bandages,** Band-Aids, gauze pads, adhesive tape and moleskin (for blisters)
**Scissors, tweezers** and a **thermometer** (note that mercury thermometers are prohibited by airlines).
**Cold and flu tablets** and throat lozenges. Pseudoephedrine hydrochloride (Sudafed) may be useful if flying with a cold to avoid ear damage.
**Insect repellent, sunscreen, lip salve, water purification tablets** and/or **iodine tincture.**
**A couple of syringes,** in case you need injections in a country with medical hygiene problems. Ask your doctor for a note explaining why they have been prescribed. ■

- **Cholera** Though no country has a cholera immunisation requirement any more and WHO has dropped cholera immunisation as a health requirement, there have been small outbreaks in China and in Baltistan in recent years. Also, travellers often face bureaucratic problems over it (eg on entering China, or on coming from African or Latin American countries), so it's wise to have it on your certificate anyhow.
- **Tuberculosis** There is some TB along the KKH. However, the TB risk to travellers is usually very low. For those who will be living or closely associated with local people, there may be some risk. As most healthy adults do not develop symptoms, a skin test before and after travel to determine whether exposure has occurred might be worthwhile. A vaccination is recommended for children living in TB areas for three months or more.

**Malaria Medication** Antimalarial drugs do not prevent you from being infected but kill the malaria parasites during a stage in their development and significantly reduce the risk of becoming very ill or dying. Expert advice on medication should be sought, as there are many factors to consider, including the area to be visited, the risk of exposure to malaria-carrying mosquitoes, the side effects of medication, your medical history and

whether you are a child or adult or pregnant. Travellers to isolated areas in high risk countries may like to carry a treatment dose of medication for use if symptoms occur. See Malaria later in this section for more details.

**Health Insurance** Make sure that you have adequate health insurance. See Travel Insurance under Visas & Documents in this chapter.

A medevac clause or policy, covering the costs of being flown to another country for treatment, is recommended (for more on medical evacuation, see Medical Problems & Treatment later in this section).

**Travel Health Guides** If you are planning to be away or travelling in remote areas for a long period of time, you may like to consider taking a more detailed health guide.

*Staying Healthy in Asia, Africa & Latin America,* Dirk Schroeder, Moon Publications, 1994. Probably the best all-round guide to carry; it's compact, detailed and well organised.

*Travellers' Health*, Dr Richard Dawood, Oxford University Press, 1995. Comprehensive, easy to read, authoritative and highly recommended, although it's rather large to lug around.

*Where There is No Doctor*, David Werner, Macmillan, 1994. A very detailed guide intended for someone, such as a Peace Corps worker, going to work in an underdeveloped country.

*Travel with Children*, Maureen Wheeler, Lonely Planet Publications, 1995. Includes advice on travel health for younger children.

Medical Advisory Services for Travellers Abroad (MASTA), a private group associated with the London School of Hygiene & Tropical Medicine in the UK, has a travellers health line (☎ (0891) 224100) where you can order a 'health brief' with information on immunisations, malaria, Foreign Office advisories and health news, for the cost of the (premium rate) call. They also offer detailed briefs for long or complex trips, plus mail-order health supplies. Also in the UK, the Malaria Reference Laboratory has a 24 hour premium rate helpline at ☎ (0891) 600350.

MASTA in Australia (☎ (02) 9971 1499 or 1300 65 55 65; fax (02) 9971 0239) offers similar services to those in the UK. Alternatively, call a clinic like the Travellers Medical & Vaccination Centre (☎ (02) 9221 7133 or (03) 9670 3969).

In the USA the Center for Diseases Control & Prevention has a travellers hotline (☎ (404) 332-4555 or 332-4559) and a free fax-back service within the USA (fax (404) 332-4565). You can also call the International Medicine Program at Cornell University Medical Center in New York (☎ (212) 746-5454). Another resource is the International Association for Medical Assistance to Travellers (☎ (716) 754-4883), 417 Center St, Lewiston, NY 14092.

There are also a number of excellent travel health sites on the Internet. From the Lonely Planet home page there are links at www.lonelyplanet.com/weblinks/wlprep.htm to the World Health Organisation and the US Center for Diseases Control & Prevention.

**Other Preparations** Make sure you're healthy before you start travelling. If you are going on a long trip make sure your teeth are OK; Pakistan and remoter China are not good places to visit the dentist!

If you wear glasses take a spare pair and your prescription. If you wear contact lenses, ask your ophthalmologist about accessories you might want in the middle of nowhere, eg ophthalmic local anaesthetic and a test and medication for corneal ulcers.

If you require a particular medication take an adequate supply, as it may not be available locally. Make a note of the generic name, rather than the brand name, which will make getting replacements easier. It's a good idea to have a legible prescription or letter from your doctor to show that you legally use the medication to avoid any problems. Keep medicines in their original, labelled containers and in your hand luggage.

MASTA (see Travel Health Guides) and SAFA (☎ (0151) 709 6075; fax (0151) 708 7211), 59 Hill Street, Liverpool LP 5SE, UK, sell travel medical kits for remote areas, and deliver worldwide.

### Basic Rules
**Food** What you put in your mouth is important, but don't get paranoid – after all, eating local food is part of the travel experience. An upset stomach is the most common health problem but it's rarely serious.

Food is quite safe in the KKH's tourist hotels, but use good sense with street food.

Bread, plentiful and varied along the KKH, is a good energy source

Places packed with travellers or locals are fine, while empty restaurants are questionable. Food in busy restaurants is cooked and eaten quickly with little standing around, and is probably not reheated. We're told that in a few street stalls in Kashgar, noodles are rinsed in river water after they've been cooked!

Go for hot, freshly made dishes; avoid salads (usually washed in untreated water); avoid undercooked meat, especially ground (minced) meat; peel fruit and vegetables yourself or wash them in water you trust, and don't buy fruit with broken skins. Even Hunza's splendid dried apricots should probably be soaked in boiled water unless you know yours have been dried and handled carefully.

Except for the long-life variety, milk is usually unpasteurised and should be treated with caution, although boiled milk is fine if it is kept hygienically. Pure cultured products like yoghurt are usually safe but again this depends on how hygienically they are kept. Brand-name ice cream from shops is OK but beware of street vendors.

A good defence against hepatitis A and E is to carry your own utensils, although even in Xinjiang restaurants 'hepsticks' are being edged out by disposable chopsticks. If you find the environmental implications of this unpalatable, you can buy your own chopsticks in department stores.

**Water** Play it safe and don't drink tap water (even, some travellers suggest, at top-end hotels); that includes not brushing your teeth in it, no ice in your drinks (a nice reminder: the Urdu word for ice is *barf*!) and keeping your mouth closed in the shower. Some travellers and tourism officials scoff at this and insist that local tap water is safe; sometimes it is and sometimes it isn't.

Even in the mountains, streams below pastureland can be contaminated with giardia.

Bottled mineral water, which is safe if the seal isn't broken, is sold in most tourist towns. But millions of unrecyclable plastic bottles represent an immense future burden on the regional environment, and sounder

**Nutrition**
If your food is poor or limited in availability, if you're travelling hard and therefore missing meals, or if you simply lose your appetite, you can start to lose weight and place your health at risk.

Keep your diet balanced. Eggs, beans, lentils (dhal), tofu and nuts are safe protein sources. Fruit you can peel is safe and a good vitamin source – though melons can harbour bacteria in their flesh. Don't forget grains (eg rice) and bread.

Along the KKH it's not always possible to find these things, so a multivitamin and mineral supplement is not a bad idea. While thoroughly cooked food is safest, when overcooked it loses much of its nutritional value. ■

alternatives are boiling, chemical treatment and filtration.

Take care with fruit juice, particularly if water may have been added. Tea or coffee should also be OK, since the water should have been boiled. Name-brand soft drinks are usually OK.

**Water Purification** The simplest way of purifying water is to boil it thoroughly. Vigorous boiling should be satisfactory; however, at high altitude water boils at a lower temperature, so germs are less likely to be killed. Boil it for longer in these environments. Restaurants can often give you 'boiled' water, but unless you see it come piping hot out of a big boiler (these are commonplace all over China) you will not know how 'boiled' it really is.

Consider purchasing a water filter for a long trip. There are two main kinds of filter. Total filters take out all parasites, bacteria and viruses, and make water safe to drink. They are often expensive, but they can be more cost effective than buying bottled water. Simple filters (which can even be a nylon mesh bag) take out dirt and larger foreign bodies from the water so that chemical solutions work much more effectively; if water is dirty, chemical solutions may not work at all. It's very important when buying a filter to read the specifications, so that you know exactly what it removes from the water and what it doesn't. Simple filtering will not remove all dangerous organisms, so if you cannot boil water it should be treated chemically.

Chlorine tablets (Puritabs, Steritabs or other brand names) will kill many pathogens, but not some parasites like giardia and amoebic cysts. Iodine is more effective in purifying water and is available in tablet form (such as Potable Aqua). Follow the directions carefully and remember that too much iodine can be harmful.

### Medical Problems & Treatment

Self-diagnosis and treatment can be risky, so you should always seek medical help. Although we do give drug dosages in this section, they are for emergency use only. Correct diagnosis is vital.

Antibiotics should ideally be administered only under medical supervision. Take only the recommended dose at the prescribed intervals and use the whole course, even if the illness seems to be cured earlier. Stop immediately if there are any serious reactions and don't use the antibiotic at all if you are unsure that you have the correct one. Some people are allergic to commonly prescribed antibiotics such as penicillin or sulpha drugs; carry this information, eg on a bracelet, when travelling .

**Hospitals** There are hospitals at Kashgar, Karimabad, Gilgit, Abbottabad, Rawalpindi and Islamabad, and clinics in many smaller towns. These are OK for routine stool and other tests, but in most cases care and standards are not what you're used to at home! For problems beyond the level of first aid – including any involving hospitalisation – get down to Islamabad as soon as possible and ask your embassy there for advice.

**Evacuation** In the case of a serious illness, the best place to head for is the airport. But if you aren't ambulatory or can't get a scheduled flight when you want it, a charter flight on short notice could cost you up to US$30,000 – hence the obvious value of a

---

### Everyday Health

Normal body temperature is up to 37°C or 98.6°F; more than 2°C (4°F) higher indicates a high fever. The normal adult pulse rate is 60 to 100 per minute (80 to 100 for children and 100 to 140 for babies). As a general rule the pulse increases about 20 beats per minute for each °C (2°F) rise in fever.

Respiration (breathing) rate is also an indicator of illness. Count the number of breaths per minute: between 12 and 20 is normal for adults and older children (up to 30 for younger children and 40 for babies). People with a high fever or serious respiratory illness breathe more quickly than normal. More than 40 shallow breaths a minute may indicate pneumonia. ■

---

medevac clause in your travel insurance (see Travel Insurance earlier in this chapter).

Most insurers have their own preferred air ambulance service, designated in the policy. These usually have offices overseas as well. Two reliable firms are SOS International (☎ (022) 476161), Geneva, Switzerland; and Asia Emergency Assistance International (☎ (0206) 781 8770), Seattle, USA.

### Environmental Hazards

**Altitude Sickness** Lack of oxygen at high altitudes (over 2500m) affects most people to some extent. Even the bus trip from Kashgar up to the Khunjerab Pass can bring on symptoms. Flying straight to a high altitude can make these problems acute. The effect may be mild or severe and occurs because less oxygen reaches the muscles and the brain at high altitude, requiring the heart and lungs to compensate by working harder.

Symptoms of Acute Mountain Sickness (AMS) usually develop during the first 24 hours at altitude but may be delayed up to three weeks. Mild symptoms include headache, lethargy, dizziness, difficulty sleeping and loss of appetite. AMS may become more severe without warning and can be fatal. Severe symptoms include breathlessness, a dry, irritative cough (which may progress to the production of pink, frothy sputum), severe headache, lack of coordination and balance, confusion, irrational behaviour, vomiting, drowsiness and unconsciousness. There is no hard-and-fast rule as to what is too high: AMS has been fatal at 3000m, although 3500 to 4500m is the usual range.

Treat mild symptoms by resting at the same altitude until recovery, usually a day or two. Paracetamol or aspirin can be taken for headaches. If symptoms persist or become worse, however, *immediate descent is necessary*; even 500m can help. Drug treatments should never be used to avoid descent or to enable further ascent.

The drugs acetazolamide (Diamox) and dexamethasone are recommended by some doctors for the prevention of AMS, however their use is controversial. They can reduce the symptoms, but they may also mask warning signs; severe and fatal AMS has occurred in people taking these drugs. In general we do not recommend them for travellers.

To prevent acute mountain sickness:

- Ascend slowly – have frequent rest days, spending two to three nights at each rise of 1000m. If you reach a high altitude by trekking, acclimatisation takes place gradually and you are less likely to be affected than if you fly directly to high altitude.
- It is always wise to sleep at a lower altitude than the greatest height reached during the day if possible. Also, once above 3000m, care should be taken not to increase the sleeping altitude by more than 300m per day.
- Drink extra fluids. The mountain air is dry and cold and moisture is lost as you breathe. Evaporation of sweat may occur unnoticed and result in dehydration.
- Eat light, high-carbohydrate meals for more energy.
- Avoid alcohol as it may increase the risk of dehydration.
- Avoid sedatives.

**Heat Exhaustion** Dehydration and salt deficiency can cause heat exhaustion. Take time to acclimatise to high temperatures, drink sufficient liquids and do not do anything too physically demanding.

Salt deficiency is characterised by fatigue, lethargy, headaches, giddiness and muscle cramps; salt tablets may help, but adding extra salt to your food is better.

Anhydrotic heat exhaustion, caused by an inability to sweat, is quite rare. It is likely to strike people who have been in a hot climate for some time, rather than newcomers.

**Heat Stroke** This serious, occasionally fatal, condition can occur if the body's heat-regulating mechanism breaks down and the body temperature rises to dangerous levels. Long, continuous periods of exposure to high temperatures and insufficient fluids can leave you vulnerable to heat stroke. You breathe and sweat away body water very fast in the mountains and in the hot plains around Kashgar.

The symptoms are feeling unwell, not sweating very much (or at all) and a high body temperature (39°C to 41°C or 102°F to 106°F). Where sweating has ceased the skin becomes flushed and red. Severe, throbbing headaches and lack of coordination also occur, and the sufferer may be confused or aggressive. Eventually the sufferer becomes delirious or has convulsions. Hospitalisation is essential, but in the interim get sufferers out of the sun, remove their clothing, cover them with a wet sheet or towel and then fan continually. Give fluids if they are conscious.

**Hypothermia** Too much cold can be just as dangerous as too much heat. If you are trekking at high altitudes or simply taking a long bus trip over mountains, particularly at night, be prepared. You should always be prepared for cold, wet or windy conditions even if you're just out walking or hitching.

Hypothermia occurs when the body loses heat faster than it can produce it and the core temperature of the body falls. It is surprisingly easy to progress from very cold to dangerously cold due to a combination of wind, wet clothing, fatigue and hunger, even if the air temperature is above freezing. It is best to dress in layers; silk, wool and some of the new artificial fibres are all good insulating materials. A hat is important, as a lot of heat is lost through the head. A strong, waterproof outer layer (and a 'space' blanket for emergencies) are essential. Carry basic supplies, including food containing simple sugars to generate heat quickly and fluid to drink.

Symptoms of hypothermia are exhaustion, numb skin (particularly toes and fingers), shivering, slurred speech, irrational or violent behaviour, lethargy, stumbling, dizzy spells, muscle cramps and violent bursts of energy. Irrationality may take the form of sufferers claiming they are warm and trying to take off their clothes. You're more likely to recognise it in someone else than in yourself.

To treat mild hypothermia, first get the person out of the wind and/or rain, remove their clothing if it's wet and replace it with dry, warm clothing. Give them hot liquids – not alcohol – and some high-kilojoule, easily digestible food. Do not rub victims, instead allow them to slowly warm themselves. This should be enough to treat the early stages of hypothermia. The early recognition and treatment of mild hypothermia is the only way to prevent severe hypothermia, which is a critical condition.

**Frostbite** Frostbite refers to the freezing of extremities, including fingers, toes and nose. It's sometimes a risk for trekkers and cyclists who cross the Khunjerab Pass early in the season, eg in April or May. It will get more relevant if talk of keeping the Khunjerab Pass open year-round for visitors comes to anything.

Signs and symptoms of frostbite include a whitish or waxy cast to the skin, or even crystals on the surface, plus itching, numbness and pain. Warm the affected areas by immersion in warm *(not* hot) water or with blankets or clothes, only until the skin becomes flushed. Frostbitten parts should not be rubbed. Pain and swelling are inevitable. Blisters should not be broken. Get medical attention right away.

**Prickly Heat** Prickly heat is an itchy rash caused by excessive perspiration trapped under the skin. It usually strikes people who have just arrived in a hot climate. Keeping cool, bathing often, drying the skin and using a mild talcum or prickly heat powder or resorting to air-conditioning may help.

**Sunburn** In the desert or at high elevations you can get sunburnt very fast, even through cloud. Use a sunscreen, hat, and barrier cream for your nose and lips. Calamine lotion, aloe vera lotion or Stingose are good for mild sunburn. Severe sunburn carries the risk of dehydration. Protect your eyes with good quality sunglasses, particularly if you are near water, sand or snow.

### Infectious Diseases
**Diarrhoea** A change of water, food or climate, even jet lag, can bring on the runs; even drinking silt-laden glacier melt-water will do it. But a few dashes to the loo with no other symptoms is nothing to worry about.

Dehydration is the main danger with any diarrhoea, particularly in children or the elderly, as dehydration can occur quite quickly. Under all circumstances *fluid replacement* (at least equal to the volume being lost) is the most important thing to remember. Weak black tea with a little sugar, soda water or soft drinks allowed to go flat and diluted 50% with clean water are all good.

With severe diarrhoea a rehydrating solution is preferable to replace minerals and salts lost. Commercially available oral rehydration salts (ORS) are very useful; add them to boiled or bottled water, which you should sip slowly all day. In an emergency you can make up a solution of six teaspoons of sugar and a half teaspoon of salt to a litre of boiled or bottled water. An alternative is rice water with some salt. You need to drink at least the same volume of fluid that you are losing in bowel movements and vomiting. Urine is the best guide to the adequacy of replacement – if you're passing small amounts of concentrated urine, you need to drink more. Keep drinking small amounts often. Stick to a bland diet as you recover.

Lomotil or Imodium can be used to bring relief from the symptoms, although they do not actually cure the problem. Only use these drugs if you do not have access to toilets eg if you *must* travel. For children under 12 years Lomotil and Imodium are not recommended. Do not use these drugs if you have a high fever or are severely dehydrated.

In certain situations antibiotics may be required: diarrhoea with blood or mucus (dysentery), any fever, watery diarrhoea with fever and lethargy, persistent diarrhoea not improving after 48 hours and severe diarrhoea. In these situations gut-paralysing drugs like Imodium or Lomotil should be avoided.

A stool test is necessary to diagnose which kind of dysentery you have, so you should seek medical help urgently. Where this is not possible the recommended drugs for dysentery are norfloxacin 400mg twice daily for three days or ciprofloxacin 500mg twice daily for five days. These are not recommended for children or pregnant women. The drug of choice for children would be co-trimoxazole (Bactrim, Septrin, Resprim) with dosage dependent on weight. A five-day course is given. Ampicillin or amoxycillin may be given in pregnancy, but medical care is necessary.

In **amoebic dysentery** the onset of symptoms is more gradual, with cramping abdominal pain and vomiting less likely; fever may not be present. It will persist until treated and can recur and cause other health problems.

**Giardiasis** is another type of diarrhoea. The parasite causing this intestinal disorder is present in contaminated water. The symptoms are stomach cramps, nausea, a bloated stomach, watery, foul-smelling diarrhoea and frequent gas. Giardiasis can appear several weeks after you have been exposed to the parasite. The symptoms may disappear for a few days and then return; this can go on for several weeks. Tinidazole, known as Fasigyn, or metronidazole (Flagyl) are the recommended drugs. Treatment is a 2g single dose of Fasigyn or 250mg of Flagyl three times daily for five to 10 days.

Metronidazole is fairly easy to obtain over the counter from pharmacies in China and Pakistan, but ask for it by its generic name and be sure of what you are getting!

**Hepatitis** Hepatitis is a general term for inflammation of the liver. It is a common disease worldwide. The symptoms are fever, chills, headache, fatigue, feelings of weak-

ness and aches and pains, followed by loss of appetite, nausea, vomiting, abdominal pain, dark urine, light-coloured faeces, jaundiced (yellow) skin and the whites of the eyes may turn yellow. Hepatitis A is transmitted by contaminated food and drinking water. The disease poses a real threat to the western traveller. You should seek medical advice, but there is not much you can do apart from resting, drinking lots of fluids, eating lightly and avoiding fatty foods. People who have had hepatitis should avoid alcohol for some time after the illness, as the liver needs time to recover.

Hepatitis E is transmitted in the same way and can be very serious in pregnant women. There are no specific vaccines for type E.

There are almost 300 million chronic carriers of hepatitis B in the world. It is spread through contact with infected blood, blood products or body fluids, for example through sexual contact, unsterilised needles and blood transfusions, or contact with blood via small breaks in the skin. Other risk situations include having a shave, tattoo, or having your body pierced with contaminated equipment. The symptoms of type B may be more severe and may lead to long term problems. Hepatitis D is spread in the same way, but the risk is mainly in shared needles.

Hepatitis C can also lead to chronic liver disease. The virus is spread by contact with blood – usually via contaminated transfusions or shared needles. Avoiding these is the only means of prevention.

**HIV & AIDS** Infection with HIV, the human immunodeficiency virus, develops into AIDS (acquired immune deficiency syndrome), which is a fatal disease. HIV is a major problem in many countries. Pakistan has reported AIDS cases and so has China, although HIV infection is uncommon in Xinjiang. Any exposure to blood, blood products or body fluids may put the individual at risk. The disease is often transmitted through sexual contact or dirty needles – vaccinations, acupuncture, tattooing and body piercing can be potentially as dangerous as intravenous drug use. HIV/AIDS can also be spread through infected blood transfusions; some developing countries cannot afford to screen blood used for transfusions (screening only began in some Pakistani hospitals in 1994).

If you do need an injection, ask to see the syringe unwrapped in front of you, or take a needle and syringe pack with you.

Fear of HIV infection should never preclude treatment for serious medical conditions.

**Intestinal Worms** These parasites are most common in rural, tropical areas. The different worms have different ways of infecting people. Some may be ingested on food, including undercooked meat, and some enter through your skin. Infestations may not show up for some time, and although they are generally not serious, if left untreated some can cause severe health problems later. Consider having a stool test when you return home to check for these and determine the appropriate treatment.

**Sexually Transmitted Diseases** Gonorrhoea, herpes and syphilis are among these diseases; sores, blisters or rashes around the genitals, discharges or pain when urinating are common symptoms. In some STDs, such as wart virus or chlamydia, symptoms may be less marked or not observed at all, especially in women. Syphilis symptoms eventually disappear completely but the disease continues and can cause severe problems in later years. While abstinence from sexual contact is the only 100% effective prevention, using condoms is also effective. The treatment of gonorrhoea and syphilis is with antibiotics. The different sexually transmitted diseases each require specific antibiotics. There is no cure for herpes or AIDS.

**Typhoid** Typhoid fever is a dangerous gut infection caused by contaminated water and food. Medical help must be sought.

In its early stages sufferers may feel they have a bad cold or flu on the way, as early symptoms are a headache, body aches and a fever which rises a little each day until it is around 40°C (104°F) or more. The sufferer's pulse is often slow relative to the degree of fever present which is unlike a normal fever where the pulse increases. There may also be vomiting, abdominal pain, diarrhoea or constipation.

In the second week the high fever and slow pulse continue and a few pink spots may appear on the body; trembling, delirium, weakness, weight loss and dehydration may occur. Complications such as pneumonia, perforated bowel or meningitis may occur.

The fever should be treated by keeping the sufferer cool and giving them fluids as dehydration should also be watched for. Ciprofloxacin 750mg twice a day for 10 days is good for adults.

Chloramphenicol is recommended in many countries. The adult dosage is two 250mg capsules, four times a day. Children aged between eight and 12 years should have half the adult dose; younger children should have one-third the adult dose.

**Insect-Borne Diseases**
Leishmaniasis is an insect-borne disease, but it does not pose a great risk to travellers. For more information on it see Less Common Diseases at the end of the health section.

**Malaria** There is a risk of malaria in Pakistan all year round, anywhere below about 2000m (ie well into the hills). This serious and potentially fatal disease is spread by mosquito bites. It is extremely important to avoid mosquito bites and to take tablets to prevent this disease. Symptoms range from fever, chills and sweating, headache, diarrhoea and abdominal pains to a vague feeling of ill-health. Seek medical help immediately if malaria is suspected. Without treatment malaria can rapidly become more serious and can be fatal.

If medical care is not available, malaria tablets can be used for treatment. You need to use a malaria tablet which is different to the one you were taking when you contracted malaria. The treatment dosages are: mefloquine – two 250mg tablets and a further two six hours later; fansidar – single dose of three tablets. If you were previously taking meflo-quine then other alternatives are halofantrine (three doses of two 250mg tablets every six hours) or quinine sulphate (600mg every six hours). There is a greater risk of side effects with these dosages than in normal use.

Travellers are advised to prevent mosquito bites at all times. The main messages are:

* wear light coloured clothing
* wear long trousers and long sleeved shirts
* use mosquito repellents containing the compound DEET on exposed areas
  (prolonged overuse of DEET may be harmful, especially to children, but its use is considered preferable to being bitten by disease-transmitting mosquitoes)
* avoid wearing perfume or aftershave
* use a mosquito net impregnated with mosquito repellent (permethrin) – it may be worth taking your own
* impregnating clothes with permethrin effectively deters mosquitoes and other insects

**Japanese B Encephalitis** This viral infection of the brain is transmitted by mosquitoes. Most cases occur in rural areas as the virus exists in pigs and wading birds. Symptoms include fever, headache and alteration in consciousness. Hospitalisation is needed for correct diagnosis and treatment. There is a high mortality rate among those who have symptoms; of those that survive many are intellectually disabled. This disease does not occur in Xinjiang, although it does occur in southern and south-west China, and is rare in northern Pakistan.

### Cuts, Bites & Stings

Rabies is passed through animal bites. See Less Common Diseases for details of this disease.

**Bedbugs & Lice** Bedbugs live in various places, but particularly in dirty mattresses and bedding, evidenced by spots of blood on bedclothes or on the wall. Bedbugs leave itchy bites in neat rows. Calamine lotion or Stingose spray may help.

All lice cause itching and discomfort. They make themselves at home in your hair

(head lice), your clothing (body lice) or in your pubic hair (crabs). You catch lice through direct contact with infected people or by sharing combs, clothing and the like. Powder or shampoo treatment will kill the lice and infected clothing should then be washed in very hot, soapy water and left in the sun to dry.

**Insect Bites & Stings** Bee and wasp stings are usually painful rather than dangerous. However in people who are allergic to them severe breathing difficulties may occur and require urgent medical care. Calamine lotion or Stingose spray will give relief and ice packs will reduce the pain and swelling. There are some spiders with dangerous bites but antivenenes are usually available. Scorpion stings are notoriously painful and can actually be fatal. Scorpions often shelter in shoes or clothing.

**Cuts & Scratches** Wash well and treat any cut with an antiseptic such as povidone-iodine. Where possible avoid bandages and Band-Aids, which can keep wounds wet.

**Snakes** To minimise your chances of being bitten always wear boots, socks and long trousers when walking through undergrowth where snakes may be present. Don't put your hands into holes and crevices, and be careful when collecting firewood.

Snake bites do not cause instantaneous death and antivenenes are usually available. Immediately wrap the bitten limb tightly, as you would for a sprained ankle, and then attach a splint to immobilise it. Keep the victim still and seek medical help, if possible with the dead snake for identification. Don't attempt to catch the snake if there is a possibility of being bitten again. Tourniquets and sucking out the poison are now comprehensively discredited.

### Women's Health

**Gynaecological Problems** Sexually transmitted diseases are a major cause of vaginal problems. Symptoms include a smelly discharge, painful intercourse and a burning sensation when urinating. Medical attention should be sought and male sexual partners must also be treated. Remember that, in addition to these diseases, HIV or hepatitis B may also be acquired during exposure. Besides abstinence, the best thing is to practise safe sex using condoms.

Antibiotic use, synthetic underwear, sweating and contraceptive pills can lead to fungal vaginal infections when travelling in hot climates. Maintaining good personal hygiene, and wearing loose-fitting clothes and cotton underwear will help to prevent these infections.

Fungal infections, characterised by a rash, itch and discharge, can be treated with a vinegar or lemon-juice douche, or with yoghurt. Nystatin, miconazole or clotrimazole pessaries or vaginal cream are the usual treatment.

**Pregnancy** It is not advisable to travel to some places while pregnant as some vaccinations normally used to prevent serious diseases are not advisable in pregnancy eg yellow fever. In addition, some diseases are much more serious for the mother (and may increase the risk of a stillborn child) in pregnancy eg malaria.

Most miscarriages occur during the first three months of pregnancy. Miscarriage is not uncommon, and can occasionally lead to severe bleeding. The last three months should also be spent within reasonable distance of good medical care. A baby born as early as 24 weeks stands a chance of survival, but only in a good modern hospital. Pregnant women should avoid all unnecessary medication but vaccinations and malarial prophylactics should still be taken where needed. Additional care should be taken to prevent illness and particular attention should be paid to diet and nutrition. Alcohol and nicotine, for example, should be avoided.

### Less Common Diseases

A number of less common diseases occur in this part of the world that you may hear about eg brucellosis, haemorrhagic fevers and hydatid disease. In general, these pose a small risk to travellers who follow the basic rules regarding hygiene and take measures to avoid insect bites. Some of these diseases are described below. Seek medical advice if you think you may have any of these diseases.

**Cholera** This is the worst of the watery diarrhoeas and medical help should be sought. There have been minor outbreaks in China and Baltistan in recent years but outbreaks are generally widely reported, so it's easy to avoid problem areas. *Fluid replacement is the most vital treatment* – the risk of dehydration is severe as you may lose up to 20L a day. If there is a delay in getting to hospital then begin taking tetracycline. The adult dose is 250mg four times daily. It is not recommended for children under nine years or for pregnant women. Tetracycline may help shorten the illness, but adequate fluids are required to save lives.

**Leishmaniasis** A group of parasitic diseases transmitted by sandfly bites. Cutaneous leishmaniasis affects the skin tissue causing ulceration and disfigurement and visceral leishmaniasis affects the internal organs. Visceral leishmaniasis occurs in Baltistan and a resurgence is occurring in China. Cutaneous leishmaniasis has been reported in Xinjiang and occurs in Pakistan. Seek medical advice as laboratory testing is required for diagnosis and correct treatment. Avoiding sandfly bites is the best precaution. Bites are usually painless, itchy and are yet another reason to cover up and apply repellent.

**Rabies** Rabies is a fatal viral infection transmitted in the saliva of infected animals; in the KKH this is mainly significant in connection with guard dogs kept by herders in remote areas eg in Baltistan. Other animals such as cats, bats and monkeys can also be infected. Any bite, scratch or even lick from a warm-blooded, furry animal should be cleaned immediately and thoroughly. Scrub with soap and running water, and then apply alcohol or iodine solution. Medical help should be sought promptly to receive a course of injections to prevent the onset of symptoms and death.

**Tetanus** Tetanus occurs when a wound becomes infected by a germ which lives in soil and in the faeces of horses and other animals. It enters the body via breaks in the skin. All wounds should be cleaned promptly and adequately and an antiseptic cream or solution applied. Use antibiotics if the wound becomes hot, throbs or pus is seen. The first symptom may be discomfort in swallowing, or stiffening of the jaw and neck; this is followed by painful convulsions of the jaw and whole body. The disease can be fatal.

**Tuberculosis (TB)** TB is a bacterial infection usually transmitted from person to person by coughing but may be transmitted through consumption of unpasteurised milk. Milk that has been boiled is safe to drink, and the souring of milk to make yoghurt or cheese also kills the bacilli. Travellers are usually not at great risk as close household contact with the infected person is usually required before the disease is passed on.

## TOILETS
We cannot recall ever seeing a public toilet in Pakistan or Xinjiang. Men don't seem to need them, being content to pee at the edge of the road or shit in a field. In Pakistan men squat to pee – an interesting cultural contrast to the west – with what modesty they might possess protected by the rear flap of their shalwar qamiz. Visiting western men will find this hard to imitate unless they too are wearing a shalwar qamiz.

For women the lack of public toilets is no laughing matter, and requires daily planning. Rural women must often settle for the cowshed. For visitors (trekkers aside), the best bet is public toilets in top-end hotels and restaurants, or periodic returns to their own hotel rooms.

Most hotel toilets used to be flushable Asian-style squats (Pakistanis call them 'Indian seat'; do Indians call them 'Pakistani seat'?), but mid-range tourist hotels are now joining the top-end ones in going over to

clean, tiled bathrooms and sit-down toilets, apparently under pressure from western group tour operators. However, it is one thing to install these and another to keep them working. In bottom-end places the squats remain.

Visitors to rural areas may still be directed to the nearest field, although in Pakistan it's increasingly a mark of prestige to equip at least one's guest room with a ceramic loo, usually Asian-style and bucket-flushed.

## WOMEN TRAVELLERS
Travel in Pakistan can be hard work for women. In traditionally-minded Muslim families, wives and daughters stay out of sight of other men – in the house, behind the veil, in special sections of buses and in the 'family' areas of restaurants. That's one reason why women travellers are regarded with such amazement, bafflement or sometimes hostility, and constantly asked, 'Where is your husband?'.

By the same token, traditionally-minded Muslim men minimise direct contact with women outside their own family – in some places (eg the Tribal Areas of the NWFP) for fear of their lives. That's why, for example, a foreign woman's questions may be answered to her male companion: generally not a sign of contempt but a habit of respect, Muslim-style.

But Pakistan isn't just populated by the traditionally-minded. Plenty of local men will willingly speak to or help a foreign woman, with no other motive than to be hospitable; some – especially in the tourist trade – do so as a matter of course. Moreover Ismaili men of the north have grown up with an outlook that westerners would consider more egalitarian, right in their own families. And western attitudes are quite common in Islamabad.

Consequently, women's experiences travelling in Pakistan range across the spectrum from heaven to hell. Every year many women travel around the country solo and love it; others, even with a male companion, have been, in the words of one, 'spat at, grabbed, groped, grappled with, sexually assaulted, ridiculed and derided, shoulder-barged and...made to feel most unwelcome and uncomfortable'.

Because many men are isolated from what westerners consider normal interactions with women outside the family, their views of 'other' women come mostly from popular culture and the media. Moreover the sexuality suppressed by tradition is inflamed by films full of guns, violence and full-hipped women (not just Pakistani and Indian blockbusters but, increasingly, B-grade western films on satellite TV). Thus women travelling on their own may be viewed as misfits, or on the make. Younger Pakistani men rarely miss the chance to point out to women visitors how sexually frustrated all Pakistani men are.

Serious harassment is rare in the north – perhaps because of Islam's injunction to be hospitable to strangers – but it does happen. There are (so far isolated) cases of sexual assault, including of women cyclists (the region from Chilas to Thakot is a place to keep your wits) and of trekkers separated from their group or travelling alone. More often harassment takes the form of shoulder rubs, bumps, gropes or just being followed in a crowded bazaar. Common sense will keep you out of some difficult situations, eg riding in the back of a crowded Suzuki at night. One letter suggests never standing with your backside to a crowd.

But women travellers also note that the risks are clearly less than in most western countries, and that isolating yourself is hardly the way to learn about the place you're visiting! It's a tightrope act for a woman to get familiar enough with a local man to learn about his life or his village, while keeping him from interpreting the conversation as an invitation and turning up at her door later. Physical signals can help or hinder; follow local practice of not shaking hands with a new male friend, and keep eye contact to a minimum.

Unaccompanied women are expected to sit at the front of the bus or in the front two seats of a minibus. The good news is that men will normally vacate these seats for women and cram themselves into the rear with the other men, and you can make a fuss if they don't. The bad news is that if these seats are already full of women, the bus might not even stop for you. If you're travelling with a man, he might be allowed up front too, provided he can avoid sitting next to a local woman!

Standing up for yourself can produce confusion, loss of attention or nervous laughter in others. This is not to say you shouldn't make a scene – as any local woman would – if you're being truly harassed. In any case westerners usually get the benefit of the doubt, and refusal to eat in the family section or sit at the front of the bus is usually tolerated.

Wearing local-style shalwar qamiz – with a light scarf to cover the hair in conservative company or in a mosque or shrine – at least wins points for attitude, and can make things easier. It's also quite comfortable, and easy and cheap to have made in the bazaar (but not blue and white: that's for schoolgirls). Those made for you in a Pakistani community back home may turn out rather different in fit and material from local versions.

Even if you don't opt for local styles, it's important, for your own stress level and as a sign of respect, to dress in a way that doesn't inflame the libidos of young men or the indignation of older ones. It would be difficult to overstate the sensitivity of this matter – see Clothing in the Planning section earlier in this chapter.

It's quite possible to travel solo in Pakistan without trouble, though you need to know yourself pretty well and be thick-skinned about being stared at. But in conservative, rural, non-Ismaili areas – essentially anywhere except Gojal and Hunza – you're better off travelling with others. Paradoxically, you're more likely than men to get a look into people's private lives; even in the most traditional areas, local women may ask you in, feed you and show you around, if there are no men around. Indeed more than one woman traveller has suggested that the very best way to ride the KKH is with other women and no men.

China, even Muslim Xinjiang, tends to be

a relief in this respect. Chinese men are at least deferential and sexual hassles are rare. Most Uyghurs seem equally uninterested in men and women foreigners.

For more on the status of women in Pakistani society, see the Society & Conduct section in the Facts About the Region chapter.

## GAY & LESBIAN TRAVELLERS

There is no visible gay/lesbian community in Xinjiang, although Ürümqi does have a small underground gay community. Conversation with Chinese people quickly turns to your spouse and children, and if you have neither you will be the object of frantic pity. Somewhat the same is true among Uyghurs. HIV is uncommon and AIDS is poorly understood.

In Pakistan, until the age of marriage, young women mix almost entirely with other young women, and young men with other young men. While it's not unusual to see women being physically affectionate with one another, it's more arresting for a westerner to see men holding hands and displaying physical affection in public, as is common here. This does not usually mean they're gay.

Homosexuality is technically against the law in Pakistan, and penalties are harsh, including jail terms and public flogging. Although the laws are apparently not much enforced, local gays and lesbians keep a very low profile. So should you.

**Organisations** Trikone is a World Wide Web site (with links to a confidential mailing list) for gay, lesbian and bisexual south Asians and friends: http://www.rahul.net/trikone/. The International Lesbian & Gay Association (ILGA, Brussels office; ☎/fax (02) 502 2471; email ilga@ilga.org) is a worldwide federation of groups and individuals, representing almost 70 countries, dedicated to achieving equal rights for lesbians and gay men. While there are no chapters in China or Pakistan, you can contact them for general information at 81 Kolenmarkt, 1000 Brussels, Belgium.

Another general resource is Amnesty International Members for Lesbian & Gay Concerns (AIMLGC; email aimlgc@igc. apc.org), c/o Amnesty International, 304 Pennsylvania Ave SE, Washington, DC 20003, USA.

## DISABLED TRAVELLERS

KKH travel would be an hour-by-hour struggle for a physically handicapped person. There are no wheelchair-accessible airports, hotels, transport or other facilities in Xinjiang or Pakistan. Disabled local people are far more in evidence (rather than institutionalised) in Pakistan than in China, or indeed than in the west, but it's not clear whether this reflects a 'Pakistani' outlook or governmental priorities.

Several western organisations offer general information on travel for the disabled, plus listings of wheelchair-friendly destinations, airports, hotels etc, though none has specific information on Xinjiang or Pakistan.

Mobility International USA (email info@miusa.org), PO Box 10767, Eugene, OR 97440, USA, publishes *You Want to Go Where? A Guide to China for Persons with Disabilities & Anyone Else Interested in Disability Issues*, with travel tips (but not for Kashgar) and information on the Chinese disability-rights movement (US$9); and *A World of Options: A Guide to International Exchange, Community Service and Travel for Persons with Disabilities* (US$35/40 including US/international postage).

RADAR, the Royal Association for Disability & Rehabilitation (☎ (0171) 250 3222; fax (0171) 250 0212) at 12 City Forum, 250 City Road, London EC1V 8AF, UK, focuses on European travel. Another UK resource is Holiday Care Service (☎ (01293) 774535; fax (01293) 784647), Imperial Buildings, Victoria Road, Horley, Surrey RH6 7PZ. Travelcare (☎ (0181) 295 1797; fax (0181) 467 2467), 35A High St, Chislehurst, Kent BR7 5QAE, specialises in travel insurance for the disabled.

A World Wide Web site for and by disabled travellers is http://www.travelhealth.com/disab.htm.

## USEFUL ORGANISATIONS
### The Royal Society for Asian Affairs
This small but venerable organisation has one of the best specialist libraries anywhere devoted to Asia, or rather to westerners' views of Asia, including many out-of-print editions. Membership is steep, however, at about UK£35 a year. They're at 2 Belgrave Square, London SW1X 8PJ (☎ (0171) 235 5122; fax (0171) 259 6771).

## DANGERS & ANNOYANCES
### Ethnic Unrest in Xinjiang
In early 1997 somewhere between 10 and 100 people died in riots in Yining, while more bombs exploded in Ürümqi, in Qorla (east of Kashgar) and on a Beijing bus. The Chinese government's response was swift and ruthless, with Uyghur sources claiming thousands of executions. As a result there has hardly been a dent in regional tourism, and there appears to be no danger for visitors.

### Sectarian Violence Around Gilgit
The Northern Areas is one of the safest parts of Pakistan. But in 1988 Sunni-Shia tension erupted in gun battles in the valleys around Gilgit, leaving at least 100 dead. There were smaller incidents in the following years. Then in 1994, electoral reforms allowed political parties to field candidates for election to local councils. Several religious rabble-rousers were elected to comfortable positions, at which point the violence abruptly subsided.

No foreigners were ever injured, but the KKH has sprouted police checkposts where foreigners must troop off the bus and sign the register. Many sign false names just for the fun of it, though these log-books have apparently been used to help embassies find their nationals in emergencies.

### Rockfall
Rockfall hazard on valley footpaths, and on the KKH and the Gilgit to Skardu road, rises sharply during rainy weather. Walkers should simply find something else to do. Rockfall on the Highway may of course ruin your plans, but it can do worse. A letter from one traveller describes a truly harrowing day

on the KKH between Karimabad and Gulmit.

A local driver said there was a rockfall but it was just a matter of scrambling across and boarding transport on the other side. But there wasn't any, so he and his companions decided to continue on foot. Soon rocks were falling around them from other slopes, and they spent six hours literally cheating death, sometimes hugging the wall, sometimes being forced down to the rising river. At one point a 5m rock smashed to the road just a metre from one of them.

Moral of the story: don't cross a rockfall hoping to find transport on the other side; the whole road is probably littered with rocks, with more to come. Go back and wait for the mountainsides to settle and the Frontier Works Organisation (FWO) to clean up the mess.

### Travel in Indus Kohistan
Indus Kohistan off the Highway is a pretty lawless place. You should seek advice from the police at Dasu/Komila, Pattan or Besham before heading up any of Kohistan's side valleys.

### Travel Elsewhere in Pakistan
In recent years a combination of sectarian and ethnic tensions, corrupt or incompetent law enforcement and a vigorous tribal arms industry has caused violence to mushroom in certain parts of Pakistan. This isn't to say you'll be dodging bullets – you just have to make sensible choices about where to go. Don't rely on tourist offices for accurate information on violence, and don't rely on the authorities to keep you away from danger: relatively few places are officially off-limits. Nearly all of the NWFP, Punjab, and Azad Jammu & Kashmir are safe, but be aware of the following hot-spots.

**NWFP** Tribal feuds and smugglers' battles are a risk to travellers who go off the main roads in the Tribal Areas, where Pakistani law has no force and the authorities are almost powerless to help you; in any case you'll need a permit to go there. It's much easier to wander into trouble without realising it in upper Swat, where there are no permit requirements.

**Sind** Foreigners should avoid Sind except for Karachi. Banditry is a major danger in the interior, and there is negligible police authority in rural Sind (and to some extent in extreme southern Punjab). Buses are regularly robbed; sometimes local trains are. Even in parts of Karachi there's a risk of being caught in the crossfire of political terrorism. At the time of research, long-distance rail travel was fairly safe.

**Baluchistan** Clan feuds and smugglers' conflicts make the interior of Baluchistan a good place to skip, except for Quetta and (at the time of research) the roads linking it to Karachi via the Bolan Pass, to the Iran border at Kuh-i-Taftan, and to Dera Ghazi Khan. Long-distance rail travel is still fairly safe.

### Petty Theft

Pakistan is one of the safest countries in the world when it comes to theft, and most Pakistanis are scrupulously honest. But to people on marginal incomes the dollars and expensive baggage of foreign visitors can be hard to resist. Don't leave valuables in your hotel room, no matter how secure it looks or how fine a fellow the manager is. Keep your money and passport with you at all times.

By contrast, Kashgar abounds with stories of theft and other problems. The bus station is a good place to keep an eye on your bags and a hand on your purse or wallet. Chinese hotels generally don't give out room keys, entrusting them instead to attendants who are not always very good about locking doors.

Vandalism is not a problem in tent sites or on most trekking routes, but don't leave things loose near villages in the Nanga Parbat and Chilas area, or anywhere in Indus Kohistan.

### Drugs

In the late 1980s Pakistan and Afghanistan together exported nearly half the world's heroin, and they remain among the world's major producers. Nudged by the US, the Pakistan government has tried to curtail poppy cultivation. But state influence is negligible in the tribal areas of the NWFP and Baluchistan, and enforcement agencies are riddled with corruption.

A few travellers come to the KKH obsessed with finding high-quality, locally-grown hashish. You'll soon recognise them, asking for stash from every local they meet and smoking with anyone who has anything. If that's not your style, say goodbye; otherwise your scope for enjoying the region will quickly narrow, and you could get into a heap of trouble. And be wary of absolutely anyone, local or tourist, who approaches you with drugs for sale.

Penalties for possession, use or trafficking in drugs are strictly enforced in both China and Pakistan, with long jail sentences and large fines frequently imposed. Legislation passed in 1994 in Pakistan makes trafficking punishable by death.

### EMERGENCIES

Your embassy in Islamabad is the best first stop in any emergency, but there are some things they cannot do for you. These include: getting local laws or regulations waived because you're a foreigner, investigating a crime, providing legal advice or representation in civil or criminal cases, getting you out of jail or even getting you better treatment there than local people get, lending money or paying your bills (though the UK

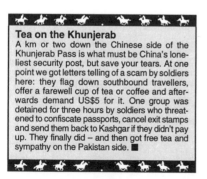

**Tea on the Khunjerab**
A km or two down the Chinese side of the Khunjerab Pass is what must be China's loneliest security post, but save your tears. At one point we got letters telling of a scam by soldiers here: they flag down southbound travellers, offer a farewell cup of tea or coffee and afterwards demand US$5 for it. One group was detained for three hours by soldiers who threatened to confiscate passports, cancel exit stamps and send them back to Kashgar if they didn't pay up. They finally did – and then got free tea and sympathy on the Pakistan side. ■

## Staying in Contact

In an emergency the simplest way for someone to reach you from outside the KKH region is by telephone to your hotel, or by telegram which can take a day or two. Of course this depends on someone knowing where you're staying!

Most foreign offices maintain 24 hour emergency operators – eg the British Foreign Office (☎ (0171) 270 3000), the US State Department Citizens Emergency Center (☎ (202) 647-5225), the Australian Department of Foreign Affairs & Trade (☎ (06) 261 9111) – who can contact your embassy in Islamabad or Beijing. Embassies naturally prefer that other means have been exhausted before they're contacted.

Obviously they'll be better able to track you down if you have let them know your plans, though few travellers actually bother. Western embassies in Islamabad and Beijing are at least willing to take note of your itinerary. They all suggest you carry the telephone numbers of your embassies in the region (see the Embassies entry in this chapter). ∎

Embassy might pay emergency travel costs in certain special circumstances).

## BUSINESS HOURS

In 1997 Pakistan's Prime Minister Nawaz Sharif shifted the weekly day off from Friday, the Muslim day of prayer and rest, to Sunday. The business community and nearly everyone else (except the clergy and some religious parties) has applauded the move, and it seems likely to stick. Now Friday is a working day, although in practice it's a half-day, with government and most private offices closing at noon or 1 pm. On Saturday, government offices close at 2 pm, private ones about 4 pm.

State banks are open from 9 am to noon on weekdays, except to 11.30 am on Friday; western banks normally stay open on Friday until about 4 pm, with an hour off for lunch. Main post offices open from 9 am to 3 pm on weekdays, except to 11.30 am on Friday; some sell stamps until 9 pm. Most museums open from 9 am to 5 pm in summer and to 4 pm in winter, except Wednesday when they're closed. Most foreign consular offices do visa business on weekdays from 9 am to

noon. In Islamabad, government officials typically turn up late at 10 am, leave early for lunch at noon, go for prayers at 1 pm, return about 2.30 pm and drift home as early as 3 pm.

In Xinjiang the Chinese-imposed day of rest is Sunday; a few offices may take a half day off on Saturday. Business hours are variable and are listed under individual towns.

## PUBLIC HOLIDAYS & SPECIAL EVENTS
### National Holidays

Except as noted, banks, businesses and government offices are closed in China or Pakistan on the following days.

1 January (China)
New Year's Day.
Late January-Early March (China)
Spring Festival or Chinese New Year, the year's biggest holiday for the Chinese, and their only three day break; calculated on the Chinese lunar calendar so dates change from year to year; the Chinese embassy in Islamabad is also closed.
8 March (China)
International Working Women's Day.
23 March (Pakistan)
Pakistan Day, celebrating the 1956 proclamation of Pakistan as a republic.
1 May (China & Pakistan)
International Labour Day.
4 May (China)
Youth Day.
1 June (China)
Children's Day.
1 July (China & Pakistan)
In China, the anniversary of the founding of the Chinese Communist Party; in Pakistan a bank holiday, but government offices and businesses remain open.
1 August (China)
Anniversary of the founding of the People's Liberation Army.
14 August (Pakistan)
Independence Day, the anniversary of the founding of Pakistan with the Partition of India in 1947; the real Northern Areas celebrations, however, are on 1 November.
6 September (Pakistan)
Defence of Pakistan Day, commemorating the India-Pakistan War of 1965.
11 September (Pakistan)
Anniversary of the death of Mohammed Ali Jinnah, regarded as the founder of Pakistan.

1 October (China)
   National Day, celebrating the founding of the PRC in 1949; in Xinjiang, a day or two off work.
9 November (Pakistan)
   Iqbal Day, honouring the poet Mohammed Iqbal, who in 1930 first proposed the idea of a Muslim Pakistan.
25 December (Pakistan)
   Birthday of Mohammed Ali Jinnah, founder of Pakistan.
31 December (Pakistan)
   Bank holiday, but government offices and businesses remain open.

## Muslim Holy Days

The Islamic calendar is lunar, and shorter than the western solar calendar, beginning 10 to 11 days earlier in each solar year. Modern astronomy notwithstanding, religious officials have formal authority to declare the beginning of each lunar month, based on sightings of the moon's first crescent. Future holy days can be estimated, but are in doubt by a few days until the start of that month, so dates given here are only approximate. They normally run from sunset to the next sunset.

These holy days are observed in Pakistan, and in a low-key way in Xinjiang; those marked with a (*) are also public holidays in Pakistan. As a result of differences in formal moon sightings, they may be celebrated on different days by Sunnis and Shias, which in the past has led to sectarian tension.

19 December 1998 to 16 January 1999; 9 December 1999 to 6 January 2000
   *Ramadan* (pronounced Ramazan in Pakistan), the month of sunrise-to-sunset fasting (see Religion in the Facts about the Region chapter for more information).
* 29 January 1998, 19 January 1999, 8 January 2000
   *Eid-ul-Fitr* (also called *Chhoti Eid* or Small Eid by Sunnis in Pakistan, *Ruza Eid* in Xinjiang), two or three days of celebrations at the end of Ramadan, with family visits, gifts, banquets, bonuses at work and donations to the poor.
* 9 April 1998, 30 March 1999, 19 March 2000
   *Eid-ul-Adha* (or Azha; also called *Bari Eid* or Big Eid by Sunnis in Pakistan, *Qurban* in Xinjiang), the Feast of Sacrifice, 40 days after the end of Ramadan, commemorating the Prophet Ibrahim's readiness to obey God even to the point of sacrificing his son. During the weeks ahead of this celebration, markets throng with goats and sheep; those who can afford it slaughter one after

early morning prayers, sharing the meat with relatives and with the poor. In Xinjiang, Uyghur men may gather to dance the *sama* to hypnotic drumbeats. This is also the season for *hajj* (pilgrimage to Mecca).
* 8 May 1998, 28 April 1999, 17 April 2000
   *Ashura*, 10th day of the month of Muharram. Shias begin 40 days of mourning the death of Hussain at Karbala. In trance-like processions, sometimes led by a riderless white horse, men and boys pound their chests and chant the names of those killed at Karbala. Some practise *zuljinnah*, flailing their backs with blade-tipped chains – awesome, and not for the squeamish – though this is disappearing. Sectarian tension is high, and visitors are not particularly welcome in Shia villages, eg all villages in Nagar, and Ganesh and Murtazaabad in Hunza.
* 17 June 1998, 7 June 1999, 27 May 2000
   *Chhelum*, 40 days after Ashura, sometimes with similar but smaller processions.
* 8 July 1998, 28 June 1999, 17 June 2000
   *Eid-Milad-un-Nabi*, the Prophet's birthday; some businesses may be closed.

## Seasonal & Regional Celebrations

Once an important part of life, celebrations associated with planting, harvesting, annual migrations or local traditions are giving way to modernisation, though you may find them celebrated privately and/or in more remote areas. Some older people of Hunza speak of the 'dreamful times' when people enjoyed community gatherings, music, dancing, courtship and a little drink.

Late February
   *Kitdit* or 'First Festival', the coming of spring, celebrated in Gojal. Houses are decorated and there are public gatherings with food and music.
Late February-Early March
   First (Wheat) Ploughing or Sowing. Called *Taghun* in Gojal and *Bo Fao* in Hunza and Nagar, this is now only celebrated privately by a few farmers in the Northern Areas, usually with food and prayers in the field. Gojalis prepare *samn*, a sweet delicacy made from fermented wheat flour. Some plough in November-December and celebrate then.
21 March
   *Nauroz* or *Navrus* ('New Days'), an adaptation of pre-Islamic vernal equinox or renewal celebrations. Polo matches may be held in Gilgit and sometimes Chalt; in smaller Northern Areas villages there is visiting, sometimes music and dancing. It's also celebrated in parts of Afghanistan, Iran and India.

13-15 April
Baisakhi, when Sikh pilgrims from India visit Panja Sahib shrine at Hasan Abdal, near Rawalpindi.

First week in May
Urs (death anniversary) of Bari Shah Latif at Nurpur Shahan village, near Islamabad; pilgrims come from Pakistani Punjab at NWFP in a carnival mood, and foreigners are tolerated.

Late June-Early July
First (Wheat) Harvest. This is called Chinir in Gojal and Ginani or Ganoni in Hunza and Nagar, and is similar to First Sowing.

11 July
Taqt Nashina ('taking of the seat'), the day the present Aga Khan assumed leadership of the Ismaili community. Of course this is only celebrated in Ismaili areas, and may include parades, games, music, dancing and fireworks on the mountainsides.

23 October
The Aga Khan's first visit to Hunza in 1960, celebrated only in Hunza; similar to Taqt Nashina.

18 November
The Aga Khan's first visit to Gojal in 1987, celebrated only in Gojal; similar to Taqt Nashina.

13 December
The Aga Khan's Birthday, celebrated by Ismailis with gatherings and speeches.

21 December
Tumishiling, a festival of renewal in Hunza-Nagar, celebrating the death of the 'cannibal-king' Shri Badat of Gilgit, whose daughter plotted with his subjects to trap him in a pit and burn him to death. Bonfires are built in some villages, and people carry fire from their own homes; there may also be music, dancing and the slaughter of sheep or goats.

Late December
Yushayas in Hunza, Nosalo in Nagar, Nos around Gilgit. During 15 days or so after Tumishiling, each household slaughters an animal and hangs it up for all to see – traditionally ensuring a winter food supply, in time for the meat to dry without spoiling; with the appearance of refrigeration, of course, this has become purely symbolic; in Bagrot, Nos is an occasion for music and dancing.

## Other Festivals

March
Rose Festival, Rose & Jasmine Garden, Islamabad.

April
Polo matches are common in Gilgit and Ghizar.

April
Spring Flower Show, Rose & Jasmine Garden, Islamabad.

July or early August
Polo on the Shandur Pass, between Gilgit and Chitral: a three or four-day jamboree with dynamite polo, folk dancing and high-jinks, and a mountain of rubbish left behind. Dates have traditionally been set only about a month ahead, but there is much talk of fixing it in early July for the sake of group tourism (it was on 8-10 July in 1997).

1 November
Northern Areas Independence Day or Jashan-i-Gilgit, commemorating the 1947 uprising against the Maharajah of Kashmir; Gilgit's major event of the year, with a week-long polo tournament from the 1st, kicked off by a tartan-clad pipe band and much good-humoured pomp.

November
Chrysanthemum Show, Rose & Jasmine Garden, Islamabad.

## ACTIVITIES

Following is an indication of the possibilities for adventure travel in the KKH region. Some reliable adventure-travel agencies (both inside Pakistan and overseas) with Xinjiang and KKH programmes are listed under Tour Operators & Trekking Companies in the Getting There & Away chapter.

### Trekking (Xinjiang)

In the Kashgar-Tashkurgan region the most accessible treks are around Kara Kul lake and the lower reaches of Mt Kongur and Muztagh Ata. This is a restricted area, for which you should have an Alien Travel Permit from the PSB in Kashgar or Tashkurgan. For visits of more than a day or so, it's sensible to make arrangements through a local agency (see the Kashgar to Tashkurgan chapter).

### Trekking (Pakistan)

Trekking in the Karakoram, which includes some of the world's highest mountains and longest glaciers, is a serious business for participants and government alike. The Tourism Division of the Ministry of Sports & Tourism defines trekking as walking anywhere below 6000m; anything above that is regarded as mountaineering.

Three types of trekking zones are defined. Treks in open zones are well removed from sensitive areas and need no permits; routes and arrangements, and guides if you want them, are up to you. Open zones near the KKH are in *certain* parts of Shimshal and the Batura Muztagh (the crest zone in Hunza-Gojal); Hoper, Hispar, the north side of Rakaposhi and Chalt-Chaprot (Nagar); Naltar, Ishkoman, Yasin, Bagrot and Haramosh (Gilgit area); across the Shandur Pass into Swat and Chitral; the Skardu area; Nanga Parbat; and the Kaghan Valley.

To trek in a *restricted* zone you need a Ministry permit and a government-approved guide or liaison officer. Permit conditions include per-head fees; a detailed application; official requirements for insurance, wages, equipment, food and transport for guides and porters; and meetings with tourism officials in Islamabad before and after the trek. An easy (but not cheap) way to arrange a trek in a restricted zone is through a trekking agency. Doing it on your own involves minimal fees but lots of time, from weeks to months.

*Closed* zones, within 48km of the Afghan border or within 16km of the Line of Control with Indian-administered Kashmir, are off-limits to foreigners.

A booklet setting out detailed regulations, permit procedures, suggested agencies and a more or less current list of 'approved' treks is *Trekking Rules and Regulations*, available from the Deputy Chief for Operations, Tourism Division (☎ (051) 820856 or 827015), Ministry of Sports & Tourism, Room 8, 13-T/U Commercial Area, Jinnah Market, F-7/2, Islamabad, Pakistan.

Major Karakoram and Hindukush treks, plus regulations, equipment, health and safety, the permit process, the complex and ticklish business of arranging porters and guides, and more are described in detail in Lonely Planet's *Trekking in the Karakoram & Hindukush*.

### White-Water Rafting

Rivers near the KKH with stretches of class IV or easier rapids (suitable for commercial rafting) include the Hunza from Sost to Passu, the Gilgit from Punial to the Indus confluence, the lower Ishkoman, the Shyok (Baltistan) from Khapalu to Gol and the Swat from Madyan to Saidu Sharif.

Two Gilgit outfits offering white-water trips for beginners, at about US$45 per person per day and with professionally trained local river guides, are Travel Walji's and Mountain Movers. The rafting season is approximately May to late June and late September to November.

### Trout Fishing

Streams and lakes all over northern Pakistan are stocked with trout. Well known reaches near Gilgit include Kargah Nala, Naltar Valley and Singhal Nala in Punial; others are in Astor, the Kaghan Valley and Swat. The season is from 10 March to 9 October. Information and licences (US$2 per person per day) are available at Fisheries offices, including one in Gilgit (which also rents tackle).

### Cycling

The KKH, at least on the Pakistan side, is in many ways a cyclist's dream. Bicycle tourists should refer to the Getting Around chapter for general information on riding the KKH, and to the cyclists' notes near the beginning of each chapter for more specific advice.

### Skiing

Simple downhill skiing facilities exist in the Naltar Valley near Gilgit and at Kalabagh near Murree. The country's biggest ski resort is at Malam Jabba in the Swat Valley. The season is from December to March. Experienced ski mountaineers can enjoy world-class touring on the Deosai Plains and on the Batura, Hispar and Biafo glaciers, in March and April.

### WORK

The only work available for passing foreigners along the KKH appears to be teaching English, especially around Gilgit and in Hunza. The demand for English teachers – and even just native speakers for conversational practice – has been climbing steadily with the growth in mostly private, English-medium primary schools and language schools. The obvious value to a visitor is the chance to stay and get more deeply acquainted with a community.

Budgets are miniscule, so you won't get rich; most likely you'd be offered free room and board with a local family, plus possibly a small salary. You should be prepared to stay and work for at least a month, although there may be brief volunteer work available too. Each school or school authority will negotiate its own conditions. School officials can at least write a letter to help you extend your visa if appropriate.

Obviously a teaching or English-teaching credential boosts your value, but there are opportunities for those without one too. Perhaps more important than a credential is a willingness to talk at length with primary-age kids about whatever interests them. The teachers may want conversational practice too, and may pick your brains about activities and games as well.

Following is a partial list of places to inquire, either in advance or as you're passing through; all are in Gilgit district. Another source of ideas is the 15 or so VSO volunteers who work in the region (and one contact for *them* is Asghar Shah, manager of the North Inn in Gilgit). Also watch for notices in backpackers' guesthouses.

Hunza Education Resource Project, Aliabad, Hunza: coordinating centre for at least 17 primary schools in Hunza and Gojal; contact Richard Barwell, Project Manager. It's Postal address is PO Aliabad, Hunza, Gilgit, Northern Areas; see the Aliabad section in the Hunza & Nagar chapter for its office location.

Naunehal Development Organisation, Jaffarabad (between Sikanderabad and Nilt), Nagar: a consortium of Nagar village organisations which has established at least eight primary schools; contact Syed Muzaffar Shah, chairman, c/o Jaffarabad Health Centre, or Raja Ali Anwar, Golden Peak Tours, Gilgit.

Pilot School, Sherqila, Punial; contact Nilusha Bardai, Principal.

Mulberry School, Gilgit; contact Asghar Shah, North Inn, Gilgit.

## ACCOMMODATION
### Reservations
Forget about booking ahead, except at top-end places. Even when you've made a booking you may find on arrival that they've never heard of you.

### Camping
In Xinjiang you can't pitch a tent with any security around larger towns, but you can camp at places like Kara Kul and below Muztagh Ata.

In Pakistan, hotels will often let you pitch a tent in their yards or on the roof and use their toilets for a small fee. Overlanders with their own transport can park and camp very cheaply at the down-and-out, government-run Tourist Campsite.

### Railway Retiring Rooms
Some major railway stations in Pakistan have retiring rooms with spartan singles/doubles from Rs 100/150, available to holders of air-conditioned or 1st class sleeper tickets. They're really only useful if you arrive late or depart very early, and even then you may find them always 'full'. You supply your own bedding. The only one near the KKH is at Taxila.

### Village Guest Houses
The Aga Khan Rural Support Programme (AKRSP) and the PTDC started a 'Village Guest House' programme under which many people around Gojal, Hunza and Gilgit converted parts of their homes into guesthouses, with a few comfortable rooms and home-cooked meals. Those that survived are now self-supporting.

Most aren't really 'homestays' since guests tend to be left to themselves and fed separately, but they're closer to grassroots level than a hotel is. Some owners speak little or no English. Not all are worth the Rs 300 or so that a double with bath usually costs.

For a somewhat out-of-date brochure listing these places, ask at PTL in Rawalpindi (☎ (051) 581480), or PTDC (☎ (0572) 2562) or the Hunza Tourist House (☎ (0572) 3788) in Gilgit. In the destination chapters we note a few that are good value.

## Hostels

The Pakistan Youth Hostels Association (PYHA), with headquarters at the Islamabad hostel (☎ (051) 826899; Garden Rd, Aabpara, G-6/4, Islamabad) and an office in Lahore (☎ (042) 878201; House 110-B, Gulberg-III) runs a dozen hostels in Pakistan, with gender-segregated dormitories, gardens where you can pitch a tent and usually cooking facilities.

A bed is Rs 45 per night in Islamabad or Lahore and Rs 40 elsewhere. The 'student price' of Rs 25 is officially for Pakistani students, but, outside the cities, *chowkidars* (caretakers) may accept foreign student cards. Guests pitch in with clean-up, and must be in by mid-evening. In summer the hostels are very popular with Pakistani students, and when they're busy you can only stay three days.

You must be a member of Hostelling International (HI, formerly the International Youth Hostel Federation) or of PYHA. If not, you can either purchase a year's membership on the spot for Rs 360 at the Islamabad or Lahore hostel, or spread it out over six stays at these or other hostels with a daily fee of Rs 60 (on top of the bed charge). Some chowkidars may be unaware of the scheme or uncertain what to do.

Along the KKH there are hostels in the Kaghan Valley, Abbottabad, the Galis and Taxila. Abbottabad's is far from town, those in the Kaghan Valley are in deplorable shape, and some are only open for a short season. But Islamabad's year-round one is good.

## Government Resthouses

These include some of the best mid-range bargains on the KKH. Also called Circuit Houses, Inspection Bungalows or Dak Bungalows, most are two- or three-unit guesthouses run by government agencies for staff on business. The best are in peaceful, isolated locations, and each has a chowkidar living nearby who can, by arrangement, prepare at-cost meals from whatever's available.

Most guesthouses near the KKH are run by the Northern Areas Public Works Department (NAPWD), the North-West Frontier Province Communication & Works Department (C&W) or Forestry Districts.

In principle they're available to tourists, at elevated rates, if no one else is using them. In practice many must be booked in district capitals or even in Islamabad or Peshawar, and the relevant chief engineer is invariably out or on holiday. The best advice may be to take your chances without a booking, though chowkidars aren't always very cheerful about it. Cyclists without bookings have been told to camp outside – though their gardens do make pretty nice camping spots!

The best resthouses and their booking offices are noted in the regional chapters.

NWFP's Sarhad Tourism is in the process of privatising all that province's resthouses, either taking them on itself or leasing them to private operators. Many bureaucrats are understandably cross at seeing one of the perks of the job disappear. The process will take years, though some resthouses, especially in Swat and the Kaghan Valley, may go private (and upmarket) during the life of this edition.

## Hotels

Most KKH hotels are cheap by western standards. They're state-run in China, mostly private in Pakistan, and with the growth of KKH tourism they now come in all cost and comfort ranges. Indeed with most new hotel construction at the upper end, the options for budget travellers are actually shrinking. At the bottom end, hotels tend towards grotty, a bit less so in China than in Pakistan.

Prices in Pakistan aren't always fixed. Two very popular areas, the Kaghan Valley and the Galis, get so crowded in summer that they're worth avoiding unless you have a booking or a tent. Hotel prices go wild then. Off season, on the other hand, you can strike some of the best bargains in the country in these places.

Price categories in this book – bottom, middle and top – are based roughly on a hotel's most basic double room, usually with attached toilet and shower. Many hotels of course have cheaper rooms than this; in fact a fairly comfortable way to travel cheaply is to stay in the dormitory rooms of better hotels. Some mainstream hotels also have cheap *charpois* (rope-beds) on the roof, if you ask.

Foreigners aren't welcome at some bottom-end places because the owner (or the state) doesn't care to adjust to western demands. In Pakistan some of these save face by saying they have no 'Form D', the government hotel-register form.

Note that many 'hotels' in Pakistan are just eating-places.

## FOOD

Food on the KKH is as varied as its ethnic groups. It can be a pleasure in Kashgar, Hunza and Rawalpindi. It's uneven in Gilgit. In Indus Kohistan you won't go hungry but you might go mad from nonstop curried mutton. Basic Uyghur and Pakistani foods are described below; local specialities are described further in the Kashgar, Gojal, Hunza & Nagar and Rawalpindi & Islamabad chapters. Longer lists of food terms are included in the Language chapter.

Remember that most Muslims avoid taking food to the mouth with the left hand. In the same vein, it's polite to accept cups of tea and plates of food only with the right hand.

In bigger towns the cook may sometimes add a side dish you don't remember ordering. It's partly goodwill, but of course you'll have to pay for it! Some travellers report being overcharged when they failed to confirm meal prices in advance and whether prices were per person or per dish.

In 1987 and 1988 hepatitis E was epidemic in western Xinjiang, and, in Pakistan, gut infections are common with foreign travellers. See the Health section earlier in this chapter for hygiene suggestions.

### Uyghur Food

*Nan* is tandoori-style bread, incredibly cheap, often sprinkled with fennel, anise, poppy or sesame seeds and served with every-thing – sometimes serving as an impromptu plate. The big, flat ones are called *ak nan* and the little 'bagels' are *gzhde*, wonderful straight out of the oven.

Mutton is the meat of choice. The common person's mutton is *shashlyk*, kebabs of fresh, marinated or minced meat sold on old-town street corners, served with nan and onions. Restaurants may also do kebabs of beef, liver or chicken.

Long, thick noodles *(laghman)* distinguish Central Asian cuisine from any other, and Uyghurs are undisputed master noodle-makers. Laghman is the base for a spicy soup (usually also called laghman, or *la-mian* to Xinjiang Chinese) with fried mutton, peppers, tomatoes and onions. In Xinjiang, *so-mian* is roughly the same ingredients on a 'bed' of noodles.

Other meat-and-dough variants include *chuchureh*, a small boiled or fried dumpling, served with vinegar or in soups; and *samsa*, a little envelope of meat and onions usually baked in a tandoori oven. Alternative fillings include potato and chickpeas.

*Plo* or 'plov' is the Central Asian version of Persian rice pilaf, consisting mainly of rice with fried and boiled meat, onions and carrots, and sometimes raisins or chickpeas, all turned over and over in a huge iron wok.

*Durap* is a heavenly concoction of chipped ice, syrup and yoghurt served in a glass, and *maroji* is vanilla ice cream, made in a butter barrel encased in ice. But try these only if you have a strong stomach; durap especially has ice made from tap water, and so carries an inherent risk.

Fruit is abundant but seasonal. May is the time for apricots, July for grapes and figs, autumn for apples, dates, pomegranates and pears. Melons and watermelons ripen in late summer but are available right into the winter.

### Pakistani Food

Pakistani food is like that of northern India but with Central Asian and Middle Eastern influences. It tends to be spicy (but not to Indian extremes) and oily. The more affluent

cook with *ghee* (clarified butter) instead of vegetable oil.

*Roti* means bread in general, mostly from unleavened whole wheat flour. No eatery is without *chapattis*, flat rounds cooked on a dry griddle, which also serve for grabbing, spooning or soaking up the bits and juices. *Paratha* is similar but thicker and fried in oil, commonly for breakfast. Nan or *tandoori roti* is like Uyghur nan. *Double roti* is western-style sliced bread from processed flour, with little food value. In Gojal and Hunza you can find several varieties of heavy wholemeal bread.

Meat *(gosht)* is usually mutton (also *gosht)* or chicken *(murghi)*, sometimes beef *(gayka gosht)*; pork is taboo for Muslims. Popular ways to cook meat, especially chicken, are *tandoori* (marinated and baked in a clay tandoor oven), *biryani* (cooked with spiced rice), *tabak* (grilled) and *karahi* (braised with vegetables and served in its own small iron wok).

*Qorma* is a braised meat curry in gravy. *Qofta* are lamb meatballs (or sometimes vegetable versions). *Qeema* is minced mutton or beef in a sauce. *Seekh kebabs* are the same as Uyghur shashlyk. *Shami kebabs* are 'pancakes' of lentils and minced mutton; a delicious Pathan variation is *chapli kebabs*, spicy 'mutton burgers' shaped like the sole of a chappal (sandal).

Vegetables *(sabzi)* are usually cooked all day, rendering them nutritionally useless and often unrecognisable. The universal vegetarian dish is lentil mush *(dhal)*. Other common accompaniments are spicy spinach *(palak)*, potatoes *(alu)*, okra *(bhindi)* and peas *(matar)*. Rice *(chawal)* can be ordered boiled *(sadha chawal)* or central Asian style *(pulau)*, fried with vegetable bits and sometimes meat.

To rescue your taste buds from a mouthful of chillies, have a dish of *dahi* (plain yoghurt) or *raita* (curd with cumin and vegetable bits) nearby.

Among spicy street snacks are *samosas* (like Uyghur samsas), *tikkas* (barbecued beef, mutton or chicken bits) and *pakora* (floured, deep-fried vegetables). If you long for something without chillies, try baked yams, popcorn, roasted or boiled corn on the cob *(sita)*, or a little glass of peppery chicken soup *(murghi kai)*.

Cheese is usually available only in pricey tinned, processed form – though you'll run across varieties of soft or hard whey cheese in the north.

Fresh fruit in the mountains includes apricots, peaches, plums, apples, cherries, mulberries and grapes. More common and less seasonal are dried apricots and mulberries. Nuts include peanuts, walnuts, almonds, pistachios and pecans.

Among common restaurant desserts are *kheer*, a milk and rice custard (often taken to break the Ramadan fast), and *kulfi*, Moghul-style pistachio ice cream. Pakistan has several decent commercial brands of ice cream, available in eateries or food shops, but the street-side 'softee' machines aren't as hygienic as they look. Food shops dispense a zillion varieties of local or imported sweet biscuits.

### Western Food

You can get good western dishes at upper-end restaurants in Gilgit and Rawalpindi, and Islamabad has everything from Italian to Tex-Mex. But almost any hotel can stir up an edible western breakfast – fried eggs *(anda frai* in Urdu, *jian ji-dan* in Chinese), boiled eggs *(ublahwa anda* in Urdu, *zhu ji-dan* in Chinese) or omelettes, white toast (or whole wheat bread in Gojal and Hunza) and jam, porridge (oatmeal) or Pakistani cornflakes, tea or awful coffee. And any place that's seen more than a few tourists has probably learned how to do chips (French fries).

### Vegetarian

The KKH can be a struggle for vegetarians. You can get by in big-town produce markets (for fruit, nuts and vegetables), in Kashgar's Chinese stalls and restaurants, Hunza and Gilgit cafes, and many upper-echelon places in Rawalpindi and Islamabad. Some hotels will stir up a vegetable entree for you, especially if you bring the ingredients. Otherwise it's rice, chapattis, dhal, sabzi (overcooked vegetables, mainly okra), yoghurt, eggs, eggs and eggs – plus whatever munchies you carry. A vitamin-mineral supplement is a very good idea.

'I am vegetarian' is *wo chi su* in Mandarin Chinese, and *me shakahari hu* in Urdu. 'Without meat' is *gushsiz* in Uyghur.

### Ramadan

Ramadan is the Muslim month of sunrise-to-sunset fasting. In Xinjiang few seem to take it seriously, and in Gojal and Hunza, Ismailis don't take part. But from Gilgit southward, getting food and drink during the day takes some planning. See Religion in the Facts about the Region chapter for more about Ramadan and how to cope with it, and Public Holidays & Special Events in this chapter for the dates, which change from year to year in the western calendar.

### DRINKS

#### Nonalcoholic Drinks

In Xinjiang you can get Chinese tea (*cha*) everywhere. Also available are little sealed containers of insipid, sweetened yoghurt.

In Pakistan, 'milky tea' (*dudh-chai*) is usually equal parts water, leaves, sugar and long-life milk brought to a raging boil – though better places serve a proper 'set', complete with warmed milk. Green tea is called *sabz-chai*; *khawa* is a sweet and delicious green tea with cardamom or other spices. The only coffee is instant, except at five-star hotels.

Bottled water and soft drinks (including imported brands) are available – but check the seal, as some dealers fill used bottles with tap water. Always safe are the little boxes of fruit juice that you punch open with a straw. *Lassi* is a refreshing subcontinental drink of yoghurt, water and crushed ice, either sweetened or salted, and in old-town Rawalpindi you'll find other thirst quenchers such as 'freshlime', made of crushed ice, salt, sugar, soda water and the juice of fresh limes. But remember that ice can carry a health risk. Vendors in Rawalpindi sell freshly squeezed fruit and sugar-cane juice, but their barely rinsed glasses are off-putting.

Tap water is not always trustworthy (see the Health section earlier in this chapter for tips on purifying it).

#### Alcohol

In Kashgar, Chinese beer, wine, brandy and spirits are available in Chinese restaurants and department stores, although Muslim Uyghurs rarely drink (in public).

Pakistan is officially dry, but on the KKH non-Muslim foreigners can drink in special lounges at top-end hotels in Rawalpindi and Islamabad. You can get a liquor permit, as long-term residents do (see the Alcohol section in the Rawalpindi & Islamabad chapter), but elsewhere on the KKH there's little liquor to get with it.

In Hunza, people brew *mel*, a coarse grape wine, and a mulberry brandy called *arak*. This so-called 'Hunza water' may be offered to you by friends.

### ENTERTAINMENT

Western films are screened in bigger cities of Pakistan (including Rawalpindi), usually in the original language. Schwarzenegger and Spielberg are big favourites.

### SPECTATOR SPORTS

The KKH's number one spectator sport is polo, and locals insist that the game was invented here. For a look at the wild and woolly Northern Areas version of polo, see the boxed text The Game of Kings in the Gilgit Region chapter.

# Getting There & Away

The northern end of the KKH is at Kashgar in China's Xinjiang Autonomous Region. Kashgar is linked by air via the provincial capital, Ürümqi, to major Chinese cities and international points. Overland, Kashgar is linked by bus (and soon by train) to Ürümqi, from where rail lines run to Chinese cities and to Almaty in Kazakhstan. A warm-weather road crosses the Torugart Pass between Kashgar and Bishkek in Kyrgyzstan, and an all-weather road runs between Ürümqi and Almaty.

The nominal southern end of the KKH is at Havelian in Pakistan's North-West Frontier Province (NWFP), but in practice it's at Islamabad, the capital, and its sister-city Rawalpindi. Islamabad has a limited number of direct international air connections, plus others via Lahore, but most are via the southern city of Karachi. Islamabad and Rawalpindi can also be reached by rail and road from southern Pakistan, India and Iran.

Note that with respect to the KKH, all domestic transport in China to Kashgar, and all domestic transport up to Islamabad in Pakistan, fall within the scope of this Getting There & Away chapter.

## AIR
### Airports & Airlines
Xinjiang's only international airport is at Ürümqi, the provincial capital. International carriers with scheduled services from Ürümqi include Xinjiang Airways (the regional carrier, devolved from state-run Air China, or CAAC) and Kazakhstan Airlines. The main headache with Ürümqi is that flights are subject to all-too-frequent delays or cancellation when the weather is rainy or dusty there.

Pakistan's main international airport is at Karachi; most major international carriers can land there, and only there. Other important international airports are at Islamabad and Lahore. Islamabad is served by Pakistan International Airlines (PIA), the national carrier, Aero Asia (a private Pakistani carrier,

now expanding from domestic into regional routes), British Airways, Saudia and Xinjiang Airways. Lahore is served by PIA, Saudia, Kuwait and Thai.

All three airports are also served by two private domestic carriers, Bhoja Air and Shaheen, although at the time of research the latter had shut down all its operations.

From Europe or Asia, flying directly into Islamabad is the most expensive option. Getting there via Lahore is usually cheaper, while the cheapest and most plentiful connections are via Karachi.

Other airports at Peshawar, Quetta, Gwadar and Pasni have Middle East links (PIA also flies to Peshawar from Tashkent).

### Buying Tickets
Some travel agencies just handle tours, while others can arrange everything from tours and tickets to car rental and hotel bookings. But if all you want is a cheap flight, then you need an agency specialising in discounted tickets.

Though the airlines' own best fares will give you a point of reference, they're rarely the lowest. Various types of discounted tickets can save you a lot and/or increase the

---

**Travellers with Special Needs**

If you have special requirements – eg you're in a wheelchair, taking the baby, terrified of flying, vegetarian – let the airline know when you book. Remind them again when you reconfirm, and again when you check in at the airport. It may also be worth ringing round the airlines before you book to find out how each one would handle your particular situation.

Airports and airlines can be surprisingly helpful, but they do need advance warning. Most international airports can provide escorts from check-in to the plane, and most have ramps, lifts, accessible toilets and telephones (but not in Xinjiang or Pakistan). Aircraft toilets, on the other hand, present problems for wheelchair travellers, who should discuss this early on with the airline and/or their doctor. ∎

## Bucket Shops & Consolidators

In London and some Asian capitals (eg Delhi and Bangkok) you'll find the lowest airfares offered by 'bucket shops' – obscure, unbonded agencies taking advantage of last-minute airline discounts on surplus seats. Many are honest and solvent, but not all.

Don't part with even a deposit until you know the date and time of your flights, the name of the airline (both outward and return), airports of departure and destination, long layovers and any restrictions. If the agent won't give you this information, go elsewhere.

Watch for 'surcharges'. Booking fees shouldn't be necessary since agents get commissions from the airlines. If you book with a credit card number you may find there's an extra charge of 1% to 2%. Ask whether all your money will be refunded if the flight is cancelled or changed to a date which is unacceptable to you. And once you have the ticket, ring the airline yourself to confirm that you're actually booked on the flight.

Increasingly, bucket shops in the UK are going respectable as 'consolidators' – official outlets for the airlines' discounted and last-minute tickets. If you have a preferred airline, this may be your best bet for a cheap ticket. Call and ask the airline who its consolidators are. ■

scope of your travel at marginal extra cost. Shop around, and start early – some cheap tickets must be purchased months in advance. Check the travel ads in major newspapers.

You're safest if an agency is a member of the International Air Transport Association (IATA) or a national association like the American Society of Travel Agents (ASTA), the Association of British Travel Agents (ABTA) or the Australian Federation of Travel Agents (AFTA). If you've bought your ticket from a member agency which then goes out of business, the association will guarantee a refund or an alternative. Member agencies must also have professional indemnity insurance (which serves as a secondary safety net).

Recommended are youth-oriented agencies like Trailfinders and Campus Travel (UK), Council Travel (USA), Travel CUTS (Canada) and STA Travel (worldwide), which specialise in finding low airfares. Most offer the best deals to students and under-26s but they are open to all, and they won't play tricks on you. All are members of their national travel agent associations.

**USA & Canada** The *Los Angeles Times, San Francisco Examiner, Chicago Tribune, New York Times, Toronto Globe & Mail* and *Vancouver Sun* have big weekly travel sections with lots of travel agent ads. The monthly newsletter *Travel Unlimited* (PO Box 1058, Allston, MA 02134) publishes the cheapest airfares from the USA for destinations worldwide.

Council Travel (☎ 800-223-7402, toll-free) and STA Travel (☎ 800-777-0112) are reliable sources of cheap tickets in the USA. Each has offices all over the country. Canada's best bargain-ticket agency is Travel CUTS, with some 50 offices in major cities. Their parent office (☎ (416) 979-2406) is at 187 College St, Toronto M5T 1P7.

Overseas offices of China Travel Service (CTS) might help with Ürümqi inquiries or bookings: 575 Sutter St, 2nd floor, San Francisco, CA 94102, USA (☎ 800-332-2831 toll-free, or (416) 398-6627); and 556 West Broadway, Vancouver, BC V5Z 1E9, Canada (☎ (604) 872-8787).

**Australia & New Zealand** STA Travel and Flight Centre are major dealers in cheap airfares, each with dozens of offices. STA's headquarters are at 224 Faraday St, Carlton, Victoria 3053, Australia (information and booking line ☎ 1300 360 960) and 10 High St, PO Box 4156, Auckland, New Zealand (☎ (09) 309 9995). Flight Centre's main offices are at Level 7, 343 Little Collins St, Melbourne, Victoria 3000, Australia (☎ (03) 9600 0799; fax (03) 9600 0733); 1/181 George St, Brisbane, Queensland 4000, Australia (☎ (07)3229 1727; fax (07) 3229 1731);

and 205-225 Queen St, Auckland, New Zealand (☎ (09) 309 6171; fax (09) 366 0809). Or you can just call ☎ 131600 to get through to your nearest branch.

Trailfinders has offices at 91 Elizabeth St, Brisbane 4000 (☎ (07) 3229 0887), and at Hides Corner, Shields St, Cairns 4870 (☎ (070) 411199), in Queensland, Australia.

## Air Travel Glossary

**Apex** Apex, or 'advance purchase excursion', is a discounted ticket which must be paid for in advance. There are penalties if you wish to change it.

**Baggage Allowance** This will be written on your ticket: usually one 20kg item to go in the hold, plus one item of hand luggage.

**Check-in** Airlines ask you to check in a certain time ahead of the flight departure (usually 1½ hours on international flights). If you don't and the flight is overbooked the airline can cancel your booking and give your seat to somebody else.

**Confirmation** Having a ticket written out with the flight and date you want doesn't mean you have a seat until the agent has checked with the airline that your status is 'OK' or confirmed. Meanwhile you could just be 'on request'.

**Discounted Tickets** There are two types of discounted fares – officially discounted (see Promotional Fares) and unofficially discounted. The lowest prices often impose drawbacks like flying with unpopular airlines, inconvenient schedules, or unpleasant routes and connections. A discounted ticket can save you other things than money – you may be able to pay Apex prices without the associated Apex advance booking and other requirements. Discounted tickets only exist where there is fierce competition.

**Full Fares** Airlines traditionally offer 1st class (coded F), business class (coded J) and economy class (coded Y) tickets. These days there are so many promotional and discounted fares available from the regular economy class that few passengers pay full economy fare.

**Lost Tickets** If you lose your airline ticket an airline will usually treat it like a travellers cheque and, after inquiries, issue you with another one. Legally, however, an airline is entitled to treat it like cash and if you lose it then it's gone forever. Take good care of your tickets.

**Open Jaw** A return ticket where you fly out to one place but return from another – an obviously handy option for KKH travel.

**Overbooking** Airlines hate to fly empty seats and, since every flight has some passengers who fail to show up, they often book more passengers than they have seats. Usually the excess passengers balance those who fail to show up, but occasionally somebody gets 'bumped'. If this happens, guess who it's most likely to be? The passengers who check in late.

**Promotional Fares** Officially discounted fares like Apex fares which are available from travel agents or direct from the airline.

**Reconfirmation** To minimise your chances of being 'bumped' from an onward or return flight due to overbooking, reconfirm directly with the airline at least 72 hours before departure – and ask about any adjustments to departure information compared with what's on your ticket. You don't have to reconfirm the first flight on your itinerary, nor any that follow stopovers of less than 72 hours. It doesn't hurt to reconfirm more than once.

**Transferred Tickets** Airline tickets cannot be transferred from one person to another. Travellers sometimes try to sell the return half of their ticket, but officials can ask you to prove that you are the person named on the ticket. This is unlikely on domestic flights, but on an international flight, tickets may be compared with passports.

**Travel Periods (Seasons)** Some officially discounted fares, Apex fares in particular, vary with the time of year. There is often a low (off-peak) season and a high (peak) season. Sometimes there's an intermediate or shoulder season as well. At peak times, when everyone wants to fly, not only will the officially discounted fares be higher but so will unofficially discounted fares – or there may simply be no discounted tickets available. Usually the fare depends on your outward flight – if you depart in the high season and return in the low season, you pay the high-season fare. ■

The Australia office of CTS might help with Ürümqi inquiries or bookings: 757-759 George St, Sydney, NSW 2000 (☎ (02) 9211 2633).

**The UK & Europe** The Saturday *Independent* and *Sunday Times* have good travel sections and ads for scores of bucket shops. Also see the Travel Classifieds in London's weekly *Time Out* entertainment magazine. The newsletter *Farang* (La Rue 8, B-4261 Braives, Belgium, ☎ (019) 699823) deals with exotic destinations; so does the magazine *Aventure du Bout du Monde* (116 Rue de Javel, 75015 Paris, France).

The UK's best known bargain-ticket agencies are Trailfinders (long-haul flights ☎ (0171) 938 3366; fax (0171) 937 9294) at 42-50 Earl's Court Rd, Kensington, London W8 6FT; Campus Travel (long-haul flights ☎ (0171) 730 8111; fax (0171) 730 6893) at 52 Grosvenor Gardens, London SW1W

## Airfares

Following is a list of the best nonstudent airfares we found. These are approximate discounted, economy fares during peak air-travel season, based on advertised rates at the time of writing. None constitutes a recommendation for any airline.

Because the KKH can make a shambles of fixed-date travel plans and because onward/return tickets are cheap in Asia, one-way fares are quoted here, though you may save even more if you buy a return ticket.

Fares to China are 10% to 20% higher in peak travel season (roughly July to September and December in North America and Europe, December to January in Australia and New Zealand); fares to Pakistan are not very seasonal.

Note that this book takes all domestic flights in China, as well as domestic flights up to Islamabad, as within the scope of the Getting There & Away chapter. Domestic fares of Aero Asia and Bhoja are similar and about 10% less than PIA's domestic fares.

| *Destination* | *Cost* | *Airline* |
| --- | --- | --- |
| Beijing-Ürümqi | Y2550 | Xinjiang Airways |
| Guangzhou-Ürümqi | Y3420 | Xinjiang Airways |
| Islamabad-Ürümqi | Y2270 | Xinjiang Airways |
| Almaty-Ürümqi | Y1660 | Xinjiang Airways |
| Ürümqi-Kashgar | Y1270 | Xinjiang Airways |
| London-Beijing | £250 | Air China |
| New York-Beijing | US$893 | Air China |
| Los Angeles-Beijing | US$683 | China Eastern Airlines |
| London-Islamabad | £239 | PIA |
| Tashkent-Islamabad | US$335 | PIA |
| London-Lahore | £269 | PIA |
| Delhi-Lahore | Rs 2830 | PIA |
| Bangkok-Lahore | US$370 | Thai |
| Hong Kong-Lahore | US$525 | Thai |
| London-Karachi | £209 | PIA |
| New York-Karachi | US$992 | PIA via Frankfurt and Lahore |
| Los Angeles-Karachi | N/A | Lufthansa |
| Tashkent-Karachi | US$320 | Uzbekistan Airways |
| Bishkek-Karachi | US$290 | Aero Asia |
| Tashkent-Peshawar | US$205 | PIA |
| Karachi-Islamabad | Rs 2640 | Aero Asia, Bhoja Air, PIA |
| Karachi-Islamabad, ord night coach | Rs 2215 | PIA |
| Karachi-Islamabad, spec night coach | Rs 2060 | Aero Asia |
| Karachi-Lahore | Rs 2160 | Aero Asia, Bhoja Air, PIA |
| Karachi-Lahore, ord night coach | Rs 1740 | Aero Asia, Bhoja Air |
| Karachi-Lahore, spec night coach | Rs 1575 | Aero Asia, Bhoja Air |
| Lahore-Islamabad | Rs 1015 | Bhoja Air, PIA |

0AG; and STA Travel (☎ (0171) 938 4711) at Priory House, 6 Wrights Lane, London W8 6TA. All have branches throughout London and the UK, and Campus Travel is also in many Hostelling International (HI) or YHA shops.

STA Travel also has offices in Paris; the main one is c/o CTS Voyages (☎ 01 43 25 00 76), 20 rue des Carmes, 75005 Paris. A reliable source of bargain tickets within the Netherlands is NBBS Reizen (☎ (071) 523 2020; fax (071) 522 6475), Schilphoweg 101, 2300 AJ Leiden, with over 50 'travelshops' and 'Budgetair' counters in post offices around the country.

CTS offices overseas might help with Ürümqi inquiries or bookings: CTS House, 7 Upper St Martin's Lane, London WC2H 9DL, UK (☎ (0171) 836 9911); and 32 rue Vignon, 75009 Paris, France (☎ 01 44 51 55 66).

**Asia** STA Travel has a branch in Hong Kong, c/o Hong Kong Student Travel (☎ 2730 3269; fax 2730 9407), 1021 Star House, Tsimshatsui, Kowloon. Other reliable budget-minded agencies in Tsimshatsui include Phoenix Services (☎ 2722 7378), 6th floor, Milton Mansion, 96 Nathan Rd; and Shoestring Travel (☎ 2723 2306), 4th floor, Block A, Alpha House, 27 Peking Rd.

STA Travel also has full-service branches in Singapore (☎ 734 5681; fax 737 2591), Bangkok (☎ (02) 281 5214; fax (02) 280 1388), Kuala Lumpur (☎ (03) 230 5720; fax (03) 230 5718), Tokyo (☎ (03) 5391 2922; fax (03) 5391 2923) and Osaka (☎ (06) 262 7066; fax (06) 262 7065).

CTS can help with flights to Ürümqi. In Hong Kong it's at 4th floor, CTS House, 78-83 Connaught Rd, Central (☎ 2853 3888; fax 2541 9777), and in Beijing at 2 Beisanhuan Donglu, 4th floor, CTS Tower (☎ (010) 6461 2591; fax (010) 6461 2593).

### Kashgar by Air

You can fly into Kashgar only from Ürümqi, and only with Xinjiang Airways (not one of the world's premier carriers: our plane said 'Air Volga'!). Flights depart once or twice

daily, year-round, subject to suitable weather at both ends. You may have to stay the night in Ürümqi.

In turn, Ürümqi has several direct international connections with Xinjiang Airways, including twice weekly from Islamabad and from Almaty, and once a week from Tashkent and from Moscow via Novosibirsk. Kazakhstan Airlines flies Ürümqi to Almaty once a week. Runway improvements are on the cards at Kashgar, with direct international connections a future possibility.

Ürümqi is linked with Beijing with several flights a day, and less frequently with Shanghai, Guangzhou (Canton) and other Chinese cities. Xinjiang Airways has irregular Hong Kong to Ürümqi flights. At the time of research China still had two-tier domestic airfares – one price for foreigners, one for locals – though there were rumours that this was to be phased out.

The cheapest international routes are usually with Air China – from Europe and North America via Beijing or Shanghai, and from Australia via Guangzhou. While quick China visas make Hong Kong a useful stop, it's cheaper to bypass it.

### Islamabad by Air

From almost anywhere, flying directly to Islamabad is the most expensive option. Getting there via Lahore is usually cheaper, while the cheapest and most abundant connections are via Karachi. All three cities are linked by multiple daily flights and bargain-rate 'night coach' flights, and same day onward connections aren't hard to get.

What's more, domestic tickets can cost up to 60% less if you buy them inside Pakistan so it's cheaper to buy them after you arrive. Larger PIA offices, eg Rawalpindi's, accept travellers cheques and Visa cards.

British Airways flies to Islamabad from London Gatwick three times a week via Manchester, and PIA has once or twice-weekly direct flights from London Heathrow, Manchester, Paris, Amsterdam, Frankfurt, Copenhagen, Rome and Beijing.

To Lahore, PIA has once or twice-weekly direct flights from London Heathrow,

Amsterdam, Frankfurt, Copenhagen, Bangkok and Singapore, and Thai flies direct from Bangkok three times a week.

To Karachi, PIA has multiple weekly direct links from London Heathrow, Manchester, Paris, Frankfurt, Kathmandu, Bangkok, Singapore and Beijing. Other international carriers with direct Karachi flights include Turkish Airlines from Istanbul, Aeroflot from Moscow and CAAC from Beijing.

Budget flights from Los Angeles, Chicago, New York and Toronto make one or more stops in Europe en route to Islamabad, Lahore or Karachi. Flights from Melbourne and Sydney connect frequently with PIA, Thai or Singapore Airlines in Bangkok or Singapore, usually to Karachi. From Auckland, Malaysia Airlines goes via Kuala Lumpur to Karachi.

PIA has three to five flights daily between Karachi and Islamabad, three or four between Karachi and Lahore, and seven to nine between Lahore and Islamabad – plus at least one 'night coach' flight every night, departing at truly awful hours but around 25% cheaper. An on-the-spot confirmed Karachi to Islamabad booking looks more problematic than Karachi to Lahore, but you may well make it on a standby ticket ('on chance').

Aero Asia and Bhoja Air also have day and night flights, cheaper than PIA's, and their night flights are sometimes at more humane hours; Aero Asia and Bhoja are even cheaper going *to* Karachi ('special night coach').

A World Wide Web site listing *domestic* timetables and fares for PIA, Aero Asia and Bhoja is http://www.khamisani.com/. PIA lists its international timetables at http://www.piac.com/.

You cannot book international flights from the PIA office in Gilgit.

**India** From Delhi, PIA has four flights a week direct to Lahore, and three to Karachi. Malaysia Airlines flies Delhi to Lahore twice a week, and Emirates does it via Dubai three times a week. PIA flies Mumbai (Bombay) to Karachi five times a week, and Indian Airlines three.

**Iran** PIA and Iran Air each have direct flights between Tehran and Karachi once a week.

**Central Asia** Xinjiang Airways flies Ürümqi to Islamabad twice a week. Uzbekistan

---

**Arriving at Karachi Airport**

Karachi's smart new Mohammed Ali Jinnah international terminal works efficiently – a great improvement over the past.

On the plane you get a health declaration and embark/disembark card, but no customs declaration. At arrivals you turn the health declaration in, swap your embark/disembark card for an entry stamp at passport control (there's a separate foreigners' queue), get your bags and stroll through the green channel at customs. By the baggage claim are several moneychangers, but wait: National Bank of Pakistan, open 24 hours a day in a little booth after customs, has the same rates but no commission.

Next door in the same building are the domestic arrivals and departures halls. A PIA ticket counter is outside to the left on ground level, and a PIA information booth is one flight up. Of Pakistan's other airlines, Bhoja Air is in the basement, Shaheen, if it is back in operation, is at ground level and Aero Asia is one flight up.

If you have a standby ('on chance') onward domestic ticket with PIA, the person to make friends with is the PIA duty manager, in the office opposite the domestic check-in desks. If your standby booking fails, PIA's refund office on the 3rd floor opens at 9 am.

On the 7th floor is a plain, 24 hour cafeteria where you can wait for the next flight out. There appears to be no place to leave luggage, for security reasons.

At least at Karachi airport, sell your rupees back before you check in, as there are no banks after immigration. Take the batteries out of your walkman, radio, camera etc, and check them through, or they'll be confiscated at airport security. Some departing passengers have been asked for photocopies of their passport at immigration, though this sounds like officials on the take. Give yourself three hours between check-in and departure. ■

## Buying an International Air Ticket in Pakistan

Travel agents are as thick as flies in Rawalpindi, Islamabad and other main cities. None come up with very big discounts on international flights, but their prices are usually better than what the airline itself is offering. You have a better chance of an honest deal from an IATA member; look for the sticker in the window. A few reliable agencies are listed under Information in the Rawalpindi & Islamabad chapter.

If you buy a non-PIA international ticket in Pakistan, you can only pay in cash rupees bought with foreign currency. You prove this by furnishing the travel agent or airline office with foreign exchange receipts totalling at least the full airline price (even if you're getting a discount). Without these, no matter how much cash you have, you'd have to exchange a further amount equal to the full price, just for the receipts. Some agents also insist on a form from the bank saying the exchange was specifically for airline tickets; others may accept any receipts less than three months old. You don't get the receipts back. Domestic tickets don't require receipts, nor do PIA international flights.

To add insult to injury, that ticket will include a whopping Rs 1500 'foreign travel tax', as well as the Rs 400 international departure tax, Rs 20 airport security tax, 20% CED, 3% capital value tax etc (though you should check this when you're quoted a fare).

After you've bought your ticket, call the airline yourself and confirm that you're booked on the flight. See the boxed text Pakistan Booking Numbers for telephone numbers for major airline booking offices.

### Departure Taxes

Pakistan's domestic departure tax is Rs 40 for economy class (more for business or 1st class), normally included in the price of the ticket. International departure tax is Rs 400 (more for business or 1st class), payable at check-in if your ticket was purchased outside Pakistan.

China's domestic departure tax is Y50,

Airways flies Tashkent to Karachi three times a week. PIA has weekly Almaty-Tashkent-Islamabad and Tashkent-Almaty-Lahore loops, plus one-stop connections from Ashgabat and Baku. Once or twice a week, Aero Asia flies Bishkek to Karachi, Avia (Turkmenistan) flies Ashgabat to Karachi, and Azerbaijan Airlines flies Baku to Karachi. PIA also has a once-weekly Tashkent to Peshawar flight.

ROBERT MATZINGER

ROBERT MATZINGER

ROBERT MATZINGER

**Cycling**
Top: The Pakistan-China border, Khunjerab Pass.
Middle: Cycling south from Passu, Gojal.
Bottom: Rush hour traffic between Sost and Khunjerab Pass.

JOHN KING

JOHN KING

BRADLEY MAYHEW

ROBERT MATZINGER

## Transport
Images of Pakistan's rolling works of art. The vividly painted trucks, although a photographer's delight, are perversely uncomfortable to ride in.

normally included in the price of the ticket. International departure tax is Y90.

### If the KKH is Closed
If snow or landslides have closed the KKH, the quickest way round is to fly Ürümqi to Islamabad; Xinjiang Airways has two direct flights weekly.

Another option is to go overland or fly either Ürümqi to Almaty (the easiest visawise; Xinjiang Airways twice a week, Kazakhstan Airlines once a week) or Ürümqi to Tashkent (Xinjiang Airways once a week), plus PIA's weekly Almaty-Tashkent-Islamabad run.

### LAND
### Kashgar by Train & Bus
**Within China to Kashgar** The marathon land journey from Hong Kong to Kashgar is by train to Ürümqi (4900km, 4½ days) and by bus from there, parallel to the old Silk Road along the northern edge of the Takla Makan desert (1480km, 1½ days).

The express train from Hong Kong to Guangzhou is about Y285. From Guangzhou to Ürümqi on a 'hard sleeper' rail berth is about Y700. Choices for the bus trip on to Kashgar are a three-day run with two overnight stops for Y233, and two 36-hour nonstop options, with soft seats (Y273) or double-decker reclining sleepers (Y380 to Y439) – all daily. Buy a ticket from the long-distance bus station in Kashgar or Ürümqi, up to three days in advance. There are also buses to Kashgar from Turfan.

The government is now at work on a railway line from Ürümqi to Kashgar, to ship in Han immigrants and bind Kashgar closer to The Motherland. One estimate says it could be done by the year 2000.

**Tibet** The road between Kashgar and Lhasa is heavily policed, making the journey problematic, though foreigners were doing it when we were there. If you're caught you may be fined and/or sent back (a favourite travellers' tale is of a traveller coming from Kashgar who, when stopped at the Ali checkpost and asked where he had come from, said instead that he was coming from Lhasa, whereupon the police 'returned' him to Lhasa!). Transport might include bus, truck, donkey, yak and one's own feet. Between September and June the cold is severe, and there are stories of westerners freezing to death in the backs of trucks or by the roadside.

An alternative route at the time of research was via Golmud (Kashgar to Golmud by bus or train, Golmud to Lhasa by CITS's overpriced bus, the price for which included a Lhasa permit). For more information see Lonely Planet's *Tibet*.

**Kyrgyzstan** From at least June to September you can cross the 3752m Torugart Pass (Chinese: Tu'ergate shankou) on a coarsely paved road to Kashgar from Kyrgyzstan. Of course you must have an onward visa (the closest place to get a Kyrgyz visa is Delhi or Beijing; China visas are available in Bishkek with a bit of work). Chinese officials insist that tourists in either direction must also have a special Torugart permit (the Torugart is formally a Class 2 or nontourist pass). Kashgar travel agencies or their Bishkek partners can get these from Ürümqi with one or two weeks' notice.

Most travellers choose the expensive option of letting an agency arrange the permit, transport to the pass and, via a partner agency on the other side, onward transport. But even the most painstaking arrangements can be thwarted by logistical gridlock, eg unforeseen closures for Kyrgyz or Chinese holidays, or the failure of your onward transport to be allowed to the top of the pass.

Kyrgyz officials may ask China-bound travellers whether they have the Torugart permit and someone to meet them. It's risky to say yes if you don't. Several travellers who did this exited Kyrgyzstan (and had their visas cancelled) but were denied entry into China and therefore stuck in limbo at the top of the pass for several days, until the Chinese relented. Hitchhikers are known to have crossed *out* of China without a Torugart permit, however. If you have time but no money for permits and travel agencies, you're better off crossing to/from Kazakhstan (see the Kazakhstan section, following).

There is a Bishkek to Kashgar bus, run by a flaky Chinese outfit, allegedly several times a month in summer. At the time of research the 700km trip was Y1400 (about US$175).

Another warm-weather Kyrgyzstan crossing, to Kashgar from Osh via Irkeshtam, is open for trade but so far not for individual tourists, although Exodus (see the list of tour operators and trekking companies later in this chapter) has taken groups this way.

**Kazakhstan** An all-weather road crosses to Ürümqi from Almaty via the border post at Korgas (Khorgos on the Kazakh side). A direct Almaty to Ürümqi bus runs six days a week in each direction, taking about 26 hours, with stops for food and bodily functions but not for sleep. Tickets are about US$55 from the main bus station in Ürümqi or Almaty. You could pay less on a succession of local buses but it's tedious (up to two or three days).

There's just one way in or out of China by rail here – the 1359km journey between Almaty and Ürümqi, on a line finished in 1992 after being delayed almost half a century by Russian-Chinese geopolitics. The trip takes 36 hours, with two nights on the train. The problem is the border crossing – not just seven to nine hours of procedures, bogey changing and waiting around with little or no water or toilets, but the systematic plunder of passengers by customs officials at the Kazakh border post of Dostyq. Tickets, from the main railway station in Ürümqi or Almaty, are about US$70 for the Chinese train (departs Almaty Saturday, Ürümqi Monday) or US$80 for the Kazakh train (departs Almaty Monday, Ürümqi Saturday).

## Islamabad by Train & Bus

You can reach the KKH by train from all over Pakistan. Most trains to the capital area go to Rawalpindi's Saddar Bazaar station. A spur of the Rawalpindi to Peshawar line runs to Havelian, the official southern end of the KKH. Pakistan Railways sells a timetable and fare book in some booking offices and station book stalls – definitely worth the Rs 5 investment.

Trains are Express, Mail or Passenger, in order of increasing frequency of stops. Classes are economy (soft seats, no compartments), 1st (soft seats, open compartments) and air-conditioned (closed compartments), though not all trains have all classes. Long-distance runs have sleepers in 1st class and air-conditioned class (which should be booked several days ahead, to a maximum of 14 and 30 days respectively). Some trains have 'economy berths' at the economy fare plus a Rs 50 berth fee. Women may book female-only carriages. At smaller stations with no reservation quota, you cannot book a berth or seat.

If you cancel your reservation you can normally get most of your fare back, minus 10% if the ticket is surrendered less than two days before departure. If you miss the train you can even get 70% back if you report within three hours.

Bedding is not provided on trains, and many travellers booking sleepers get caught out. Air-con sleeper ticket holders can theoretically hire bedding, soap, towel and toilet paper from reservations offices at Rawalpindi, Peshawar, Lahore and other centres.

A student ID card gets you a 50% discount, and nonstudent foreign tourists can get 25% off – theoretically. Go to the Commercial Department, often in a separate building from the ticket office, and if it's open and the appropriate bureaucrat happens to be there, you can get a form to take to the ticket seller. As you must do this every time you buy a ticket, you're best off buying as much rail travel as you can at one go.

**Within Pakistan to Islamabad** The cheapest route to the southern KKH is by air to Karachi and then by train to Rawalpindi or Lahore. At the time of research the train journey from Karachi was fairly safe (see the Dangers & Annoyances section in the Facts for the Visitor chapter). The problem is booking the train, as sleepers can get booked a week or two ahead, though it's easier to get one to Lahore than to Rawalpindi. Otherwise you must travel unreserved (no fun) and try to get the conductor to upgrade you.

A 1st/air-con Karachi to Rawalpindi sleeper is Rs 679/1634; there are four daily expresses, the *Tezgam* and *Awam* (26 hours) being the best. The *Abaseen* and *Quetta* expresses take about 34 hours from Quetta to Rawalpindi via Lahore; a 1st/air-con sleeper is Rs 646/1287. There are seven trains daily from Peshawar to Rawalpindi, though the afternoon *Rahmkar Railcar* is quickest (3½ hours), with Rs 40 unreserved seats. An economy/1st/air-con Lahore to Rawalpindi seat is Rs 80/154/282, with three express trains (six hours).

Swarms of cheap buses and minibuses connect Rawalpindi with Peshawar and Lahore along the Grand Trunk Road at all hours of the day and night. Bus travel from further south in the Punjab is possible by linking shorter trips, though it's not much fun. Travel by road in Sind and extreme southern Punjab is inadvisable (see the Dangers & Annoyances section in the Facts for the Visitor chapter).

Best bets from Lahore to Rawalpindi (five hours, about Rs 110) are the air-conditioned coaches of the Tourism Development Corporation of the Punjab (three a day), and minibuses of New Flying Coach, New Khan Road Runners and Skyways to Rawalpindi, or Citylinkers to Islamabad (at least hourly). The same operators also come from Peshawar all day long for about Rs 50. See the Rawalpindi & Islamabad chapter.

**India** Daily express every Monday and Thursday link Lahore with Amritsar in India. The *Amritsar Express* leaves Lahore City railway station at 11 am, stopping for at least two hours at the Wagah crossing and reaching Amritsar about 3 pm; the return trip leaves Amritsar at 9.30 am, arriving at Lahore about 2 pm. There are also slower daily Lahore to Wagah trains. Lahore to Amritsar is Rs 32 in economy class.

You can cross by road as well as by rail at Wagah. Fewer passengers to process at the border means the bus is quicker than the train (and it's more frequent too), though Lahore

to Amritsar still takes most of half a day. On each side you must clear immigration, customs and two further security checks, and walk across 100m of no man's land. The border is open from 9 am to 3 pm Pakistani time.

There are no direct buses, but plenty to/from the border on both sides. Number 12 minibuses leave from Lahore City railway station all day for Rs 9 (there are two No 12s; make sure yours is going in the right direction); normally you must change at Jallo for the remaining 5km. There are occasional direct buses between the border and Amritsar, or you may have to take a rickshaw 3km to/from Attari, with regular buses between there and Amritsar.

**Iran** The weekly *Taftan Express* between Quetta and Zahedan in Iran, via the border post at Taftan (Mirjave on the Iran side), leaves Zahedan Monday morning at 9.30 am and Quetta Saturday at noon, taking about 30 hours. A slower service leaves Zahedan Thursday and Quetta Tuesday, taking at least 34 hours. A first class sleeper is Rs 514. Take plenty of drinking water in summer as train supplies often run out. Border formalities have been known to take eight hours. West of Zahedan it's 600km of dusty bus rides to the next-nearest railhead.

A better option is the 14-hour overnight Quetta to Taftan bus, at Rs 250. Several air-con buses depart daily from Quetta bus station between 4 and 6 pm. Frequent Iranian buses make the two hour trip between Mirjave and Zahedan. If you must spend the night in Taftan the PTDC motel has dorm beds and doubles and the Hayat Hotel has rooms for about Rs 200.

The border is open from 9 am to 1 pm and 3 pm to sunset. The Bank of Pakistan there keeps normal hours so if you're crossing late in the day or on Sunday you should change money in Quetta or Taftan bazaar. A branch of Melli (State) Bank is on the Iran side.

### Driving

You can bring your own car, van, bus or motorcycle into Pakistan duty-free, for up to three months. You'll need a *carnet de passage en douane* – essentially a passport for the vehicle – plus registration papers, liability insurance and an International Driving Permit. For more information on paperwork, insurance and the availability of petrol and spare parts, ask your automobile association before leaving home. On entry, you sign a form saying you promise not to sell the vehicle while you're in Pakistan.

Contrary to what some sources say, it's also possible to drive your own vehicle in China. We met a family who had driven their van from Kathmandu, across Tibet and to Kashgar, but it took them months of detailed preparation, reams of paperwork (including, they said, 22m of faxes!) and lots of money. They had to buy a tour package that included some nights in hotels, and take along a Chinese 'minder' who knew little about the places they wanted to go.

### Bicycle

It's almost impossible to get a straight answer about bringing a bicycle into China (see the boxed text), but in any case no cyclist for years has been prevented from bringing one in or out at Tashkurgan. There's no problem with bringing a bicycle in or out of Pakistan, though you're expected to mention it on your visa application.

Your bike can get to the KKH by air. You can dismantle it and put it in a bag or box, but it's easier just to wheel it to the check-in

---

**Chinese Bicycle Permit?**
Visa information from the Chinese embassy in London says 'foreign tourists are not supposed to bring into China their bicycles and any vehicles'. Other sources say all you need is an import permit, which you can get on arrival at the border, in return for a fee and a written promise to take it back out when you leave. Some travel agents, who ought to know better, say only Guangzhou allows them. But cyclists have arrived permit-less by air at Beijing and had no problem, and at least some land borders are major bicycle thoroughfares, with no-one asking for permits or fees; this is certainly the case at Tashkurgan. ∎

---

desk, where it should be treated as baggage (you may have to remove the pedals and turn the handlebars sideways). However, Xinjiang Airways has in the past told cyclists that their bikes were not baggage but cargo and would be charged at 1% of the ticket price for each kg of weight! Check with the airline well ahead of time – preferably before you buy a ticket from them.

Before you leave home, go over the bike with a fine-toothed comb and fill your kit with every imaginable spare. You won't be able to find that crucial widget when your steed breaks down in the back of beyond.

For more on what to bring, and on cycling the KKH itself, see the Getting Around chapter and the boxed Cyclists' Notes in each regional chapter.

### TOUR OPERATORS & TREKKING COMPANIES

In this section we list companies that can help you make arrangements for travel or trekking along the KKH (both Xinjiang and northern Pakistan). We have tried to differentiate between overseas companies marketing off-the-shelf tours and treks, and Pakistan companies that can help you set up your own programmes, either in advance or after you arrive – though things are rarely so clear-cut, since some overseas outfits will make partial arrangements and some in Pakistan have their own ready-to-go programmes.

These companies can in turn be distinguished from local agencies which you might use for one-off arrangements such as hotel bookings or air tickets, and which are listed under individual towns.

### Tour Operators Overseas

For those with more money than time, numerous overseas companies offer general, special-interest and 'adventure-travel' group tour packages ranging from air-conditioned minibus trips between posh hotels, to multiweek truck or jeep safaris, to serious trekking and mountaineering. Following is a list of some reputable ones.

Allibert (☎ 01 48 06 16 61; fax 01 48 06 47 22), 14 rue de l'Asile Popincourt, 75011 Paris, or contact ☎ (04) 76 45 22 26; fax (04) 76 45 27 28, route de Grenoble, 38530 Chapareillan, France

Asian Pacific Adventures (☎ (213) 935-3156, toll-free 800-825-1680; fax (213) 935-2691), 826 S Sierra Bonita Ave, Los Angeles, CA 90036, USA

Encounter Overland (☎ (0171) 370 6845; fax (0171) 244 9737), 267 Old Brompton Rd, London SW5 9JA, UK: truck/bus safaris

Exodus (☎ (0181) 675 5550; fax (0181) 673 0779), 9 Weir Rd, London SW12 0LT, UK; Exodus has an Australia office (☎ (02) 9925 5439 or toll-free 1-800-800724; fax (02) 9251 5432), Suite 5, 1 York St, Sydney, NSW 2000

Explore Worldwide (☎ (01252) 319448; fax (01252) 343170; email info@explore.co.uk), 1 Frederick St, Aldershot, Hants GU11 1LQ, UK; Explore's Australasia agent is Adventure World (☎ (02) 9956 7766; fax (02) 9956 7707), 3rd floor, 73 Walker St, North Sydney, NSW 2059, Australia, and (☎ (09) 524 5118, toll-free ☎ 0800-652 954; fax (09) 520 6629; email discover@adventu reworld.co.nz), 101 Great South Rd, Remeura, Auckland, New Zealand

FSC (Field Studies Council) Overseas (☎ (01743) 850164; fax (01743) 850178), Montford Bridge, Shrewsbury SY4 1HW, UK: an educational charity dedicated to environmental understand-ing, FSC runs about 50 trips a year to places of special wildlife or botanical interest

Geographic Expeditions (☎ (415) 922-0448, toll-free 800-777-8183; fax (415) 346-5535), 2627 Lom-bard St, San Francisco, CA 94123, USA: for-merly InnerAsia, pioneering itineraries (eg it took the first western groups across the Torugart Pass)

Hann Overland (also called Hinterland Travel; ☎ (01883) 743584, 743861; fax (01883) 743912), 2 Ivy Mill Lane, Godstone, Surrey RH9 8NH, UK: truck/bus safaris

Himalayan Kingdoms (☎ (0117) 923 7163; fax (0117) 974 4993), 20 The Mall, Clifton, Bristol, BS8 4DR, UK

KE Adventure Travel (☎ (017687) 73966, 72267; fax (017687) 74693; email: keadventure@enter-prise.net), 32 Lake Rd, Keswick, Cumbria CA12 5DQ, UK: Karakoram trek specialists

Mountain Travel (☎ (415) 527-8100; fax (415) 525-7710), 6420 Fairmount Ave, El Cerrito, CA 94530, USA

REI (☎ (206) 891-2631, toll-free 800-622-2236; fax (206) 395-4744), PO Box 1938, Sumner, WA 98390, USA: environmentally aware trekking and cycling trips

Steppes East (☎ (01285) 810267; fax (01285) 810693), Castle Eaton, Cricklade, Swindon, Wiltshire SN6 6JU, UK

The Globe Granite (UK ☎ (0171) 286 3029; email globegranite@btinternet.co.uk), c/o Mountain Travels Pakistan, listed under Trekking/Touring Companies in Pakistan: unique long-distance horseback expeditions in the Northern Areas

Voyages Jules Verne (☎ (0171) 616 1000; fax (0171) 723 8629), 21 Dorset Square, London NW1 6QG

Wilderness Expeditions (☎ (0545) 271074, 274711; fax (0545) 273756), Kluverskamp 29, 7271 XM Borculo: 'extreme adventure tourism', including trekking/climbing in the Tian Shan and around Xinjiang's Muztagh Ata, and expeditions in the Takla Makan desert

Wilderness Travels (☎ (415) 548-0420, toll-free 800-368-2794; fax (415) 548-0347), 801 Allston Way, Berkeley, CA 94710, USA

World Expeditions (☎ (01753) 581808; fax (01753) 581809), 101c Slough Rd, Datchet, Berkshire SL3 9AQ, UK

## Trekking/Touring Companies in Pakistan

Most of these companies can arrange a tour or trek, usually in advance but sometimes upon arrival.

Adventure Center Pakistan (☎ (0572) 2409; fax (0572) 3695; email ikram@acp-glt.sdnpk. undp.org), PO Box 516, Gilgit

Adventure Foundation (☎ (0992) 5526), No 1 Gulistan Colony, College Rd, Abbottabad; also through Adventure Inn (☎ (051) 272536; fax (051) 274625) Islamabad: founded to promote special-skills training and Outward Bound-style adventures for young Pakistanis; can arrange small-group adventure travel given enough notice

Adventure Tours Pakistan (☎ (051) 252759; fax (051) 252145), House 551, St 53, G-9/1, PO Box 1780, Islamabad; (☎ (0572) 2663) Airport Rd, Gilgit

Adventure Travel (☎ (051) 272490, 822728; fax (051) 821407; email snmalik@adven-ture.sdnpk.undp.org), 15 Wali Centre, 86 South Blue Area, PO Box 2062, Islamabad; and 3 Wali House, Khomer, Jutial, Gilgit

Alpine Club of Pakistan (☎ (051) 562887, contact Manzur Hussain), 509 Kashmir Rd, Rawalpindi: information on mountaineering, guides for 'green' trekking, occasional expeditions

Baltistan Tours (☎ (051) 270338; fax (051) 278620), PO Box 1285, Islamabad; (☎ (0575) 2626) Sat-ellite Town, Skardu

Concordia Expeditions (fax (051) 584566, attention No 1084) PO Box 1800, GPO Rawalpindi; and (☎ (0572) 47010) Karimabad

Concordia Tours & Trekking Services (☎ (051) 223849, 823371; fax (051) 823351, 823364), 35 Chughtai Plaza, West Blue Area, Islamabad; (☎ (0575) 2947) Naya Bazaar, Skardu

Concordia Trekking Services (☎ (0575) 3440, 2707), PO Box 626, Skardu 16100

Golden Peak Tours (☎ (051) 256660; fax (051) 811478), Flat No 2, 12-K Chaudhry Plaza, G-8 Markaz, Islamabad; (☎ (0572) 4295; fax (0572) 55900) Chinar Bagh Link Rd, PO Box 531, Gilgit 15100

Himalaya Nature Tours (☎ 811478; fax 811478), House 5, St 45, F-7/1, Islamabad; (☎ (0572) 2946) Chinar Bagh Link Rd, Gilgit

Himalaya Treks & Tours (☎ (051) 563014, 515371; fax (051) 563014), 112 Rahim Plaza, Murree Rd, PO Box 918, Rawalpindi; (☎ (0575) 2528), College Rd, Skardu

Hindukush Trails (☎ (051) 821576, 277067; fax (051) 275031, 277067), House 37, St 28, F-6/1, Islamabad; (☎ (0533) 2112) Mountain Inn, Chitral

Indus Guides (☎ (042) 630 4190; fax (042) 872529) 7-E Egerton Rd, Lahore

Jasmine Tours, (☎ (051) 507127; fax (051) 584566; email ali@porik.sdnpk.undp.org), 2nd floor Ishaq Market, 24 Canning Rd, Saddar Bazaar, Rawalpindi: tour agency

Karakorum Explorers (☎ (051) 441258; fax (051) 442127), House 1295, St 90, I-10/1, PO Box 2994, Islamabad; (☎ (0572) 47073) Ganesh

Karakurum Treks & Tours (☎ (051) 829120; fax (051) 271996), 1 Baltoro House, St 19, F-7/2, PO Box 2803, Islamabad; (☎ (0572) 2753), Airport Rd, Gilgit; (☎ (0575) 2856) Satellite Town, Skardu

Mountain Movers (☎ (051) 470519; fax (051) 470518), PO Box 985, Rawalpindi; (☎ (0572) 2967; fax (0572) 55900) Airport Rd, Gilgit

Mountain Travels Pakistan (☎ (051) 264213; fax (051) 260469), House 1-A, St 22, F-7/2, PO Box 2014, Islamabad; (☎ (0575) 2750) Satellite Town, Skardu

Nazir Sabir Expeditions (☎ (051) 853672, 252580; fax (051) 250293; email nazir@nse.sdnpk. undp.org), House 487, St 52, G-9/1, PO Box 1442, Islamabad; (☎ (0572) 2562, 2650), Gilgit; (☎ (0572) 45048), Aliabad; (☎ (0575) 3346) Airport Rd, Skardu

Pakistan Adventure Travel Service (☎ (051) 414489; fax (051) 584566 attention 1231), E-block 251/B, Satellite Town, Rawalpindi; c/o Madina Guest House, Gilgit

Pakistan Guides (☎ (051) 524808, 525633; fax (051) 539497, 524808; email guides@paknet1.ptc.pk) 62/2 Bank Rd, 3rd floor, PO Box 1692, Rawalpindi 46000

Pamir Tours (☎ (0572) 3939; fax (0572) 2475), PO Box 545, Gilgit: tour agency

Panorama Travels & Tours (☎ (051) 815266, 817424; fax (051) 822313), 8 Safdar Mansion, Blue Area, PO Box 1064, Islamabad: tour agency

Rakaposhi Tours (☎ (021) 586 4848; fax (021) 587 0652), 12-C 31st Commercial St, Phase V, Defense Housing Authority, Karachi: tour agency

Sitara Travel Consultants (☎ (051) 564750, 566272; fax (051) 584958; email info@sitarapk.ibrain. brain.net.pk), 232 Khadim Hussain Rd, PO Box 63, Rawalpindi; Airport Rd, Gilgit

Siachen Travels & Tours (☎ (0575) 2649, 2844), PO Box 622, Skardu

Trans Asian Tours (☎ (051) 859367; fax (051) 822313), PO Box 2914, Islamabad; (☎ (0572) 3419), Chinar Bagh Link Rd, Gilgit

Trans-Pakistan Adventure Services (☎ (051) 274796; fax (051) 274838), 8 Muzaffar Chambers, Fazl-e-Haq Rd, PO Box 2103, Islamabad; Chinar Bagh Link Rd, Gilgit

Travel Walji's Ltd (Adventure Pakistan) (☎ (051) 270745, 820908; fax (051) 270753; email walji@twlisb.sdnpk.undp.org), 10 Khayaban-e-Suhrawardy, PO Box 1088, Islamabad; (☎ (0572) 2665; fax (0572) 2663), Airport Rd, Gilgit; (☎ (0572) 47045), Karimabad; (☎ (0575) 3468) College Rd, Skardu

## Trekking/Touring Companies in China

Xinjiang Mountaineering Association (European Dept ☎ (0991) 381 0878; fax (0991) 218365), 1 Renmin Lu, Ürümqi 830002

Kashgar Mountaineering Association (☎ (0998) 282 3680; fax (0998) 282 2957), 8 Tiyu Lu, Kashgar 844000

Kashgar Travel Agency (☎ (0998) 282 2593, 282 2181; fax (0998) 282 2525), 1 Jiefang Nan Lu, Kashgar 844000

# Getting Around

Note that with respect to the KKH, all domestic transport in China to Kashgar, as well as domestic transport up to Islamabad in Pakistan, falls within the scope of the Getting There & Away chapter

## AIR
### Domestic Air Services
Pakistan International Airlines (PIA), the national carrier, has daily flights linking Islamabad to Gilgit and to Skardu. For the prolonged, stunning views of the western Himalaya and High Karakoram, these may be the best airfare bargains in the world. Between Islamabad and Gilgit, 8125m Nanga Parbat – 8th highest mountain on the planet – is straight out of the window (on the right northbound, left southbound, and the best seats are towards the rear). Naturally the flights are very popular, and you should try to book at least a week ahead in summer.

The Islamabad to Gilgit flight (Rs 850 with departure tax, 1¼ hours) is in ageing, prop-driven Fokker Friendships – though PIA thankfully has plans to phase these out.

**Beware the Old Fokkers!**
If, after waiting weeks for a flight to or from Gilgit, you board and find empty seats, it may be because the old Fokkers get less lift in hot summer air and can't take a full load. Enjoy your flight. ■

The Islamabad to Skardu flight (Rs 1015 with departure tax, 1½ hours) is in Boeing 737s. With Gilgit's airstrip due for extension, jets will eventually go there too.

Schedules are the same year-round, though the weather isn't. The flights require near-ideal weather so they're very often cancelled, and all bookings are effectively standby. Backlogs of a week or more are common even in summer. Most Skardu flights and essentially all Gilgit flights get cancelled in winter. Don't rely on leaving the Northern Areas by air if you have an onward flight to meet!

Another air approach to the KKH is by daily Fokker from Islamabad to Saidu Sharif

---

**Booking a Northern Areas Flight**
Try to buy your ticket at least a week ahead in summer. Bear in mind that even if your flight day dawns clear as a bell, if it's the first clear day after a spell of cloudy weather, all those people whose flights were cancelled theoretically have priority over you. Your ticket should have a 'serial number': this is your place on the waiting list.

Beginning the day before your nominal departure, check at PIA every morning to see if your number has come up. When it does, get the ticket 'confirmed', which means you're on the manifest for the next day's flight – pending the weather, of course. You may have to leave the ticket and collect it later the same day. If you're not there when your number comes up, you're dropped from the list. No one else can present your ticket for you.

The final decision to fly is made only hours before the scheduled departure time. If your flight is cancelled, you're automatically confirmed for the next one.

Official tourist-priority seats are a thing of the past, but Rawalpindi PIA staff may help you jump the queue if you catch their eye and look distressed, and in Gilgit you may be moved up without even knowing it. You'll then be participating in what everybody knows is a fairly, shall we say, loosely-run ticketing system, under which staff hand out confirmed Northern Areas tickets at their 'discretion'.

Note that Gilgit is not linked to PIA's country-wide computer network, which means that if you book a flight out of Gilgit from anywhere else – even if you get a ticket – you should insist that they call the Gilgit office while you are standing there. ■

**PIA Air Safari**
Every Saturday PIA runs a spectacular 1¾ hour 'Air Safari' loop flight from Islamabad up near K2 and back, with views of Nanga Parbat, Rakaposhi, Masherbrum, Haramosh and Concordia along the way. Window seats are Rs 9000, middle seats Rs 4600, aisle seats Rs 2400; with one or two friends you could purchase three in a row and swap around. Like all Northern Areas flights, these are very weather-dependent. Travel agencies may offer discounted tickets. ■

in the Swat Valley, from where it's a few hours by bus to Besham in Indus Kohistan.

Rawalpindi has a special Northern Areas ticket office; this and other large PIA offices accept travellers cheques and Visa cards for payment. Northern Areas and Chitral flights are the only ones with two-tier pricing, ie subsidies for locals. Travel agents cannot offer discounts on these flights.

Private carriers, Aero Asia and Bhoja Air, are now giving PIA competition on certain domestic routes, though not to/from Chitral, Saidu Sharif, Gilgit or Skardu. Another airline, Shaheen, had shut down all operations at the time of research.

**Helicopter Flights** A PIA foray into scheduled helicopter services (eg Islamabad to Abbottabad and Islamabad to Murree) collapsed for lack of interest. A Gilgit agency, Pamir Tours (see the Gilgit Region chapter), organises pricey Islamabad to Gilgit and other Northern Areas charter flights.

### TRAIN
Pakistan's rail system ends where the KKH begins. You can round out your journey with a three hour, Rs 22 ride (unreserved economy class) in an ancient carriage between Rawalpindi and Havelian (the official southern end of the Highway), but that's about all. See the Getting There & Away chapter for more about Pakistan's trains, including student and tourist discounts.

### ALONG THE KKH
Although you can take a train up to the southern end of the KKH or a plane into the middle of it, the cheapest way to get around is on the road itself. Long-distance buses and minibuses cover the whole thing, and in Pakistan they'll stop almost anywhere for a passenger. For medium and short hops, the roads are ruled by Toyota minibuses.

Pakistan's formerly state-run transport system is in a state of flux, with lines being privatised and many new private lines springing up. One result is that towns may now have more than one bus depot. Bus stations all tend to be utterly chaotic; at least in Pakistan, the best way to attract help may just be to call out the destination you want.

South of Gilgit, don't be surprised if your bus stops for prayers at Friday lunchtime, with driver and male passengers rolling out prayer mats by the roadside or visiting a local mosque.

### Bus
In the Northern Areas, the government-run Northern Areas Transportation Company (Natco) and several private companies run coaches between Rawalpindi, Gilgit, Skardu and the China border. Further south, the most comfortable intercity trips are in big air-conditioned Hino buses run by private outfits like New Khan Road Runners, Skyways and Citylinkers.

Then there are Pakistan's rolling works of art: chrome-sequinned vintage Bedford buses and trucks, vividly painted with poetry, Koranic passages and technicolour landscapes; equipped with tinted windows, dangling chains and musical horns; and decorated with buttons, badges, plastic fluting, laminated photos of Ayub Khan, the Aga Khan or the Ayatollah Khomeini. Though a

**Watch Your Neighbours**
Stay alert if you're travelling by bus on a winding mountain road. Passengers, particularly children, often throw up without warning.

**Segregation of Women**
On most passenger transport in Pakistan, women and families are seated separately, in the front seats beside the driver. If a man and woman are travelling together, the man takes the seat next to the driver. Western couples are often asked to rearrange themselves or even to sit apart, not to force Muslim habits on foreigners nor for the women's comfort, but because Muslim men may be acutely uncomfortable sitting next to a foreign woman. ■

photographer's delight, they're perversely uncomfortable to ride in.

Chinese buses, all government-run, are marginally maintained, tired old crocks, equipped with bad-tempered drivers.

### Minibus
Natco and private operators run 15-seat Hi-Ace and 21-seat Coaster minibuses on many regional and long-distance routes in Pakistan. They're faster and a bit pricier than buses. Coasters are the more comfortable of the two. The more common Hi-Ace, now (mis)used on roads once reserved for 4WD pickups, crams 21 people into a space meant for 15. Your view of the scenery is also limited, an important factor in the Northern Areas.

**Schedules & Booking** Only long-distance buses, eg Sost to Gilgit, Gilgit to Skardu and Gilgit to Rawalpindi, run on even an approximation of a fixed timetable. Only government and private Gilgit to Skardu and Gilgit to Rawalpindi buses and minibuses can be booked ahead, and only by a few days. Natco buses *from* Rawalpindi to Gilgit cannot be booked ahead.

Most other vehicles go when they're full, so departures can be lengthy affairs, with drivers honking up and down in search of passengers. Chinese buses seem to be repeatedly loaded, fuelled and repaired after everyone is on board.

**Concessions** If you ask, and have a student card, Natco gives a 50% student discount between Gilgit and Rawalpindi (except for their 'deluxe' service). They may not give it unless you booked the seat in advance.

It's always worth flashing your student card. While you may get little more than a snarl, local buses may give you a discount – but only after your green plastic has been passed around the whole bus to admire.

### Suzuki & Datsun Pickup Trucks
The most common short-haul transport in northern Pakistan is the converted Suzuki light-duty pickup, holding eight to 10 people. Don't let them charge you extra for a cab seat.

Private Datsun pickup trucks with seats for 10 to 12 are common in Kohistan. They're handy for scenic routes, as they'll stop anywhere to pick you up or let you off, and you pay only for the distance you go. Views are nonexistent unless you're brave enough to hang off the back! Some drivers try to charge more for a seat in the cab.

### Wagon
Old 15-seat Ford wagons are still common in Indus Kohistan, privately operated on set regional routes.

### Jeep
Where mountain roads permit nothing else, 4WD passenger-cargo jeeps and Land Cruisers serve remote Pakistani villages. Smaller jeeps are said to seat seven but we were once on one with 24 people attached to it.

### Cross-Border Transport
For many people the whole point of visiting the KKH is making the spectacular trip between Xinjiang and the Northern Areas over the Khunjerab Pass. A government bus or Land Cruiser is the normal way to do it.

China-to-Pakistan travellers ride buses of

## KKH Distances

Signs, maps, officials and drivers all tell you different numbers, each with the utmost certainty. The following distances in km are probably accurate to within about 5%.

|  | Kash | Tash | Khun | Sost | Kari | Gilg | Chil | Besh | Abbt | Rwpi |
|---|---|---|---|---|---|---|---|---|---|---|
| Kashgar | – | 290 | 420 | 505 | 595 | 700 | 835 | 1040 | 1190 | 1300 |
| Tashkurgan | 290 | – | 130 | 215 | 305 | 410 | 545 | 750 | 900 | 1010 |
| Khunjerab Pass | 420 | 130 | – | 85 | 175 | 280 | 415 | 620 | 770 | 880 |
| Sost | 505 | 215 | 85 | – | 90 | 195 | 330 | 535 | 685 | 795 |
| Karimabad | 595 | 305 | 175 | 90 | – | 105 | 240 | 445 | 595 | 705 |
| Gilgit | 700 | 410 | 280 | 195 | 105 | – | 135 | 340 | 490 | 600 |
| Chilas | 835 | 545 | 415 | 330 | 240 | 135 | – | 205 | 355 | 465 |
| Besham | 1040 | 750 | 620 | 535 | 445 | 340 | 205 | – | 150 | 260 |
| Abbottabad | 1190 | 900 | 770 | 685 | 595 | 490 | 355 | 150 | – | 110 |
| Rawalpindi | 1300 | 1010 | 880 | 795 | 705 | 600 | 456 | 260 | 110 | – |

the Xinjiang Tourism Authority from Kashgar to the Pakistani border post of Sost. Pakistan-to-China travellers ride Natco or PTDC vehicles from Sost to the Chinese border post of Tashkurgan and buses of the Tashkurgan or Kashgar municipal transport authority on to Kashgar. The trip takes two days either way, with an overnight stop in Tashkurgan.

You can hire your own Land Cruiser (nine passengers) for the trip, and even do the trip in one very long day – but only from a government agency such as CITS, Natco or PTDC, since only their drivers have permits to cross the border.

There are usually as many vehicles as necessary to meet demand, and prices are uniform. All must return empty, an absurd and wasteful consequence of China-Pakistan trade agreements.

For more on fares, timetables and border formalities, see the Kashgar to Tashkurgan and Khunjerab Pass & Gojal chapters.

### DRIVING & RENTAL

It's not hard to hire your own vehicle and driver. In Pakistan a private hire is called a 'special', and is a great bargain if you've got enough friends to fill it. Another advantage is that you can ask the driver to stop for photos and other impulses – and to slow down!

You can often hire a Suzuki or other vehicle right off the street (but if you just want a seat, be sure you're not hiring the whole vehicle). In the north, jeeps and Suzukis for hire normally have a separate stand; they also loiter around the bus station and filling stations. Jeep drivers in touristed places like Hunza and Swat have formed cartels with fixed rates for common routes.

Jeeps or Land Cruisers can also be hired from several agencies in Kashgar; from PTDC in Gilgit, the Kaghan Valley and Rawalpindi; or privately (ask your hotel-wallah). They may be hard to find on short notice in summer. Typical Land Cruiser rates from PTDC at the time of writing were about Rs 300 a day plus Rs 5 per km (or Rs 1000 per day all in), or fixed totals for common destinations.

Natco at Sost will rent you a minibus or even a bus (and driver).

Avis has cars for hire in Islamabad and Rawalpindi, some of them through Travel Walji's. Bottom-end rates are Rs 760 a day plus Rs 2.75 per km and Rs 200 collision damage waiver; or Rs 55 per hour plus Rs 5.5 per km with a driver. Pakistani companies are cheaper, but check the small print carefully. You'll need a credit card as a deposit. Avis (c/o Walji's Travel ☎ (0572) 2665;

Airport Rd), can also get you a car and driver in Gilgit.

## BICYCLE

The KKH is a spectacular trip for cyclists who are super-fit and ready for the unexpected. One called the Pakistan side a dream road; said he, 'Where else in the world can you find an incredibly scenic paved road from almost sea level to almost 5000m?'. On the China side, permits are no longer needed to cycle the Kashgar to Khunjerab road (you may be told to buy a travel permit to stop at Kara Kul, but see the Kashgar to Tashkurgan chapter for details). In towns, some cyclists have found themselves more welcome on a bike than on foot: many Asians regard people who walk great distances in the heat as slightly mad.

But you won't be the first: the manager of Tashkurgan's Ice Mountain Hotel, where most passing cyclists seem to stay, estimated he saw over 50 of them in the month before we were there, which works out to almost two a day.

The itinerary most often suggested by cyclists we met is to fly to Islamabad, bus to Gilgit, cycle to Kashgar and return by bus (or hop off the return bus at the border for a smoking downhill to Sost). Most who have cycled the KKH rate Indus Kohistan (Chilas to Besham) their least favourite part: intervals between decent food and rest are long, summer weather is scorching, people are anarchic and suspicious of outsiders, and men tend to have distorted ideas about western women.

The boxed Cyclists' Notes in each regional chapter are based on information from half a dozen helpful Lonely Planet correspondents. Note that distances there can only be trusted to within perhaps 5% because of variations in the way people calibrate their odometers.

Cyclists will also find current news and advice in good hotel guest books along the way – including those at the Ice Mountain Hotel (Tashkurgan), Mountain Refuge (Sost), New Hunza Tourist Hotel (Karimabad), Kisar Inn (Altit), North Inn and others (Gilgit) – but

### Cycling Tips

Two of the most common annoyances are: kids running along with you, begging for pens and pulling your brakes when you go slowly. Dogs, especially in China. Never try to cycle away from a dog. We encountered a dog with only three legs who went 33km/h. If you just stop, dogs will (usually) not dare to attack you.

While most of the KKH and the Gilgit to Skardu roads are 'paved', the pavement is usually rough and washboard-like with plenty of holes. You also have to be prepared for regular unpaved landslide areas which can stretch for kilometres.

All in all, plan for a 30-50% drop in your average daily mileage. In Europe we can usually do about 100km a day over long periods, while in Pakistan we managed only 50-60km with the same effort.

You definitely need a good, reliable bike. We used our 15-year-old travelling bikes which had already survived several tours all over Europe, and made sure they were in tip-top shape. We took additional features like a third brake (handy for the long downhills and it also meant we didn't have to bring spare parts for the brakes), a frame enforcement (which gets rid of frame vibrations at high speeds) self-made paniers of extra size, and the strongest 32-622-wheels we could find.

Most importantly, I know every screw and part of our two bikes so I know what they can withstand and how they can be repaired. Our bikes are pretty low-tech and compatible with the most simple and cheap cycle parts which meant that we could get spare parts in most of the major towns along the KKH – although we still carried 3.5kg of repair tools and parts. You will be in big trouble if you have the ultimate high-tech bike and one of the parts fails in the middle of the Chinese desert stretch. That's one reason I would strongly advise against taking the KKH on with a brand new bike. Every new bike (even the most expensive ones) has weaknesses you have to find out about. Know your bike in detail before you set off.

Finally, a note on flats. There is a plant, common in Kohistan and around Skardu, which spits thorns into the sand. We had about 20 punctures in this area – seven in one day alone – so make sure you have enough puncture repair stuff and spare tubes.

**Robert Matzinger**

unfortunately not in Kashgar, nor south of Gilgit.

For information on getting your machine to the KKH, see the Bicycle section in the Getting There & Away chapter.

For its members, the Cyclists' Touring Club (☎ (01483) 417217; fax (01483) 426994; email cycling@ctc.org.uk) in the UK publishes useful, free information booklets on cycling in China, in Pakistan and on the KKH. Contact them at Cotterell House, 69 Meadrow, Godalming, Surrey GU7 3HS or at their World Wide Web site, http://www.ctc.org.uk.

### Equipment

A mountain bike is considerably easier and more comfortable than a touring bike. On the latter the KKH, though largely sealed, is just bumpy enough to discourage you from a good run-up for the next hill; in the spring you may also find that winter weather has made hash out of many stretches. If you do take a touring bike, take the fattest tyres you can fit on your rims. A small pump may be adequate, but a big one comes in handy for discouraging dogs.

Water supplies are vital, and each rider should be equipped to carry a minimum of three litres.

Tent and stove are handy in the thinly populated region between Ghez and Sost, but you can manage without them, especially if you're planning to cycle only in Pakistan. The reduced weight will let you cycle far enough to always find some sort of shelter and food. A bivvy bag or even a groundsheet will do for the few places where you might have to sleep outdoors.

Similarly, a stove is not 100% essential: you could carry chapattis, tinned cheese and biscuits and get your hotel to boil some eggs for you. If you do bring a stove, note that methylated spirits (methyl alcohol) is unobtainable at least in Pakistan; kerosene is readily available along the KKH, but should be filtered before use.

### Purchase & Rental

Several shops in Kashgar sell Chinese-made mountain bikes for the equivalent of around US$70. Travellers have bought these, cycled to the Northern Areas and sold them at no loss. Doing this in the other direction is more problematic, as bikes in Gilgit are scarcer and considerably more expensive.

We know of only one Northern Areas outfit that rents mountain bikes: Himalaya Nature Tours in Gilgit.

### Safety & Security

See Dangers & Annoyances in the Facts for the Visitor chapter, particularly about rockfall hazard after prolonged rain.

Stories of bike theft abound in China, including Xinjiang, so always lock up. So skilled are locals, it is said, that while you're snoozing on the bus they can remove your bike from the roof rack without even disturbing the tarpaulin. Cyclists moving on by train may find that their Cannondale has magically turned into a Flying Pigeon during the journey. Pakistan is safer but bike thefts happen there too.

### HITCHING

Hitching is possible on well travelled roads in Xinjiang and northern Pakistan. Though it's relatively safe here – at least for men – hitching is never entirely without risk, and we don't recommend it. If you do decide to flag a lift, note that it's not always free; although some drivers just like the company, others hope for the equivalent of the bus fare. Nobody knows the thumbs-up sign; just wave.

Most truck drivers in Pakistan are Pathans, who are usually very helpful and friendly. But quite a few Pakistani trucks drive off the road every year, so have a good look at your driver first! Gojal people say some truckers are fond of the Chinese wine that turns up at Sost, and there are plenty of speed-freaks on the long hauls. The closest thing to a central loading yard in any KKH town is Airport Rd in Gilgit, though Besham has a big repair yard.

A few car drivers have been known to offer a lift and then, on arrival, demand payment.

## LOCAL TRANSPORT

You can get around central Kashgar by taxi or motorcycle sidecar, or to the outskirts on pony-carts navigated by boys with cheating hearts.

Local transport in northern Pakistani towns is commonly by fixed-fare Suzuki. Those in Rawalpindi have conductors; elsewhere, tap on the cab window or stomp on the floor when you want out. There are also motor-rickshaws and horse-drawn tongas with negotiable fares (plus some fixed-route tongas) in old-town Rawalpindi; taxis, Suzukis and fixed-route minibuses and buses run on the main roads and in Islamabad.

Bicycles can be hired in Kashgar and Gilgit.

# Kashgar to Tashkurgan

The Tarim Basin is a 1500km-long depression covering most of southern Xinjiang and consisting almost entirely of a hostile desert called Takla Makan (roughly 'Desert of No Return' in the Uyghur language) with a string of oases round the edge. Kashgar (Uyghur: Qashqar; Chinese: Kashi) is one of these oases, about 1300m above sea level in a cul-de-sac formed by the Tian Shan, Pamir and Kunlun ranges. Despite its isolation, Kashgar has seen plenty of traffic over the last 2000 years, as a major Silk Road town and a crossroads for invading armies. 'Kashgaria' is the historical name for the western end of the Tarim Basin.

### History

Kashgaria's terrain, people, languages and religion have more in common with Kazakhstan, Kyrgyzstan and Tajikistan, and even northern Pakistan, than with China. But over the centuries Imperial China has come again and again to control its frontiers or police the Silk Road. History in the Tarim Basin is mainly about conflicts between the Chinese and the indigenous nomadic tribes.

The Han dynasty was here, protecting its new trade routes to the west, until the 1st century AD, when the prospering oases fell to northern nomadic warrior tribes, Mongols and later Turks. Imperial power was not reasserted until the Tang dynasty in the late 7th and 8th centuries. Even then, empires were jostling each other; in the 8th century an Arab expedition reached Kashgar, and a Tang army crossed the Pamirs and occupied Gilgit and Chitral for several years in an attempt to deal with Arab and Tibetan expansion.

Tang control in Kashgaria was ended in 752 by the Turks, and the area ruled by a succession of tribal kingdoms – early Uyghur, Qarakhan and Karakitai – for more than four centuries. It was during the mainly Uyghur Qarakhan dynasty in the 9th to 12th centuries that Islam, spreading east from

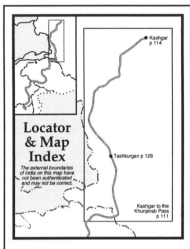

### Highlights

- The traditional crafts and quiet courtyards of Old Kashgar
- Kashgar's mind-boggling Sunday Market
- Kumtagh, the sand dunes of the Ghez River
- Beautiful Kara Kul lake, nestled between two Pamir giants

Persia (Iran), took hold here. At its peak, Qarakhanid Kashgar is said to have had 18 madrassas (Islamic academies). The tomb of the Qarakhan ruler Sutuq Bughra Khan, who first embraced Islam in 934, still stands at Artush.

In 1219 Kashgaria fell to the Mongol Empire of Genghis Khan, and for another century the Silk Road flourished. At the end of the 14th century a Turkic warlord of Samarkand, Timur (called Tamerlane in the west), sacked Kashgar in the course of an Asian rampage. Until the 18th century Kashgaria remained under the control of

Timur's descendants or various Mongol tribes.

In 1755 China was back, in the form of a Manchu army, and Kashgar became part of the Qing dynasty. Qing rule was oppressive, and resentment soon boiled over. In 1847 the independent Karakoram state of Hunza helped the Chinese put down a revolt in Yarkand. In the 1860s and 1870s Muslim uprisings exploded across China like a string of firecrackers. In 1865 Yaqub Beg seized Kashgaria and proclaimed a short-lived independent Turkestan (see the boxed text Yaqub Beg). Upon his demise Kashgaria became part of China's newly created Xinjiang ('New Dominions') Province.

At this time British India, probing north from Kashmir, discovered Tsarist Russia expanding south. In 1882 an agreement pried from the Qing government allowed Russia to open a consulate in Kashgar. A British Agency in Gilgit, opened briefly in 1877, was urgently reopened after the Mir (ruler) of Hunza entertained a party of Russians at Baltit Fort in 1888. Britain set up its own Kashgar office in 1890.

For the next half-century Kashgar was at the centre of the so-called Great Game to establish political dominance in eastern Turkestan. In the end, boundary agreements gave Russia most of the Pamirs, though the Tarim Basin remained in Chinese hands.

The revolution of 1911 ended China's dynastic history, but the new Republic became a stage for four decades of civil war, with local warlords holding sway. After the 1917 Bolshevik revolution Russia was forced out of its Kashgar listening post, and not allowed back until 1925.

Despite this official absence, Soviet political and economic influence remained strong in the region.

In 1931-34 a ferocious anti-Chinese insurrection burned across Xinjiang, contained in the end by an improbable coalition of Chinese soldiers, immigrant White Russians and covert Soviet troops (the young USSR lived in fear of a Japanese invasion across China). Were it not for the duplicity of Xinjiang's Manchu governor, Kashgar

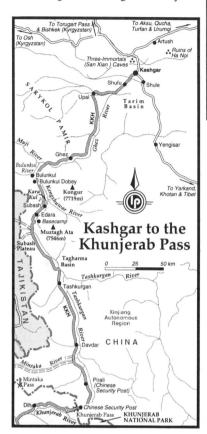

Kashgar to the
Khunjerab Pass

might well have fallen under Soviet control at this time, joining the Central Asian republics.

Xinjiang fell to the Nationalist Chinese (Kuomintang) in 1941. At the end of WWII, Xinjiang declared independence as the Republic of East Turkestan, aided and encouraged by Mao Zedong in exchange for Uyghur resistance to the Nationalists. But after Mao's founding of the Peoples' Republic of China in 1949, the fledgling state collapsed when most of its leaders died in a mysterious plane crash, en route to Beijing to negotiate with the new regime.

## Yaqub Beg

In the early 1860s, in response to insurrections elsewhere in China, Uyghurs and Chinese Muslims rose up and seized the region around Kulja (present-day Yining, in what is now north-western Xinjiang) from the rule of the Qing (Manchu) dynasty.

In 1863 a former ruler of Kashgar left his exile in Kokand in present-day Uzbekistan, in hopes of taking advantage of the pandemonium and re-staking his claim there. His military officer, an adventurer named Yaqub Beg who claimed direct descent from Timur (Tamerlane), instead manoeuvred himself into power, and within four years emerged as supreme ruler of Kashgar and a swath of Xinjiang stretching to Ürümqi, Turfan and beyond.

Great Britain, keen for a foothold, flattered Beg with diplomatic recognition, and Russia established trading ties. Beg made the most of it, playing the two empires off against each other. But his game ended when Russia, eager also to maintain relations with the Manchus, in 1871 closed the borders of its new Central Asian territories and seized Kulja. Six years later, Beg died in mysterious circumstances, his regime collapsed and Britain quickly switched its overtures to the Manchus. ∎

Xinjiang was subsequently declared an 'autonomous region', an Orwellian sleight of hand that has failed to change anything very much. A cycle of violence continues, attracting little outside notice. Riots in Kashgar in the 1970s and uprisings in 1981 and 1990 may have left scores dead. A bomb did minor damage in Kashgar in 1993. In 1996 a Uyghur in Khotan killed 16 Chinese policemen with a machine gun, and separatists blew up an armaments depot near Ürümqi and a railway bridge in eastern Xinjiang. In early 1997, somewhere between 10 and 100 people died in riots in Yining (Gulja), while bombs exploded in Qorla (east of Kashgar) and on public buses in Ürümqi, killing at least nine.

The government's response has been ferocious, with exile Uyghur sources claiming hundreds or thousands of executions since 1996. But tourism has continued through Kashgar without a ripple.

### Time

A constant concern for visitors is clock time. Officially all China runs on Beijing time but here, 3500km from Beijing, people set their watches to unofficial 'Xinjiang time', two hours earlier. You must run on both times, always checking which is meant (Uyghur: *Beijing waqt?*; Chinese: *Beijing shijian?*). Note that airline schedules and government office hours are always given in Beijing time.

### Business Hours

Business hours in Kashgar and Tashkurgan are roughly 10 am to 2.30 pm and 5 to 9 pm in summer, and 10 am to 2 pm and 3.30 to 7.30 pm in winter (Beijing time), Monday to Saturday. Some offices close on Wednesday afternoon. Many locally run shops are open Sunday and closed Monday.

### KASHGAR

*Pop (est): 180,000   Tel Area Code: 0998*

For two millennia Kashgar has been a Silk Road trading centre, and even today it remains just a big market town, with impromptu street corner negotiations, perpetual bazaars and hotel room deals with Gilgit traders. Some things haven't changed since medieval times – blacksmiths, carpenters and cobblers work by hand in the old quarter, and from surrounding fields come wheat, maize, beans, rice, cotton and fruit in profusion. Id Kah Mosque stands over the town as it has since 1442.

But in most ways the past is decidedly gone – symbolically confirmed by the huge statue of Mao Zedong and the 'Military Administration Zone' garrison compounds around town. High-rises sprout, department stores multiply. Sleaze, including prostitution, has arrived in the wake of tourism. Vehicle noise and fumes now put Kashgar in a league with most other Chinese cities.

The British and Russian consulates were closed in 1949. The British office, called

### Cyclists' Notes, Kashgar to Tashkurgan

There's no permit requirement just to cycle the Kashgar to Tashkurgan road. Officially an Alien Travel Permit is needed to stop at Kara Kul lake, but at the time of writing nobody was checking for them there. They're available at Kashgar and Tashkurgan Public Security Bureau (PSB) and at checkposts; at Ghez, cyclists who revealed plans to stop at Kara Kul were made to buy one.

Food is scarce between Kashgar and Tashkurgan – mainly bread, dumplings and tea. Water is scarce in the Kashgar plain, and one of the driest stretches of the KKH is between Kara Kul and the Khunjerab Pass. Checkposts make good overnight stops, and it's no longer illegal to stay in private homes.

The Highway on the China side has kilometre posts, probably representing distances from Ürümqi. Major climb southbound: 120km from near Upal to Subash. Major climb northbound: much of the 70km from Tashkurgan to the Subash Plateau.

**Kashgar to Ghez, about 120km** Kashgar itself has wide roads and separate bike lanes. Overall the road south from Kashgar is fairly level for 70 or 80km, then climbs increasingly steeply to Ghez. Upal, about 50km from Kashgar, has melons, samosas and other snacks. The Ghez checkpost has basic food and accommodation.

**Ghez to Kara Kul, about 70km** Above Ghez the road climbs steeply for 40km through a canyon where landslides may block the road during rainstorms. Travellers exploring the sand dune area at the top of the canyon have been warned off by mounted police. From there it's a gradual uphill, then steep for a few km, to Kara Kul lake. A lakeside hotel and yurt site has overpriced beds and decent food. Camp away from it, as those who spurned the offer of a yurt have been hassled. There is also an unappealing truck stop at Kara Kul.

**Kara Kul to Tashkurgan, about 100km** The 30km rising road to the Subash Plateau (at about 4000m the second highest point on the KKH) is a long grind but not outrageously steep for most of the way. About 60km from Kara Kul is Kekyor checkpost, now apparently abandoned. A grotty truck stop perches on the steep climb south out of the Tagharma Basin. Tashkurgan is the only place between Kashgar and Sost with real restaurants. The Ice Mountain Hotel at Tashkurgan has a good guestbook full of cyclists' tips.

**Tashkurgan to Pirali, about 100km** The bumpy road goes slightly downhill, then rises toward the Pirali checkpost. Cyclists have spent the night at the settlement of Davdar, which also has a grotty truck stop. Soldiers at Pirali, about 45km from Tashkurgan, might let you stay the night. ■

Chini Bagh (Uyghur for Chinese Garden), was first occupied in 1890 by George Macartney. In 1898 he brought a bride from his native Scotland, and over the next 17 years Catherine Macartney made Chini Bagh an island of gardens and European hospitality. A 15 minute walk away was the Russian consulate, never blessed with a Lady Macartney. The imperial rivalry across the Pamirs was matched by personal rivalries across town – for information, Chinese sympathies, even Silk Road antiquities. Both consulates later reopened as tourist hotels, but have nearly disappeared under subsequent construction.

Kashgar's future may imitate its past. In 1983 barter trade resumed across the borders with the old Soviet republics. In 1986 tourism

surged with the opening of the Khunjerab Pass. In 1992 a rail link was finally completed between Ürümqi and Almaty. In October 1996 a Pakistani truck caravan made a symbolic trading trip via Kashgar to Bishkek and Almaty. It's not hard to imagine a new high-tech Silk Road crossing the Tarim Basin one day.

Peak tourist season (and peak demand for rooms and transport) is from late June to September – with saturation at weekends as tourists arrive for the Sunday market. If you're coming from Pakistan, Chinese brusqueness will come as a shock, though you'll find an echo of Pakistani cheer in younger Uyghur men. It's also nice to see the female half of the human race out in the open again.

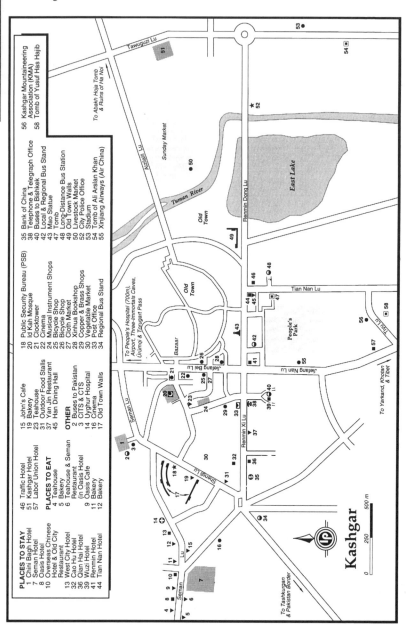

**PLACES TO STAY**
1 Chini Bagh Hotel
7 Seman Hotel
8 Oasis Hotel
10 Overseas Chinese
   Hotel & Old City
   Restaurant
13 West City Hotel
32 Cao Hu Hotel
36 Qian Hai Hotel
39 Wuzi Hotel
41 Renmin Hotel
44 Tian Nan Hotel

46 Traffic Hotel
51 Kashgar Hotel
57 Labor Union Hotel

**PLACES TO EAT**
4 Teahouse
5 Bakery
6 Teahouse & Seman
   Restaurant
   (in Oasis Hotel
9 Oasis Cafe
11 Bakery
12 Bakery

15 John's Cafe
19 Bakery
23 Teahouse
31 Outdoor Food Stalls
37 Yan Jin Restaurant
45 Han Dining Hall

**OTHER**
2 Buses to Pakistan
3 CITS & CTS
14 Uyghur Hospital
16 Cinema
17 Old Town Walls

18 Public Security Bureau (PSB)
20 Id Kah Mosque
21 Clocktower
22 Cinema
24 Musical Instrument Shops
25 Bicycle Shop
26 Bicycle Shop
27 Cloth Market
28 Xinhua Bookshop
29 Copper & Brass Shops
30 Vegetable Market
33 Post Office
34 Regional Bus Stand

35 Bank of China
38 Telephone & Telegraph Office
40 Buses to Bishkek
42 Local & Regional Bus Stand
43 Mao Statue
47 Tomb
48 Long-Distance Bus Station
49 Old Town Walls
50 Livestock Market
52 City Police Office
53 Stadium
54 Tomb of Ali Arslan Khan
55 Xinjiang Airways (Air China)

56 Kashgar Mountaineering
   Association (KMA)
58 Tomb of Yusuf Has Hajib

Kashgar

## Orientation

Official (Chinese) street names are given here. The main streets out from the centre are Renmin Dong Lu and Renmin Xi Lu (East and West People's Rd), and Jiefang Bei Lu and Jiefang Nan Lu (North and South Liberation Rd). The perimeter road on the northwest is Shengli Lu (Victory Rd).

The heart of town is around Id Kah Mosque and the main bazaar. Uyghurs live mainly north of the centre and Chinese in brick compounds to the south. The budget travellers' enclave is on the west side, with mid-range hotels, travel help and good food. The Sunday market grounds are east of town.

Buses from Pakistan go to the Seman Hotel and/or the Chini Bagh Hotel, on request. If you arrive by air, a Y8 shuttle bus will bring you to the Xinjiang Airways and Air China (CAAC) booking office on Jiefang Nan Lu, which isn't convenient to anything at all. Or you can pick up local transport; see the Getting Around section later in this chapter. The airport is 12km north-east of the centre.

## Information

**Tourist Offices/Travel Agencies** There isn't really a 'tourist office' here. The state-run China International Travel Service (CITS) and China Travel Service (CTS) are basically travel agencies. Both can arrange air tickets or transport, but they're not reliable sources of information on off-route places. CITS (☎ 282 5390; fax 282 3087) is up two flights of stairs in a building inside the Chini Bagh Hotel gate. CTS (☎ 283 2875; fax 282 2552) is up two more flights in the same building. CTS is consistently cheaper than CITS.

From his John's Cafe (☎ & fax 282 4186), opposite the Seman Hotel, knowledgeable John Hu organises bookings, tickets, transport and excursions at competitive rates. The cafe looks like the best place in town to meet travellers and swap information.

The Kashgar Mountaineering Association (KMA) (Uyghur: *Takka chkesh*; Chinese: *Dengshan xiehui*) is a government liaison office for expeditions and group sports travel, and will help individuals with guides or vehicles, though both are scarce in high season. The office (☎ 282 3680; fax 282 2957) is far away at 8 Tiyu Lu (Sports Rd), off Jiefang Nan Lu beyond CAAC.

The city-owned Kashgar Travel Agency (☎ 282 2593; fax 282 2525), on the 2nd floor of the Renmin Hotel, can arrange sightseeing and some trekking trips (including one to K2 base camp on the China side).

**Police** A city Public Security Bureau (PSB) office is on Renmin Dong Lu, past East Lake.

**Travel Permits & Visa Extensions** The Division of Aliens and Exit-Entry Administration of the regional PSB is at PSB headquarters on Shengli Lu. Alien Travel Permits *(waibin tongxing zheng)*, for areas not freely open to foreigners, are Y10. You can get your Chinese visa extended here too; price depends on nationality, ranging from Y45 to Y120. Some staff speak English. The office is open weekdays only, from 9.30 am to 1.30 pm and 3.30 to 8 pm (Beijing time).

**Money** Tourist hotels, and the Bank of China on Renmin Xi Lu, will change travellers cheques and cash in major currencies. Exchange rates are uniform throughout China. The bank can also give cash advances on major credit cards in a matter of minutes, and is open weekdays from 9.30 am to 1.30 pm and 4 to 8 pm, and Saturdays from 11 am to 3 pm (Beijing time). You can only sell *renminbi* (RMB) back at exit points, eg the Tashkurgan borderpost.

Uyghur moneychangers loiter outside Chini Bagh Hotel and in the bazaar. There's little to be gained from dealing with them because their rates are so similar to the bank's, and plenty to be lost because some are accomplished cheats. If you insist, to minimise chances of a rip-off, trade a round sum for quick calculations; have it ready in your pocket to avoid fumbling in an open purse or wallet; tell the dealer what you have but don't pull it out; insist on his money first, take your time counting it, and don't let him recount it.

**Post & Communications** The post office on Renmin Xi Lu is open daily from 10 am to 8 pm (Beijing time). Buy stamps downstairs, but hand overseas letters to the international desk upstairs. There's a Y2.30 charge for each letter you pick up from poste restante there.

Across the road is the telephone & telegraph office, open daily from 9.30 am to 8 pm (Beijing time). Upstairs is for international calls, faxes and cables, and downstairs for telegrams and domestic calls. Kashgar now has International Direct Dialling (IDD), so calls go through fairly fast. Make your calls here: IDD prices from tourist hotels and agencies are all grossly inflated.

You can make local calls for a few mao at numerous shops with small 'PUBLIC TELEPHONE' signs .

**Airline Offices** The Xinjiang Airways and Air China (CAAC) ticket office (☎ 282 2113), at 49 Jiefang Nan Lu, is open Monday to Saturday from 10 am to 1.10 pm and 4.30 to 7.30 pm, and Sunday from 11 am to 1 pm (Beijing time). This is also the terminus for the airport bus.

**Newspapers & Magazines** Forget it – even *China Daily* seems to get here only in travellers' rucksacks.

**Laundry** You can get your wash done for reasonable per-piece rates at tourist hotels as well as at the Oasis Cafe and the laundry next door.

**Medical Services** The main Chinese hospital is People's Hospital (Renmin yiyuan) on Jiefang Bei Lu north of the river. There's a hospital of traditional Uyghur medicine on Seman Lu east of the Seman Hotel, but travellers say it's pretty filthy.

**Dangers & Annoyances** Travellers have lost money or passports to pickpockets at the Sunday market, in the ticket scrum at the long-distance bus station and even on local buses, so keep yours tucked away.

**Language Help** An enterprising Uyghur named Ablimit Ghopor has assembled an extensive English-Uyghur pocket dictionary, which he hawks from the neighbourhood of the Oasis Cafe.

### The Sunday Market

Once a week Kashgar's population swells by 50,000 as people stream in to the Sunday market, one of Asia's most mind-boggling bazaars. By sunrise the roads east of town are a sea of pedestrians, horses, donkey carts, bikes, trucks, cars, buses and belching motor-rickshaws, everyone shouting *boish-boish!* (coming through!). In arenas off the road, men test-drive horses or look into the mouths of sheep and goats. Sellers sit by rugs and blankets, clothing and boots, hardware and junk, tapes and boomboxes, and of course hats.

This traditional livestock market has mutated into a vast social event, and thence into a tourist attraction. Increasing numbers of foreigners arrange their visits around it, with hotel occupancy soaring on weekends. It can be a photographer's dream (bring three times as much film as you expect to use) although, especially in July to August, it's hard to get a shot that doesn't have another tourist in it.

The grounds are a 10 minute walk from the Kashgar Hotel, or 30 or 40 minutes from the Seman Hotel. The livestock market is south of the main road, just east of the river bridge; try to see this by 8.30 or 9 am (Beijing time). A pavilion east of the bridge was conceived as a meeting place for Central Asian and Russian traders, but it's now mostly carpet showrooms. At the rear of this is the cloth market.

Taxis, sidecar motorcycles and donkey carts lurk outside tourist hotels on market day, though traffic may prevent them from taking you right into the heart of the market. At the time of research a sidecar from the Seman was Y5, a taxi about Y10. Ask for Yekshenba bazaar (Sunday market). John Hu

## Peoples of Kashgaria

Xinjiang is home to over a dozen of China's 55 official minorities, and many ethnic groups are represented in Kashgaria. A walk in Kashgar's bazaar reveals an array of faces from Chinese, Slavic and Turkish to downright Mediterranean – surmounted, incidentally, by an incredible variety of hats.

With the exception of Chinese, Russians and Wakhi Tajiks (Ismailis), nearly all are Sunni Muslims, though not as self-consciously devout as those in Pakistan. Though Mandarin Chinese is the official language, Xinjiang's *lingua franca* is Uyghur, a Turkic dialect written in both Arabic and Latinised scripts (the latter introduced for a time in an unpopular Chinese attempt to reduce illiteracy).

**Uyghurs** Uyghurs (pronounced 'WEE-gur') consider themselves Xinjiang's indigenous people. The first Uyghur empire, in the 8th century, ruled from the Karakoram to Siberia's Lake Baykal. Later branches include the Buddhist 'Yellow Uyghurs' of Gansu, Buddhist Karakhoja Uyghurs of Gaochang (near Turfan) and the great Muslim Qarakhan dynasty that held sway from Balasagun (now Burana in Kyrgyzstan), Talas (now Zhambyl in Kazakhstan) and Kashgar.

Uyghurs were the first Turkic people to settle down, and are today known as skilled oasis farmers (they invented the *karez* system of underground channels still in use in the region). They are easily distinguishable from other Turkic peoples here, being larger, darker and more Mediterranean-looking. The men's four-sided skullcap is a giveaway, though some older men wear a tall black cotton hat with a narrow fringe of fur at the bottom.

The last Chinese census counted 7.2 million Uyghurs in Xinjiang. While Uyghurs remain a majority in the Tarim Basin, an Ürümqi to Kashgar railway line now under construction seems likely to change that. The Eastern Turkestan Union in Europe estimates that there are a further half-million Uyghurs in the former Soviet Central Asian states, plus a total of about 75,000 in Pakistan, Afghanistan and émigré communities in Saudi Arabia, Turkey and the west.

Uyghurs consider themselves Xinjiang's indigenous people, and their Mediterranean features make them easily distinguishable from other peoples in the region.

**Kyrgyz** The summer villages and small camel caravans of the Kara Kul region are mostly Kyrgyz, who have retained some of their ancestors' nomadic ways. 'Kyrgyz' is one of Asia's oldest ethnic names, going back to the 2nd century BC when the ancestors of modern Kyrgyz are said to have lived in the upper Yenisey river basin in Siberia. They migrated to the mountains of what is now Kyrgyzstan from the 10th to 15th centuries, some fleeing wars, some in the ranks of Mongol armies.

Kyrgyz have noticeably Mongolian features. Older Kyrgyz men may wear an embroidered white, tasselled felt cap, or in winter a round, fur-trimmed hat. Of course the great majority of Kyrgyz today live in Kyrgyzstan. One estimate puts their number in Xinjiang at 147,000, with a sizeable community in Afghanistan too.

**Tajiks** Most in evidence near the Pakistan border are Sarykol and Wakhi Tajiks – mild, rather European-looking people renowned as skilled herders. Wakhi Tajiks also live in northern Pakistan and eastern Afghanistan and of course in Tajikistan. Most of China's roughly 20,000 Tajiks live in Tashkurgan Tajik Autonomous County, south of Kashgar. Tajiks are relatives of present-day Iranians and speak a dialect of Persian, while all other Central Asian peoples speak Turkic languages.

**Others** Some Kazakhs live in Xinjiang, though mostly in the north. There are also some Uzbeks. Han Chinese are dominant in government but still a minority in southern Xinjiang. It's a surprise to encounter occasional Slavs, descendants of White Russians who fled after the 1917 Bolshevik revolution. ■

offers a free one way minibus shuttle after breakfast.

If the tourist crush gets to you, try the Sunday market at Khotan (see Yarkand & Khotan in the Around Kashgar section).

## Id Kah Mosque

The big yellow-tiled mosque is one of the largest in China, with a peaceful courtyard and gardens for 20,000 worshippers. It was built in 1442 as a smaller mosque on what was then the outskirts of town. During the Cultural Revolution, China's decade of political anarchy from 1966 to 1976, Id Kah suffered heavy damage, but has since been restored. Its central veranda has a carved and finely painted ceiling.

It's acceptable for non-Muslims to go in. Local women are rarely seen inside but western women are usually ignored if they're modestly dressed (arms and legs covered and a scarf on the head). Take your shoes off if you enter covered, carpeted prayer areas, and be discreet about photos. Some travellers refer to a Y3 entrance fee for foreigners but we weren't charged.

In front of the mosque is Id Kah Square, swarming on sunny days with old men in high boots and long black coats, women with brown veils over their heads, and quite a few down-and-outers.

There are also more than 90 neighbourhood mosques throughout the city.

## Abakh Hoja Tomb

Kashgar's best example of Muslim architecture is an elegant mausoleum built in the mid-17th century for the descendants of a Muslim missionary named Muhatum Ajam (or Makhtum Azan). With its tiled dome and four minarets, it resembles a bright, miniature Taj Mahal.

Beneath the tiled stones in the main chamber are more than 70 graves, including those of children. They include that of Muhatum Ajam's grandson, Abakh Hoja, a Uyghur aristocrat and spiritual leader who ruled southern Xinjiang for 16 years in the 17th century and is sometimes called the 'patron saint of Kashgar'. Another grave is that of Abakh Hoja's granddaughter, known to the Chinese as Xiang Fei (see the boxed

### Where Is Old Kashgar?

Kashgar is again looking like a Central Asian hub, firmly on the tourist trail and with trade links to Pakistan, central China, and the former Soviet republics of Kazakhstan and Kyrgyzstan. There is talk of upgrading the airport and adding international connections. Beijing's embrace grows fonder, with a railway line on the march from Ürümqi. The 'town' has become a city, conceding a lane at a time to high-rises, shattering traffic and other 'modernisations'. But traditional Kashgar is still here if you look for it:

- At the Sunday market, of course.

- In the old bazaar, a dusty labyrinth of blacksmiths, farriers, carpenters, jewellers, tea shops, bakeries and noodle shops, behind a wall of department stores opposite Id Kah.

- Along the roads east of Jiefang Bei Lu, some sporting bright renovated or new buildings in traditional style and, off these roads, narrow alleys lined with adobe houses.

- In the food stalls that materialise every afternoon at the south end of Shengli Lu, and in the nearby vegetable market.

- Inside Id Kah Mosque.

- On the road along the south wall of Id Kah, which Uyghurs call Üstangbuyi ('riverside', after a long-gone stream), at the end of the day: merchants and artisans winding down, night hawkers setting up, men sipping tea on balconies, darkening stalls with everything from plimsolls to brassware, tiny barbershops, mullahs in turbans, caged thrushes singing their hearts out, swifts darting, kids tumbling. ■

## Fragrant Consort

The most celebrated occupant of Abakh Hoja's mausoleum is his granddaughter Ikparhan, widow of a Yarkandi prince and better known to Chinese as Xiang Fei (Fragrant Consort). In 1759 she led Uyghurs in an abortive revolt against the Qing emperor Qian Long, and was then taken off to Beijing as an imperial concubine. There, says the legend, the emperor fell madly in love with her. Two years later, while Qian Long was out of town, his mother the empress dowager ordered Xiang Fei to commit suicide, which she did. Legend also says her body now rests here. The 'official' version is that Xiang Fei died of old age and is buried in China's Hebei Province. ■

text Fragrant Consort). Behind the mausoleum is a vast graveyard.

The mausoleum is a half-hour bike ride or a two hour walk north-east of town. There is a Y10 admission fee, plus Y1 for bicycle parking.

### Tomb of Yusuf Has Hajib

Yusuf Has Hajib (or Yusup Khas Hajip, lived *ca* 1019-85) is perhaps the best known Uyghur scholar, thanks to *Kutad Kubilik*, or *The Wisdom of Royal Glory*. This encyclopedic look at Qarakhan political, economic and cultural life, cast in the form of a 13,290-line lyric poem, is a classic of Uyghur literature. He presented it in 1070 to the Qarakhan ruler, who awarded him the title Has Hajib, meaning 'royal adviser'. Strangely, there is no trace of the original, only very old copies in libraries in Vienna, Cairo and Namangan (Uzbekistan).

The striking, purple-domed mausoleum is a 1993 restoration of a building enlarged many times over the centuries and then smashed up during the Cultural Revolution. It's Xinjiang's most important Uyghur monument, though there's little to see besides the huge, elaborate gravestone inside. The complex is open daily from 9.30 am to 8 pm (Beijing time). Entry, from Tiyu Lu, is a steep Y8 (plus Y2 for photos). Modest dress is probably not essential.

### Tomb of Ali Arslan Khan

Another historical site is this tomb and small mosque, fairly modest considering they mark the grave of a Qarakhan ruler, Ali Arslan Khan (ruled 970-998). At the end of Renmin Dong Lu, go almost a km south. The tomb is in a weedy courtyard behind a minaretted gate on the right. You may be asked for a few mao donation.

### People's Park

South of the Mao statue is People's Park (Renmin gongyuan), a weedy arboretum with avenues of tall poplars, a horrible little zoo, and Uyghurs playing billiards, chess and *shiang chi* (Chinese chess). East of the park, 200m down a back lane, is a decaying old tomb, which, according to local people, may have been for a 19th century imam (religious leader).

### Old Town Walls

At the east end of Seman Lu stands a 10m-high section of the old town walls, at least 500 years old. Another rank of them is visible from Shengli Lu. Construction around, on and in them makes access impossible, and there's clearly no interest in preserving them. Another small section is on the way to East Lake.

### East Lake

East out Renmin Dong Lu is a willow-lined artificial lake, a popular spot for migratory birds and a good place for a picnic or a peaceful walk among the weeds. In the summer you can rent little boats.

### Three-Immortals Caves

Twenty km north of Kashgar is one of the area's few traces of the flowering of Buddhism, the Three-Immortals (San Xian) Caves, three grottoes high on a sandstone cliff, in one of which you can make out some peeling frescoes. The cliff is too sheer to climb, so it's a bit of a disappointment. CTS's half-day trip to San Xian is cheapest at about Y50 for four or five people in a Land Cruiser.

## Ha Noi & Mor Pagoda

At the end of a jarring 35km drive north-east of town are the ruins of Ha Noi, a Tang dynasty town built in the 7th century and abandoned in the 12th. Little remains but a great solid pyramid-like structure and the huge Mor 'Pagoda' or stupa. CTS or Kashgar Travel Agency will take you to Ha Noi on a half-day excursion for about Y25 per person.

## Pigeon Swap

You may notice flocks of birds wheeling over the city, signalled from house-tops with flags, whistles or hoots. Pigeon-raising is popular here, and on warm evenings there is a quiet pigeon market *(keptey bazari)* in Id Kah Square, where young men buy and sell birds by the light of oil lamps and candles.

## Places to Stay

Accommodation is tighter on the days preceding the Sunday market than afterward. Off-season, or for stays of more than a few days, or for students, you may be able to coax some discounts. No hotel in Kashgar accepted credit cards at the time of research. Except at very bottom-end places, Chinese-style squat loos are a thing of the past.

**Bottom End** Hotels currently uninterested in foreigners include the *Oasis*, *West City*, *Cao Hu*, *Wuzi* and *Labor Union*, and the *Jiaotong Lüshe* (or *Traffic Hotel*) at the long-distance bus station.

The *Chini Bagh Hotel* (Chinese: Qini-wake; ☎ 282 2103) is a five storey tower where the British consulate's front gate used to be. Triples/quads with shower are Y30/25 per bed. Clean doubles with shower in the main building are Y120; quieter ones with TV in the annex are Y180. The complex has Chinese and Uyghur restaurants and a coffee shop. At the rear is the original consular house, now tarted up as VIP suites.

The *Seman Hotel* ('si-MAAN'; ☎ 282 2147; fax 282 2861) is a 500 bed complex in three buildings and three one-storey blocks (the latter are all that remain of the old Russian consulate). Dorms of two to six beds, some with old Russian bathtubs, are

Y20 per person. Doubles with bath range from Y100 to Y280. Hot water is unpredictable, room security is dubious and 2nd floor rooms are above a karaoke bar. For Y10 you can use the murky outdoor swimming pool.

Across the road (on the site of a building bombed by militants in 1993) the government-owned *Overseas Chinese Hotel* (☎ 283 3262) has dorm beds for Y25, doubles and triples with bath, TV and telephone for a negotiable Y100 and up, but medieval management and plumbing.

At the *Tian Nan Hotel*, on Renmin Dong Lu near the long-distance bus station, doubles/triples are Y60/50 per bed. Showers are communal and hot water unreliable. The *Renmin Hotel* (☎ 282 3373), on the corner of Renmin Dong Lu and Jiefang Nan Lu, has small, dreary doubles with telephone, TV and bath, overpriced at Y190.

**Middle** The *Kashgar Hotel* (☎ 282 2367/8; fax 282 4679), also called Kashgar Guesthouse, is a spacious, dusty 200 room compound with Chinese and Uyghur restaurants and a beer garden. Carpeted doubles with telephone and hot shower are Y200, or Y250 with TV and bathtub. Quads with bath and TV are good value at Y200. The drawback is that it's 3km east of the centre, although taxis (about Y10 to the centre) and motorcycles linger at the gate. The No 10 bus goes to Id Kah and back, or you can rent a bike.

The high-rise tower in Chini Bagh's front yard is the *Kashgar-Gilgit International Hotel* (☎ 282 4173; fax 282 3842), a joint venture between CITS and Gilgit's Northern Areas Trading Cooperative. It's poor value for tourists; comfortable but damp doubles with bath are Y208.

**Top End** Kashgar is sprouting gaudy new hotels aimed at Chinese *nouveaux riche and PLA officers. One of the smartest is the Qian Hai* (☎ 282 2922), off the street at Renmin Xi Lu 48, with plush doubles with telephone, TV and bath from Y440, and a clean restaurant.

## Places to Eat

**Cheap & Quick** The pavement along Shengli Lu north of Renmin Xi Lu overflows in late afternoon and evening with Chinese, Hui (Chinese Muslim) and Uyghur stalls offering good food at minuscule prices. Hygiene is sometimes dubious, but you can't go wrong dipping your own spoon into hot laghman or jiaozi (dumplings in boiling broth). Check out huo guo, a tasty mini-casserole of noodles, vegetables or meat served up in colder weather, which looks pretty safe if it's on the boil. You might also find plov, mutton shashlyk or meatballs in broth.

**Chinese Food** Across from the Seman Hotel are *John's Cafe* and the *Oasis Cafe*, with big quasi-Chinese menus from which you can satisfy a raging hunger for under Y15 (they also do chips and adequate western breakfast, and John's whips up 'Kashgar pizza' and good desserts, in a 'street cafe' atmosphere). A more traditional Chinese restaurant is the *Tian Nan*, around the corner from the hotel of the same name; the sign says 'Han Dining Hall'. Some glitzier versions are in a row at the south end of Shengli Lu. Figure at least Y40 per person for a blow-out Chinese meal.

**Uyghur Food** The *Old City Restaurant*, beside the Overseas Chinese Hotel, has good Uyghur (and Chinese) food at local prices (Y5 to Y10 per dish). There's no English

menu and little English among staff, so ordering is a struggle unless you go for Uyghur standards like laghman or chuchureh. Or try fentang, a savoury Hui soup of meat, vegetables, rice noodles and garlic. The *Traffic Hotel* has a surprisingly good, clean Uyghur restaurant, where a meal is about Y30, though zero English is spoken.

The *Chini Bagh*, *Seman* and *Kashgar* hotels have clean Muslim dining halls where you can eat fixed Uyghur meals during limited hours. Most other Uyghur eateries seem uninterested in western customers, hygiene is marginal and your meal is likely to be accompanied by kung fu videos. 'Muslim Restaurant' on many grotty places just means no pork is used.

For information on Uyghur dishes, see Food in the Facts for the Visitor chapter.

**Self-Catering** The best way to eat vegetarian is to self-cater. A small vegetable market on Shengli Lu, and an impromptu one outside the bus station, have fresh fruit and vegetables, hard-boiled eggs (usually dyed red), steamed yams and yellow figs. Early in the morning, bakeries churn out stout nan bread (the flat ones are *ak nan*, the bagels *gzhde*). Department stores may have dried or preserved fruit, biscuits, sweets, peanut butter, bulk honey and nuts. Dried fruit isn't always clean; soaking it in boiling water reduces (but doesn't eliminate) the risk of illness.

Yoghurt is available in insipid, sweetened, drinkable tubs made in Kashgar. But Uyghur women still sell the real thing – thick, tasty yoghurt – in ceramic bowls for under Y1, around 8 to 9 am (Beijing time) in the bazaar and the streets near the Seman and Chini Bagh hotels. Bring your own spoon and scrape away the top crust.

---

### Mongolian Hot-Pot

Everybody claims they can make you Mongolian-style hot-pot (shuan yan rou). The best (though not the cheapest) is still at its original home, the Yan Jin Restaurant (no English sign, but a red doorway) on Renmin Xi Lu. In the middle of your table a brass pot heated by a gas fire keeps broth nearly boiling. You add herbs and salt and dip in rice noodles, cabbage and meat slivers till they cook, and drink the broth afterward – a great group meal, though a bit hot for midsummer. The cost depends on the ingredients you order. Vegetarian versions are possible too. ∎

---

**Alcohol** Local and Beijing beer is available in non-Uyghur restaurants, and department stores carry beer, Chinese wine, brandy and white lightning (a potent rice liquor). A regional favourite is wine from Turfan – red or white, both of them sickly sweet like sherry.

## Things to Buy

**Books** The Xinhua Bookshop on Jiefang Bei Lu has everything from English primers to Stalin posters, as well as maps of the Kashgar region, China and the world, in Chinese or Uyghur.

**Film & Processing** You can get western-brand print film and Chinese black & white, plus some western E6 slide film, in department stores and a growing number of shops and kiosks. Colour print processing is available but of poor quality.

**Souvenirs** For serious shopping go to the bazaar; Sunday market prices tend to be higher. The citizens of Kashgar have been selling things for 2000 years, so be ready to bargain. It helps to listen in on what local people pay (a good reason to learn Uyghur numbers).

Look for hats, copper/brass ware and handicrafts along the south side of Id Kah Mosque. On the road south to the post office are dowry chests, brightly painted cradles and hardware of every kind. Uyghur knives with colourfully inlaid handles are a big favourite with tourists but don't try to fly out of Kashgar with them in your hand luggage!

The bazaar has a depressing lineup of snow leopard pelts. Aside from the moral issue of buying the skins of an endangered species, bear in mind that you may not be able to import such items into your own country.

Hotel gift shops have convenient selections of outrageously overpriced souvenirs.

**Musical Instruments** Beautiful long-necked stringed instruments run the gamut from junk to collector's items. They include the two-string *dutar*, larger three-string *khomuz*, small *tambur* and elaborately shaped *ravap* with five strings and a lizard-skin sounding board. The small reed horn is a *sunai* or *surnai*. A *dab* is a type of tambourine. Two shops on the street north from the post office sell these plus miniature tourist versions.

**Gold** An arcade of goldsmiths is just south-west of Id Kah Mosque. At the rear of some you can see young apprentices at work making jewellery.

**Carpets** There are a few dealers in the bazaar and some bargains in small shops, but most have moved out to the Sunday market pavilion. Regionally, the best carpets are said to be in Khotan.

## Getting There & Away – Air

So far, the only place you can fly to/from is Ürümqi, in a Russian-made Tu-154 jet, for Y1270. There are no discounts. Flights go once or twice a day. Try to book at least a week ahead in summer, at the Xinjiang Airways ticket office (☎ 282 2113) at 49 Jiefang Nan Lu.

These flights are sometimes cancelled because of wind or sandstorms (in which case you could easily spend less money and arrive sooner on a fast bus). If yours is cancelled, just show up for the next flight and you get priority; there's no need to change the ticket (but you must change any ticket for a connecting flight out of Ürümqi).

You can buy tickets here for other domestic flights too. Runway improvements and international connections are on the cards.

## Getting There & Away – Land

**Pakistan** The starting point for the 500km bus trip to Sost is the Chini Bagh Hotel. At the time of research a ticket was Y270, from the customs shed beside the hotel (open daily from 9.30 am to 1.30 pm and 4 to 8 pm, Beijing time). Departure is officially 10 am Beijing time, but usually more like 10 am local time. Landslides in the Ghez Valley can cancel departures at any time of year but especially in July and August.

Bring water, snacks and warm clothes, as nights can be cold in any season. Sit on the east side for the overall best views. Everything that goes on top of the bus is customs-inspected before departure and then locked up for the journey, so carry on whatever you want for the overnight at Tashkurgan, plus whatever you declared to customs on entering China.

An alternative is to hire a Land Cruiser or minibus to Sost – still a two day trip, though you might do it in one long day. All the agencies listed in the Information section earlier in this chapter can arrange it, eg Y800 to Y1000 per person for four in a Land Cruiser, possibly more when demand is high, eg the Monday after Sunday market. If you have enough friends to fill it, a minibus is even cheaper.

**Ürümqi** You can make the 1480km trip to Ürümqi in a nonstop, soft-seat or 'half-sleeper' coach (Uyghur: *ali mashina*; Chinese: *haohuache*) for Y273, or an upper/lower berth in a sleeper coach (Uyghur: *qarvatlik mashina*; Chinese: *wopoche*) for Y380/439 respectively, in 36 hours. You can also go in an ordinary bus (Uyghur: *adetki mashina*; Chinese: *putongche*) in three days, with grim overnight stops at Aksu and Qorla, for Y233.

These are foreigners' prices, though by the time you read this China's abolition of two-tier bus prices may finally have taken hold in Kashgar. At the time of research you could already pay local price *from* Ürümqi, or in Khotan for fast buses from there to Ürümqi.

All depart daily from the long-distance bus station – ordinary and soft-seat buses at 11.30 am, 3 and 9 pm, and sleepers at 9 am, 1.30 and 6 pm (Beijing time). Tickets are sold up to three days ahead, at window Nos 5, 6, 7 and 8 at the station or more expensively through CITS or CTS. Sleepers sell out quickly. There have been instances of theft and pack-slashing at the bus station, so keep an eye on your bags.

A railway line is on the way, projected to link Kashgar and Ürümqi as early as the year 2000.

**Kyrgyzstan** Chinese border formalities take place at a new checkpost, nicknamed Topa ('dust'), 60km south of the Torugart Pass. You must have a Kyrgyzstan visa (nearest source: Delhi or Beijing). Chinese border officials may insist that you have a special Torugart permit as well. Don't ask at Kash-

gar PSB, who may just say you can't cross the Torugart at all.

KMA, CITS, CTS and John Hu (see Information) can get the permit (but not a visa) and take you as far as the top of the pass, from where it's straightforward to hitch a truck into Kyrgyzstan. For those entering China they can also arrange, via Kyrgyz partners, to confirm the permit and meet you at the pass. For four people in a Land Cruiser, permits included, CITS and KMA wanted about Y1100 per person, CTS and John Hu under Y500, plus fax or telephone costs.

A Chinese outfit runs a bus between Kashgar and Bishkek, though the operation seems flaky. We were told a bus departs every Tuesday morning but when we appeared, they said 'er...next Tuesday'. The office (☎ 282 6693) is upstairs at the Wuzi Hotel (Wuzi binguan), a block south of the post office. Tickets are Y1400, but it might be wise not to buy one until you see a bus being loaded! Little English is spoken, but 'bus to Bishkek' is *Bishkeke avtobusi* in Uyghur, and the Chinese characters for this are:

# 我去比什凯克

Some travellers have hitched out on their own without a permit. Get an early start: the border is only open until noon, Beijing time. You might bag a ride in a truck if you wait north of People's Hospital, but all goods get shifted to Kyrgyz trucks at Topa; or you can hire a Y100 taxi to Topa. There, ignore the Kyrgyz drivers offering to take you to Bishkek for US$500, and instead get on the Chinese shuttle bus to the pass. On the Kyrgyz side you'll find taxi and truck drivers who'll take you for US$20 per person to Naryn (from where a public bus is US$4 to Bishkek) or all the way to Bishkek for US$50. You're highly unlikely to *enter* China this easily.

For more on the Kashgar to Bishkek journey and paperwork, see Kashgar by Train & Bus in the Getting There & Away chapter, and pick up a copy of Lonely Planet's *Central Asia*.

**Other Buses** Most other buses depart from the long-distance bus station. Ticket window

Nos 1 to 4 are for Yengisar, Yarkand and Yecheng (Qarghillik); 5 to 8 are for Khotan, Tashkurgan and Ürümqi. A bus stand by People's Park is for local and regional buses and motor-rickshaws; another regional bus stand is just out on the road to Tashkurgan.

**Hitching** You might hitch a lift between Kashgar and Tashkurgan, but expect waits of anything from hours to days. You won't save much money, as drivers expect something equivalent to the bus fare. From Tashkurgan to Pakistan you'll probably have to wait for an empty seat on a bus. Hitching to Kyrgyzstan is possible; see Kyrgyzstan in this section.

**Bicycle** At least two Uyghur shops on Jiefang Bei Lu sell Chinese mountain bikes for the equivalent of US$60-100. We met a traveller who had bought one, cycled across the Khunjerab and sold it in Karimabad at no loss. See the Getting Around chapter about cycling between Kashgar and Pakistan.

**Getting Around**
**To/From the Airport** A Y8 bus leaves from the Xinjiang Airways ticket office 2½ hours before each flight departure, and one meets each incoming flight. along with swarms of overpriced vans and underpowered motor-rickshaws. A taxi is about Y30. Local bus (not minibus) No 2 goes from the stand by People's Park to the airport all day long.

Airport' is *aydrum* in Uyghur, *feijichang* in Chinese.

**Other Local Transport** A few local minibus routes are handy, as noted elsewhere in the text, though none run through the town centre. The fare depends on distance travelled but is nowhere more than about Y1. Taxis and sidecar motorcycles hang out at tourist hotels. Snarling two-stroke motor-rickshaws have appeared too, and although cheaper are uncomfortable for long trips.

**Bicycle Rental** One gear clunkers can be hired outside Chini Bagh for Y2 per hour or Y20 per day, or at the Kashgar Hotel for Y3 per hour. A deposit of several hundred yuan is required; don't leave your passport instead, as some ask you to do. Be sure your bike comes with a lock. Note that riding can be hazardous in Kashgar's undisciplined traffic.

**AROUND KASHGAR**
**Artush**
Artush or Artux (Chinese: Atushi), an hour's ride north-east of Kashgar, is a Kyrgyz market town and the centre of Kyzylsu Kyrgyz Autonomous County. It has a large bazaar, heavy on cloth and clothing. It's famous locally for figs, best in late summer or early autumn. Also here is the 10th century tomb of Sultan Sutuq Bughra Khan of the Qarakhan dynasty, the first local ruler to convert to Islam.

Local Kashgar minibus No 9 passes the Seman and Chini Bagh hotels on its way to the end of the line near People's Hospital, where you can get a regional minibus to Artush for about Y20. The official foreigners' hotel is *Kejou Binguan*.

## Yarkand & Khotan

These and other towns south-east of Kashgar were stops on a Silk Road branch along the south side of the Takla Makan Desert, and from time to time were also little mini-kingdoms. Yarkand, four hours from Kashgar, has a small indoor Sunday bazaar.

The craftspeople of Khotan were celebrated throughout Asia for their rugs, silk and carved jade, and to some extent still are. The 4th century Chinese pilgrim Fa Hsien described Khotan as a highly developed centre of Buddhism, with no fewer than 14 large monasteries. Khotan, 12 hours from Kashgar by bus, has a Sunday market to rival Kashgar's, smaller but without the tourists.

**Places to Stay** Hotels are pretty spartan. In Yarkand the *Shache Binguan* (Hotel Yarkand) has dorm beds for Y20. A small hotel with no English sign, beside the Altun Darvaza gate into the old town, has beds for under Y10.

The official tourist hotel in Khotan is the *Hetian Binguan* (Hotel Khotan), and beside the bus station is a small hotel called *Bakht Meymonkhanasi* (no English sign) with beds for under Y10.

**Getting There & Away** From Kashgar's station, buses go frequently to Yarkand for Y29. One bus goes daily at 9 am (Beijing time) to Khotan for Y87. When buying tickets use the Chinese names: Shache for Yarkand, and Hetian for Khotan.

## KASHGAR TO KARA KUL

To Chinese, the road from Kashgar to the Pakistan border is the China-Pakistan Highway (Zhong-Pa Gong Lu). After 80km across the flats and a sharp 70km climb, it runs for 250km to the border in a high valley through the eastern Pamirs. This is a region

of sublime scenery and weather extremes, a 2000-year-old passage for trade, plunder and religious ideas, and a geopolitical vortex even now.

As you leave Kashgar, the main attraction, rising from the plain to the west, is the luminous rampart of the Pamirs. An hour down the road, through gauntlets of dusty poplars, is a food stop (a pretty silly place for one, whichever direction you're headed) at **Upal** (Chinese: Wupa'er). Three km off the road here is the small tomb of Mahmud Kashgari, an 11th century scholar famous for writing the first dictionary of Turkic languages (see the boxed text).

Most settlements on the Kashgar plain are Uyghur. Most from the Ghez canyon to Kara Kul are Kyrgyz.

An hour and a half from Kashgar you enter the canyon of the Ghez River (Uyghur: Ghez Darya), with wine-red sandstone walls at its lower end. The scattered adobe houses are the same colour, and during heavy rainstorms the Ghez River itself can run red. The white giant to the south is a shoulder of Mt Kongur, at 7719m the highest peak near the road until you reach Pakistan's Hunza Valley.

**Ghez** itself is a lonely military checkpoint, plus a few shops and tea shops. Photographing soldiers or buildings here might result in

---

### Mahmud Kashgari

Mahmud Kashgari was born in the 11th century into an aristocratic family at Barskhan (or Barskoön) on the shore of Lake Issyk-Kul in present-day Kyrgyzstan; museums there refer to him as Mahmud Barskhani. According to legend he was the only family survivor of a vicious Qarakhan court struggle, and took to wandering, all the while gathering information on the traditions, customs and speech of the peoples he encountered. In Baghdad in 1072-74 he compiled his notes into *Divan Lughat at-Turk* (A Glossary of Turkish Dialects), an Arabic encyclopedia-dictionary of Turkic speech, including specimens of pre-Islamic poetry. The original manuscript has never been found, but a 15th century Persian copy was discovered in this century in Istanbul. ■

confiscated film. Upstream the canyon grows immense, steep and lifeless, forbidding even on a sunny day. The road is cut into sheer walls, or inches across huge tilted boulder fields. A hot spring is inside a plain brick building by the river, near the top of the canyon.

At the top of the canyon, two to three hours above the Kashgar plain, the landscape changes abruptly. The Ghez seems to lose its way in a vast wet plain ringed with white sand dunes, a strangely beautiful spot that locals call Kumtagh (sand mountain). Travellers who have stopped here and headed up the Muji Valley to the north-west have been sent back by mounted police – probably because of the copper mines about 60km up the valley.

The terrain is typical of the Pamirs: high, broad, treeless valleys strung between glacier-rounded mountains, with rivers often pooling into shallow lakes. The word *pamir* refers to pasturage, the valleys' main historical use. The corridor north-west to Muji and south to the Pakistan border is a pamir valley, the **Sarykol Valley**. The rampart of snowy peaks along the east side is the Sarykol or Taghdumbash Pamir.

Just to the south, near the Highway bridge over the Kengshuwar River, is a yellow obelisk from the days of China's Cultural Revolution; it reads 'Long Live Chairman Mao'. Past the bridge, at the foot of Mt Kongur, is **Bulunkul Dobey**, an outpost of the larger Kyrgyz settlement of Bulunkul, 3700m above sea level. An hour south of this is Kara Kul (or Karakol Lake) – properly Lesser Kara Kul, as there's a bigger lake of the same name 150km north-west in Tajikistan – and two small sister lakes across the road, Besekh Kul and Shor Kul.

## KARA KUL

Many travellers come to Kashgar hoping to rub shoulders with Kyrgyz nomads in the pastures around Kara Kul (Chinese: Kalakuli Hu). This is one of the most beautiful places in western China, the deep blue waters *(kara kul* is Uyghur for 'black lake') nestled between two Pamir giants, 7546m Muztagh

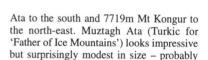

**Permit for Kara Kul?**
Officially Kara Kul is a restricted area, for which you need an Alien Travel Permit, even for a day trip. However, at the time of research nobody was checking them, nor discouraging contacts between locals and foreigners. Nevertheless, PSB is pleased to sell you a permit, in Kashgar for Y10 or Y20 and in Tashkurgan for Y50! Cyclists heading south through the Ghez checkpoint were asked, 'Kalakuli?'; those who said 'yes' had to fork over Y10 for a permit. ■

Ata to the south and 7719m Mt Kongur to the north-east. Muztagh Ata (Turkic for 'Father of Ice Mountains') looks impressive but surprisingly modest in size – probably because all the available vantage points are themselves over 3700m!

This is officially a restricted area, for which you need a travel permit, but see the boxed text.

There are several Kyrgyz summer villages in the area; the nearest, just south of the lake, is Subash. You can walk around the lake in half a day; the downstream outflow can be forded at the village nearby. At Subash or elsewhere you can arrange an excursion by horse to high pastures *(jailuu)*, about three hours from the lake at the foot of Muztagh Ata, for about Y150/day.

With a tent you could spend days at the lake or on the flanks of Muztagh Ata. To walk up to Muztagh Ata base camp it's easiest to head south on the highway for about 14km, then east for 2km to Edara village (which some maps also call Subash). From there it's a climb of about 15km to the base camp, at 4550m. Be prepared for the worst kind of weather, no matter what it looks like when you start.

The lake is at 3700m and nights are below freezing even in summer; one camper awoke to find snow on the ground at lakeside in the middle of August! Beware also of summer sandstorms, which can rise in a minute and disappear as fast. Go between late May and early October; at other times the whole place may be deserted.

## Places to Stay & Eat

Unless you make advance arrangements, the main alternative to camping is a small, spartan hotel by the lake, with mock-up yurts and a few rooms, decent but overpriced meals and malodorous toilets. A bed is Y40 if they smell a tour group, otherwise negotiable. Campers and cyclists who opt instead to pitch their own tents should move 15 minutes off around the lake to avoid hassles.

The yurt site has become a bit of a tourist trap. On arrival you may be surrounded by Kyrgyz trying to sell you everything from stones to a bed in their yurt. In Subash or elsewhere you might trade tea, salt, postcards etc for bread, yoghurt or yak's milk. KMA runs a food tent at Muztagh Ata base camp during climbing season (July-August).

## Getting There & Away

Local Kashgar to Tashkurgan buses will stop at Kara Kul, though some travellers have had trouble flagging one down again when they were ready to return or move on. You can catch the bus to Kashgar if it stops to let tourists take photos of the lake. Wait to buy your onward fare on the onward bus, as drivers like cash in the hand and will probably charge you local price. Seats are also available as far as Kara Kul on the bus to Pakistan, on a standby basis for Y43. You may be asked to show a travel permit.

CTS and Kashgar Travel Agency offer Kara Kul day trips, one for under Y300 per person with four in a Land Cruiser; CITS charges about Y500, with a guide and lunch. An overnight adds at least Y200 per person for bed, dinner and vehicle charges. KMA can arrange more interesting trips, such as an overnight at Subash with local walks, a night or two at Muztagh Ata base camp, or various five to seven day treks on the mountain.

## KARA KUL TO TASHKURGAN

On the high (around 4000m), very broad ground west of Muztagh Ata, called the **Subash Plateau** (Subash Daban), the Highway makes its closest approach (about 10km) to Tajikistan. At the turn of the century this area was still in dispute, never having been properly mapped. Two hours south of Kara Kul is a military checkpoint at **Kekyor**, lately looking abandoned. From there across the marshy **Tagharma Basin** it's about an hour to Tashkurgan.

Settlements from Kara Kul to Kekyor are Kyrgyz, those on to Tashkurgan are Sarykoli Tajik. One question that comes repeatedly to mind here is: How can sheep graze on gravel?

## TASHKURGAN

In the Uyghur language, *tash kurgan* means 'stone fortress'. The ruins of a huge mud-brick fort still stand on the edge of town, and although this one is estimated to be about 600 years old, local lore says Tashkurgan has been a citadel for over 2300 years. The Greek philosopher-scientist Ptolemy (90 to 168 AD) mentioned Tashkurgan in his *Guide to Geography* as a stop on the road to China. The Chinese Buddhist pilgrim Hsuan Tsang wrote about its fortress in the 7th century, when it was the furthest frontier outpost of the Tang dynasty.

Tashkurgan has little else to offer, although if you're coming from Pakistan, you'll delight in (a) public conversations with women, and (b) beer (which may knock you back considerably at this elevation).

This is the site of the Chinese customs and immigration post. It's also the administrative centre of Tashkurgan Tajik Autonomous County, stretching from Muztagh Ata to the border and home to most of China's Tajiks. Tashkurgan is about 3200m above sea level and 290km from Kashgar.

## Orientation & Information

Tashkurgan has just two main roads, with a small bazaar on a side street between them. Customs and immigration are south of town. Your bus (if you're southbound) or a free shuttle bus (if you're northbound) will take you the 500m to/from the bus station – though you could walk there and back repeatedly in the time it usually takes for the bus to set off.

The Bank of China at customs is the only place in Tashkurgan to change money,

Tashkurgan

To Kashgar

0    200    400 m
Approximate Scale

Old Town

Fort

Steps

1 Pamir Hotel
2 Schoolyard
3 Bakery
4 Cinema
5 Hospital
6 School
7 Friendship Restaurant
8 Dragon Restaurant
9 Huanche Restaurant
10 Bakery
11 Ice Mountain Hotel
12 Jiaotong Binguan
13 Bus Station
14 Radio Mast
15 Public Security Bureau (PSB)
16 Post Office
17 Vegetable Market
18 Bank of China
19 China Customs & Immigration

To Pakistan

accepting cash in most major currencies (but not travellers cheques). It's open daily from 8 am to 2 pm and 5 to 8 pm (Beijing time).

The PSB is south of the bus station. Reception for the foreign affairs section is inside the right-hand entrance, and is open from 10 am to 2 pm and 5 to 8 pm (Beijing time).

**Fort**

Tashkurgan's one attraction is the massive, crumbling fort north-east of town, on the only hill in the Tashkurgan River's flood plain. Most of its multi-layered walls and battlements are still intact. The simplest route is from the east end of town, but a shorter one is through the schoolyard west of the Pamir Hotel or up an incongruous flight of steps to the east. Enterprising locals may demand Y5, though the whole area is open.

**Places to Stay**

You'll probably be dropped at the filthy *Jiaotong Binguan* (Transport Hotel) at the bus station, where doubles/quads are Y30/15 per bed.

The best budget bet is the *Ice Mountain Hotel* across the road, unusual in China for

RICHARD I'ANSON

RICHARD I'ANSON ROBERT MATZINGER JOHN KING

RICHARD I'ANSON

**Kashgar**
Top: The hills are alive, Xinjiang style.
Middle: Scenes from Kashgar's astonishing Sunday market.
Bottom: Close shaves at the Sunday market, Kashgar.

BERNARD NAPTHINE

ROBERT MATZINGER

ROBERT MATZINGER

## Kashgar

Top Left: Sparkles and smiles, Uyghur girls, Kashgar.
Top Right: Detail of a prayer house, Kashgar.
Bottom: Brilliantly coloured textiles illuminate Kashgar's streets.

its hospitable atmosphere (it's run by a Gojal Pakistani). Cyclists especially should read the good guestbook. Dorms are Y15 and Y20 per bed, rooms Y30 per bed. Toilets and cold-water washrooms (no showers) are communal.

Tour groups prefer the *Pamir Binguan* (or *Pamir Hotel*), where dorm beds are Y15, plain cold-water triples are Y90 and comfortable doubles with bathtub and hot water (an hour in the morning and an hour in the evening) are Y180.

### Places to Eat

The *Pamir Binguan* restaurant offers a set menu of little hot and cold dishes (Chinese or Uyghur). You can eat well for Y15 but it's easy to spend more, so check prices before you tuck in. Dinner may be accompanied by a diverting dance and music show if there are groups staying. Chinese breakfast is Y20. The *Ice Mountain Hotel* does meals from June to September.

Tashkurgan's nonhotel restaurants are like meterless taxis: agree on a price before you commit. Gouging tourists is a local sport, though you should be able to fill up for Y15-Y30. Little English is spoken so unless there's a menu, go into the kitchen and point to the raw ingredients you want. The lineup changes from year to year. Two fairly clean places are the Tajik *Friendship Restaurant*, with good laghman (even meatless if you ask) for about Y10, and the Chinese *Dragon Restaurant*. The Ice Mountain guestbook has an ongoing debate over whether the *Huanche Restaurant* is a rip-off.

Several bakeries open early enough to beat the bus, with hot nan bread and free tea. Fruit stalls have melons in late summer.

In 1987-88 hepatitis E was epidemic in southern Xinjiang. This is now history but Tashkurgan may still be one of the easiest places on the KKH to catch a stomach infection.

### Getting There & Away

A bus takes passengers from Sost on to Kashgar about 9.30 am (Beijing time) for Y77; locals pay about Y25, although two-tier pricing appears to be on the way out here. You can buy tickets to Kashgar the day before departure from a bus company official outside customs, or you can get one on the bus. On departure you may also be hit up for an exorbitant Y5 baggage charge. The trip takes six to seven hours.

Foreigners are not ordinarily allowed to ride anything else to Kashgar, although one customs official was offering a car the same day for Y200 per person! Hitching from Tashkurgan is also frowned upon. Further away, everybody loosens up.

Seats as far as Tashkurgan on the Kashgar to Sost bus are sold on a standby basis for Y63, but you risk finding no seat on a later bus to Sost. You can also expect a sour face from the driver, who won't have you on his customs manifest.

A public bus runs between Kashgar long-distance bus station and Tashkurgan daily except Sunday, for Y52. On their return to Kashgar these may also stop at the bus stand near the Bank of China.

### TASHKURGAN TO THE KHUNJERAB PASS

The level stretch along the Tashkurgan River to Pirali is grand and picturesque in fine weather, with muscular-looking peaks along the west side of the valley and lots of horse and camel traffic. Settlements from Tashkurgan over the Khunjerab Pass and into Gojal are Wakhi Tajik.

About an hour south of Tashkurgan is **Davdar**, the largest permanent Tajik settlement along the Highway. South of Davdar the road passes the mouth of an enormous opening westward into the Pamir – the **Mintaka Valley**, once a major Silk Road branch and historically one of the main routes to Hunza and on to Kashmir. About 75km up the Mintaka Valley, a jeep track enters Afghanistan's Wakhan Corridor.

**Pirali**, the former Chinese customs post and now just a security checkpoint, is 1½ hours from Tashkurgan at about 4100m. South of here the Pamir gradually becomes the Karakoram.

# The Khunjerab Pass & Gojal

Depending on whom you ask, *khun jerab* is Wakhi for either 'Valley of Blood' or 'Valley of the Khan'. The broad, fertile Khunjerab Pass was for centuries used by Kyrgyz and Tajik herders, until Hunza raiders and slave-traders hounded them out in the late 18th century, after which Hunza's rulers declared the area to be 'royal' pasturelands – so either version fits.

A steady trickle of horseback commerce crossed the Khunjerab (Chinese: Hong-qilapu) until the 1950s, when China-Pakistan hostility closed the border. By the mid-1960s the two countries had made amends and set to work on a road over the pass. 'Khunjerab Top' (4730m) was opened to official traffic and trade in 1982, and to tourists in 1986, though travellers had already discovered it.

The crossing is not only between countries and between watersheds (rivers flow north into the Tarim Basin and south to the Arabian Sea) but also between two of the world's major mountain ranges, the Pamir and the Karakoram. In the two to 2½ hours from Pirali to Sost the transition is evident, from rounded Pamir valleys to the deep, angular gorge of the Khunjerab River.

The Khunjerab and Ghujerab rivers merge below the Khunjerab Pass to form the Hunza River, the only stream to cut across the high spine of the Karakoram. It does so in Gojal (the historical name (still used) for the region usually described as 'upper Hunza'), which extends from the pass to where the river turns west into 'Hunza proper'. The High Karakoram is consequently more accessible here than anywhere else on the KKH. At Passu and Gulmit several major glaciers reach nearly to the Highway.

'The scenery is stern and impressive, but too gloomy and harsh to be really sublime,' wrote the British explorer Reginald Schomberg in 1935. Mountains with razor-edge summits and bare walls drop sheer to the river, and the wind drives up the valley even

**Locator & Map Index**

The external boundaries of India on this map have not been authenticated and may not be correct.

The Khunjerab Pass & Gojal p 131

Sost p 134
Afiyatabad (New Sost) p 135

Around Gulmit & Passu p 138

Gulmit p 141

### Highlights

- Highway-nudging glaciers
- The vanishing habitat of Marco Polo sheep and snow leopards
- Trekking with heart-stopping views above Passu and Gulmit
- The unparalleled hospitality of the Wakhi Tajik people

on brilliant days. But if you're fit, this is the place to climb up and get a feeling for the highlands. The clearest and most storm-free weather is in early autumn.

The Hunza River picks its way among great fans of alluvium carried down by smaller streams, and most villages are built on these fertile deposits. The larger tributaries also bring down soil and rocks, often suddenly and destructively. Huge floods periodically destroy river-front fields and orchards. In 1974 a mudslide from Shishkut Nala (a nala is a tributary canyon) backed up the Hunza River for 20km, despite Pakistan

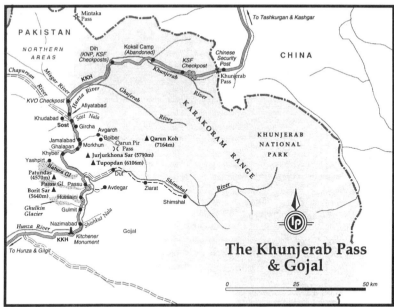

The Khunjerab Pass & Gojal

Air Force attempts to bomb it loose. The resulting lake lasted for over three years, during which time the valley practically filled up with sand and gravel, leaving it grimmer than when Schomberg saw it.

## Wildlife Conservation

The alpine region between Pirali and Dih is the only habitat of the curly-horned Marco Polo sheep, of which there are now only a few hundred in the world. The pass is also home to Himalayan ibex, golden marmot, wolf, snow leopard, the rare Tibetan wild ass and more (see the Flora & Fauna section in the Facts About the Region chapter).

Both China and Pakistan have set aside nature reserves here. On the Pakistan side is the 2270 sq km Khunjerab National Park (KNP), where officials, conservationists and local people have been struggling – mainly with each other – since its founding in 1975 (see the boxed text following). In 1984 the Chinese established the 15,000 sq km Tashkurgan nature reserve; the Highway runs within it from about Tashkurgan to the border.

## People

Like the people of Hunza proper, Gojalis are Ismaili Muslims and were for several centuries loyal subjects of the Mir of Hunza. But their Persian-influenced language is unrelated to Burushashki, the speech of Hunza (except in a few villages, eg Khudabad, Nazimabad and those of the Misgar Valley, where Burushashki predominates).

Most Gojalis are Wakhi Tajik (one of seven Tajik tribes in central Asia), descendants of nomadic herders from Afghanistan. Traditionally they have depended on the raising of sheep and yaks, and to a lesser extent on farming. They're certainly the most warm-hearted people on the KKH, with easy greetings and hospitality for both men and women visitors.

## Khunjerab National Park

The Khunjerab Pass came under the control of the *mirs* (rulers) of Hunza in the late 18th century. The mirs controlled all hunting and grazing rights there, as well as trade across the pass. In 1974, when Hunza was formally merged with Pakistan, the central government assumed control of this land.

The following year, at the urging of wildlife biologist Dr George Schaller, Prime Minister ZA Bhutto declared a swathe of grassland across the Khunjerab, Ghujerab and Shimshal valleys a national park, to protect the remaining Marco Polo sheep there. The government promised compensation to local people whose traditional grazing rights had thereby suddenly evaporated, though none was forthcoming. Little else was done until 1989, when an international workshop urged a strict ban on grazing and hunting in a 'core area' of the park.

Most local people who depend for their livelihood on grazing yaks and other animals in those valleys refused to cooperate, and the Khunjerab Village Organisation (KVO) – a coalition of Gojal communities who use the Khunjerab and Ghujerab valleys for grazing – filed suit seeking to reverse the grazing ban. The suit was eventually lost, and herders and hunters ejected, but with the help of the government's main consultant on the park, the Worldwide Fund for Nature (WWF), a process of community consultation was set in motion.

In 1992 a ground-breaking agreement was reached between the KVO and the Northern Areas administration on joint management of the park, including revenue sharing and the training and employment of local people in wildlife conservation jobs. A great deal remains to be worked out. Local mistrust is thawing only slowly (and Shimshalis still refuse to acknowledge the existence of a protected area at all), but the precedent could eventually make 'wildlife conservation with a human face' a reality in this and other parks in Pakistan.

The park extends along both sides of the KKH from the Khunjerab Pass to Sost, and along the China border, but don't look for brochures, or smartly dressed park rangers, or gift shops selling Marco Polo sheep cuddly toys just yet. About all you may see along the KKH are several community checkpoints looking for evidence of illegal hunting.

You aren't likely to see much by just hopping off the bus, and the Khunjerab Security Force (KSF) may frown on impromptu walks, since so much of the park is along the Chinese border. You might catch sight of ibex grazing near the highway very early or late in the day, in the off-season. Forget about Marco Polo sheep, as you'd probably have to trek at least three days away from the KKH to see them, and nobody is likely to give you a permit for that anyway.

The Khunjerab National Park Directorate (☎ (0572) 55061) is in Jutial (Gilgit). By 1998 WWF-Pakistan plans to open a Gilgit Conservation & Information Centre next door, with a database on Pakistan's protected areas. WWF-Pakistan's Gilgit office (☎ & fax (0572) 4127) is at PO Box 592, 543-A Shahrah-e-Quaid-e-Azam, across the road from the Tourist Cottages. WWF in Gilgit also sells the excellent *An Ecotourist's Guide to Khunjerab National Park*. ■

### Gojal Food

Gojal specialities are similar to those of Hunza (see the Hunza & Nagar chapter) but with Wakhi names. One of the best local items is wholemeal bread, available in some hotels. *Kamishdoon* (called *phitti* in Hunza) is a heavy round loaf baked under coals. *Dildungi* is a slightly risen tandoori-style flatbread. *Kulcha* is a Kashmiri-style flat-bread made with lots of milk and eggs, mainly for ceremonial occasions. *Kurutemoch* is a thick noodle soup made with dried cheese.

### ACROSS THE PASS

This region has historically been admired more for pastures than passage, and from Pirali to the top in warmer weather you'll see herds of shaggy domesticated yaks or cow-yak hybrids called dzu, and clusters of Tajik yurts.

The pass itself is long and flat. At the summit is a plaque commemorating the 1982 opening. At this point you're about 400km from Kashgar and 880km from Rawalpindi. Something besides the time zone changes at the top, namely the side of the road you drive on (China is right-hand drive, Pakistan left-hand), so it's probably a good thing that everybody stops for a photo break here!

Scattered down the Pakistan side are deserted concrete buildings – hostels for Chinese KKH workers, built in the late 1960s when the road was being laid to Gulmit. At **Koksil** the ruins of a Chinese

### Cyclists' Notes, Khunjerab Pass & Gojal

Altitude is the challenge here, not distance. Food is scarce all the way from Tashkurgan to Sost. Water is scarce from Tashkurgan to Khunjerab Top. The road is wide and fairly well maintained. Major climb southbound: 40km from Pirali to the pass. Major climbs northbound: the first 4km or so out of Ganesh; 50km from Dih to the pass, especially the last 17km of switch-backs.

**Pirali to Khunjerab Pass, about 40km** A gradually increasing grade, quite steep by the time you near the top.

**Khunjerab Pass to Sost, 85km** The road on the Pakistan side knots itself into switch-backs for 17km, then descends steeply to Dih, about 50km from the top; from there it's a gentle descent to Sost. Strong winds can make the going very hard or very easy. Abandoned KKH work camps make camping spots, and Dih has a national park resthouse where you might pitch a tent. Those without camping gear might stay the night at a road-works camp or at the KVO checkpost about 8km above Sost. The guestbook at the Mountain Refuge in Sost has current comments from cyclists.

**Sost to Passu, about 40km** A gentle downhill ride. The Hunza Dreamland Hotel at Gircha (a few km south of Sost) and the Greenland Hotel at Morkhun avoid the Sost crowds and have hot showers. Khyber, about 20km from Sost, has a small inn. Passu's Batura Inn has good 'rumour-books' with cyclists' comments.

**Passu to Gulmit, 16km** Sharp climbs include the 4km from Passu south to Yashvandan, or the 5km north from Hussaini to Yashvandan. Near Hussaini a bouldery link road climbs to a small hotel at Borit Lake; you may have to carry your steed up.

**Gulmit to Ganesh, 34km** The road is fairly level but often plagued with rockfall damage. Karimabad is a steep 2km climb on a link road a few km west of Ganesh. ∎

THE KHUNJERAB PASS & GOJAL

work camp straddle the river at a large side-canyon. Below this the valley walls are 'black, crumbling rock' (this is how the Turki words *kara koram* translate) and the river cuts through deep beds of gravel, the residue of repeated mud and rock slides.

About 50km below the top are Khunjerab Security Force (KSF) and KNP/Forestry checkposts at **Dih** (or Dhee). If you're coming from China you'll get a warm welcome. There is a *KNP Resthouse* at Dih, which might be available to the public if no officials are using it, as with other government resthouses in the Northern Areas, but booking is through the KNP Directorate in Gilgit (see the boxed text Khunjerab National Park). It's 35km from Dih to Sost, through some of the narrowest gorges on the KKH.

The Khunjerab Village Organisation (KVO) is a partner with the park administration in wildlife conservation efforts in the park. KVO also has its own 'Khunjerab Buffer Zone Wildlife Conservation Project', with volunteer wardens on the lookout for illegal hunting of Himalayan ibex, snow leopard and blue sheep, and a checkpost outside the park boundary.

### SOST & AFIYATABAD

In 1996 Pakistani customs and immigration shifted several km upstream to what is now called Afiyatabad or New Sost, though many hotels and other facilities remain at 'old' Sost. Both are frenetic, depressing strips of hotels, teashops, vehicles and men who seem to be waiting for Godot. A permanent urine smell suffuses Afiyatabad, whose scores of small shops all appear to specialise in Chinese crockery. This is not a useful place to stock up for the trip to China.

Most travellers never see the village of Sost (also spelled Sust), at 3100m on a ledge above the Highway, or the trails into Sost Nala.

### Information

The Northern Areas Transportation Company (Natco), Pakistan Tourist Development

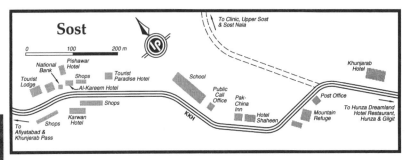

THE KHUNJERAB PASS & GOJAL

Corporation(PTDC) and other long-distance transport is at Afiyatabad.

The National Bank at Sost, open from 9 am to 1.30 pm (open to noon Friday and closed Sunday), accepts cash and travellers cheques in US$, UK£ and DM only, and buys back rupees in limited amounts (eg up to about US$100 worth). Alam Money Changer at Afiyatabad – just a shop beside the Four Brothers Hotel, open daily from 7 am to 8 pm – will do the same and buy/sell RMB; cash rates are a bit better than the bank's. The post office is near the south end of Sost.

A village clinic dispenses medications and first aid; take the track near the Mountain Refuge hotel for about 400m and turn left.

### Day Trip to the Pass
It's possible to visit Khunjerab Top as a day trip – normally two hours up and 1½ hours down. The air at 4730m is very dry, cold and thin, but it feels like the top of the world. Take lots of water and know how you're getting back down! Don't rely on passing traffic. Natco will rent you a 4WD pickup (holds five), Land Cruiser (10) or Hi-Ace minibus (14) for Rs 1500, or a Coaster (19) for Rs 3000. Be sure the heater is working; one traveller found a blizzard blowing at the top in mid-June.

### Hikes Above Sost
At the intersecting paths near the clinic, turn right through fields to upper Sost and Sost Nala. The compact houses, walled fields,

poplars, fruit orchards and the dramatic canyon are very different from the scene along the road.

If instead you go straight at the intersection, it's 3km up to a 400m irrigation tunnel dug by villagers in 1985, one of hundreds of regional self-help projects started with the aid of the Aga Khan Rural Support Programme (AKRSP, see the Economy section in the Facts about the Region chapter). From here there are several good half to full-day walks above Sost Nala, with fine views of the valley.

### Khudabad
Across the Hunza River is Khudabad village and the narrow Khudabad Nala. A bridge spans the river near Afiyatabad. A walk to the village and back takes an hour, while the nala can be a full day's trek.

### Places to Stay
Everything is overpriced, but places at Afiyatabad tend to be very negotiable; we list posted prices. Many hotels will let you pitch a tent and use their toilets and water for a fraction of the room cost. You could throw a bag down almost anywhere, except that most open space near the road is used as a toilet too!

**Bottom End** The *Mountain Refuge* (☎ 46219) at Sost is the most congenial place on either strip, with communal dinner and a 'rumour book' with travellers' tips. Dorms are Rs 50 per bed and doubles Rs 150, with squat loo

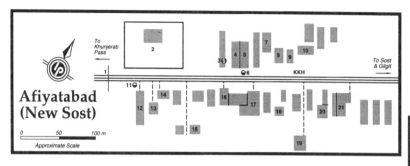

Afiyatabad
(New Sost)

0    50    100 m

Approximate Scale

**PLACES TO STAY**
4    Four Brothers Hotel
      & Restaurant
5    Fairy Land Hotel
7    Hotel Al-Mahmood
8    Siachen Hotel &
      Restaurant
12   PTDC Motel
13   Everest Inn
14   Badakhshan
      Hotel

18   GMJ Hotel & Restaurant
19   Asia Star Hotel
20   Park Hotel
21   Sky Bridge Inn

**PLACES TO EAT**
9    Fruit Stalls
10   Teahouses

**OTHER**
1    Gate

2    Customs Yard
      for trucks
3    Alam Money Changer
6    Nellum
      Transport
11   PTDC Transport
15   Immigration Office
      (temporary
      location)
16   Natco Office
17   Customs

and cold water (hot-water doubles at Rs 400 and up have plumbing you'd expect for half the price, but you can stay in a cheaper room and take a hot shower for Rs 10 or so extra).

Several places have grim doubles with squat toilet and bucket wash for under Rs 200, eg the *Al-Kareem* at Sost and the *Everest Inn*, *Fairy Land*, *Badakhshan*, *Park* and *GMJ* hotels at Afiyatabad.

**Middle** Above about Rs 300 you can expect an attached bathroom with western toilet. At Sost, the *Khunjarab Hotel* (☎ 46213) has comfortable doubles for Rs 400, but cold showers; hot ones are Rs 500. Rooms at the *Tourist Lodge* are grotty but Rs 400 gets a hot shower.

A fair deal at Afiyatabad is *Hotel Al-Mahmood*, favoured by Kashgar traders, where plain singles/doubles with hot shower are Rs 200/300. The *Asia Star Hotel* is a better choice than many, with clean, carpeted rooms for Rs 350/400. The *Four Brothers Hotel* has doubles for Rs 250.

The group-oriented *Hunza Dreamland*

*Hotel Restaurant* (☎ 46212) has Rs 35-per-bed dorms, plus doubles with western loo and cold/hot shower for Rs 250/350, but it's 2km south of Sost.

**Top End** In Afitayabad clean doubles at the group-oriented *Sky Bridge Inn* are Rs 550. Singles/doubles at the *PTDC Motel* (☎ 46240) are Rs 900/1000.

**Places to Eat**

Most hotels have basic Pakistan road food: gosht, dhal, chapatti and tea, with full-blast satellite TV. Afiyatabad has little *teahouses* with rock-bottom prices and dubious hygiene, and travellers say the *Four Brothers Restaurant* is OK.

The *Mountain Refuge* serves filling Hunza-style dinners – rice, noodle soup, vegetable and dessert for Rs 70, or with meat for Rs 110 – and western-style breakfasts. Book dinner ahead of time if you're not staying there.

THE KHUNJERAB PASS & GOJAL

### Getting There & Away

**Kashgar** Natco does the four hour trip to Tashkurgan, and a Chinese bus takes you from there to Kashgar the next morning. Note that landslides and snow can cancel these trips even in summer. It's a good idea to carry a day's water and snacks.

Get a Tashkurgan ticket the day before or on the morning. Natco (open 7 am to 7 pm) runs vehicles to suit the size of the crowd – 4WD pickup, Land Cruiser, minibus or bus. The price at the time of research was Rs 950 per person in any vehicle, and tourists pay the same as locals. Since prices are uniform, you won't save much by booking your own. PTDC mainly hires minibuses for groups, though they'll take a minimum of five people (but not Pakistanis!) at passenger rates.

A Natco vehicle swings by the tourist hotels in old Sost around 8 to 8.30 am, PTDC will do the same, and the Mountain Refuge offers free transport to/from Customs on request. Vehicles are usually loaded by 9 am, but departure awaits Customs and Immigration formalities, usually between 10 am and noon. You might hitch to Sost from Passu in time to depart the same morning, though it's easier to stay the night in Sost.

**Gojal, Hunza & Gilgit** Most transport south leaves early in the morning. A Natco bus leaves daily for Gilgit about 5 am (summer) and 7.30 am (winter), taking five hours and stopping everywhere in between. The Gilgit fare is Rs 80, paid on board. The bus doesn't go to Karimabad but stops on the KKH at Ganesh.

Nellum Transport goes to Gilgit for Rs 100 from in front of the Fairy Land Hotel at 9 am and 4 pm, but doesn't stop en route. You can hire a Suzuki (holds eight to 10), eg to Passu for Rs 400 or Karimabad for Rs 800, but not much further; or a Land Cruiser from Natco, eg Rs 1000 to Karimabad or Rs 2500 to Gilgit.

Passu is six to seven hours away on foot.

### Getting Around

There's no regular transportation between Afiyatabad and Sost. A Suzuki for hire is about Rs 50. There are even a few, pricier taxis.

### MORKHUN

Gojalis in the villages north from Khyber sometimes distinguish their turf as 'upper Gojal', whose people are directly descended from Wakhi Tajiks of the present Wakhan Corridor region. By contrast, they say, those beyond Passu are a mixed bag of Tajiks from Badakhshan and migrants from Hunza and further south.

Most Gojalis are Wakhi Tajik, the most warm-hearted people on the KKH.

The Boiber Valley above Morkhun (10km south of Sost) is probably the most historical part of Gojal, although trekkers and mountaineers are about the only foreigners who have heard of it. Tajiks from Wakhan arrived in the Sost area but fled into this valley from the forces of Taj Mughal, the 16th century Ismaili ruler of Yasin, Punial and Gilgit. There they founded Avgarch, coming down in summer to till fields along the Hunza River. After Taj Mughal's little empire collapsed, Gojal came under the control of the mirs of Hunza, and Avgarchis settled in the Hunza River valley, building a fort at Gircha. For more on Gojal's history under the mirs, see the Hunza & Nagar chapter.

Nowadays in the 'Avgarchi' villages along the KKH (Gircha, Jamalabad, Morkhun and Ghalapan) there is talk of eco-friendly tourist development, with proposals for hotels and homestays, a road to Boiber, glacier trips by horse and yak, and more. So far, though, it feels pretty remote.

### Valley Walk

Avgarch (3200m), on a footpath up the rugged, boulder-strewn Boiber Valley, is probably Gojal's oldest permanent Tajik settlement. If you're fairly fit you can reach Avgarch and return to Morkhun (2750m) in about six hours, including rest time, or push on to Boiber village and return in about eight hours. Stay away on rainy or windy days, when rocks hurtle down scree fields like artillery shells.

From Jamalabad, adjacent to Morkhun, a link road climbs the north side of the valley. You cross the river twice, then climb out of the valley to Avgarch – either doubling back at the second bridge to Yasinband, a hair-raising vertical ascent on ledges and juniper-wood steps, or carrying on up-valley for ¾ hour to a marginally less perilous climb.

Avgarch has about 100 houses, an ancient mosque, and two small forts dating from perhaps the 18th century, when Avgarchis had to defend themselves from Kyrgyz raiders. Villagers winter over here, busy just keeping themselves and their animals alive. In spring, some descend to tend crops at Morkhun and take their children to school, while the rest till fields here.

It's another ¾ hour across the valley to the smaller, weather-beaten settlement of Boiber (3500m) on the south side of the valley. From here it's possible to trek over the Qarun Pir pass to Dut in Shimshal Valley (the traditional access to Shimshal from the Hunza Valley), or up-valley toward the Qarun Koh glacier. Return along the Boiber stream, or along livestock trails high on the south wall of the valley, with fine views of Avgarch but several muscle-straining side-nala crossings.

A guide is recommended, even on a day trip, not only for safety – at dangerous scree-field crossings and in the final climb to Avgarch – but for potential local hospitality. Ask at the Dreamland Hotel or at the 'Khunjrab S F' shop front just south of the hotel, the office of the Khunjerab Students Welfare Federation (an early actor in the push for eco-friendly development here) and their unlicensed but locally competent travel agency, Qarun Tour & Trek.

### Places to Stay & Eat

The gloomy *Greenland Hotel* at the north end of Jamalabad has serviceable doubles with hot shower for a negotiable Rs 250. At Khyber, the *Khyber Inn* has dorm beds for Rs 60 and spartan triples with squat loo and hot water for Rs 200. Both serve basic meals for guests.

### Getting There & Away

The only way we know to visit Morkhun is by hitching or by hopping off a Sost to Gilgit bus.

### MORKHUN TO PASSU

As the valley widens north of Passu the KKH crosses a makeshift girder bridge over the **Batura Glacier** stream. The glacier itself nearly reaches the road, though its dirty grey ice looks more like rocky soil. This is one of the Karakoram's larger glaciers, extending 60km back into the cluster of 6000m to 7000m-plus peaks called the Batura Muztagh. It advances and retreats from year to year. In 1976 it ground up the original

Chinese bridge, which was then replaced by the present 'permanently temporary' girder bridge.

East of this bridge is the yawning **Shimshal Valley**, once one of the remotest places in the old state of Hunza. It was from upper Shimshal, even as late as the 1890s, that raiders harried caravans heading to Kashmir. In 1985 an Aga Khan-funded valley road was begun, that will eventually reach 45km to Shimshal village. At the time of research it had arrived at Dut, 15km or 1¼ hours by jeep from Passu, from where trekkers can reach Ziarat in one day and Shimshal on the second (take a Shimshali guide). The conservative Shimshalis are not uniformly thrilled at the arrival of tourism.

Ten minutes from the bridge over the Batura stream, at the north end of Passu, is a windy plain full of broken-down buildings. From 1968 until 1979 this was a camp for Chinese KKH workers.

### PASSU
Sitting between the black Batura Glacier and the white Passu Glacier, this is the place to stop if you like to walk. Passu, at 2400m, is the base for some dramatic hikes and longer treks.

Although it's one of the oldest settlements in Hunza-Gojal, a kind of geographical curse has prevented Passu from growing into a town. As glaciers periodically dammed the Shimshal River and then broke, floods have gradually torn away Passu's river-front land. The 1974 mudslide at Shishkut Nala created a lake that submerged parts of the village and choked the valley with sand and gravel. At one time Passu had extensive orchards, a polo field and nearly five times its present population, mostly on land that is no longer there.

The highest point of the 'cathedral' ridge across the river is 6106m Tupopdan (Wakhi for 'hot rock', because in winter its slopes shed the snow quickly). On lower slopes are messages, spelled out with painted rocks, dating from the Aga Khan's 1987 visit to Gojal.

The village is below the Passu Inn, where buses usually stop. Buses will also drop or collect you at hotels further out on the KKH.

### Tajik Cultural Museum
For Rs 30 you can see a modest exhibit of old Tajik tools, houseware, furnishings and clothes in a traditional Passu house. Ask at the giftshop opposite the Passu Inn.

### Hikes
No excursion longer than a day should be undertaken without sound advice and weather information, and preferably a reliable guide. Foreigners who think of these trips as dawdles frequently get into trouble here. For budget-minded help finding a guide, ask any of Passu's wise hotel-wallahs.

Hiring your own help is tricky. Porters' wages are based on 'stages' corresponding very roughly to changes in elevation; thus the wage for an overnight climb to Avdegar (six stages) would be more than for three days' walk to Shimshal (five stages). Guides

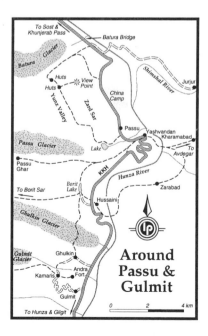

Around Passu & Gulmit

are normally paid per day, though many unfairly demand these per-stage fees. A local student might want Rs 150 per *stage* to show you trails and act as an interpreter, but Rs 150 to Rs 250 per *day* would be more reasonable.

**Glacier Views** An easy trail goes to the lake below Passu Glacier from the stone barns half a km south of the Passu Inn. Better views of this beautiful glacier are from the Yunz Valley and Passu Ghar trails.

In the other direction, the toe of the Batura Glacier is 4km north of the Batura Inn. The views improve as you climb the moraine (glacial rubble) along its south side.

**Yunz Valley** The massive caramel-coloured rock behind Passu is Zard Sar ('Yellow Top'). A vigorous six to seven-hour loop climbs to the glacial Yunz Valley behind it, offering excellent views of both the Batura and Passu glaciers. This is a hot, strenuous walk with no water along the trail. Note that the old trail up to Yunz Valley was destroyed by a landslide, and you must now start from the lake below Passu Glacier.

Skirt around the lake and follow cairns west up gravel and then scree to the top of a rock formation half an hour from the lake. From here the trail over the glacier's lateral moraine, west up a small parallel valley and north up to Yunz Valley itself is fairly clear. From a pair of huts an hour up Yunz Valley, a steep 1½ to two hour detour climbs to Zard Sar, with views over the Hunza Valley (stick to the track: a tourist is said to have fallen to his death from here in 1996).

At the end of Yunz Valley, keep right and descend steeply past more huts to the valley and moraine beside the Batura Glacier. From here it's still two or three hours down and across the low plateau to the right, back to Passu. There are camping areas at Zard Sar and around the second huts.

**Passu Ghar** This hike climbs about 700m in elevation to shepherds' huts along the south side of the Passu Glacier and back, in six to seven hours. The trail leaves the KKH at a highway sign half a km beyond the Shisper

Hotel, where power lines cross the road. The huts are about two hours beyond the bottom of the glacier.

**Borit Lake & Beyond** A walk from Passu to Borit Lake and back takes four to five hours. From the Passu Ghar trail, branch left near the bottom of the glacier.

Over the years the once-big lake has grown swampy and brackish (*borit* is Wakhi for 'salty'), possibly because the underground seepage that feeds it has decreased as the glaciers recede. Villagers of nearby Ghulkin have organised themselves to keep hunters from threatening migratory waterfowl, mainly tufted ducks, which rest here in April and May and again in October and November.

A long and strenuous day trip above Borit Lake takes you to Borit Sar, the ridge between the Passu and Ghulkin glaciers, with awesome, nearly 360° views of Passu and Ghulkin glaciers and the Batura Muztagh. There's no water on the way.

A return option from the lake is simply to walk half an hour down the bouldery jeep road to the KKH and hitch back to Passu. The lake also makes a good overnight stop on a walk between Passu and Gulmit (see Places to Eat section).

**Zarabad & Hussaini** This trip crosses the Hunza River on two long suspension bridges, and has good views of the Passu and Ghulkin glaciers from the other side. It takes four to five hours from Passu to Hussaini, plus a hitchhike or walk back (8-10km along the KKH or via Borit Lake).

From the KKH, at the first hairpin, turn south of the Shisper Hotel, a trail drops to the right of a settlement called Yashvandan. Climb the far side of the ravine, following a path (marked by cairns) to the river bed, then up another path on the bank, to the first bridge, about 1km from Yashvandan. It's just a cluster of cables with planks and branches woven in. On a windy day it will make you feel like Indiana Jones.

On the far side a trail branches left at another cairn, but you should continue

THE KHUNJERAB PASS & GOJAL

straight on. Climb toward the canyon walls and cross the shallow valley as high as possible, to the small village of Zarabad. A dramatic narrow track then crosses a sheer rock face to the second bridge.

Hussaini, back on the other side, is in a hollow below the KKH. It has a warm spring by the river's edge, used by Hussaini women for doing their wash (so tourists are probably not welcome to bathe). At the north end of the village is a white shrine to Shah Talib, a Muslim missionary active in the 17th or 18th century. A path climbs to the Highway near the shrine.

**Avdegar** East across the river is pasture called Avdegar at 3600m, with stupendous views from Sost to Shishkut, the entire length of the Passu Glacier and the highest peaks of the Batura Muztagh. It's a demanding, relentlessly steep overnight trip. Start at dawn to avoid the harsh midday sun on the way up.

Cross the bridge, as to Zarabad, but bear left toward the village of Kharamabad. A trail above the village heads left and up to a deep ravine, where there is a fresh spring just below a waterfall plunge-pool (another spring further on dries up in autumn). Cross the stream about 100m below the pool to find the upward trail. Higher up, the way is very easy to lose among yak tracks or, nearer Avdegar, in scree. Those with any energy left the next day could make the difficult climb to the 4000m ridge above Avdegar for even more sublime views.

If you prefer a day trip, you can make a gaspingly dry and very vertical one to the juniper-dotted slope halfway to the ridge and return to Passu in about 10 hours.

**Yashpirt** This pasture and summer encampment up the north side of Batura Glacier is accessible in one day from Passu. Opposite is the awesome Batura Wall icefall, calving thunderously around the clock. Above Yashpirt, on a moderate grade, are further meadows.

Climb the south moraine and cross the glacier, for which you might want local guid-

ance. The poor herders you may meet are hospitable, though the smaller your group, the warmer the welcome. In any case don't go expecting to be fed by them: carry the food you'll need, and consider taking items like sugar, salt, tea, oil, matches, etc as gifts or in trade for yoghurt or cheese. A locally known companion can smooth the way (guides were charging anything from Rs 300 to 500 a day at the time of research).

### Places to Stay & Eat
The Passu V O has put a good two page sheet in every hotel, offering good tips on social and environmental awareness in the Passu area.

**Bottom End** Recommended are the *Batura Inn's* cheap, good food, good attitude and 'rumour books' full of advice about the area. It's 800m north on the KKH, in a corner of the old KKH work camp (it started as a canteen for Chinese officers). Four-bed dorms without toilet are Rs 40 and 50 per bed, doubles Rs 100 and 200, and camping free. Spartan rooms with cold shower at *Passu Peak Inn*, 1.5km north of the village, are good value at Rs 75 per bed.

**Middle** We like the tranquil atmosphere and good meals at Ahmed Karim's small *Village Guest House No 1* in the village. A dorm in traditional style (raised sleeping area around a stove) is Rs 75 per bed and doubles are Rs 200 with shared facilities or Rs 250 with your own. Behind it is *Village Guest House No 2* (also signposted Dreamland Guest House), devoid of No 1's warmth.

Doubles at the *Passu Inn*, by the KKH bus stand, are Rs 150 with cold shower, and Rs 250 and up with hot shower; a local-style dorm is Rs 100 per bed. The drowsy *Shisper Hotel*, 1.5km south on the KKH, has dorm beds for Rs 40, cold-shower doubles for Rs 100, and several hours more sunshine than the others. An *NAPWD Resthouse* is opposite the Passu Inn.

Above Borit Lake, the *Borith Lake Hotel* has a small shop, simple meals, a Rs 50 per bed dorm and two modest doubles for around

Rs 250, or pitch a tent for Rs 50. It should be open from May to September, but some travellers have found it closed, so don't bank on it.

**Top End** With its very comfortable doubles and glossy dining room, the *Passu Tourist Lodge* is aimed at groups, but if there are vacancies a double for individuals is Rs 500. One owner is a disaffected cook from Gilgit's Serena Lodge, so the food's good. It's 2.5km north of Passu on the KKH.

### Getting There & Away
The Sost to Gilgit bus passes after 6.30 am and the Gilgit to Sost bus passes after 1 pm; put your bags beside the road and they'll stop. You could even walk to Gulmit, about 15km (four hours) via Borit Lake.

### GULMIT
With a library, a museum and the mirs' traditional second home, Gulmit ('GOOL-mit') is the closest thing to a town in Gojal, and its unofficial capital. It's very picturesque in spring and early summer when the fruit trees bloom, and there are many fine walks. The village is centred on its old polo ground, 700m off the KKH, though several hotels are down on the Highway. The village has a small civil hospital.

### Cultural Museum
A unique collection of Hunza history is packed in a dusty house near the Marco Polo Inn – maps, utensils, musical instruments, a stuffed snow leopard, gems, firearms (including the matchlock gun said to have injured the British commander at the Battle of Nilt in 1891) and even a tapestry of the Last Supper. If it isn't open, ask at the Marco Polo Inn. Admission is Rs 25.

### Library
Adjacent to the *jamaat khana* is a library than includes English-language books on history, education and religious studies.

### Old Gulmit
The mir's palace is at the north end of the polo ground. Until the early 1970s the Mir

of Hunza lived here for three months of the year, presiding over local *durbars* (councils); now it's being renovated. A cluster of houses to the left of the palace is the original village. The tallest of these is said to be Gulmit's oldest, probably 100 to 200 years old; before the palace was built the mir stayed in it on his Gulmit sojourns. To its left are the carved lintels of an old Shia mosque from the early 19th century, before Gojalis converted to Ismailism.

### Hikes
The following day hikes can be done with minimal gear and no assistance. If you want a guide, any able-bodied Gulmiti will be able to help, altho ugh they have a tendency to badly underestimate walking times for a downlander!

**Kamaris, Andra Fort & Gulmit Glacier** A twisting track behind Gulmit climbs for an hour to friendly Kamaris village, with views up and down the valley. A half hour walk north-east from Kamaris brings you to the marginally interesting ruins of Andra Fort, built about 200 years ago to defend Gulmit in Hunza's war with the neighbouring state

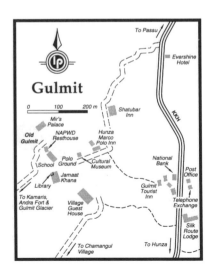

THE KHUNJERAB PASS & GOJAL

of Nagar. Ask local people for Andra Gelah ('geh-LA').

The track continues past Kamaris for another hour, north-west to the base of the Gulmit Glacier. A long day or overnight option is to continue on the footpath along the south side of the glacier, an area known locally as Zherav, where there are some shepherds' huts. Stay away on windy or rainy days, when rockfall hazard is high.

**Ghulkin Village** From Kamaris a footpath crosses the stream below Gulmit Glacier, then becomes a jeep track up to Ghulkin village, and returns to the KKH. The loop from Gulmit takes four to five hours.

**Borit Lake** From Ghulkin a footpath crosses the grey Ghulkin Glacier to Borit Lake, two hours away. It's 1.25km across the glacier, the way marked by a cairn on the south moraine and a big cleft or dip in the north moraine. The glacier crossing can be tricky, and it might be worth a few rupees to get someone in Ghulkin to show you across. Alternatively, the lake is about five hours (12km) from Gulmit via Kamaris. See the Passu section earlier for trip ideas and possible accommodation there.

### Places to Stay & Eat

The *Gulmit Tourist Inn* (formerly Tourist Cottage; ☎ 46119) on the KKH has a handsome local-style dorm for Rs 60 a bed. Doubles are priced for groups – Rs 300 with cold shower or Rs 400 and 750 with carpets and hot shower – but it remains a comfortable base for local walks.

Also priced for groups is the monster *Silk Route Lodge* (☎ 46118) across the road; basic singles/doubles are Rs 730/870. Opposite the link road, the seedy *Evershine Hotel*

has doubles with hot water for Rs 100. The *Shatubar Inn* stands empty on the link road.

Up by the polo ground, the *Village Guest House* (formerly *Village Hotel*; ☎ 46112) is good value, with quiet doubles with shared toilet and hot shower for Rs 200, more comfortable ones with attached facilities for Rs 350, and a peaceful orchard. The nearby *Hunza Marco Polo Inn* (☎ 46107) has posh doubles with hot shower and western toilet for Rs 750, a few cheaper ones in local style and 'culture shows' for groups.

### Getting There & Away

A local minibus departs Gulmit for Gilgit about 6 am. The Sost to Gilgit bus passes after 7 am and the Gilgit to Sost passes after 12.30 pm. It's a four to five hour walk to Passu – about 15km via Borit Lake. To Karimabad on foot along the KKH is said to take at least nine hours.

### GULMIT TO GANESH

At the Shishkut Bridge south of Gulmit, Nazimabad village is the southernmost settlement in Gojal, though the majority of people there are Burushashki speakers.

Perhaps the most obscure monument in British history is about 10 minutes south of the bridge, a bit downstream of where the gorge turns west. Across the river, a small stone tablet marks the passage in August 1903 of Lord Kitchener, on a tour of the frontier areas of British India as the army's new commander-in-chief. The tablet was erected by Mir Nazim Khan of Hunza (great-grandfather of the present mir), probably to flatter the British who had installed him after their invasion of Hunza in 1891. It's on a level with the Highway, about 3m above the tenuous old track – forerunner of the KKH – that Kitchener took.

# Hunza & Nagar

For natural beauty, the Hunza Valley is the centrepiece of the KKH. The continuous sweep from the Hunza River through mighty, grey-brown scree slopes and up to snowy peaks (including 7790m Rakaposhi, which seems to loom everywhere) is a reminder of the river's deep slice across the Karakoram. The very edge of the primordial Asian continent is exposed here (see the Geology section in the Facts about the Region chapter). In spring everything is green shoots and white blossoms in endless tiers, and autumn is a riot of yellow poplars, reddening orchards and maize drying on rooftops.

Snaking across the slopes are Hunza's hallmark, the precision-made stone channels on which its life depends. Carrying water from canyons to tiny, rough-walled fields 8km away, they have transformed a 'mountain desert' with few horizontal surfaces into a breadbasket. Their paths on the high rock faces are revealed by thin lines of vegetation, and patches of green are visible on the most improbable walls and ledges. Irrigation sustains orchards of Hunza's famous apricots, as well as peaches, plums, apples, grapes, cherries and walnuts; fields of maize and wheat; and the ever-present poplars, a fast-growing source of fodder, firewood and timber.

Added to the beauty is a kind of mythology about Hunza's isolation and purity, spawned by James Hilton's 1933 novel *Lost Horizon*, nourished in films about the lost kingdom of Shangri-la, and fostered in the 1970s by media stories of extraordinary health and longevity. The KKH itself has put an end to Hunza's isolation, and while the Garden of Eden image ignores a rather bloody and disreputable history, this hardly alters Hunza's appeal. Westerners find more in common culturally with Hunzakuts than with anyone else in Pakistan, and the feeling seems mutual.

'Hunza' is commonly (and inaccurately) used for the entire broad valley. In fact two

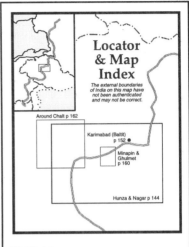

Locator & Map Index

The external boundaries of India on this map have not been authenticated and may not be correct.

Around Chalt p 162

Karimabad (Baltit) p 152

Minapin & Ghulmet p 160

Hunza & Nagar p 144

## Highlights

- Hunza Valley, the centrepiece of the KKH
- Majestic snowy peaks, including 7790m Rakaposhi
- Baltit Fort, redoubt of Hunza rulers for seven centuries
- Fruit in abundance from a former mountain desert

former princely states, Hunza and Nagar ('NAH-gr'), with shared language and ancestry, face one another across the river. Hunza refers to the villages on the north bank from Khizerabad to Ghareghat (or sometimes as far as Nazimabad). Gojal is sometimes described as part of Hunza too.

Smaller but more populous Nagar occupies the entire south side of the valley and the north side around Chalt, and includes Rakaposhi and the lower Hispar Glacier. Although it enjoys less media fame, Nagar is home to some of the best treks in the Karakoram (many of them set out in Lonely

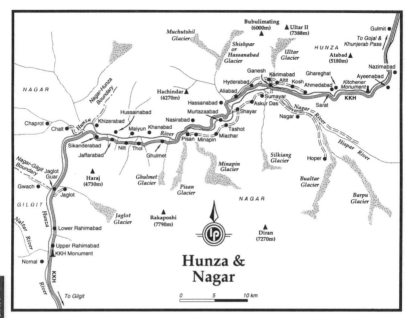

Hunza &
Nagar

0          5          10 km

Planet's *Trekking in the Karakoram & Hindukush*).

### History

(Early oral histories of the Northern Areas were typically based on a count of generations. Except for certain moments in the Islamic calendar, it is only in recent times that local scholars have tried to attach calendar dates to these histories. As a result of overestimates of the length of a generation, local accounts tend to give considerably earlier dates than those deduced by western historians. We have tried to be consistent with the latter.)

The Hunza (ancient name Kanjut) Valley lies on a branch of the Silk Road from Kashgar to Kashmir.

The valley's earliest settlers may have come from an ancient village called Gor, in the hills across the Indus River from Chilas. The first villages were at Ganesh, Altit and Baltit (now known as Karimabad).

The origins of the separate Hunza and Nagar kingdoms are obscured by legend, but they're probably offshoots of Gilgit's Trakhan dynasty. From a marriage of royal cousins of that dynasty in the 15th century came twin sons, Maglot and Girkis, later to become the rulers, respectively, of Nagar and Hunza. From infancy, so the story goes, the little princes had a mutual hatred, and as kings they led their people into frequent bloody battles with one another. Over the centuries their royal descendants have continued the feud, even as their families intermarried.

Girkis and all his family except one daughter, Nur Bibi, were finally killed in a Nagari raid. To save the royal bloodline, the story goes that the *wazirs* (ministers) of Ganesh, Altit and Baltit wandered for seven years in search of long-lost relatives, until guided to Badakhshan in Afghanistan by a white crow. From there a distant cousin was brought back, married Nur Bibi and became

**Cyclists' Notes, Hunza & Nagar**
Food, water and accommodation are plentiful and the road is wide and paved. No major climbs southbound. Major climb northbound: the first 15km east of Ganesh. Otherwise the ride is on a gentle grade with few long or steep hills.

**Ganesh to Minapin turning, about 25km** Karimabad is a sharp but paved 2km climb from just west of Ganesh; northbound riders can spread this out on the mostly paved link road to Karimabad from 2km west of Aliabad. If you're not stopping, Ganesh, Aliabad and Murtazabad have small hotels, and Aliabad has a camp site. From the bridge over the Hunza River it's an unpaved 3km to Minapin, with a steep down-and-up at Minapin Nala.

**Minapin turning to Chalt turning, about 25km** There is food and shelter at Ghulmet Nala, about 5km west of Pisan. Chalt is about 4km (fairly level but unpaved) off the KKH, and has simple accommodation.

**Chalt turning to Gilgit, about 55km** Basic food and rope-beds are available at Jaglot Guar, about 14km from the Chalt turning or 42km from Gilgit. The shortest route into Gilgit from the north is via a tunnel and two suspension bridges (turn off the KKH at Dainyor), although oscillations on the bridges can make cycling very tricky! A good 'rumour-book' for cyclists is at the North Inn in Gilgit. ■

Mir Ayesho I *(ayesho* means 'sky-born' in Burushashki).

Under Ayesho's grandson, Mir Ayesho II, Shia Islam came to the valley as the result of alliances with Baltistan's Maqpon dynasty. Ayesho II's grandsons fought with one another, with Shah Abbas in Baltit defeating Ali Khan in Altit to confirm Baltit as Hunza's capital.

In the 18th century Shah Abbas' grandson, Mir Shah Salim, and most of his subjects in Hunza and Gojal converted to Ismailism, although the doctrine had probably arrived in Chitral and Gilgit several centuries before with Taj Mughal (see the History section in the Gilgit Region chapter). Shah Salim is credited with bringing irrigation techniques to the valley. He also extended Hunza's influence north into Xinjiang, and began paying annual tributes of gold dust to China. As mir, his son Shah Ghazanfar in 1847 helped the governor of Xinjiang put down a rebellion in Yarkand.

The valley's modest agricultural output had for years been supplemented by raids on caravans between Kashgar and Kashmir, and by slave trading. Yaqub Beg, who proclaimed an independent Turkestan republic in Xinjiang in the 1860s (see the boxed text Yaqub Beg in the Kashgar to Tashkurgan chapter), put a temporary end to the raids.

This economic blow led Hunza and Nagar to declare allegiance to the British-aligned maharajah of Kashmir, probably for the subsidies they got in return. Kashmiri troops moved into Chalt.

In 1886 Safdar Ali, Shah Salim's great-grandson, became mir of Hunza in accordance with the valley's age-old customs – by murdering his father and three brothers. Within two years he conspired to eject the Kashmiris from Chalt, resumed the caravan raids and played host at Baltit Fort to a party of Russian 'explorers'. British India, spreading north from Kashmir, had grown aware of Russia expanding into Central Asia, and Hunza now began to look like a loose cannon on deck.

Britain decided to improve supply lines from Kashmir and reopen its old agency at Gilgit, and gradually became entangled in Hunza-Nagar's bloody politics. Within five years a British-Kashmiri force had occupied the valley and installed its own mir, Nazim Khan, in Hunza (see the following boxed text). A British garrison remained at Aliabad until 1897. In Hunza, Nazim Khan ruled until his death in 1938, and his son Ghazan Khan until 1945.

Within weeks of the formal partition of India and Pakistan in August 1947, an uprising in Gilgit against the maharajah of

**HUNZA & NAGAR**

## The 'Pacification' of Hunza & Nagar

The Crown's agent at Gilgit was Captain Algernon Durand, who apparently believed that, to counter Russian influence in India, sooner or later all its frontier tribes would have to be subjugated or bought off.

In 1889 Durand visited Hunza's Mir Safdar Ali and Nagar's Mir Zafar Khan, proposing British access up to Shimshal in Gojal, and an end to Hunza's caravan raids, in exchange for more subsidies. Both agreed. Nevertheless, in the following year, Hunza plundered a Kyrgyz camp in the Pamirs, and in 1891 Uzar Khan, eldest son of the Mir of Nagar, began making threatening noises towards the British. Moreover, he had just had two of his 12 brothers murdered and was plotting against the others.

Durand moved troops to Chalt and built a sturdy bridge across the Hunza River. The mirs protested, but they were already undone: both royal families were increasingly terrorised by Uzar Khan, and both mirs had already advised several sons and nephews to take refuge with the British. Durand in fact arrived at Chalt with Uzar Khan's youngest brother, Sikander.

On 21 December 1891 a combined British and Kashmiri force crossed the river and next day, at Nilt, encountered Uzar Khan's Hunza-Nagar irregulars at a fort beside a deep ravine. After dynamiting the gate the invaders rushed in, and the defenders fled through hidden passages beneath the fort. (Durand, seeking a view of the action, had stood up and taken a shot in the groin – made, he later discovered, of a garnet slug encased in lead, standard issue in Hunza. The gun allegedly used for this deed is in the Gulmit Museum.)

The British, despite some casualties, congratulated themselves on a splendid little fight. Then it was discovered that the men of the valley had destroyed the trails by which they escaped across the ravine, and had regrouped in a stronger position on the other side. For 17 miserable days the British, unable to advance, sat in the fort trying this and that.

Finally, a party of Kashmiris slipped out at night and stormed the far side before breakfast, and opposition evaporated. Zafar Khan surrendered at Tashot and Durand's army – with the help of Humayun Beg, Safdar Ali's disaffected wazir (prime minister) – crossed the river and marched into Baltit.

While they languished at Nilt, the British had received, and rejected, an appeal for negotiations from Safdar Ali. He then fled with his family, including his brother Nafiz Khan and stepbrother Nazim Khan, as well as Uzar Khan and several hundred others, to Xinjiang.

Arriving at Baltit Fort, the British found that Safdar Ali had taken most of its treasure with him, though they ransacked what was left. The spoils from years of plunder included antique chain armour, a Parisian music box, Dutch engravings, even a European armchair, plus an extensive library and a cache of guns, powder and garnet bullets. Overlooking superior British firepower and the embarrassing layover at Nilt, a London *Times* correspondent, EF Knight (who had already forsaken his objectivity by volunteering for a command at Nilt), declared the episode 'one of the most brilliant little campaigns in military history'.

But local notables urged the British to bring back Safdar Ali, who they felt was the only one capable of uniting the squabbling clans of Hunza. A delegation of locals was dispatched to Xinjiang, but Safdar Ali refused to return nor to allow Nafiz Khan to go, sending the delegation back instead with the hapless Nazim Khan.

In January 1892 the British installed Nazim Khan as Mir of Hunza, and the ageing Zafar Khan was reinstated as Mir of Nagar. About a year later Nafiz Khan appeared, insisting he was the rightful heir to Hunza's throne, but Nazim Khan banished him to Khudabad (opposite Sost in Gojal), where his descendants still live. Uzar Khan was sent back by the Chinese, and jailed in Kashmir. Safdar Ali was allowed to stay in Xinjiang and died a poor man at Yarkand in 1930. ■

*Reference for illustration supplied by Baltit Fort Cultural Centre*

Nazim Khan, installed by the British as Mir of Hunza in 1892.

Kashmir, who had opted to join India, brought Hunza and Nagar into Pakistan. They remained semi-autonomous until 1974 when they were merged with Pakistan, reducing their rulers to district officials.

Many older Hunzakuts still fondly recall their last mir, Muhammad Jamal Khan, who died two years after the formal dissolution of the old princely states. His son Ghazanfar Ali still occupies the royal house in Karimabad. Nagar's last mir still lives in Nagar village.

## People

Although Nagaris and Hunzakuts have common ancestors, there is no consensus on the place of their origin. A persistent legend is of descent from Alexander the Great ('Sikander'), or those of his officers who are alleged to have stayed behind in the 4th century BC. There is little to support this, but it is startling to occasionally see Mediterranean features, sandy hair and blue eyes.

Most people here still think of themselves as subjects of their respective mirs, rather than as Pakistanis. They are not fond of the down-land Pakistanis that the KKH has brought, but even in remote areas they are very hospitable to foreigners.

The two kingdoms also have a common language, Burushashki, but nobody is sure where it came from. Wakhi is spoken in upper Hunza (Gojal); in lower Nagar (in common with Gilgit) Shina is also used. Many people speak Urdu and English.

Hunza and Nagar also once shared the Shia faith, but Hunza is now almost entirely Ismaili (except for Murtazaabad, Ganesh and a few other pockets). Older shamanistic beliefs also linger, especially about mountain spirits or fairies who live on the highest peaks and behave capriciously toward humans. You can still see children and young women with dark eye make-up, to ward off spirits that may enter the eyes and other body orifices.

Hunzakut men and women wear the long shirt and baggy trousers called *shalwar qamiz*. The women's outfits are brightly coloured and many wear embroidered pillbox

Older Hunzakut men are easily identified by the Hunze wool cap.

caps with a *dupatta*, or shawl, thrown over them. Older men wear the distinctive Hunza wool cap, basically a tube of cloth with the edges rolled tightly up. In cold weather men may put on a *chogha*, a handsome embroidered woollen cloak with oversize sleeves.

## GANESH
### Tel Area Code: 0572

Ganesh ('GUN-ish') is the oldest settlement in Hunza & Nagar, and despite having been cut to pieces by the KKH, it has a lovely village centre full of classic Hunza architecture. Ganeshkuts were once famous for their raids against Nagar. In the 19th century Ganesh was the main Hunza hold-out against Ismailism and, except for five or six Ismaili families, is all Shia today. With cultural ties to Hunza and religious ties to Nagar, the village nowadays seems friendless.

Most travellers know the place only as Karimabad's bus stop. Sost to Gilgit buses drop you at a clutch of shops, cafes and hotels by a monument to KKH construction-worker 'martyrs' (casualties). It's a 2km walk up to Karimabad.

HUNZA & NAGAR

## Hunza Food & Drink

Hunza food is closer to western food than anything else on the KKH. Meals can include things like potatoes, rice, whole-wheat bread and noodle soup, with oil and spices used sparingly. But there's more to Hunza cooking than that, as you'll see if you're lucky enough to be invited home for dinner. A few Karimabad restaurants also make an attempt at it for foreigners.

Note that if you're China-bound, Karimabad is the last good place to stock up for the trip.

**Milk Products** These include milk *(mamu)*, yoghurt *(dumanu-mamu)* and *diltar*, a cultured buttermilk left after yoghurt is churned for butter. A soft cheese called *burus*, which settles to the bottom of diltar kept warm for several days, is good for upset stomachs. *Kurut* is a sour, hard cheese made by boiling and drying diltar.

Yoghurt and burus are available by request at some hotels. At least one of Karimabad's bakeries, Happy Bakery, sells burus and local butter. You're most likely to get kurut from shepherds in the high valleys, in trade for things like tea, salt or sugar.

**Bread** *Phitti* is a thick wholemeal bread, baked in coals. Some hotels can order it for you, and several bakeries in Karimabad sell it. *Chhapshuro* is a kind of 'Hunza pizza': meat, tomatoes, onions and sometimes other items like burus, traditionally cooked into a thick chapatti but sometimes just sandwiched between two chapattis and fried.

*Burushapik* ('cheese-chapatti') is burus cooked into a wholemeal chapatti, the outside covered in apricot kernel oil, and served cold – good and very filling. *Burutze berikutz* is similar but with sweet herbs (coriander, mint) added, and served in small pieces.

**Soup** *Daudo* is a noodle soup with vegetables, thickened with egg and whole-wheat flour. It comes in many varieties, eg *kurutze daudo*, with kurut, and delicious *haneetze daudo*, with nuts or crushed apricot kernels, garlic and onion. Apricot soup is made from dried apricots, flour and water.

**Fruit** Most of the Northern Areas' dried fruit comes from Hunza, and dried Hunza apricots are found in bazaars all over Asia. There are at least 22 varieties of apricots, and the best trees are said to be heirlooms. Apricots usually ripen by June. Wholesalers sort theirs on the floor so unless you know yours were dried and handled carefully, you should soak them in boiling water to reduce the risk of illness.

Mulberries also appear in June, and peaches, plums, apples, grapes, cherries and walnuts in early autumn. A great travel snack is dried mulberries.

**Drink** *Tumuro*, or *chumuru*, is a wild alpine herb similar to sage, collected and brewed into a tea that is said to cool and clear the head, especially at high elevation.

Despite Muslim prohibition and disapproval from the Aga Khan, some Hunzakuts carry on pre-Muslim traditions by brewing a rough grape wine called *mel*, and a potent mulberry firewater called *arak*. Arak ('Hunza water') may be offered to you by friends, though your stomach may not like it. Some shops also sell nonalcoholic Pakistani beer. ■

### Ganesh Village

Older Ganeshkuts frown on outsiders but if you ask around you may be welcomed into the village, one of the least modernised in Hunza. Around a central pond are several richly carved wooden mosques, 100 to 200 years old, each donated by a Ganesh clan, and a timber-and-stone watchtower from the days of war with Nagar.

West across the fields is a flag-decked *ziarat* to an early Muslim holy man named Bulja Toko – who never came to Hunza, but featured in a villager's dream. Food is left here on Fridays for the poor to take. Two km

west, Ganesh's sister-village of Tsil Ganesh has a Balti-style *imam barga*, a hall used for the Shias' Ashura and Chhelum observances.

### The 'Sacred Rocks of Hunza'

About 1.5km east of Ganesh, on the KKH, are several stony rises marked by a sign with this name (which was probably invented at the Ministry of Tourism). Locally the site is called Haldekush. The rocks, with pictures, prayers and writing from as early as the 1st century AD, are a kind of 'guest book' of the valley. In addition to local traditions they tell of Buddhist pilgrims, kings of the Kushan

Empire at Taxila, a 6th century Chinese ambassador, 8th century Tibetan conquerors and even KKH workers! Look up for fine views of Altit Fort and Ultar Peak (see the Baltit & Karimabad section later in this chapter).

### Places to Stay & Eat

The *Karakoram Highway Inn* (☎ 47095) has barren triples with squat loo and cold shower for Rs 100/bed. At one-third the price, local drivers prefer the dismal *New Ganesh Hotel*.

At Garelt, 1.5km west on the KKH, Pakistan Tourism Development Corporation's (PTDC) *Hunza Motel* – marring valley views from every angle – has singles/doubles for Rs 900/1000. Across the road the *Golden Peak View Hotel*'s doubles are ridiculously overpriced at Rs 600.

### Getting There & Away

Aliabad minibuses scout Ganesh for passengers to Gilgit around 5 to 6 am. The Natco bus passes through at about 8 am on the way to Gilgit, and after about 11 am on the way to Sost. Free jeep shuttles from Karimabad's New Hunza Tourist Hotel and Altit's Kisar Inn often meet these buses; other jeeps lurking at Ganesh were asking Rs 120 to Karimabad at the time of research. Passenger Suzukis ply between here and Aliabad for Rs 5.

### BALTIT & KARIMABAD
#### Pop (est): 10,000   Tel Area Code: 0572

Baltit has always been the capital of Hunza, and its magnificent fort, on a throne-like ridge with Ultar Nala yawning behind it, has always been the kingdom's focal point. The fort, started over 750 years ago, served as the royal palace until 1945, when sounder quarters were built below it in what came to be called Karimabad (for Prince Karim, the present Aga Khan). The name is now also used for Baltit and the complex of ancient tribal hamlets around it.

Since the arrival of KKH tourism and overseas aid, Karimabad has grown and prospered, and the bazaar has filled with hotels, restaurants and a growing number of travel agencies, 'art' dealers, dried-fruit shops and underqualified 'guides' in pursuit

of customers among the armies of tourists that now pass through. The old village has lost its innocence, and much of its charm; for that you must take time to explore the surrounding countryside.

Before electricity, Karimabad filled each evening with the sound of diesel generators. Now that a big Norwegian hydro generator is in place in Hassanabad Nala, it fills on most evenings with the sound of satellite TV and Indian musicals.

### Orientation

Karimabad is perched high above the KKH. Vehicle access from the KKH includes paved New Ganesh Rd to the lower end of the bazaar from just west of Ganesh, and a mostly paved road to the top of the bazaar from just west of Aliabad. A path climbs from the upper bazaar to Baltit Fort. Old Ganesh Rd, the original access road from Ganesh, is now just a dusty footpath.

### Information

The National Bank (☎ 47050) on New Ganesh Rd, open daily except Sunday from 9 am to 1.30 pm, accepts US$, UK£ and DM cash or travellers cheques. Alam Money Changer (☎ 47109) in the lower bazaar has better cash rates, accepts almost any major currency and is open from 8 am to 8 pm daily.

The post office, up a steep flight of steps in the bazaar, is open from 8.30 am to 4 pm Monday to Saturday, except to noon Friday. A telephone exchange (open until 10 pm) and a grotty hospital are on Old Ganesh Rd below the Mountain View Hotel. Shops may open as early as 7 am and close as late as 9 pm.

Travel agencies include Walji's Travel (☎ 47045) atop the Tourist Park Hotel, and Concordia Expeditions (☎ 47010), a trekking agency misleadingly signposted 'Tourist Information Office', up the road from the gate of the Hill Top Hotel.

### Baltit Fort

Baltit Fort, a potent symbol of Hunza's history and identity, dates from the 13th century, although the present imposing exterior probably goes back less than 150 years.

HUNZA & NAGAR

## A History of Baltit Fort

By the mid-13th century (as confirmed by carbon-14 dating) a few one-storey buildings and a defensive tower were in place on a tall moraine overlooking the Ultar stream, from where its precious water supply could be controlled. The tower was probably similar to those still seen in villages near the KKH in Indus Kohistan. Over the centuries more houses and towers were added, and the result was fortified.

According to local history, Mir Ayesho II of Hunza (great-grandson of the legendary Girkis), in an effort to cement an alliance with Baltistan's powerful Maqpon dynasty in the 17th century, married Sha-Khatun, daughter of the Balti ruler Abdullah Khan. Abdullah Khan sent artisans to build a fort at Altit. The princess then came with her court to live in Hunza, bringing along her own artisans to improve Baltit Fort. The Balti-style renovation of the fort continued under Ayesho II's son, Mir Sultan. The name 'Baltit' presumably dates from this time.

The fort took on its present appearance only in the last century or so, mostly at the hands of Mir Nazim Khan. Outer walls were added, to shore up the old ones and/or to give a more imposing appearance. Around 1900 the building was tarted up as a royal palace. While the 1st floor, and the women's areas and mir's bedroom on the 2nd floor, were left as they were, the mir fixed up many of his own rooms with western furnishings like wallpaper and drapes, added fireplaces, balconies, carved ceilings and coloured window glass.

He had the outer walls whitewashed, dramatically raising the fort's visual impact from all over the valley. Also added were a dais on the roof (where royal councils were held in good weather, with the distraction of fabulous valley views) and the 'lantern', or skylight, that some visitors mistakenly take as an original Balti feature.

Nazim Khan's grandson Mir Muhammad Jamal Khan moved down to modern quarters in Karimabad in 1945, leaving the fort for almost half a century at the mercy of random visitors, many of whom helped themselves to what was left or scribbled their names on the walls.

Surveys were begun in 1985 with an eye to restoration, with money from the Aga Khan Trust for Culture (AKTC) and other sources. Ghazanfar Ali, son of the last mir, agreed to donate the fort to the AKTC. A public foundation, the Baltit Heritage Trust (BHT), was created as part of the legal mechanism to shift the fort to public ownership, and to search for long-term funding for the project.

The AKTC's Historic Cities Support Programme got involved in 1992 with a wider effort to control the rush of tourism-driven development around Karimabad, especially unregulated construction in areas of valuable farmland and unspoilt views. In this they were aided by a team of architects, engineers and social workers called Karimabad Planning Support Services (KPSS), the closest thing to a village

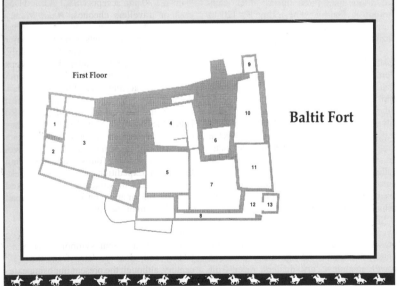

First Floor

**Baltit Fort**

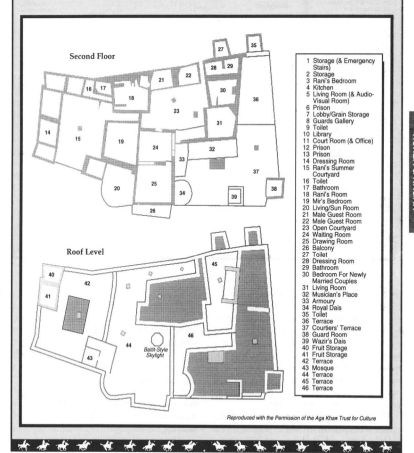

planning department. A conservation area has been defined within Karimabad. Related programes now under way include rehabilitation of private homes near the fort and new water supply and sanitation systems.

The fort's restoration took place from 1990 to 1996 in overlapping stages – structural engineering, architectural preservation and modern additions for safety and new uses. On 29 September 1996 the restored fort was inaugurated (and handed over to the BHT) with a level of hoopla probably never before seen in Hunza. Pakistan president Farooq Leghari did the honours, and the Aga Khan attended.

The work has generated a corps of local people trained in conservation principles and techniques, plus related subjects like archeology, structural engineering and public administration. It has also generated interest in (but not yet any money for) other conservation projects such as Altit Fort and the mosques at Ganesh. Finally, it has given a big nod to local traditions in the face of full-tilt economic and social change.

Those with more interest in this and other projects in Karimabad can contact the Aga Khan Trust for Culture (☎ (022) 909 7200; fax (022) 909 7292), 1-3 Avenue de la Paix, 1202 Geneva, Switzerland. ■

**Second Floor**

1 Storage (& Emergency Stairs)
2 Storage
3 Rani's Bedroom
4 Kitchen
5 Living Room (& Audio-Visual Room)
6 Prison
7 Lobby/Grain Storage
8 Guards Gallery
9 Toilet
10 Library
11 Court Room (& Office)
12 Prison
13 Prison
14 Dressing Room
15 Rani's Summer Courtyard
16 Toilet
17 Bathroom
18 Rani's Room
19 Mir's Bedroom
20 Living/Sun Room
21 Male Guest Room
22 Male Guest Room
23 Open Courtyard
24 Waiting Room
25 Drawing Room
26 Balcony
27 Toilet
28 Dressing Room
29 Bathroom
30 Bedroom For Newly Married Couples
31 Living Room
32 Musician's Place
33 Armoury
34 Royal Dais
35 Toilet
36 Terrace
37 Courtiers' Terrace
38 Guard Room
39 Wazir's Dais
40 Fruit Storage
41 Fruit Storage
42 Terrace
43 Mosque
44 Terrace
45 Terrace
46 Terrace

**Roof Level**

Baltit-Style Skylight

HUNZA & NAGAR

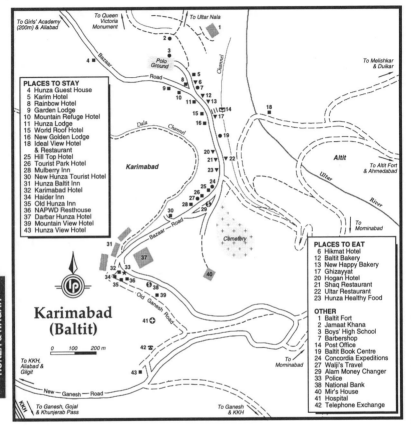

**PLACES TO STAY**
4 Hunza Guest House
5 Karim Hotel
8 Rainbow Hotel
9 Garden Lodge
10 Mountain Refuge Hotel
11 Hunza Lodge
15 World Roof Hotel
16 New Golden Lodge
18 Ideal View Hotel
   & Restaurant
25 Hill Top Hotel
26 Tourist Park Hotel
28 Mulberry Inn
30 New Hunza Tourist Hotel
31 Hunza Baltit Inn
32 Karimabad Hotel
34 Haider Inn
35 Old Hunza Inn
36 NAPWD Resthouse
37 Darbar Hunza Hotel
39 Mountain View Hotel
43 Hunza View Hotel

**PLACES TO EAT**
6 Hikmat Hotel
12 Baltit Bakery
13 New Happy Bakery
17 Ghizayyat
20 Hogan Hotel
21 Shaq Restaurant
22 Ultar Restaurant
23 Hunza Healthy Food

**OTHER**
1 Baltit Fort
2 Jamaat Khana
3 Boys' High School
7 Barbershop
14 Post Office
19 Baltit Book Centre
24 Concordia Expeditions
27 Walji's Travel
29 Alam Money Changer
33 Police
38 National Bank
40 Mir's House
41 Hospital
42 Telephone Exchange

## Karimabad (Baltit)

By the time KKH travellers first saw it in the 1980s it was an abandoned shell, stripped of anything of value and verging on collapse. In the early 1990s it was effectively taken apart stone by stone and reassembled, in a painstaking British-Pakistani effort using the most advanced preservation principles, while also retaining the unique construction and earthquake-proofing techniques pioneered by the fort's own builders.

The result is quite splendid and the renovation work almost invisible. Several rooms have exhibits of clothing and old photographs, plus utensils and furnishings donated by local people. A cultural centre and library occupy discreet corners. Visitors are given a half-hour tour of the building by polite, knowledgeable local staff (you cannot go in without one). It doesn't have the same buzz as scrambling around on your own, as visitors could do in the past, but you'll learn a lot more about it.

Now the bad news: the entry fee for outsiders is an over-the-top Rs 200, which is meant to cover fort maintenance and staff salaries. Locals pay Rs 50, an equal hardship on some of them. Nobody seems to have thought of youth/senior discounts.

The fort is open year-round, daily from 9 am to 1 pm and 2 to 5.30 pm. Tickets are sold at a small office/cloakroom/souvenir shop below the fort. No photography is allowed inside. See the boxed text on page 150-151 for more on the fort's history and layout.

### Around Karimabad

**Near the Fort** The house over the path to Baltit Fort is actually an old family mosque from the days when Hunza was Shia, and belongs to the descendants of Mir Nazim Khan's wazir (prime minister). It was formerly in a spot just below the fort, but in the 1930s the mir decided he wanted that spot, so the wazir's family moved it to its present odd location.

**Mir's House** Above the Tourist Park Hotel a road leads to the modern residence of Ghanzanfar Ali, who would today be mir if Hunza were still independent.

**Cemetery** Just after you cross under the aqueduct near the Hill Top Hotel, a right turn takes you to Karimabad's cemetery, with low-altitude valley views; the walled part is for royal graves.

**Mominabad** There are traces of an ancient caste system in the Northern Areas in which musicians and artisans ranked low. In the past they were often segregated in their own villages. Though quite ordinary-looking, Mominabad (old name Berishal), near a turn on the Ganesh to Karimabad road, was such a village. Its people even speak their own dialect, Berishki. With tourism on the rise, local musicians may be low-caste but they're getting rich.

**Channel Walks** It's amazing how many irrigation channels come out of a single canyon, and how far they go. A three or four hour walk along the main channels *(gotsil)* from Ultar Nala is a good way to see Hunza. Try to avoid the delicate side-channels.

Climb past the polo field, bearing left beside the channel. The path goes down the valley all the way to Hyderabad Nala. There,

scramble down the stream-bed to the link road. Turning back toward Karimabad, you can soon drop to the Dala channel that goes all the way back. You can go right on around Karimabad, past Mominabad to the headworks behind Baltit Fort, although the channel goes underground for part of the way.

Both channels distribute water from Ultar Nala. There are seven channels running to the west and five to the east from Ultar Nala. The velvety appearance of Ultar water is the result of minute flakes of mica.

**Queen Victoria Monument** There is a monument to Queen Victoria at the top of the rock face behind Karimabad, probably erected by Nazim Khan, and it can be reached in an hour from Baltit. Take the channel path above the polo ground. Five minutes out, cross the channel and climb stone steps beside an old watchtower. At the top of the village, scramble to a shallow cleft with some very large boulders. Go straight up to the base of the cliff *before* crossing over to the monument; avoid a diagonal crossing of the face because the top Ultar water channel spills down it. In Burushashki the monument is called *Malikamu Shikari* ('ma-li-KA-mu shi-KA-ri').

### Ultar Meadows

A climb to the meadow beside Ultar icefall will give you an appreciation for how vertical things are here. It's a strenuous day trip or an easier overnight. Some people hire a local guide, for around Rs 300 per day – useful but not essential. But going alone is *not* recommended; in the last five years several solo hikers have disappeared, and others have been injured.

Enter Ultar Nala from the top of Baltit village and follow a steep and often difficult trail up the moraines on the west side of the stream. There is a spring 15 minutes beyond the village, just past the channel headworks. The meadows are three to four hours up, about 800m to 900m above Karimabad at the foot of the rumbling icefall, in an awesome amphitheatre of peaks. One black pinnacle, 6000m Bubulimating (named for a hapless princess named Bubuli, left there by a demon king), or 'Lady Finger', is so sheer that snow doesn't stick to it. To its right, on the backbone of the Karakoram and 4.5 vertical km above you, is Ultar II (7388m). Until it was scaled by a Japanese team in 1996, Ultar II was one of the world's highest unclimbed peaks.

Shepherds drive flocks up to the meadows and live in the stone huts all summer, and you should ask before camping near their animals. And now, as one traveller said, you can go up with little more than your wallet: from May to October the *Lady Finger Campsite*, below the huts, serves basic food and even rents tents and bags for staying the night. Ask around to be sure it's still there though.

On the return trip, water channels look like good trails but often leave you with some dangerous descents, and may pose a rockfall hazard to others below. If you must use a channel, walk *in* it if you can, so as not to damage it. Rockfall risk is also high after prolonged rain, high winds or a thaw. Do not walk on the dangerously crevassed glacier.

The Ultar stream comes from the glacier, and as the sun rises and warms the glacier, the flow increases substantially; an ankle-deep crossing at 9 am can turn waist-deep and dangerous in a few hours, putting you in a bad spot on the way down. The best solution is to start before sunrise and aim to return by midday or the next morning. In July and August, when thunderstorms can roll through, the stream is even more swollen.

Carry water: the thrashing stream can be hard to approach. Take extra layers, even on a hot day, against the icy wind off the glacier.

**Hon** West and four to five hours up from the huts is a 4500m north-south ridge called Hon, with incredible views across to Nagar, Golden Peak and Rakaposhi. This is only really feasible as a day trip or overnight from the meadows. It's not a technical climb but does require great care. There is no water en route, nor at Hon.

For another, slightly less vertical, day hike above the meadow, turn right off the Hon trail about two-thirds of the way to the ridge, crossing a stream coming down from the right. About 1km up is a camp site with equally fine views.

### Places to Stay

Most new hotel development in Karimabad is designed (and priced) for tour groups, but several venerable bottom-end places are still good value. Except at the top end, rates are very negotiable outside peak season.

**Bottom End** In this range you can expect squat loos and cold showers, except as noted. Hotels with dorm-style beds for Rs 40-50 include *New Hunza Tourist Hotel, Old Hunza Inn, Garden Lodge* and *Karimabad Hotel*; *Garden Lodge* also has a cheaper dorm-tent. You can pitch your own tent and use the facilities for free at *New Hunza Tourist Hotel* and for Rs 20-30 at *Garden Lodge, Hunza Guest House* and others.

*New Hunza Tourist Hotel* (☎ 47108) has gloomy doubles with toilet for Rs 120 and 150. The communal meals are a good place for meeting travellers, and Manzoor Hussain's jeep is available for excursions. Also good value is the *Old Hunza Inn* (☎ 47020), with triples at Rs 40/bed; in 1980 this was Hunza's first private guesthouse. The nearby *Haider Inn* was under renovation when we visited. The *Garden Lodge* (☎ 47093), in a quiet garden off the upper bazaar road, has doubles/triples for Rs 200/250 and a shady dining room with good food. A sprawling *Northern Areas Public Works Department (NAPWD) Resthouse* has Rs 150 doubles.

*Hunza Lodge* (☎ 47061) has dusty doubles with fine views for a negotiable Rs 200, pricier ones with western toilet, and erratic service. The glum *Rainbow Hotel* is Rs 100 for a double with shared loo, no showers, and zero service when the TV is on. Truly bottom of the heap are the Rs 40 beds at the three room *Karimabad Hotel*.

**Middle** In the middle and top ranges you can expect plain, clean rooms with attached western toilets and hot showers, except as noted. The *Karim Hotel* (☎ 47089) at the top of the bazaar has clean Rs 250 triples (some share toilets), Rs 300 doubles, a six bed local-style room for Rs 400, OK food on a sunny patio with fine views – but videos downstairs in the evening. Nearby, the *Mountain Refuge* (☎ 47088) has two Rs 300 doubles and a Rs 400 quad with squat loo and hot shower.

Good value in this range is the quiet *Hunza Guest House* (☎ 47022), with rooms clustered around shared facilities and several small eating spaces. A six bed local-style room is Rs 130, a double with squat loo Rs 240, comfortable doubles Rs 320-560, and the food is good. It's beyond the bazaar on the Aliabad road, north of Karimabad.

The *Tourist Park Hotel* (☎ 47045) has a warren of single/double rooms around a quiet courtyard for Rs 450/500. Next door, the *Hill Top Hotel* (☎ 47010, 47060) just keeps growing, with Rs 400/500 rooms around a grassy terrace, the occasional venue for 'culture shows' of Hunza music. In the lower bazaar the old *Mountain View Hotel* (☎ 47053) has overpriced doubles for Rs 600 and Rs 900, though travellers praise the food.

In the middle of the bazaar are the *World Roof Hotel*, where doubles with a balcony and great views are Rs 500, and the earnest *New Golden Lodge*, where a double with squat loo and hot shower is Rs 300. Clueless staff at the *Mulberry Inn* asked Rs 400 for a double, and Rs 200 to pitch a tent in the garden!

**Top end** The well-run *Hunza Baltit Inn* (☎ 47113; fax Gilgit (0572) 55900) has bright rooms for Rs 750/950 with views up to Baltit Fort. They're also taking over the unfinished behemoth next door.

The booby prize goes to the pretentious, unsightly *Darbar Hunza Hotel* (☎ Gilgit (0572) 4238), owned by the Hunza royal family and trying to be four star with rooms for Rs 2800/3200. Also out of the question for individual travellers is the *Hunza View Hotel* (☎ 47098), sticking out below the tele-phone exchange; big rooms are Rs 1050/1250 and up. All have satellite TV.

### Places to Eat

See the boxed text titled 'Hunza Food & Drink' earlier in this chapter. Most tourist hotels can also do a good approximation of a western breakfast.

*Ultar Restaurant* is a kind of multilevel outdoor dining room with a big menu of cheap Hunza dishes. The cuisine is definitely not haute, service is snail's-pace and arithmetic is not one of their strengths, but this is one way to sample local food and enjoy views of Altit and Duikar. Enter from the bazaar, near the Altit turning.

Several grotty shacks serve basic local and Pakistani dishes, boiled eggs, chicken soup etc. One that we can recommend is *Ghiz-ayyat*, to the right of the post office steps. Since the arrival of satellite TV, other dives with cheap food and dubious hygiene now serve mainly as auditoria – eg the *Hogan Hotel*, *Shaq Restaurant* and the ironically named *Hunza Healthy Food*.

*Happy Bakery*, opposite the Mountain Refuge, often has phitti, burus and local butter. Others with phitti include *Baltit Bakery* and *New Happy Bakery*. These are also good places for dried fruit, snacks and trekking supplies.

The *Old Hunza Inn* does cheap and generous local/western dinners (eg daudo, vegetable, rice, chapatti, chips, sometimes traditional items like burushapik). *New Hunza Tourist Hotel* also offers bargain local-style set meals if there are enough guests. If you're not staying at these places, book dinner in the morning. By arrangement, the *Tourist Park Hotel* does Hunza-style dinners in the owner's home, right in the middle of the hotel complex.

When there are enough guests the *Hill Top Hotel* has buffet breakfast/lunch/dinner for Rs 80/130/150, open to nonguests too. *Hunza Baltit Inn* serves good fixed meals for Rs 100/155/180. The *Mountain Refuge* was building a restaurant when we visited, although prices looked high. Other hotels have restaurants roughly in line with room

HUNZA & NAGAR

quality; even the worst of them can produce chicken curry, dhal and boiled potatoes.

Self-caterers will find fresh fruit and vegetables less plentiful here than in Gilgit.

**Drinks** If you don't like the look of Karimabad's murky water, fill your bottle at a clear spring 15 minutes beyond Baltit village on the Ultar trail, just past the channel headworks, or buy bottled water in the bazaar.

### Entertainment

Traditional dances are occasionally performed at the Hill Top or other upper-end hotelsby local musicians. Hunza music is called *hareep*, and there are different versions for weddings, festivals, polo matches and other events. It's rarely performed now except privately. Instruments include large drum *dadang*, small bongos *dadamal*, horn *surnai*, pipe *tutek* and flute *purelo*.

### Things to Buy

The Baltit Book Centre in the bazaar has a respectable collection of Northern Areas and Central Asia books in English (plus pirate copies of the 1st edition of this book!).

The bazaar is lined with 'art galleries' and 'handicraft' shops, not all of them run by local people. Keep your money in the community by going for the smaller, less pretentious ones run by older men. Hunza-Nagar wool is renowned for durability, though it's being displaced by factory imitations. The best deals are in general shops, though selection is probably larger in Gilgit.

A place just above the Baltit Hunza Inn calling itself 'Women Welfare Shop' has no relationship at all with local women nor their welfare, and should be avoided.

### Getting There & Away

Local jeep drivers have formed a cartel, with a rota system and fixed prices for standard tourist destinations, although your hotelwallah may have his own vehicle available for local trips.

Minibuses to Karimabad depart around 3 pm from Gilgit's Jamaat Khana Bazaar (be sure they aren't just going to Ganesh). They run up and down the Karimabad bazaar around 5 to 6 am in search of passengers to Gilgit; the fare is Rs 60. Natco's Sost to Gilgit bus passes through Ganesh about 8 am.

The only convenient Karimabad to Sost transport is to hitch or take the Natco bus at Ganesh – passing through en route to Sost after about 11 am – or to hire a vehicle through your hotel.

### Getting Around

It's a 2km climb to the bazaar from Ganesh on the KKH. A free jeep shuttle from the New Hunza Tourist Hotel often meets Sost to Gilgit buses. Other jeeps lurking at Ganesh were asking Rs 120 at the time of research. Passenger Suzukis do an Aliabad-Karimabad-Ganesh loop all day for Rs 5-10.

### ALTIT, DUIKAR & MELISHKAR

Little Altit village (population about 2000) offers a respite from the increasing hustle of Karimabad, though it too is starting to prosper from the tourist trade. Jealous Karimabad hotel-wallahs will tell you Altit is 'too far'. A stiff hike above Altit brings you to the practically airborne summer villages of Duikar and Melishkar.

### Altit Fort

This is a miniature, unrenovated, graffiti-covered (and slightly older) version of Baltit Fort. It costs Rs 25 to enter. Through doors with carved lintels are two family rooms in traditional style, with sleeping and sitting platforms around the cooking area. Outside one is an ancient shitter with a 300m sheer drop to the Hunza River. On the roof is a handsome, wood-and-stone watchtower, too dangerous to climb. The fort is open daily from 8 am to about 6 pm.

Local people dislike outsiders wandering in Altit's old village centre – eg through the gate opposite the pool – and resent tourists taking photos of them on their rooftops from the fort (the rooftop was traditionally as private a place as the inside of a house). Please be discreet in any case.

## Melishkar & Duikar

At about 3000m, Melishkar is said to be Hunza's highest village. It and Duikar are a punishing two to 2½ hour climb from Altit, past cheerful hamlets and gravity-defying terraced fields. The reward is immense valley views. For a sublime experience, come up for sunset and a moonlit overnight stay.

If you can tear yourself away from the view, there is an even better one from Khosht, a promontory leaning out over Ultar Meadows and the glacier, and a five hour round trip walk from Melishkar.

## Places to Stay & Eat

Altit's *Kisar Inn* (☎ 47041) has a shady courtyard and a guestbook with good tips among hash-heads' ravings. Dorms are Rs 40/bed (Rs 50 in local style with loo) and doubles Rs 200 (Rs 300 with western toilet and shared hot shower), or pitch a tent for Rs 30. There are good local dishes in the rooftop restaurant.

Other Altit accommodation includes at least two *Village Guest Houses* at about Rs 300 per double – Amir Jan's opposite the Kisar Inn and Wilayat (☎ 47039) at the east end of the old polo ground. Near Wilayat is the top-end *White Apricot Lodge*. The *Ideal View Hotel & Restaurant* on the Karimabad to Altit road has a few singles/doubles for Rs 50/80 with shared loo, but it's too far from anywhere.

To accompany Melishkar's views, the *Eagle Nest Hotel* has comfortable rooms and first-rate Hunza food from May to October. Doubles with western toilet and hot water are Rs 200 to 500, double tents Rs 100 and 150, dorm-tents Rs 50 and 75 per bed, or pitch your own tent for Rs 50. It's very popular, so ask at the Kisar Inn (same owner) to see if there's room. At Duikar, *Edelweiss Lodge* has two barren doubles with loo and cold shower for a negotiable Rs 80/bed, but minimal views.

## Getting There & Away

Tracks run to Altit from Karimabad bazaar (25 minutes on foot) and from New Ganesh Rd. Kisar Inn's free jeep shuttle often meets Sost-Gilgit buses at Ganesh. A hired jeep from Ganesh is Rs 300. Suzukis run between Altit and Ganesh/Aliabad in the morning. An early-morning minibus runs between Altit and Gilgit for Rs 65.

Altit Fort is a five to 10 minute walk east of Kisar Inn. Turn right after the jamaat khana and pass the old village pool to the fort gate. Fort is *gela* ('geh-LAH') in Burushashki.

The turning for Melishkar is just before (west of) Altit, about 20 minutes walk from Karimabad bazaar. A gate there is for the collection of road-maintenance tax by Altit villagers. On foot Melishkar is 2½ hours up a rough, very dusty jeep track, or two hours on a shorter but very steep footpath that leaves the jeep track soon after the gate. A jeep from Karimabad is Rs 750; Kisar Inn charges Rs 500 for a jeep from Altit.

A fast (about two hours), dramatic route back to Karimabad is directly across the dry slopes between Duikar and Ultar Nala. The path is below the upper water channel and points roughly toward Baltit Fort. A trail crosses the nala behind the fort, to the path into the village.

## ALIABAD

Aliabad's characterless bazaar, strung for 1.5km along the KKH, is a transport hub and, since 1974, the Hunza Valley's administrative headquarters. It's an awkward base unless you're trekking in Hassanabad Nala.

## Orientation & Information

There's a small telephone exchange in the centre. The post office is at the east end, 200m beyond the petrol station. The office of the Hunza Education Resource Project is down a track to the right of the Rakaposhi Inn, then east on a footpath by an irrigation channel. The link road to Karimabad joins the KKH 2km west of the bazaar.

## Hassanabad Nala

Three km west of Aliabad is deep Hassanabad Nala. Trails up both sides of the nala allow you to reach the toes of two glaciers in reasonably straightforward day trips. More than about three hours up either side gets you into glacier walking, for which a local guide is essential, since routes over the glaciers change from year to year.

The trail up the west side of the nala follows the channel feeding the big 'hydel' plant that generates most of Hunza's electricity. You can turn left after 3km into the first side canyon and left again after 3.5 to 4km, and climb to the high pastures called Hachindar, about five hours from the KKH. Or it's about three hours from the KKH straight up Hassanabad Nala to sandy camping spots below the toe of Muchutshil Glacier.

A trail also climbs from behind a highway maintenance camp along the east side of Hassanabad Nala to the toe of Shishpar (also called Hassanabad) Glacier, about three hours from the KKH. One traveller wrote that a simpler approach is to walk beside the irrigation channel from above the link road 2km west of Aliabad (this channel also runs east to Hyderabad).

### Places to Stay & Eat

Three places in a row in the centre are only for the desperate. Best of the lot is the *Karakuram Lodge* (☎ 45024), with a moderately clean restaurant, cold-shower doubles for Rs 150 and a garden where you can pitch a tent for Rs 10. The *Shishper* and *Prince* hotels have grotty triples for about Rs 100. Nearby, opposite the telephone exchange, is the similar *Jubilee Hotel & Restaurant*.

West of the centre, *Rakaposhi Camping* (☎ 45083) is a spacious walled garden with two-person tents and a small dorm, but we never found anyone there. Across the road is a *Village Guest House* (☎ 45016) with comfortable doubles and triples for Rs 300. Top of the line is the nearby *Rakaposhi Inn*, where comfortable doubles with western loo and hot shower are Rs 800.

### Getting There & Away

Minibuses leave Aliabad for Gilgit as early as 5 am, first scouting Karimabad and Ganesh for passengers. Suzukis go all day to/from Ganesh for Rs 5 and Karimabad for Rs 10.

### MURTAZAABAD

Along with Ganesh, Murtazaabad is one of the few villages in Hunza with a sizeable Shia population. The village centre is just off the KKH, 8km down-river from Aliabad. In an orchard 100m east of the centre, the *Eagle Nest Hotel* (☎ 45089) has a few plain, quiet doubles with squat loo for a negotiable Rs 200.

There are several hot springs near the village, regularly used by local people for bathing and laundry. Friday and Sunday, when people also come from outside Murtazaabad, are the busiest. For more information, ask at the Eagle Nest. 'Hot spring' is *garum bul* ('gah-ROOM bool') in Burushashki.

Some passenger Suzukis come to Murtazaabad from Aliabad, or you can hire one, or hitch the through traffic.

### UPPER NAGAR

That part of Nagar visible from Karimabad is strung together by a jeep road from the Hassanabad-Shayar suspension bridge up to the glaciers at Hoper. Much of it is in the shadow of its own peaks, giving it a slightly gloomy atmosphere. It's more densely populated than Hunza, but the location makes for heavier snows and more water, so there's no need for Hunza's meticulous irrigation.

Tourism has hardly made a dent here, for better or worse. Some Nagaris would like a cut of Hunza's growing tourism-related prosperity, but fate doesn't seem to be on their side. At the time of research the people of Sumayar and Nagar villages had been engaged for several years in disputes over grazing and mining rights in the hills above, and had let the jeep road between them go unmaintained.

The main attraction easily accessible from Hunza and the KKH is the glaciers at Hoper, but even that was being strangled by Nagar villagers (or drivers at any rate), annoyed that Hunza drivers were getting all the business to 'their' Hoper. Traffic-stopping rockfalls just below Nagar village were curiously frequent.

## Orientation & Information

Opposite Ganesh the Nagar (also called Hispar) River joins the Hunza River. About 12km upstream the valley divides, south to the fertile Hoper Nala and south-east to the remote Hispar Nala. Hoper's glaciers reach nearly to this confluence.

A paved road climbs from the KKH east of Ganesh, up the east side of the Nagar River. A track continues toward Hispar Glacier and another crosses to Nagar village and up to Hoper. The jeep track west from Nagar village to Shayar will eventually be repaired between Nagar and Sumayar. A tenuous track also runs along the south bank of the Hunza River from Shayar to Minapin.

## Nagar Village to Shayar

It's a two hour drop from Nagar to Sumayar, a fairly level two hour walk on to Shayar (with views across to Hunza), then a precipitous down-and-up at the Shayar- Hassanabad suspension bridge. This area has few of the conveniences found along the KKH. There are stories of stone-throwing kids but Nagaris dismiss them as 'Hunza propaganda'.

**Nagar village** was the capital of the state of Nagar, and the old mir still lives here. It has a hospital, a police post and a few basic shops and restaurants. An *NAPWD Resthouse* has doubles for Rs 150.

Camping is not advisable near **Sumayar** but it's good in the meadows three hours up Sumayar Nala (the narrow canyon you look right into from Karimabad), with views of 7270m Diran and the Silkiang Glacier. A footpath leaves the jeep track near a power-house, initially following the channel. In the afternoon after freezing nights there is a rockfall hazard in the nala. **Askur Das** has a tea shop and small restaurant.

## Hoper

After the hard-scrabble agriculture below, the area from Nagar village to Hoper looks fertile and lovely in spring. Hoper (or Hopar) is a cluster of villages around a natural bowl at a bend of the Bualtar Glacier, 19km from the KKH. Opposite Hoper the white Bualtar is joined by the Barpu Glacier. From here you can hike beside the Bualtar or cross it and climb to summer villages along both glaciers. This is also a base for treks into the high, glacier-draped peaks called the Hispar Muztagh.

At the end of the road is a tent camp and soup kitchen called the *Hoper Hilton*, where you can pitch your tent or take a bed in one of theirs for Rs 100; a few double rooms are Rs 300 and 400. A two person tent at the nearby *Hoper Inn* is Rs 200. The managers of both can help with information (including glacier crossings) and local guides, but beware of other 'friends' who later demand a guide fee. A two room *NAPWD Resthouse* here must be booked in Gilgit.

## Getting There & Away

When the road is clear, a daily minibus and assorted jeeps run between Hoper and lower Bank Rd in Gilgit. At the time of research a jeep hired from Karimabad was Rs 950 for the return trip to Hoper. Regular cargo jeeps go in via Hassanabad to Sumayar and via Ganesh to Nagar village, heading back early the next morning.

On foot, Nagar village is about three hours, and Hoper five to six hours, from Karimabad via Ganesh. A footpath over the ridge on the Nagar side of the KKH bridge shortens this a bit. From Hassanabad via Shayar, Hoper is a very long day's walk.

## MINAPIN

Down-river from Murtazaabad the KKH crosses into Nagar. From Pisan, just on the Nagar side, a jeep track heads east for 3km across Minapin Nala to Minapin. Literally at the foot of Rakaposhi, this is the start of a steep glacier-side climb to one of the mountain's expedition base camps, with some of the grandest mountain panoramas you can find near the KKH. Even nontrekkers will appreciate the scenery from the village.

## Rakaposhi Base Camp via Minapin Glacier

This trek is best done between July and September, when days are long and water

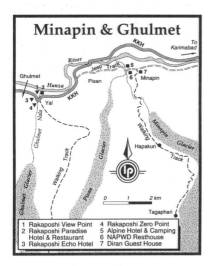

**Minapin & Ghulmet**

1 Rakaposhi View Point
2 Rakaposhi Paradise Hotel & Restaurant
3 Rakaposhi Echo Hotel
4 Rakaposhi Zero Point
5 Alpine Hotel & Camping
6 NAPWD Resthouse
7 Diran Guest House

available; even then, nights are cold. Rakaposhi is also subject to sudden, chilling storms. Start early to avoid frying your brain on the long climb to Hapakun. A local guide is a good idea, especially in the spring when the trail is eroded and dangerous. Beyond Tagaphari a guide is essential at any time. Local guides have worked out a fixed-rate rota system; contact your hotel-wallah.

The trail starts near the Diran Guesthouse. The first few km climb the Minapin Glacier's terminal moraine to the path along its west side. The path gives wide views of the glacier, and eventually of the entire Rakaposhi-Diran crest-line. Four to five hours up are huts at Hapakun. Camping is free on common land with water and a cooking area, or for a small fee on a few private patches.

On the second day the trail rises through forest for three or four hours to the base camp at Tagaphari, a meadow in a glacier-side valley 1500m above Minapin. At least one hut here is for trekkers. Climb a bit further up the ridge to blow your mind with views across a vast ice field to Diran (7270m) and Rakaposhi (7790m), and south across the Hunza Valley to the Shishpar and Ultar glaciers and the Batura Muztagh.

A retired Diran guide named Mohammad Gul is employed by a Lahore environmental outfit called Green Earth Organisation (GEO) to keep the Rakaposhi and Diran base camp areas clean, and to rent out stoves and sell kerosene (to minimise the use of scarce wood).

### Places to Stay & Eat
First across Minapin Nala as you enter the village is the down-at-heel *Alpine Hotel & Camping*, with two doubles with squat loo and cold shower for Rs 100, camping for Rs 30 and a dining room. You may not like sharing the garden with the owner's beehives. Across and up the road is an *NAPWD Resthouse* with doubles for Rs 150.

East beyond a big mosque is the best bet, *Diran Guesthouse*, with a local-style dorm for Rs 60/bed, two singles/doubles at Rs 300/400 and a too-posh complex of new rooms for Rs 400/500, all surrounded by a peaceful walled orchard. All rooms have western toilets and 24 hour hot showers.

### Getting There & Away
Minibuses depart Minapin for Gilgit after about 7am, and come to Minapin from lower Bank Rd in Gilgit around 1 to 2pm, for about Rs 50. Minapin is a 45 minute walk from the KKH.

### GHULMET
The starting point for another Rakaposhi climb is the village of Ghulmet (pronounced 'ghool-MET'; this spelling is used instead of the often seen 'Gulmit' to avoid confusion with the village in Gojal). At its eastern end is Ghulmet Nala, out of which Rakaposhi rises in a single unobscured sweep, 6000m above the road and begging to be photographed.

### Rakaposhi Base Camp via Ghulmet Glacier
Although there's a base camp up this trail (used by a Japanese expedition in 1979) and the views are outstanding, it's a long, steep slog with no water and poor camping on the way. The trail begins behind the hamlet of

JOHN KING

JOHN KING

BERNARD NAPTHINE

**Hunza & Nagar**
Top: The view of Altit fort and the Hunza Valley from Melishkar village.
Right: Hunzakut girl, Hunza Valley.
Bottom: The ancient site of Baltit fort, Hunza.

JOHN KING

JOHN MOCK

ROBERT MATZINGER

**Hunza & Nagar**
Top: Cheerful smile among the old goats, near Karimabad, Hunza.
Left: The much photographed sheep pen, Ultar, Hunza.
Right: Suspension bridge, Naltar, Hunza. Fortunately alcohol is prohibited.

Yal on the east side of Ghulmet Nala, and climbs a high ridge between the Ghulmet and Pisan glaciers. See the Minapin section above for tips on weather and on finding guides.

### Places to Stay & Eat
Several makeshift places jockey for your attention by the KKH bridge over Ghulmet Nala. *Rakaposhi View Point* and *Rakaposhi Echo Hotel* have tents for Rs 30/bed, or you can pitch yours for free; both close only in December and January. *Rakaposhi Paradise Hotel* has four plain doubles for a negotiable Rs 300, plus tent space for Rs 10-20. *Rakaposhi Zero Point* is a refreshment stand.

### GHULMET TO CHALT
The nala and village west of Ghulmet are called **Thol** (pronounced 'tole'). A prominent landmark is the green-roofed ziarat to Shah Wali, a Shia preacher who passed through in the late 18th century. Nearby is a small timber-and-stone house with carved door and a 'skylight' in the Balti-Tibetan style of Baltit Fort. Local people claim this was Shah Wali's house.

West of Thol are the nala and stone fort at **Nilt** that nearly derailed the British invasion of 1891. A path from the south side of the KKH (east of a sign reading 'Mountaineering Institute & Alpine Club') leads 300m up to the fort, a nondescript low structure now used as homes, and closed to the public. The Mountaineering Institute is a kind of clubhouse where army officers have run training programmes for Pakistani mountaineers.

Next comes **Jaffarabad**, headquarters for the Naunehal Development Organisation, Nagar's answer to the Aga Khan Rural Support Program (see the Economy section in the Facts about the Region chapter). Naunehal, founded in 1994 by 16 Nagar villages, has established at least eight English-medium primary schools, two health centres and a posse of volunteers who patrol the Minapin-Sikanderabad area for illegal hunting, especially of ibexes.

Westward the KKH arches around fertile **Sikanderabad**. Across the Hunza River is

**Khizerabad**, and west of that a small nala marks the western end of Hunza. Further west, scratched into the valley walls hundreds of metres high, is the 'road' that was Hunza's link to the outside just a generation ago.

Here the KKH runs along the southern edge of the primordial 'Asian Plate' into which the Indian subcontinent drove 50 million years ago, giving rise to the Himalaya chain. Although there's no simple line, Asia, roughly speaking, is to the north, and to the south are remnants of a chain of volcanic islands trapped between the two continents (see the Geology section in the Facts about the Region chapter).

### CHALT
In a wide bowl where the Hunza River turns south, Chalt sits across the mouths of two large valley systems. This is the only part of Nagar north of the river, and the best-endowed in terms of weather, water, pasture and tillable land. The mir of Nagar still keeps a house here. People of Chalt speak Shina (in common with Gilgit, Chilas and Kohistan), Burushashki, Urdu and sometimes English.

The Chaprot Valley, with some fine day-hikes, has brought out the poet in visitors and residents alike. The misanthropic 20th century explorer Reginald Schomberg called it 'lovely, more beautiful than any other valley in the Gilgit Agency'. Safdar Ali, mir of Hunza at the time of the British invasion, said Chalt and Chaprot were 'more precious to us than the strings of our wives' pyjamas'.

### Orientation & Information
From the KKH a jeep crosses the river and runs 3 or 4km to Chalt, with a left fork crossing the Chaprot River to a small bazaar with shops, a post office and a telephone exchange. A new bridge and road will soon enter Chalt from the west.

### Ghashumaling
Ghashumaling ('ga-SHU-ma-ling') is a lovely area in a lower Chaprot tributary. With easy trails and mulberry, peach, apple and walnut orchards, even local people come up for

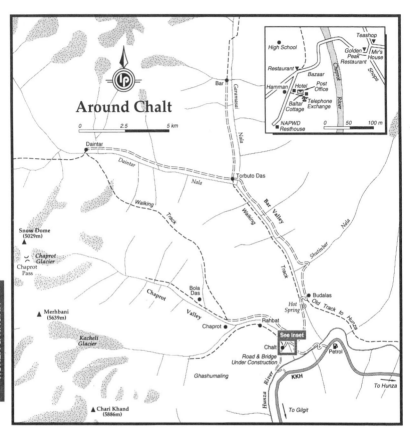

**Around Chalt**

picnics. A walk can take from two hours to all day. From Chalt bazaar take the path past the high school and up the south side of the valley. At the head of the canyon, about 12km up, are pine forests and the small Kacheli Glacier.

### Chaprot Valley

From the bazaar, cross the Chaprot River and turn left. About 150m up take the left fork, which climbs the north side of Chaprot Valley. It's an hour's walk to Chaprot village (actually a collection of hamlets). From there it's three to four hours on a mule track through summer villages to pastures at the head of the valley, a good overnight destination. In summer, horses can be hired at Chaprot.

### Bar Valley

From the bazaar, cross the river, turn left and at the next fork keep right into Bar Valley (also called Garamasai or Budalas Valley). After 3km a path continues up the west side of the valley while the jeep track crosses a bridge to Budalas. Just below the bridge is an undeveloped hot spring, sometimes used for laundry but too hot to soak in.

On the east side of Bar Valley, about 3km upstream from the bridge, the track crosses **Shutinbar Nala**. It's a steep 8-10km up Shutinbar to a glacier at its head, and there are abandoned ruby mines in the canyon.

Further up Bar Valley is Torbuto Das, about 13km from Chalt at the confluence of the Daintar and Garamasai (or Tutu Uns) nalas. West past Daintar village and about 9km from Torbuto Das, in a lovely meadow called **Taloybari**, local herders have set up a simple camping area, with food available. This is a long day's walk from Chalt; jeeps to Daintar can also be hired in Chalt.

North up Garamasai Nala from Torbuto Das is Bar, or Barkot, village, trailhead for treks to the Toltar and Baltar glaciers flowing down from 7168m Kampir Dior. Local moves since 1990 to protect Himalayan ibex in the upper Bar and adjacent watersheds were among the Northern Areas' first community-based wildlife conservation efforts. Local ex-hunters are now employed as game wardens, and of the income from government-regulated trophy hunting, 75% now goes to the people of the valley. Since 1990 ibex populations have increased in the valley.

**Places to Stay & Eat**

*Baltar Cottage* in Chalt bazaar has a few spartan rooms. In a walled apricot orchard beyond the hotel, an *NAPWD Resthouse* has two doubles for Rs 150 and 200, or you can pitch a tent for Rs 50 in the garden. In addition to meals at the resthouse by arrangement, there are shops and some small, gloomy restaurants in the bazaar, and a tea shop and the Golden Peak restaurant east of the bridge.

The Bar Valley NGO (an association of villages) has boarded the ecotourism bandwagon, and you may find Daintar and Bar villagers ready to put you up for around Rs 60 per person or let you pitch a tent for Rs 40.

**Getting There & Away**

Chalt-bound minibuses and passenger jeeps depart in the early morning from lower Bank Rd in Gilgit for Rs 30, returning next morning. One or two Suzukis go to Aliabad each morning from the chowk on the east side of the Chaprot River bridge, for Rs 30.

## CHALT TO GILGIT

Below Chalt the Hunza River turns south. Ten minutes drive down-river from the Chalt turn-off, road-cuts above the Highway are early 1960s attempts at a highway by Pakistan army engineers. Across the river is the KKH's precarious precursor, a now-abandoned jeep road that follows the oldest caravan trails.

A few minutes southward the Highway passes a clutch of cafes and a road-maintenance base called Jaglot Guar. The *Hunza Hotel* and other cafes here have rope beds and basic food.

Two or 3km later, a jeep road climbs up to Jaglot village, the starting point for another Rakaposhi trek, a day's climb up the north side of Jaglot Nala toward 4730m Haraj, Rakaposhi's western arm. Down by the river are camps of nomads, known as Mohans, who pan small amounts of gold from the river, mercury-treat it and sell it in the Gilgit bazaar.

About 25 minutes down-river from Chalt, at the south end of Rahimabad village – and almost exactly midway between Kashgar and Rawalpindi – is a monument to KKH workers, topped with an old pneumatic drill used for setting explosives. In Urdu script on the pedestal are the words of Pakistan's favourite philosopher-poet, Allama Mohammed Iqbal (who in the 1930s first proposed a Muslim state in India): 'God has given man integrity, faith, and a strong mind, and if he sets himself to it he can kick a mountain to powder or stop a river in its tracks.'

As the road comes out into the basin where the Hunza River joins the Gilgit River, the view back up the Hunza Valley is dominated by Kampir Dior, 70km north on the crest of the Karakoram. Dainyor, at the confluence, is the southernmost Ismaili village on the KKH.

# Gilgit Region

Gilgit is administrative headquarters for the 70,000 sq km Northern Areas, and the hub of the KKH, with information, transport, westerner-friendly hotels and restaurants offering a welcome break from sabzi, dhal and chapatti. It swarms with visitors from May to October.

Except for spring blossoms and autumn colours, the scenery around Gilgit (at 1500m) is austere and brown. In summer it's almost too hot for hiking near Gilgit but, as in the rest of the Karakoram, above about 2000m you can find glacier-fed valleys with pine and juniper forests and luxuriant meadows. A web of nearby valleys fingers Rakaposhi, Nanga Parbat and other giants.

## History

**Early History** From the 1st century AD, Gilgit was part of the Buddhist Kushan Empire at Taxila, and remained Buddhist after the Kushans' demise in the 3rd century. The Chinese pilgrim Fa Hsien found hundreds of active monasteries in the course of his journey from Xinjiang to Taxila in 403 AD. A few traces remain, including a bas-relief Buddha on a cliff-face near Gilgit and pictures scratched onto riverside rocks at Chilas.

Sanskrit inscriptions on a boulder at Dainyor list Tibetan rulers of the 7th and 8th centuries. In the 8th century a Tang Chinese army occupied Chitral and the upper Gilgit River basin for three years before the Tibetans drove them out. According to the Dainyor stone, local rulers in turn expelled the Tibetans.

The shift from Buddhism to Hinduism to Islam in this region is tangled in folklore. Gilgit's last Buddhist ruler is said to have been a cruel cannibal-king named Shri Badat, who ate a baby for breakfast every day – although the story and even the name have echoes in a variety of south Asian legends. The story goes that his daughter

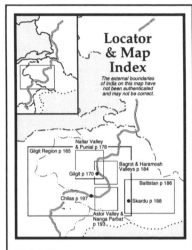

## Locator & Map Index

The external boundaries of India on this map have not been authenticated and may not be correct.

Naltar Valley & Punial p 178

Gilgit Region p 165

Bagrot & Haramosh Valleys p 184

Gilgit p 170

Baltistan p 186

Chilas p 197

Skardu p 188

Astor Valley & Nanga Parbat p 193

## Highlights

- No-holds-barred polo and the world's highest polo ground at Shandur Pass
- Giant Buddhas carved on rockfaces in Gilgit and Skardu
- The remote and ancient kingdom of Khapalu in Baltistan
- Two thousand years of petroglyphs at Chilas

plotted with a Persian demi-god named Azur Jamsher to trap him and burn him to death, after which the two married and founded a lineage that continues today with the Hunza and Nagar royal families.

In any case Gilgit appears to have been ruled more or less continuously from perhaps the 15th or 16th century to the 19th by the so-called Trakhan (or Tara Khan) dynasty. The dominant tribe or caste was the Shins, who may have originally been Hindu and come from the lower Indus Valley. Their language, Shina, is still the common speech.

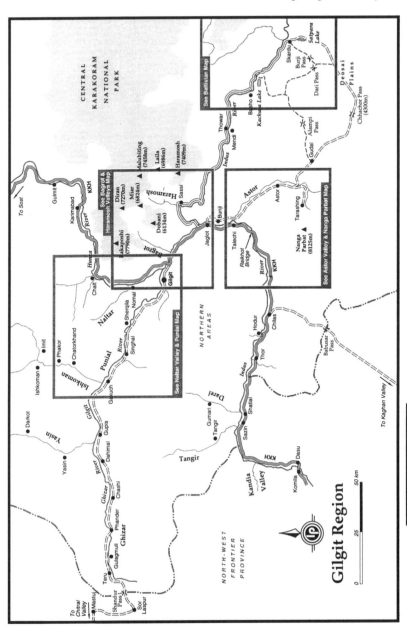

Gilgit Region

### Cyclists' Notes, Gilgit Region

Gilgit is 10km off the KKH via Jutial. Most people cycling the KKH start or finish here, avoiding the headaches of Indus Kohistan. Good 'rumour-books' are at the North Inn and Mountain Refuge in Gilgit. Cars driving onto the suspension bridges connecting Gilgit with the KKH via Dainyor set them into a waving motion that can knock you over – just grab the nearest rope and hang on!

Gilgit to Shatial has no long climbs in either direction, but lots of lung-busters under 3 or 4km long. There is a significant risk of dehydration and heat stroke between Raikhot Bridge and Shatial, one of the KKH's driest stretches, and ferociously hot in summer too. Roadside rivulets tend to be geothermal – warm and sulphurous.

The Gilgit to Chitral crossing via the Shandur Pass takes about eight days, and is too rough for anything but a mountain bike. There are plans to pave the road from Gilgit west to Gakuch. It's already paved from Chitral east to Buni, with plans to extend this to Mastuj. The Chitral side is the steepest.

For notes on crossing the Babusar Pass between Chilas and the Kaghan Valley, see the Kaghan Valley section of the Hazara chapter.

**Gilgit to Raikhot Bridge, 80km** Jaglot, about 20km south of Gilgit, has cheap serais and a small hotel. The best overnight stop between Gilgit and Chilas is the scenic NAPWD Resthouse at Talechi, about 62km from Gilgit or 67km from Chilas; book it in Gilgit or Chilas, or camp out in the garden. Don't count on finding food there. Cyclists report astronomical prices and shifty staff at the Shangri-La Midway House by Raikhot Bridge.

**Raikhot Bridge to Chilas turning, 54km** Gonar Farm has one or two serais. At several slide-zones, the road is holed, bumpy and occasionally washed out.

**Chilas turning to Shatial, 63km** Shatial has a basic inn where some cyclists have been turned away, and a primitive resthouse with a sleepable veranda. ■

In perhaps the 16th century, Taj Mughal, ruler of Badakhshan in Afghanistan, crossed from Chitral and briefly seized Gilgit. In honour of his victory he built a stone monument above Jutial, which is still there. Taj Mughal is also credited with bringing Ismailism to the region. Shia Islam may have arrived via Baltistan and Kashmir in the 16th or 17th century.

As the Silk Road fell out of use in the 16th century the region split into feuding mini-kingdoms, the main ones being Gilgit, Hunza, Nagar and four in the upper Gilgit basin – Punial, Ishkoman, Yasin and Ghizar. In the 17th century most were vassal to Baltistan.

**The Dogras & the British** The last local ruler at Gilgit was a tyrant from Yasin named Gohar Aman, famous for selling a large part of the town's population into slavery. He was dethroned in 1841 by Dogra soldiers of Kashmir on behalf of the Sikh Empire in the Punjab, but they proved so disagreeable that

he made a comeback in 1848. He fortified the town (a remnant is the tower within the present militia barracks) and ruled until he died, 10 years later.

After that the Dogras came back, under new management. In 1846 the British had won the first of two quick wars with the Sikhs and annexed Sikh territories in the Kashmir Valley, Ladakh, Baltistan and the vassal state of Gilgit. Packaging them up as 'the State of Jammu and Kashmir', they sold it for £750,000 to a Dogra prince named Gulab Singh and declared him the first maharajah of Kashmir. Thus Muslim Gilgit found itself with a Hindu master, who received grudging tributes from local rulers and kept his garrisons beefed up.

Then Britain discovered Russians snooping in the Pamirs and Afghanistan, and began to have doubts about the maharajah. In 1877 Kashmir was put under control of the Indian Foreign Office and a British 'political agent' arrived in Gilgit to look over the Kashmiri governor's shoulder. This arrangement proved awkward and the Agency was closed down after a few years – only to reopen in 1889 as Britain's anxiety mounted. The new 'PA' was a no-nonsense soldier named Algernon Durand, who lost no time in taking charge and putting everyone in their places.

Durand conducted his own foreign policy in the region. Soon after his invasion of Hunza in 1891 (see the boxed text The Pacification of Hunza & Nagar in the Hunza & Nagar chapter), he put a garrison at Chilas to control the Babusar Pass to the Kaghan Valley, one of two tenuous supply routes for Gilgit (the other was the Burzil Pass from Kashmir).

Gilgit, like Kashgar, was an outpost in the 'Great Game', the imperial hide-and-seek between Britain and Russia, well into the 20th century. A succession of political agents managed by grace or guile to stay in charge, and in 1935 Britain actually leased back the entire Agency from Kashmir.

A local militia, the Gilgit Scouts, was mobilised. The were drawn heavily from sons of local royalty, and were raised and dressed in their own tartan. They were probably as much a symbolic warning to the Russians and a vehicle for intrigue as a defence force.

**Partition** In the 1930s and 1940s demands mounted both for Indian independence and for a separate Muslim homeland. In the end, Britain agreed to split the Raj into two separate countries, a Muslim-majority Pakistan and a Hindu-majority India.

An awkward problem was the hundreds of princely states with direct allegiance to Britain, who theoretically stood to regain their original sovereignty. Most were coaxed to join India or Pakistan. Kashmir – with a Hindu ruler, a Muslim majority and a lovely vale beloved by both Hindus and Muslims – was the biggest hot potato. Hoping for his own independence, Maharajah Hari Singh stalled.

Two weeks before 14 August 1947 which was to mark the end of the empire, the last political agent handed over the Gilgit Agency to a new Kashmiri governor, Ghansar Singh. As the day came and went, Gilgit held its breath while the maharajah dithered.

Then, on 26 October, a band of Pathan (Pashtun) Afridi tribesmen from the North-West Frontier Province (NWFP) marched into Kashmir proclaiming a *jihad*, or holy war, and everything came unglued. Hari Singh fled to Delhi, acceded to India and

---

**The Gilgit Uprising**

Several groups had anticipated Hari Singh's accession to India. A clique of Muslim officers in the Maharajah's own army, led by Colonel Mirza Hassan Khan, had been conspiring to seize Kashmir for Pakistan, but word had got out and Hassan was transferred to Kashmir's 'Siberia', the Bunji garrison south of Gilgit.

Meanwhile, Major Mohammed Babar Khan of the Gilgit Scouts and several fellow-officers (and, according to some, their British commander) had hatched their own rebellion.

Within days of the Maharajah's decision, a mob gathered in Gilgit from neighbouring valleys. The governor called Bunji for help, and who should be among the reinforcements but Colonel Hassan. On 1 November Babar Khan arrested Ghansar Singh and the rebels asked to join Pakistan.

Within a few days the Scouts, and Muslim soldiers of the Kashmiri army, joined the war with India. In the following months the Scouts took Baltistan and Hassan got to the outskirts of Srinagar.

The fledgling Indian air force at one point bombed Gilgit, no easy task in the narrow valleys. Gilgitis like to tell the story of the Scouts' pipe band, who mocked the Indian pilots by defiantly tootling up and down the airfield the whole time.

Memories of the 'Uprising' are still alive in Gilgit. Hassan, Babar and another leader of the Gilgit Scouts, Maj Safiullah Beg, are buried in the town's maple-shaded municipal park, Chinar Bagh, and many of their offspring are local politicians and entrepreneurs. Of course it's not 14 August but 1 November that Gilgit celebrates as Independence Day, with spontaneous music and dancing and a week-long polo tournament. One of the best polo teams every year is from the Gilgit garrison of the Northern Light Infantry (NLI), successor to the Gilgit Scouts. ■

asked for military help. India accepted, subject to an eventual vote by Kashmiris.

The people of the Gilgit region would have none of this and staged their own rebellion, arresting the new governor and demanding to become part of Pakistan (see the boxed text on previous page). In Kashmir the two newborn countries went to war. It ended in January 1949 with a United Nations ceasefire, under which Pakistan got temporary control over what came to be called the Northern Areas, plus a slice of western Kashmir it calls Azad (Free) Kashmir, while India got Ladakh and the Kashmir Valley. The ceasefire line became the de facto border.

**After Partition** India and Pakistan again fought over Kashmir in 1965 and 1971, and almost again in 1990. Pakistan's official position is that, until the referendum promised by India is held, Kashmir doesn't belong to anyone – although its leaders are as repelled as India's at the idea of an independent Kashmir. Hope for a solution to the impasse has ebbed and flowed over the years.

The Burzil Pass was closed by the 1948 ceasefire, leaving only the Babusar Pass to link the Northern Areas with Pakistan. It is surprising to realise that Gilgit was only firmly linked to the outside world some 25 years ago, by a civilian air corridor and the first stages of the KKH.

The Northern Areas' 1.6 million people (other estimates say 1.2 million) remain in limbo. For Islamabad to call this a province would concede the status quo of a divided Kashmir. It is instead a 'Federally Administered Area,' governed by a council of locally elected or appointed members, but headed by a federally appointed official answerable only to Islamabad (see the Government section in the Facts about the Region chapter). With much justification, local people bemoan this inferior status – eg they have no representation in Pakistan's parliament – although 1994 political reforms have given the Northern Areas a structure that

very much resembles the country's constitutional provinces.

## People

Whatever their tribe, nearly everyone with roots longer than a generation in the watersheds around Gilgit, as well as south in Indus Kohistan to Pattan, speaks Shina ('shee-NA'), the language of the Shins. But Gilgit's crossroads position has filled its bazaar with people from all over Asia, forcing Gilgitis to be multilingual. It is not unusual to hear Uyghur, Wakhi, Burushashki, Pashto or even Persian in the bazaar. Urdu and English are widely spoken.

All brands of Islam are represented: Ismailis in the Gilgit, Ghizar and Hunza valleys; Shias in Nagar, Punial, Bagrot and Haramosh; Sunnis in Chilas and southward. They all overlap in Gilgit, with inevitable tension.

## GILGIT
### Tel Area Code: 0572

Gilgit is of interest mainly for its people, though there are historical spots and a few good day-trips, and the bazaar is eclectic and lively. The shopkeepers, from all over Pakistan and Xinjiang, are part of its attraction. In search of a sale or a chat, it's their 'Muslim duty' to ask you in and serve you sweet tea till your kidneys burst.

Gilgitis have not always been this kind to one another. This is the only town in the region with substantial populations of all branches of Islam, and tensions have frequently surfaced. In 1988 Sunni-Shia hostility exploded into virtual warfare at Jalalabad in Bagrot. Sectarian battles erupted around Gilgit in 1992, 1993 and 1994, leading to curfews of a week or more.

Curiously, since political reforms in 1994 gave limited political power to local branches of religious-based parties, and as development money has become more evenly distributed in the region, the situation has calmed dramatically, in stark contrast to Punjab's escalating sectarian bloodshed. There is more dialogue, shops are starting to stay open late again, and football matches are back on the calendar.

In fact the only major violence since then united everybody against the government. In 1996 the authorities responded to demands for a local militia with a hugely popular recruitment campaign (soldiering is honourable here, and unemployment high). But back-door hiring of men from outside the Northern Areas led to protests. An officer fired into a crowd and killed at least one man, and an angry mob burned down a magistrate's office and ransacked the Deputy Commissioner's office.

Gilgit is becoming a city, its headlong growth owing more to its position on modern trade routes to China and Central Asia than to tourism, which remains low. An extension of the airport runway is on the cards, which will allow jets to land, making the region more accessible for more of the year. But public services haven't multiplied nearly as fast as hotels – eg Gilgit doesn't yet have a sewage system – partly because of lopsided expenditure on law enforcement. Electricity and water remain unreliable and vulnerable to heavy weather.

The town wakes up early to muezzins in scores of mosques calling the faithful to dawn prayers. Plaintive and charming for the first few days, the overlapping, amplified chants soon lose their appeal for the average infidel.

## Orientation

Gilgit is on the south bank of the Gilgit River, 10km west off the KKH via the military cantonment at Jutial. A back road also comes from the KKH at Dainyor, via a tunnel and two swinging bridges, over the Hunza and Gilgit rivers.

The bazaar is essentially a single 2km street full of shops, increasingly punctuated by cul-de-sac 'markets' which replace one or two shops with a dozen. Shopkeepers from nearby villages cluster together, eg in Bank Rd for Nagar and Jamaat Khana Bazaar for Hunza. South-west up Bank Rd are government offices, and further up are several villages, the biggest of which is Barmas. The airport is east of the bazaar.

Many larger streets have two names, one common and one official. These include (official name in parentheses) Jamaat Khana Bazaar (Sir Aga Khan Rd), Bank Rd (Khazana Rd; *khazana* is Urdu for 'bank'), Hospital Rd (Alama Mohammed Iqbal Rd) and Jutial Rd (Quaid-i-Azam Rd or Shahrah-i-Quaid-i-Azam).

## Information

**Tourist Offices** The Pakistan Tourism Development Corporation (PTDC) (☎ 2562), at the Chinar Inn on Babar Rd, has brochures and can help with bookings and tours, but that's about it. There's no Gilgit map. PTDC also has a small office at JSR Plaza.

To book any of the Northern Areas Public Works Department (NAPWD) Resthouses between the Khunjerab Pass and Chilas, see the Administrative Officer, office of the Chief Engineer at NAPWD (☎ 3375), on Bank Rd opposite the National Bank.

**Police & Foreigners' Registration** Police headquarters (SSP or Senior Superintendent of Police; ☎ 3356) is across the Pul Rd bridge. The Foreigners' Registration Office (FRO), at Khomer Chowk, is open from 8 am to 3 pm from April to September, 9 am to 4 pm the rest of the year, but to noon on Friday and closed Sunday.

**Money** National Bank is off Bank Rd, and Habib, Allied and Soneri banks are in a row in Saddar Bazaar. All do foreign exchange. Hours are 9 am to 1.30 pm (Soneri also from 3 to 5 pm), except closed Friday afternoon and Sunday. National Bank accepts travellers cheques or cash in US$, UK£, DM, FF, C$ and Japanese yen. At a pinch, some merchants will change US dollars cash.

Alam Money Changer (☎ 2605) in JSR Plaza has better cash rates than the banks, accepts most major currencies and is open from 8 am to 8 pm daily.

**Post & Communications** The post office is in Saddar Bazaar. Hours are 8 am to 2 pm,

GILGIT REGION

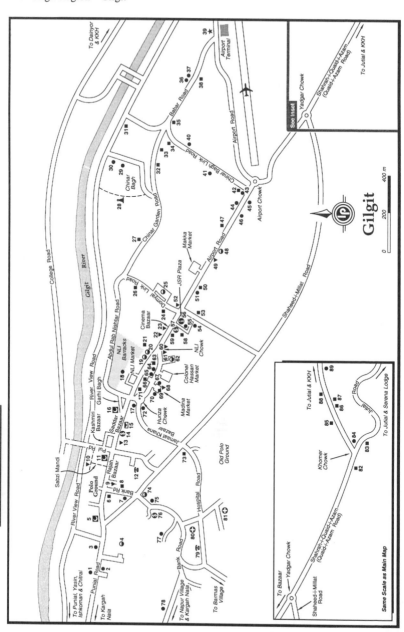

Gilgit

**PLACES TO STAY**

| | |
|---|---|
| 6 | NAPWD Resthouse |
| 8 | Golden Peak Hotel & Restaurant |
| 21 | Madina Guest House (new annex) |
| 24 | Alflah Hotel |
| 26 | Mir's Lodge |
| 27 | Mountain Refuge |
| 31 | Riveria Hotel |
| 32 | PTDC Chinar Inn & PTDC Tourist Information |
| 33 | Hunza Inn |
| 34 | Chinese Lodge |
| 35 | Mekkah Hotel (under construction) |
| 38 | Hunza Tourist House |
| 42 | Park Hotel |
| 47 | Shaheen Hotel (under construction) |
| 50 | Top Moon Hotel |
| 53 | Diamer Hotel |
| 58 | JSR Hotel |
| 59 | Skyways Hotel |
| 63 | Madina Guest House |
| 66 | New Kashghar Inn |
| 69 | Taj Hotel |
| 71 | Ibex Lodge |
| 73 | New Lahore Hotel |
| 82 | North Inn |
| 83 | Gilgit Gateway Hotel |
| 85 | Tourist Hamlet Hotel |
| 86 | Horizon Guest House |
| 87 | Hotel (under costruction) |
| 88 | Tourist Cottages |

**PLACES TO EAT**

| | |
|---|---|
| 9 | Haidry Tea Shop |
| 10 | Hassan's Yoghurt Shop |
| 13 | Salar Restaurant |
| 22 | Pathan Hotel |
| 23 | Yoghurt Shops |
| 49 | Patthan Restaurant |
| 52 | Baig's Restaurant |
| 60 | Pathan Restaurant |
| 61 | Kadahi Shop |
| 68 | Cafe Burushal |

**OTHER**

| | |
|---|---|
| 1 | Nazir Khan's Shop |
| 2 | Ehsan Cloth House |
| 3 | Kakakhel General Store |
| 4 | Natco Bus Yard for Punial & Wesward |
| 5 | Imamia Mosque |
| 7 | British Cemetery |
| 11 | Jama Mosque |
| 12 | Telephone Exchange |
| 14 | Allied, Soneri & Habib Banks |
| 15 | Post Office |
| 16 | Moti Mosque |
| 17 | Bicycle Rental |
| 18 | Gohar Aman's Tower |
| 19 | Natco Bus Yard |
| 20 | K-2 Travels |
| 25 | General Bus Stand |
| 28 | Uprising Memorial |
| 29 | Town Hall |
| 30 | Northern Areas Council |
| 36 | Aga Khan Rural Support Programme (AKRSP) |
| 37 | IUCN-Pakistan |
| 39 | Police |
| 40 | Golden Peak Tours |
| 41 | Himalaya Nature Tours |
| 43 | Hunza Handicrafts |
| 44 | Xama Shop |
| 45 | Mountain Movers |
| 46 | Walji's Travel (Adventure Pakistan) |
| 48 | Tai's Transport |
| 51 | Mountaineering Equipments |
| 54 | PIA Booking Office |
| 55 | Sargin Travel |
| 56 | PTDC Information Office & Pamir Tours |
| 57 | Alam Money Changer |
| 62 | Mashabrum Tours |
| 64 | National Music Centre |
| 65 | Gilgit Colour Lab |
| 67 | Pak Hunza Handicrafts |
| 70 | North News Agency |
| 72 | GM Beg Sons |
| 74 | Minibuses to Chalt & Thol & Minapin |
| 75 | NAPWD Office |
| 76 | National Bank |
| 77 | Library |
| 78 | Fisheries Office |
| 79 | Telephone Exchange |
| 80 | District Hospital |
| 81 | Women's Hospital |
| 84 | Foreigners' Registration Office (FRO) |
| 89 | WWF-Pakistan |

Saturday to Wednesday. Stamps are sold in front. Poste restante, at the side, is also the place to get your outgoing mail franked while you wait (as a precaution against stamp theft).

You can make overseas calls from a government public call office (PCO) just off Rajah Bazaar, and make calls or send telegrams from the main exchange in upper Hospital Rd. Both are open 24 hours a day. The government PCO charges less than private ones for local calls.

Gilgit has (IDD), International Direct Dialling, though only government and a few private places can afford the connection.

Some hotels will place calls for you at an inflated rate.

Pamir Tours (fax 2475) and the Serena Lodge (fax 55900) will send and accept international faxes.

**Travel Agencies** There are a number of travel and trekking agencies awaiting your business; following are some reliable ones. Many also have Islamabad or Rawalpindi offices (see the Tour Operators & Trekking Companies section in the Getting There & Away chapter). Walji's and Mountain Movers can also organise local white-water trips.

**GILGIT REGION**

**Gilgit Telephone Numbers**
At the time of writing Gilgit was in the throes of a conversion to a digital exchange and longer telephone numbers – not all of them yet operational. ■

**Libraries** Off upper Bank Rd, in the renovated home of the early British political agents, is the Gilgit Municipal Library. Many of its 20,000 volumes are in English, heavy on colonial tastes and modern Americana, with much on the Northern Areas. You can also browse through some western magazines and English-language Pakistani papers. Senior Librarian Sherbaz Ali Khan is a good source of local information. Hours are 9 am to 3 pm daily, except 8 am to noon on Friday, and closed Saturday.

**Environmental Organisations** WWF-Pakistan's Gilgit office (☎ & fax 4127) is at 543-A Shahrah-i-Quaid-i-Azam. Here you can buy the good *An Ecotourist's Guide to Khunjerab National Park*. IUCN-Pakistan (☎ & fax 2679) has an office on Babar Rd near the airport. The Khunjerab National Park Directorate (☎ 55061) is in Jutial near the KKH. By 1998 WWF plans to open a Conservation & Information Centre next door, with a database on Pakistan's protected areas.

Adventure Centre Pakistan (☎ 2409), c/o GM Beg
    Sons bookshop, Jamaat Khana Bazaar
Golden Peak Tours (☎ 4295), Chinar Bagh Link Rd
Himalaya Nature Tours (☎ 2946), Chinar Bagh
    Link Rd
Lost Horizon Treks & Tours (☎ 4202), c/o Horizon
    Guest House
Mountain Movers (☎ 2967), Airport Rd
Pamir Tours (☎ 3939), JSR Plaza
Walji's Adventure Pakistan (☎ 2665), Airport Rd

**Medical Services** The District Hospital is in upper Hospital Rd. Nearby is a Women's Hospital, with female doctors. Foreign women can go to either, though the former has more specialists. A western-staffed, privately

funded Vision International eye hospital (☎ 2878), on River View Rd 2km east of the twin suspension bridges, can help with non-eye problems in extreme situations.

Of the bazaar's pharmacies ('medicos'), one in front of the New Kashghar Inn looks clean and well stocked.

**Gohar Aman's Tower**
On the grounds of the Northern Light Infantry (NLI) barracks, a white tower is all that remains of a fort built by Gohar Aman in the 1850s. You can get up close to it in the playing field behind NLI Market.

**British Cemetery**
In lower Bank Rd is an overgrown graveyard surrounded by barbed wire. Captain George Hayward, a British explorer murdered in Yasin in 1870 by a son of Gohar Aman, is among those buried here. Ask for the key from Ghulam Ali, who lives in a shack at the corner of the cemetery and has a cloth shop across and just down the street (key is *chabi* in Urdu).

**Uprising Memorial**
By Chinar Bagh, the town park, is a rather touching memorial to those who rose against the maharajah in 1947. The graves are those of local heroes Mohammed Babar Khan and Safiullah Beg of the Gilgit Scouts and Mirza Hassan Khan of the Kashmir Infantry.

**Horseriding**
You can hire a horse from Horse Club Dainyor, at the Travel Lodge Hotel on the north side of Dainyor, for Rs 20 per hour or Rs 1000 per day.

**Fishing**
You can pick up a fishing license for US$2 per person per day at the Fisheries Office (☎ 2374) on the Napur road, where you can hire fishing equipment.

**Places to Stay**
**Bottom End** At this end, expect shared squat loos and showers, with hot water in the morning and evening. Even the cheapest

places often have satellite TV in the dining room!

*Madina Guest House, Mountain Refuge, Hunza Inn, Horizon Guest House, Tourist Cottages* and *Tourist Hamlet* have dorms for Rs 50-60/bed; *Golden Peak Hotel*'s are Rs 80. These and other places also have gardens where you can pitch a tent.

*Madina Guest House* at NLI Chowk is a peaceful meeting place with ultra-basic doubles/quads for Rs 140/200 and doubles/triples with toilet and shower for Rs 180/250. The food, both western and Pakistani, gets good when the place fills up. Another good bet is the *Mountain Refuge* (☎ 2513) in lovely 'Sufi Garden' on Chinar Garden Rd, where doubles are Rs 100-125 with shared facilities or Rs 150 with their own; more comfortable 'family' rooms are across the road.

*Horizon Guest House* (☎ 4262), run by an Astori man and a New Zealand woman, has sunny doubles/triples with loo and shower for Rs 200/250. It's out at Khomer Chowk but worth the trip for the first-class food. Nearby is *Tourist Cottages* (☎ 55087), with run-down rooms with shared loo and cold showers at Rs 70/bed.

*New Lahore Hotel* (☎ 3327) is a surprisingly peaceful place on lower Hospital Rd, with doubles with squat loo and hot shower for Rs 200 and a garden where you can pitch a tent for Rs 60.

Unexceptional doubles with loo and shower are Rs 200 at the *Top Moon Hotel* (☎ 3828) on Airport Rd, and Rs 150-200 at *Chinese Lodge* on Chinar Bagh Link Rd. Noisy, semi-clean doubles/quads with squat loo and no shower are Rs 170/260 at the *New Kashghar Inn* in Cinema Bazaar and Rs 150/200 at the *Alflah Hotel* (☎ 3447) by the general bus stand.

A comfortable *NAPWD Resthouse* is on the corner Bank and Punial roads, but its Rs 150 doubles are usually booked out in summer; check with the NAPWD Chief Engineer's office on Bank Rd.

Half a dozen other local hotels have filthy rooms and no interest in foreigners.

**Middle** Hotels in this range and above have attached western toilets and hot showers, except as noted.

Good value in the bazaar is the well-run *Taj Hotel* (☎ 3716) in Madina Market, with clean singles/doubles for Rs 200/300 and cheaper multi-bed rooms. *Hunza Inn* (☎ 2814), on Chinar Garden Rd near the park, has comfortable rooms for Rs 400/500 (plus some small ones with cold shower for Rs 100/200), guide and transport services, bicycle rental, and a pleasant garden. Show this book to the good-natured manager, Abdullah Baig, for a 10% discount.

Two hotels out at Khomer Chowk have comfortable rooms and very good food: *North Inn* (☎ 55660), where doubles are Rs 250 and 350, and *Gilgit Gateway Hotel* (☎ 55014/55467), at Rs 400. Also out here is the *Tourist Hamlet Hotel* (☎ 55140), with a garden and carpeted doubles for Rs 400 and up.

On Bank Rd, *Golden Peak Hotel & Restaurant* (☎ 3890) occupies the quiet garden and dilapidated old summer house of the mir of Nagar; singles/doubles with squat loo are Rs 150/250 with dinner. On NLI Rd, the *Ibex Lodge* includes an old building where Gilgit Scouts officers plotted their uprising against the maharajah, but shadeless Rs 150 singles with shared facilities and Rs 250 and Rs 500 doubles with bath are poor value.

Basic doubles with shared squat loo are Rs 250 and carpeted doubles/triples with western toilet Rs 300/380 at the *JSR Hotel* (☎ 3971) on JSR Plaza. Seedy doubles/triples/quads with squat loo and cold shower are poor value for Rs 200/250/350 at nearby *Skyways Hotel* (☎ 3026).

Singles/doubles at the mammoth *Park Hotel* (☎ 2379) on Airport Rd start at Rs 210/350, but if the power fails you listen to the diesel generator all night. Nearby, the monster *Hotel Shaheen* is under construction.

**Top End** *Mir's Lodge* (☎ & fax 2875) on Domyal Link Rd has Rs 400/500 rooms on the sunny side or Rs 500/650 and up in the shade, cheaper outside peak season. Another well-run place is *Hunza Tourist House*

(☎ 3788; fax 2475) on Babar Rd, whose well-furnished Rs 600 doubles get booked out in summer. The food at both places is pricey but very good.

PTDC's *Chinar Inn* (☎ 2562) has rooms for Rs 750/850. In Jutial, *Serena Lodge* (☎ 55894/9) at Rs 2100/2700 may not be the place for budget travellers but, with good buffet dinners (see the Places to Eat section) and a free shuttle bus, it might be worth a visit. Several other top-end places are on the main road opposite Jutial Cantonment, but public transport is awkward.

Gilgit will soon be saturated at the top. Rising at Khomer Chowk is the *Rupal Hotel* (☎ 55471) with big rooms, three restaurants, fine views up the Gilgit Valley and the Northern Areas' first lifts. Other giants on the way are the Riveria Hotel on River View Rd and the Mekkah Hotel on Babar Rd.

### Places to Eat

Hygiene is problematic if you must eat with your fingers or scraps of chapatti, although even the lowliest place has a washstand, and something on the menu that's steaming hot. A bigger risk is drinking tap water from communal tumblers. At some lower-end places, afternoon food may be recycled in the evening.

Vegetarians can get by here, but meatless fare tends to be dreary. Some hotels will stir something up by request, especially if you bring the ingredients. In this angler's paradise, it's a pity nobody serves fish (commercial fishing is illegal), although they'll cook it if you catch it.

**Restaurants** Gilgit's most visible eatery is the *Pathan Hotel* in Cinema Bazaar, its back room full of men tucking into chapli kebabs ('mutton-burgers') and other Pathan dishes. Stick to hot-off-the-fire items; recommended is half a braised chicken (karahi murgi), enough for two for under Rs 100. Poor imitations include the *Pathan Restaurant* at NLI Chowk and the *Patthan* (sic) *Restaurant* on Airport Rd. Also at NLI Chowk is a tiny, nameless place doing only karahi gosht –

mutton braised with vegetables, served in its own cooking pan (and thus very hygienic).

The *Salar Restaurant* (☎ 2660) in Saddar Bazaar serves Pakistani standards and interesting 'Chinese' items – eg mantou (steamed buns) and strange but tasty fried noodles – in clean, low-key surroundings. Earnest *Cafe Burushal*, in Madina Market, has good biryanis plus toasted sandwiches, burgers and soups at modest prices. Opposite JSR Plaza is *Baig's Restaurant* – gloomy but clean, with good Pakistani dishes.

**Hotel Restaurants** Best at the budget end is *Horizon Guest House*, with good vegetarian and meat dishes, and careful hygiene (eg salads washed in purified water). How does a Lebanese pita sandwich or kidney bean hotpot sound? Very good mid-range hotel food – Pakistani, Chinese and western – is a few steps away at the *North Inn* and the *Gilgit Gateway Hotel*. Also recommended are the chicken biryani and other Pakistani dishes at the *Taj Hotel* in Madina Market.

*Mountain Refuge* serves a Hunza-style sit-down dinner for about Rs 55. The *JSR* and *Park* hotels have clean restaurants with modestly priced but ho-hum Pakistani and western dishes. *Mir's Lodge* and *Hunza Tourist House*, at mid-range (Rs 150-200 for a meal), have very good a la carte and fixed-menu Pakistani and Chinese food. The *Serena Lodge* has daily all-you-can-eat lunch (Rs 240) and dinner (Rs 250) buffets, sometimes with a theme, eg Hunza food, barbecue.

An informal survey of Gilgit-area VSO volunteers names the Park Hotel for the best dhal, Hunza Tourist House for the best chips and breakfasts and North Inn for superior spring rolls!

**Self-Catering** Stands on Airport Rd and on the approach to the Pul Rd footbridge sell fruit and vegetables, especially in the evening. A vegetable market *(sabzi mandi)* is along the west side of Jama Mosque.

Apricots usually appear in June. The best dried apricots are in small general stores. Wholesalers sort them on the floor, so unless

**The Best Tea Shop in Town**
*Haidry Tea Shop* is in an alley off Rajah Bazaar, around the corner from Bank Rd. This tiny one-man operation serves fresh black tea with milk, sugar, cardamom and ginger, in meticulously washed glasses, for Rs 2. ■

you know where yours came from you should soak them in boiling water to reduce the risk of illness. Apples, pomegranates, walnuts and Gilgit's own peaches appear in early autumn.

Fresh nan bread is sold right from the tandoor ovens in the sabzi mandi and elsewhere, but it's gone soon after 7 am.

You can buy yoghurt *(dahi)* at general stores on either side of an auto repair yard opposite the Skyways Hotel. Bring your own container or take it away in a plastic bag; Rs 10 buys enough for one. An older yoghurt shop is Hassan's, at the back of the sabzi mandi (tell him *pita* or *jata* – to drink there or take away). Bad batches do happen, so taste before you pay.

Numerous bakeries and general stores have biscuits, sweets, jam, cornflakes, soup mixes, long-life milk and tinned processed cheese. There is no alcohol available, even in top-end hotels.

### Things to Buy
**Books** The Northern Areas' best-known bookshop is GM Beg Sons (formerly Mohammad Book Stall; ☎ 2409) in Jamaat Khana Bazaar, with hard-to-find works on the region plus handicrafts, postcards and newspapers. A small branch is at Serena Lodge. North News Agency (☎ 2524) in Madina Market has a modest collection of Northern Areas books in English, and some Lonely Planet titles. Hunza Handicrafts, by the Park Hotel, has books among the curios and second-hand camping gear.

### Camping Equipment Sales & Rental
Some travel agencies have gear for use by clients (though sleeping bags are scarce). A

shop on Airport Rd called Mountaineering Equipments (☎ 3842) has down jackets, sleeping bags and pads, stoves, tinned food and other expedition leftovers. Hunza Handicrafts has miscellaneous stoves, clothing and climbing gear for rent or sale. Adventure Centre Pakistan, in Jamaat Khana Bazaar, rents tents, and Himalaya Nature Tours, on Chinar Bagh Link Rd, rents mountain bikes for about Rs 400/day (for use on paved roads only), as well as stoves and tents. Horizon Guest House rents camping gear and sells woolly New Zealand thermal underwear.

**Handicrafts** Gilgit's oldest handicrafts shop is honest Pak Hunza Handicrafts (the sign says 'Hunza Handcrofts') at No 7, Madina Market. This and a clutch of shops around Hunza Chowk are full of gemstones, old musical instruments, hats, waistcoats, embroidered choghas, and wool by the yard. A Northern Areas bargain is the durable, handwoven wool *(patti* or *pattu)* of Hunza and Nagar – coarse, thick and tight, with an uneven grain – for Rs 100-300 per yard. Some shopkeepers push cheaper, machine-woven varieties.

By the Park Hotel is the Xama shop (☎ 3558), with a good collection of old jewellery, silver, carpets and flintlocks. An Afghan shop at JSR Plaza has similar items.

**Film & Photo Processing** Gilgit Colour Lab (☎ 2567), in Cinema Bazaar, sells and processes colour print and E6 slide films. It also has video cassettes, and can do passport and other photos.

**Music** National Music Centre (☎ 3462) is a tape shop in Cinema Bazaar with interesting Pakistani music, both traditional and modern fusion.

### Getting There & Away – Air
The PIA office at JSR Plaza is the place to book the spectacular flight to Islamabad. Theoretically this goes every day but it's highly weather-dependent, so the waiting list can get very long. The booking procedure is straight out of Kafka; see the Getting Around

chapter, especially the boxed text Booking a Northern Areas Flight.

### Getting There & Away – Bus, Minibus & Jeep

Long-distance operators include Natco and K-2 Travels at NLI Chowk; Mashabrum Tours in Cinema Bazaar; Sargin Travel at the JSR Hotel; Hameed Travel at the Skyways Hotel; and Tai's or Nellum Transport on Airport Rd. Natco also has a yard just off Punial Rd. The general bus stand – also called *Jaglot adda* (Jaglot station) – is up Domyal Link Rd from JSR Plaza with connections to Nomal/Naltar, Bagrot, Jaglot/Astor and Chilas.

Much regional transport starts where people from outlying areas have their shops – eg Jamaat Khana Bazaar for Hunza, lower Bank Rd for Nagar, Garhi Bagh (the little wedge of park at the east end of Saddar Bazaar) for Haramosh and Bagrot, and Punial Rd for the upper Gilgit River basin.

Details of transport to the valleys around Gilgit are in the following sections on Naltar, the upper Gilgit River basin (Punial, Ishkoman, Yasin and Ghizar), Bagrot, Haramosh, and Astor. For connections to Chitral, see the section on Punial, Ishkoman, Yasin & Ghizar later in this chapter.

**Rawalpindi** Natco's 9 am and 3 pm 'air-con deluxe' buses are Rs 370, the 2, 5 and 7 pm 'deluxe' buses Rs 320, and the 11 am and 9 pm normal services Rs 276. A 50% student discount is available on all but air-con deluxe. Mashabrum Tours has daily buses for Rs 300 at 1, 4 and 6 pm. Sargin and Hameed each run Coasters for Rs 380 at 3 and 5 pm. Departure times and fares may vary with the season.

The trip takes 14 to 17 hours, punctuated by numerous police checkposts where foreigners must troop out and sign the register. Natco and Mashabrum Tours go to Pir Wadhai bus stand, and Sargin and Hameed to Rajah Bazaar. All vehicles go with two drivers. Sit on the left for the overall best views unless you're squeamish about heights.

**Hunza, Nagar & Gojal** Minibuses depart from Jamaat Khana Bazaar to Aliabad and Karimabad until mid-afternoon, and from lower Bank Rd to upper Nagar in the morning and to Chalt and Minapin around midday. Nellum Transport has morning minibuses to Sost for Rs 100. A single Natco bus departs daily for Sost at 8 am, for Rs 90/100 (normal/deluxe), stopping everywhere en route.

**Skardu** A Natco bus departs daily at 6 am. Mashabrum Tours has a 7 am bus, and 8 and 10 am Hi-Ace minibuses. K-2 Travels has daily morning and afternoon Coasters. The fare is about Rs 100. The trip takes about six hours, and the best views are on the right side going to Skardu.

**Hiring Your Own** For jeep or minibus rental ask the travel agencies listed under Information, or your hotel-wallah. At the time of research you could hire a Land Cruiser one-way to Skardu or Sost for about Rs 3000.

### Getting Around

**To/From the Airport** Cheapest is a passenger Suzuki to Airport Chowk plus a 10 minute walk. A hired Suzuki all the way is Rs 20-30. Several hotels have free airport transfers, though outside peak season they may not meet every flight.

**Suzukis** For a few rupees, passenger Suzukis go to Jutial from in front of the post office, and to Dainyor from the east end of Garhi Bagh. They can be flagged down anywhere, though they don't run much beyond 9 or10 pm. Suzukis also run west from Punial Rd.

**Serena Shuttle** From July to September, Serena Lodge runs a free evening pickup and return service (for nonguests too) from stops at Hunza Chowk, near the Hunza Inn, and near the Park Hotel. Times are posted.

**Bicycles** One-gear bikes can be hired for jaunts around Gilgit for about Rs 15 an hour (and sometimes a security deposit) from the

Hunza Inn and from a bike shop just off Hunza Chowk.

## AROUND GILGIT
### Kargah Buddha & Kargah Nala
A large standing Buddha carved on a cliff-face in Kargah Nala, west of Gilgit, may date from the 7th century. From Punial Rd it's a 5km hike, or you can jump off a Rs 6 minibus to Baseen, or hire a Suzuki for a three hour return trip for Rs 200. A 10 minute walk up the left side of Kargah Nala is Shuko Gah (*gah* is Shina for 'tributary valley'), and the Buddha is high above this gully. Local kids may 'guide' you there.

On up Shuko Gah is Napur village, the ruins of a monastery and stupa, and a cave where Buddhist birch-bark texts (now called the Gilgit Manuscripts) were found in the 1930s. Cave is *kor* in Shina. A return option with valley views is to continue on this high path to Barmas village, and then down into Gilgit, in about two hours.

The jeep track further on up Kargah Nala passes a series of 'hydel' stations generating Gilgit's electricity. Beyond the last one a trail climbs past small villages and side-canyons. The canyon eventually opens up, the river now meandering past a village and cultivated fields. Beyond the village a crumbling guard tower marks the old boundary between British control and the territory of Darel.

From here, trails run over 4000m to 5000m passes, east down the Sai Valley to Jaglot on the KKH, south into the Indus Valley or south-west into the Darel Valley. But the people of these valleys have a reputation for lawlessness, and these treks are definitely not recommended.

### Jutial Nala & Taj Mughal Monument
The Gilgit Valley is rather grand, but impossible to appreciate from town. A fairly easy two hour hike along a high water channel gives a fine panorama of the valley, plus Rakaposhi and other peaks.

Take a Jutial Suzuki to the end of the line, below Serena Lodge. Half a km uphill past the Serena, turn right and then left up the nala. Climb till you see a stream going off to

the right – the headworks of the water channel. Several km west along the channel, you can scramble 100m up to Taj Mughal's monument. Continue west and descend from Barmas village to Gilgit. A variation is to climb into Jutial Nala, two hours up to pine forests and excellent Rakaposhi views. Another is to continue west along the channel to Napur and the Kargah Buddha.

These walks are hot in July-August. If there has been more than a few hours of rain in recent days, *stay away*, as the hillsides are very prone to rock slides.

### Dainyor
A small village at Gilgit's back door and perhaps Pakistan's southernmost Ismaili village, Dainyor has some interesting historical items. From Saddar Bazaar, Suzukis go to Dainyor bazaar on the KKH, via two dramatic bridges and a tunnel.

Overlooking the Hunza River is a *ziarat* to a 17th or 18th century Shia preacher named Sultan Alib. Villagers will show you inside and ask you to leave a few coins for upkeep. Get off the Suzuki when it tops the climb after the tunnel, and double back on a footpath above the road.

From Dainyor bazaar it's 1.5km south on the KKH to a melancholy cemetery on the left, with the graves of 88 Chinese KKH workers who never made it home.

In Dainyor is a huge rock with Sanskrit inscriptions about a line of Tibetan princes who ruled here in the 7th and 8th centuries. It's on the property of one Rafidullah, who'll show it to visitors for a few rupees. From the bazaar go 1km north on the KKH to a jeep road on the right. Up the road about three-quarters of a km, Rafidullah's house is on the left. If you get lost ask for 'old writing stone' – *likitu giri* in Shina.

## NALTAR VALLEY
Naltar was the Gilgit Agency's 'hill station', where British colonial administrators went when the summer heat grew oppressive. Most guides who know the valleys around Gilgit call this the loveliest. Its perfect alpine scenery is accessible for overnights, or even

a fast day trip by jeep from Gilgit. Accommodation is booked out in July and August, but feasible out of season; we found it deserted in mid-May.

The valley meets the Hunza River at Nomal, 25km north of Gilgit. A jeep road climbs a stony canyon beside the tumbling Naltar River, 7 or 8km to lower Naltar village *(kilini Naltar* in Shina), and 6 or 7km more to upper Naltar *(ajini Naltar)* at about 3000m. Here the valley opens out and begins to look alpine. The village at upper Naltar is actually called Jagot. Across the river is a Pakistan air force winter survival school.

From upper Naltar it's a beautiful 12km hike on a bad jeep road, via Gujar settlements at Beshgiri and Bangla and two smaller lakes, up to Naltar Lake (called Kuto in Shina) and dense pine forests. No guide is necessary. Beyond this are more pastures and summer settlements. Naltar is also the start of a five or six day trek west to Phakor in the Ishkoman Valley, for which a guide *is* recommended.

### Places to Stay & Eat

Nomal has no accommodation since its *NAPWD Resthouse* burned down, but its

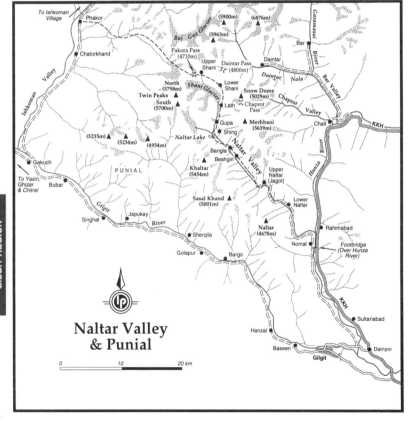

**Naltar Valley & Punial**

garden is a nice place to pitch a tent. There's nothing at lower Naltar.

At upper Naltar the *Hilltop Hotel* has small doubles with squat loo (no showers) for Rs 200 and chilly beds in their tent for Rs 50, or you can pitch your tent for Rs 30. Basic meals taste pretty good at this elevation. Next door is the seedy *Prince Hotel*, which we found closed in May. A pricey-looking hotel is under construction upstream.

Cross to the west side for a well-sited *NAPWD Resthouse* with Rs 150 and Rs 200 doubles, an NLI barracks, an Air Force Resthouse and the *Pasban Inn* with big, dusty doubles with squat loo for Rs 300. Gujar kids with sticky fingers mean that hotel gardens are best for camping.

At Naltar Lake is the *Lake View Hotel* camp site, and a place known as *Red Stone Huts* with a kitchen and a tent with spaces on the ground (no huts for tourists). Both are open from June to September.

### Getting There & Away

From Gilgit's general bus stand, at least two or three passenger jeeps go each afternoon to Naltar for Rs 35-40, but be sure yours goes to upper Naltar or be prepared to hike up from lower Naltar. Gilgit to upper Naltar takes two to 2½ hours by jeep. Hiring one was Rs 1300 return at the time of research. Most Gilgit travel agencies have Naltar packages.

Several afternoon buses to Nomal (returning in early morning) are of use only to hikers since few jeeps start here for Naltar. An alternative is to get off any KKH bus about 1km down-river of the KKH monument at Rahimabad, climb down to the river and cross a small footbridge to Nomal bazaar. On foot, upper Naltar is six to seven hours above Nomal.

### Getting Around

At upper Naltar you can hire a horse for around Rs 500 for a day trip to Naltar Lake and back, or Rs 1100 for an overnight; ask your hotel-wallah.

## PUNIAL, ISHKOMAN, YASIN & GHIZAR

The Gilgit River basin upstream of Gilgit is mainly familiar to trekkers and anglers. Most overlanders who pass through are on their way to/from Chitral, although the upper basin offers some of the Northern Areas' most peaceful getaways.

Once a nest of feuding kingdoms, the region is still a surprising patchwork of people and languages, with hardly anything big enough to be called a town. The old valley-kingdoms are Punial ('poon-YAAL'), above Gilgit; Ishkoman ('eesh-KO-man'), entering from the north about 80km up the Gilgit River; Yasin ('ya-SEEN'), which enters at about 110km; and Ghizar ('GHUH-zr'), stretching west to the Shandur Pass into Chitral. See the Gilgit Region and Naltar Valley & Punial maps. Politically, this comprises the district of Ghizar.

The mountains here are the Hindu Raj, an arm of the Hindukush (to geographers, the Karakoram range only begins east of Ishkoman). The reaches just above Gilgit are hot in summer and unexceptional to look at, but the upper valleys are isolated and grandly beautiful. The route is dotted with ancient petroglyphs of ibex and other animals.

Tourist development is minimal, and food is limited and basic; consider carrying your own, especially in Ishkoman and Yasin. No permits are necessary except for trekking in restricted zones upstream of Imit in Ishkoman and to the north of Ishkoman and Yasin in Chitral's upper Yarkhun Valley.

Most Punialis speak Shina. In Ishkoman you can hear Shina, Khowar (Chitrali) and Wakhi. The good-natured Yasinis speak the purest form of Burushashki, the speech of Hunza, which suggests that this obscure language was once used across a wide area; about 25% speak Khowar. Shina and Khowar are the tongues of Ghizar. A few Pathans and Gujars live in Ishkoman and Ghizar. Some Urdu, but little English, is spoken.

The region is 80-85% Ismaili (it was through here that Ismailism arrived from Afghanistan). Most others are Sunni, with some Shias in Yasin. The only visible women

GILGIT REGION

are Ismailis, who dress in bright colours and pillbox caps (which seem to get taller the further west you go), and are unveiled and relaxed in public.

## Punial

Tidy, proud **Sherqila**, about 40km from Gilgit and across the river, has a watchtower, a big Aga Khan-funded girls' school and an English-language primary school built and equipped with help from Canadian agencies and individuals. Visitors willing to spend some time at the primary school talking with the children are welcome. **Singhal**, 53km from Gilgit, has a spiffy AKESP hospital. Singhal Gah is a well-known trout reach.

The valley broadens at the growing district headquarters of **Gakuch** (also with good trout fishing), 16km beyond Singhal. There's little reason to stop except to catch onward transport. Occasional camels grazing beside the road apparently belong to the Pir of Chatorkhand (see the Ishkoman section below). Just beyond Gakuch yawns the mouth of the Ishkoman Valley.

**Places to Stay & Eat** *Shandur Tourist House*, west end of Gakuch, has four clean Rs 200 doubles with shared toilets and no showers; ask at the gun shop in front. For the same price *Ghizar Tourist House*, just off the central bazaar, has two filthy doubles with squat loo. 'Charpoi & chapatti' places include the *Snowdrop Inn, Hazara Inn* and *Rajab Hotel & Restaurant* in the centre. The food's best at Rajab or Ghizar Tourist House.

Golapur, Singhal and Gakuch have heavily used *NAPWD Resthouses*. Locals insist you can safely pitch a tent by the river anywhere upstream of Gakuch.

## Ishkoman

**Chatorkhand**, 25km from Gakuch, is the traditional seat of the Pir of Chatorkhand, head of a line of hereditary religious leaders who came from Bukhara in Central Asia in the early 19th century.

Ishkoman is best known for treks. A five to six day trek crosses from Naltar Valley, over the 4710m Pakora Pass to **Phakor**, upstream of Chatorkhand. Others go west to

Yasin, and a spectacular, week-long one runs through a restricted zone near the Afghan border to the Chapursan Valley, which enters the Hunza Valley near Sost. See Lonely Planet's *Trekking in the Karakoram & Hindukush* for more on these treks.

**Places to Stay** There are *NAPWD Resthouses* at Chatorkhand and Imit (about 30km beyond Chatorkhand).

## Yasin

The Yasin and Ghizar rivers join near Gupis to form the Gilgit River. Across a new Chinese-built bridge, 25km north of Gupis, is **Yasin** village. From here it's 40km to the valley's highest village, **Darkot**, beyond which is the Darkot Pass (a restricted trekking zone) into Chitral's upper Yarkhun Valley.

By the time he died in 1857, the Yasini ruler Gohar Aman (see the Gilgit history section earlier in this chapter) held everything down to Astor, but six years later Kashmiri soldiers retook it all, and massacred some 1200 people at Yasin village.

**Places to Stay** Yasin village has a *NAPWD Resthouse*, and a few km north at Taus is a small serai.

## Ghizar

This peaceful, ruggedly beautiful valley meets the Yasin Valley at **Gupis**, 37km up the Gilgit River from Gakuch (the valley is

### Shandur-Hundrup National Park

This 518 sq km park consists of the Hundrup River valley – including a world-class trout stream – and a separate patch at the Shandur Pass. It was declared a national park by the Chief Secretary of the Northern Areas in 1993, partly in the hope of keeping an environmental lid on the annual Shandur Pass polo tournament and the mess left by its 12,000-plus spectators. It's still going through the Pakistan government's official review process, so it's only a 'paper park': visitors will find nothing to indicate even its boundaries, and despite clean-up efforts by tour operators and others, rubbish continues to deface the meadows and nalas around Shandur Lake. ■

sometimes called Gupis too). Distances and times seem to stretch out in Ghizar, surely the best place between Gilgit and Chitral to put your feet up.

Just beyond Gupis is Khalti Lake – just a naturally dammed-up spot on the Ghizar River. A 3½ hour drive past Gupis, to the south behind **Chashi**, is Chashi Gol *(gol* is Khowar for a side-valley). Half an hour later, where the valley opens wide, is **Phander** ('FUN-dr'). An hour on at **Gulagmuli** village, Hundrup Gol gapes to the south. With the Shandur Pass area, this canyon forms Shandur-Hundrup National Park, one of Pakistan's newest parks.

If you want to linger, places to do it are Phander and **Teru**, 3100m high and at the foot of the Shandur Pass. Horses can be hired at Phander for local trips.

**Places to Stay & Eat** In Gupis bazaar are serais called *Kakakhel Hotel* at the west end, and the *Snow Leopard Inn* near the east end, where rooms with shared toilets are Rs 250 and beds in big tents are Rs 30. Neither looks very congenial for women. Gupis also has an *NAPWD Resthouse*, and we found a resthouse or inn under construction beside Khalti Lake.

About 2km east of Phander bazaar, overlooking Phander Lake, is a good-value *NAPWD Resthouse*. Across the road the *Over the Lack Hotel* has doubles for Rs 200 or whatever the market will bear when the resthouse is full. *Phander Tourist Inn*, in the village, has doubles for about Rs 150, cheaper beds in tents, and charpois for Rs 30. Along with other Northern Areas beauty spots, Phander Lake will soon be defaced by a new *PTDC Motel*.

Teru has only a sublimely primitive *NAPWD Resthouse*. About 5 or 6km beyond Teru at Barsat is a serai for about Rs 50/bed.

### The Shandur Pass

The 3810m Shandur Pass, 106km beyond Gupis, is actually broad enough to have several lakes, and a polo ground where the best players from Gilgit and Chitral meet every summer, part of a three or four day festival of polo and merry-making.

Chitral Scouts soldiers are stationed year-round at the pass. Sign their register and enjoy a free cup of tea, a nice hello (or goodbye) to Chitral. The first Chitrali settlements beyond the pass are Sor Laspur and Mastuj.

### Getting There & Away

The road is paved only to the Gilgit 'suburb' of Baseen (with plans to pave it to Gakuch); wide and roughly graded to Gupis; and narrow and jeep-only from there to the Shandur Pass.

Natco buses leave from Gilgit's Punial Rd bus yard for Yasin at 8 and 9 am (Rs 76, six to seven hours), for Gupis at 9 and 10 am (Rs 55,

### Over the Shandur to Chitral

To get to or over the Shandur Pass you'll probably have to hire a jeep (four or five passengers) in Gilgit or Gupis – or Chitral or Mastuj coming from the other side.

At the time of research, Gilgit to Shandur was about Rs 4500, Chitral to Shandur about Rs 3000. A direct Gilgit to Chitral trip (400km) was Rs 6000-8000, with one or two overnight stops and about 22 hours of driving. Arranging it through an agency or hotel jacks up the price, so you're better off dealing directly with drivers, who in any case scout tourist hotels in Gilgit and Chitral. Those returning home may ask less. (Well known on this route is 'driver Yaqub' of Gupis, who scouts Gilgit's Madina Guest House and Chitral's bazaar, Al-Farooq Hotel and Tourist Lodge, and puts passengers up at his home.)

The Shandur Pass is normally open from June to October. If you get to Teru and the pass is closed by snow or nobody's driving, you could walk the roughly 40km on to Sor Laspur, a 1½-day trip. You might even be able to hire a horse and guide. The track is rough and narrow to Sor Laspur, graded to Buni, and paved to Chitral town. From Sor Laspur, daily jeeps are Rs 50 to Mastuj, and Mastuj to Chitral is easy by passenger/cargo jeep.

During the Shandur polo tournament in July, hitching to the pass is pretty easy. ■

five to six hours), for Gakuch at noon (3½ to four hours) and at least to Singhal at 2 pm. You might catch these a bit earlier at Natco's NLI Chowk station.

Less predictable but more interesting are daily cargo and passenger jeeps leaving from shops along Punial Rd (see the Gilgit map). Departure points vary from year to year, but at the time of research Kakakhel General Store was the place to ask about Gupis, Phander and Teru (Rs 182 per person for Phander or Teru); show up by noon and

## The Game of Kings

Polo is the most popular sport in the Northern Areas and Chitral, eclipsing even cricket as a topic of conversation and a crowd-puller . It's thought to have originated in pre-Christian times as a form of military training for elite royal troops – probably in Persia, although many locals will tell you it started in the Northern Areas (polo is Balti for 'ball'). Teams might number up to 100, like miniature armies.

It certainly didn't come cheap; major costs like the upkeep of ponies could eat up a sizeable part of a mir's annual budget. Today most tournaments are government-supported.

The rules are relatively simple. Each team has six players. One of them begins the game by taking a ball and stick in one hand and galloping up the field towards the other team like a man possessed. At the halfway line he throws the ball up and, with a bit of skill, hits it far towards the opposition's goal. Horses foam at the bit, sticks clash together, players hang off their mounts to get into the best position to smack the ball. Whenever play nears the side-lines, spectators flee for their lives as balls and mallets fly through the air. The

Polo is the most popular sport in the Northern Areas and locals will tell you the game originated here.

aim is of course to score a goal, whereupon a band of drummers and *surnai* pipers goes mad, and the teams change ends.

Traditionally the game continues until one team has scored nine goals, but nowadays an hour's play with a 10 or 15-minute halftime break is the norm. If a horse or player is injured and forced to retire, his opposite number must also leave the game.

Northern polo ponies are beautiful animals with astonishing stamina (there are no horse changes), but mountain polo can be a cruel game. Horses are routinely hit or cut by balls moving at blinding speed, or by mallets. Pakistani friends say several horses drop dead of heart failure every season, in the middle of games. Local people appear to take it in stride, but westerners don't.

The best places and times to catch a game are:

- Gilgit from April to early May and in October-November, especially the Uprising Day tournament in the first week of November.
- Skardu, especially the Pakistan Independence Day tournament in the second week of August.
- Chitral in late May or during the district tournament in mid-September.
- At the world's highest polo ground, the Shandur Pass, during the Chitral vs Gilgit tournament each July. This dates from 1936, and has been an annual, heavily touristed event since 1989. Most sizeable travel agencies in Gilgit and Chitral and a number of national agencies now have package tours, and their own Shandur encampments, for the event.

**Bradley Mayhew**

you're off the same day. For rare jeeps to the Shandur Pass, Mastuj (Rs 270) or Chitral town (Rs 320), ask here or across the road at Ehsan Cloth House. Nazir Khan's shop also has Gupis connections.

Travelling in short hops gives you a good, cheap look at these beautiful valleys, but it can also mean long waits and midnight departures on whatever comes through. If you get a seat at all, you'll share it with petrol cans, sacks of flour and lots of cheerful people.

For Ishkoman, ask in Gakuch (at the auto-parts shop opposite the Snowdrop Inn) about daily passenger jeeps for about Rs 40 to Chatorkhand and Imit, leaving around midday.

On most days, cargo jeeps go from Gupis to Phander and/or Teru for Rs 200-250 if they're full.

### Gilgit to Chitral Travel Times

Following are approximate travel times by jeep from Gilgit to Chitral via the Shandur Pass.

| | |
|---|---|
| Gilgit to Singhal | 2 hours |
| Singhal to Gakuch | 1 hour |
| Gakuch to Gupis | 1½ hours |
| Gupis to Phander | 4 hours |
| Phander to Teru | 2½ hours |
| Teru to Sor Laspur | 4 hours |
| Sor Laspur to Mastuj | 2 hours |
| Mastuj to Buni | 2 hours |
| Buni to Chitral town | 2 hours |

**Side Trips**

| | |
|---|---|
| Gakuch to Chatorkhand | 2 hours |
| Chatorkhand to Imit | 1½ hours |
| Gupis to Yasin | 1 hour |

## BAGROT VALLEY

Fifteen km down-river from Gilgit, a broad alluvial fan marks the Bagrot ('ba-GROTE') Valley. Its lower reaches are like a marbled moonscape, and a ride up the narrow, perched road in an overloaded cargo jeep is unforgettable. The upper valley is huge, rugged and densely cultivated. The Shina-speaking, Shia Muslim Bagrotis see few foreigners except passing trekkers.

**Oshikandas** is a mainly Ismaili village on the road from Gilgit, at the valley mouth. Across the river is mainly-Shia **Jalalabad**, scene of the heaviest fighting in 1988 Shia-Sunni violence. Bagrot's main village is **Sinakkar**, two hours from Gilgit. At the end of the jeep road, 1½ hours on, is the last year-round village, **Chirah**, with a view of Hinarche Glacier and a series of ridges cul-minating in Diran peak (on the other side of which is Nagar). The prominent peak to the south-east is 6134m Dobani.

A four to five hour walk above Chirah is **Dar**, and the same distance again is **Gargo**. These are 'temporary' villages where a large part of the valley's population goes with their goats and sheep each summer. For advice on treks starting at Chirah (for which a local guide is essential), see Lonely Planet's *Trek-king in the Karakoram & Hindukush.*

### Places to Stay

Due to open in 1998 is *Bagrote Sarai*, on a ledge above Chirah with postcard-perfect views of Diran and Hinarche Glacier. Beds in their tents are Rs 100 each, and doubles with windows all round, and separate loo and hot shower, are a steep Rs 500. They also rent gear and can arrange local guides and porters.

### Getting There & Away

From Garhi Bagh in Gilgit, cargo jeeps go in the early morning to Chirah via Dainyor in under an hour, returning the next morning. The adrenalin rush from the ride alone is worth the price. Avoid mid-day passenger jeeps to Sinakkar, which isn't far enough. Bagrote Sarai plans its own Rs 50 passenger jeeps, departing about 2 pm. Walji's in Gilgit organises overnight trips and local hikes around the valley.

## HARAMOSH VALLEY

An hour south of Gilgit the Skardu road leaves the KKH and heads up the Indus River. The Haramosh Valley circles north

GILGIT REGION

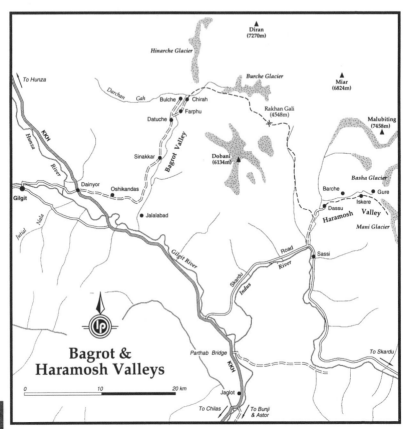

## Bagrot & Haramosh Valleys

and west around 7409m Haramosh peak, descending to the road just where the Indus turns south, near the bus-stop village of **Sassi**.

Like Bagrotis, the Shina-speaking people in the valley are unused to foreigners and have little to offer visitors. There's no food or lodging, though alpine meadows and the glaciers at the feet of Haramosh, 6685m Mani, 6986m Laila and 7458m Malubiting await trekkers; see Lonely Planet's *Trekking in the Karakoram & Hindukush*.

Fit walkers equipped with sleeping bags, tent and all the food they need can have a look at the lower reaches. From Sassi, head

downriver 1 or 2km to where a jeep road turns north off the road, by a bridge over the Phuparash River. Follow the jeep road about 8 level km along the Phuparash, cross and climb the bluffs to **Dassu**, and ask for a place to pitch your tent.

Next day you could follow a footpath 4 steep km up to **Iskere**, at about 2500m, where most of Dassu's population lives from May until December, grazing goats and cutting timber.

### Places to Stay & Eat

There are none beyond the highway. Sassi has a cafe and several seedy roadhouses.

**Getting There & Away**

A daily minibus departs for Sassi from Garhi Bagh in Gilgit at about 3 pm, for Rs 35, returning the next morning. Skardu-bound buses also stop at Sassi.

## BALTISTAN

Rising at Mt Kailas in Tibet, the Indus flows north-west almost to Gilgit in a deep trench dividing the Himalaya from the Karakoram, and the Indian subcontinent from Asia. Before turning south it drains Baltistan, or 'Little Tibet', an arid land inhabited by people who today speak classical Tibetan and in the 17th century were masters of the Northern Areas.

Near the Balti capital of Skardu the Indus is joined by the Shigar and Shyok rivers, flowing down from the Baltoro Muztagh, a segment of the Karakoram backbone containing the densest mass of glaciers and high mountains on earth, including 8611m K2, second only to Mt Everest.

Since 1949, after the first India-Pakistan war, Baltistan has been a subdivision of the Northern Areas. In recent years specially trained Indian and Pakistani troops have skirmished around the Siachen Glacier in Baltistan's eastern corner. But away from this zone are mind-bending scenery, world-class treks, two national parks and villages that seem hardly touched by the 20th century.

Until an air route was opened from Islamabad in the 1960s, Baltistan was still almost medieval in its isolation. From 1972 to 1985, simultaneous with construction of the KKH, Pakistan army engineers cut a road up the canyon of the Indus that is even more harrowing than the KKH, and often littered with rocks from the peeling mountainsides. Ride this road to feel genuinely small.

### History

Buddhism probably came to Baltistan in the 3rd century with Gandharan missionaries, and again when this was part of the 8th and 9th century Tibetan Empire. Islam arrived in the 15th or 16th century, probably from Kashmir. Baltistan then consisted of several small kingdoms, of which the most important

---

**Central Karakoram National Park**

The highest density of high peaks and long glaciers on earth, combined with difficult access and limited facilities, have given the central Karakoram a reputation as one of the planet's last unspoiled wilderness areas.

Naturally there are also unparalleled opportunities for trekking and mountaineering, and it is the escalating impacts of these activities that led to the establishment in 1993 of the 9738 sq km Central Karakoram National Park. This is by far Pakistan's biggest protected area, stretching north into Gojal, west to Haramosh and Rakaposhi, south almost to Skardu and Khapalu, and east to the crest of the High Karakoram. The area is also to be nominated as a UNESCO World Heritage site.

The central Karakoram already gets a conservatively estimated 20,000 to 25,000 visitors a year – mainly trekkers, climbers and their retinues of cooks, porters and guides. About half of the region's mountaineering expeditions, and two-thirds of the treks, make their way up the mighty Baltoro Glacier, with trekkers bound for the 'inner sanctum' of Concordia – surrounded by four over-8000m peaks – and K2 base camp. The park also takes in the Biafo and Hispar glaciers, together a continuous ice corridor 114km long, and 10 of the world's 30 highest peaks, including K2.

Details of the park's management, including its relationship with surrounding communities, remain to be worked out. But visitors may soon have to pay an entry fee (US$1 has been proposed), perhaps with vouchers sold at a dozen 'gateway' villages plus other centres like Gilgit and Skardu. Three-quarters of this money will go to gateway communities for trail maintenance, waste disposal and eventually, it is hoped, local initiatives such as visitor education and wildlife-viewing trips. There is already a good deal of community involvement in conservation efforts, eg bans on hunting in parts of Shigar, the Hushe Valley and the Rakaposhi area, and on the cutting of green wood in many areas of Baltistan.

Until there's an official park headquarters, inquiries about the current situation can be made at offices of IUCN, the World Conservation Union, in Gilgit (Babar Rd, ☎ & fax (0572) 2679; email mail@iucn-glt.sdnpk.undp.org) and Islamabad (House 26, St 87, G-6/3; ☎ (051) 270686; fax (051) 270688; email mail@iucn-isb.sdnpk.undp.org). ■

GILGIT REGION

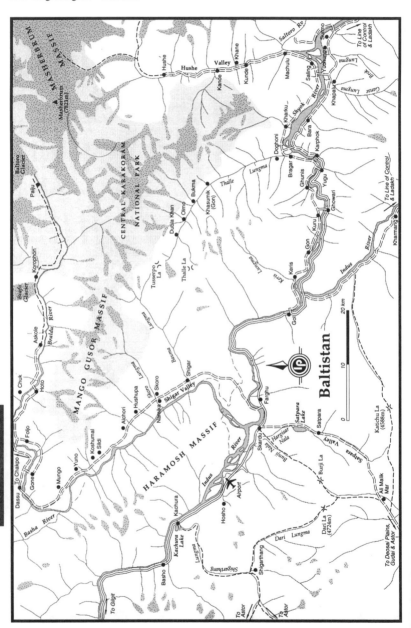

were Rondu and Skardu on the Indus, and Khapalu, Shigar and Astor. Skardu's Maqpon dynasty gradually absorbed the others.

The most famous Maqpon raja (king) was Ali Sher Khan, who ruled from about 1590 to 1630, conquering Ladakh and much of the Gilgit and Hunza valleys. After his death, rule passed from his squabbling sons to his grandson, Shah Murad, who ruled from 1650 to about 1690, extending Balti control as far as Chitral. Baltis claim this is when they taught the Gilgitis and Chitralis how to play polo! These distant lands were lost in the 18th century.

In 1840, using a quarrel between Raja Ahmad Shah and his son as an excuse, 21,000 Hindu Dogra tribesmen in the service of Raja Gulab Singh of Kashmir laid siege to Skardu's fort. Ahmad Shah was tricked out and captured, and his son installed as puppet raja in a cruel Dogra reign. By artful politicking Gulab Singh remained a friend of the British after they defeated the Sikhs in 1846, and was made maharajah of the newly created State of Jammu & Kashmir, which included Baltistan and the rest of the Northern Areas.

When, in 1947, Maharajah Hari Singh chose to align Kashmir with India, Gilgit rose in revolt. The Gilgit Scouts militia and rebel soldiers of the maharajah's army tried to liberate Kashmir, and Pakistan and India went to war. The Scouts took Skardu in August 1948. Since the UN ceasefire, most of Baltistan has been under Pakistani administration, with Ladakh in Indian hands.

The poorly defined eastern end of the Line of Control tempted India in 1982 to send troops onto the Siachen Glacier, which Pakistan regards as part of the Northern Areas. The two countries have militarised the area, skirmishing repeatedly in what has come to be called 'the highest war on earth'.

## People

Balti people are a mix of Tibetan, Mongol and the descendants of Northern Areas peoples taken prisoner in Baltistan's 17th century heyday. They stand out with their short stature, leathery hide and friendly disposition. Relatively few Baltis live in Skardu, which seems to be full of Gilgiti traders and bureaucrats.

About 60% of Baltis speak an archaic form of Tibetan, seasoned with Arabic and Persian; a few Balti phrases are included in the Language chapter at the back of this book. The second most widely spoken language is Burushashki. Villagers of the Satpara Valley, above Skardu, whose ancestors probably came from Astor, speak Shina. Urdu and some English are spoken in Skardu and larger villages.

Everyone is Shia Muslim and not a woman is visible in Skardu. Men and women visitors alike should dress conservatively; shorts are out, and even bare arms put orthodox backs up. Many people of Shigar and Khapalu belong to the Nurbakhshi sect, whose women are unveiled and as open and brightly dressed as the Ismailis of Hunza.

### The Gilgit to Skardu Road

An hour south of Gilgit the road leaves the KKH and crosses a bridge and a spit of rock into the Indus valley. Ten minutes from the bridge is a perfect panorama of the entire Nanga Parbat massif. Fifteen minutes later the Indus is at its northernmost point. Another 15 minutes on is the fuel stop of **Sassi**.

About 3½ hours from the KKH (2½ hours from Skardu) is the regional centre of **Thowar**. Across the river is **Mendi**, capital of the ancient Rondu kingdom. Below **Basho** the Indus valley opens up into the vast Skardu Valley, and an hour later you're in the Skardu bazaar.

In good weather the 170km trip takes six to seven hours, with at least five police checkposts. In rainy weather (eg summer storms and winter drizzle) multiple slides may block it completely.

**Places to Stay & Eat** Thowar has an *NAPWD Resthouse* with Rs 160 doubles. Bring your own snacks and water – food stops are pretty dismal.

GILGIT REGION

## Skardu

*Tel Area Code: 0575*

The vast, flat Skardu Valley, through which the Indus meanders, is 40km long, 10km wide and carpeted with sand dunes, and a gritty wind always seems to be blowing. The brown mountains give no hint of the white giants beyond. Skardu, at 2290m, is on a ledge at the foot of Karpochu, a rock sticking 300m out of the plain.

The town has been a mountaineer's haunt for over 150 years, and a military headquarters since Partition, but it's also the base for many classic Karakoram treks (described in detail in Lonely Planet's *Trekking in the Karakoram & Hindukush*), and even some good day trips. Hot mid-summer is prime mountaineering season, so jeeps and hotel space may be hard to find then. Walking and trekking can be pleasant even in October, when prices start to fall and the weather is clear and cold. From November to March, temperatures drop to freezing.

Hotels get booked out in the second week of August, when Skardu hosts a big tournament of Baltistan's polo teams to celebrate Pakistan's Independence Day.

**Orientation** Along the main road is Naya (or New) Bazaar and in the back streets the more interesting Purana (or Old) Bazaar. Reference points are Yadgar Chowk, with a monument to the uprising against the maharajah of Kashmir, and Hussaini Chowk near the 17th century aqueduct. The cheaper hotels are near Yadgar Chowk. Government offices are well east or south of the bazaar. The airport is 14km west on the road to Gilgit.

**Information** PTDC (☎ 2946) is at the K2 Motel, but you'll get more help from your hotel-wallah. National Bank near Yadgar Chowk is the only bank doing foreign exchange, but you can also change money at the Rockman souvenir shop in Kazmi

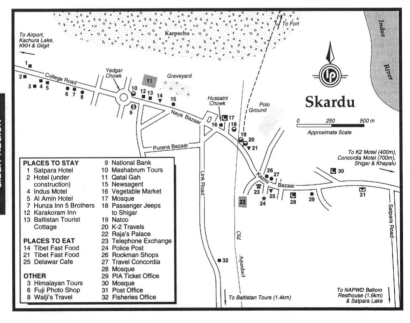

| PLACES TO STAY | | |
|---|---|---|
| 1 Satpara Hotel | 9 | National Bank |
| 2 Hotel (under | 10 | Mashabrum Tours |
| construction) | 11 | Qatal Gah |
| 4 Indus Motel | 15 | Newsagent |
| 5 Al Amin Hotel | 16 | Vegetable Market |
| 7 Hunza Inn 5 Brothers | 17 | Mosque |
| 12 Karakoram Inn | 18 | Passenger Jeeps |
| 13 Baltistan Tourist | | to Shigar |
| Cottage | 19 | Natco |
| | 20 | K-2 Travels |
| PLACES TO EAT | 22 | Raja's Palace |
| 14 Tibet Fast Food | 23 | Telephone Exchange |
| 21 Tibet Fast Food | 24 | Police Post |
| 25 Delawar Cafe | 26 | Rockman Shops |
| | 27 | Travel Concordia |
| | 28 | Mosque |
| OTHER | 29 | PIA Ticket Office |
| 3 Himalayan Tours | 30 | Mosque |
| 6 Fuji Photo Shop | 31 | Post Office |
| 8 Walji's Travel | 32 | Fisheries Office |

Bazaar. A government telephone exchange in Kazmi Bazaar is open daily from 7 am to 12.30 am, and has scratchy IDD connections. Beside it is a police post (☎ 2444). The post office, PIA and the Pakistan army are well east of the bazaar.

Theoretically, Baltistan's NAPWD Resthouses can be booked via the Skardu and Ghanche district Chief Engineers in Skardu, but you'd probably have better luck with the Chief Engineer in Gilgit. Or try your luck without a booking, but be ready to camp in their gardens if necessary.

Several trekking agencies have branch offices here, including Travel Concordia (also called Concordia Trekking Services, in Kazmi Bazaar), Walji's (west of Yadgar), Himalaya Tours & Treks (behind the Indus Motel) and Baltistan Tours south of the bazaar. Though reliable, they're organised and priced for groups. SM Abbas Kazmi, owner of Travel Concordia (☎ 3440), is a respected scholar of Baltistan's culture and history.

There's a Fuji **photo shop** two doors west of the Hunza Inn 5 Brothers which sells film and does processing.

**Karpochu** Ali Sher Khan probably built the fort on the east end of this rock in the 17th century, but the Dogras trashed and rebuilt it. It's a half-hour climb to the partly reconstructed fort, with fine valley views. Some sources call it Askandria, possibly a Dogra name. The path starts between Natco and Tibet Fast Food. From the polo ground there is also a track around the base of the rock.

You can get to the summit (and the ruins of more fortifications, and amazing views) by a steep, dry, two or three hour scramble up the west end of the rock from near the Satpara Hotel. Use care, as this route has some false paths taking you near unprotected and dangerous drops.

**Raja's Palace** The old royal residence, still occupied, is down a drive near the police post.

**Qatal Gah** The brightly painted complex behind the Baltistan Tourist Cottage includes a mosque, an *imam barga* (a hall used only during the Shia festivals of Ashura and Chhelum) and a vast graveyard. It's said to be a little replica of one in Iraq. Except during the two festivals, foreigners can visit if they're conservatively dressed.

**Places to Stay** *Baltistan Tourist Cottage* (☎ 2707) – also known by its old name, Kashmir Inn – has budget prices and a good cook, and is a good place to swap tales. Manager and teacher Mohammad Iqbal is a source of budget-minded help. Cold-water dorms with shared loo are Rs 40/bed, cold-water doubles Rs 120 and hot-water doubles/triples Rs 150/200. The nearby *Karakoram Inn* (☎ 2449) has so-so doubles with hot shower for Rs 200.

The *Indus Motel* (☎ 2608) west of Yadgar Chowk has clean doubles for Rs 300 with squat loo and cold shower, or Rs 500 with western toilet and hot shower, and good food, though they try a bit too hard to keep locals out. Ask for a back room, with views toward Satpara Lake. The *Satpara Hotel* (☎ 2951) has the same choice for just Rs 100 and 200, but rooms to match the price. The *Al Amin Hotel* is similar.

Someone could make a nice place out of the *Hunza Inn 5 Brothers* (☎ 2570), with doubles with shared facilities for Rs 150, triples/quads with squat loo and cold shower Rs 250/300, and a overrun, weedy garden. Singles/doubles at PTDC's *K2 Motel* (☎ 2946; fax 3322) are Rs 650/750 and Rs 900/1000. The *Concordia Motel* (☎ 2547) is Rs 650/750. Both are a long walk from the bazaar.

Three km south of the bazaar is NAPWD's *Baltoro Resthouse*, where doubles with hot shower are Rs 160, but public transport is nonexistent. A big hotel is under construction opposite the Satpara Hotel. Out by the airport is the *Pioneer Hotel* with rates like the K2 Motel. There are also other hotels under construction there.

**Places to Eat** *Baltistan Tourist Cottage* has good chips, omelettes, roast and karahi chicken, and the pricier *Indus Motel* does tasty biryanis, tomato soup and Pakistani standards. Hygiene is suspect at many dark eateries, but *Delawar Cafe* by the police post offers dhal, curries and other basics in clean surroundings. Burgers, soups, chips and ersatz Chinese food are not bad at two apparently unrelated places called *Tibet Fast Food*, in Naya Bazaar and by Natco. For decent coffee, herbal tea and ice cream, try Rockman in Kazmi Bazaar. Skardu is hard word for vegetarians, but there's fruit in summer, and many general stores and bakeries to keep you going.

**Getting There & Away – Air** Weather permitting, Boeing 737s depart daily at 11.30 am to Islamabad. For information on the tedious booking procedure, see the Getting Around chapter, especially the boxed text Booking a Northern Areas Flight.

**Getting There & Away – Road** Mashabrum Tours (☎ 2616) has a shop-front near Yadgar, and Natco and K-2 Travels (☎ 2855) have ticket offices by the aqueduct. Jeeps hang out at Yadgar Chowk, available for anything from local trips to safaris across the Deosai Plains.

Ageing buses depart for Gilgit from Mashabrum Tours at 6 am and Natco at 6.30 am. Mashabrum has Hi-Aces at 8 and 10 am; K-2 Travels has Coasters at 9 am and 1 pm. The fare is about Rs 100. For the best views, sit on the left side heading for Gilgit. A single Natco bus goes to Rawalpindi at 1 pm for Rs 390, taking at least 22 hours.

For Shigar and Khapalu transport, see those sections.

**Getting Around** A taxi to the airport is about Rs 100. Suzukis can be hired for less from Yadgar chowk. Head out at least two hours before the 11.30 am flight departure for Islamabad. There don't seem to be any passenger Suzukis going up and down the bazaar.

### Around Skardu
**Satpara Lake & Buddha** Nine km south of Skardu is pristine Satpara Lake, a dry, moderately steep three hour (8-9km) walk up

Hargisar Nala from the bazaar, on a jeep road or beside the irrigation channel above the aqueduct. Some locals say the lake isn't safe for swimming because of water snakes.

Across Hargisar Nala from the track is a big sitting Buddha carved on a rock in about the 7th century, in the same style as the one near Gilgit. About 200m beyond the Baltoro Resthouse turning and a cluster of government offices, and just past an AKRSP office, turn right on a small path. Near the end of this is a footbridge across the nala, and a track up to the Buddha. There and back is a detour of about an hour.

A jeep track runs past the lake and 6 to 8km on to Satpara village, populated by Shina-speakers who don't mix much with the Baltis. Roughly 25km beyond the village, the track crosses the Ali Malik Mar Pass onto the Deosai Plains. The more popular trekking route goes from Skardu up Burji Nala, to the west of Hargisar.

The first accommodation you come to at the lake is the small but earnest *Lakeview Hotel*, with two Rs 220 doubles (no showers), tent space for Rs 25, and basic food. The overpriced *Sadpara Lake Inn* has Rs 500 doubles with western toilet and hot shower, two-person tents (no beds) for Rs 200, space for yours for Rs 40 and pretty good food in a lakeside dining room. Some of their rooms are used by PTDC and called *Satpara Hut*. Hotels are open from May to October. Rising on the opposite side of the lake is a 60 room *PTDC Motel*.

You can hire a Suzuki for about Rs 300 for the round trip from Skardu bazaar.

**Kachura Lake** Thirty km north-west of Skardu (an hour by jeep), off the road to Gilgit, this small lake is known mostly for the hyper-expensive *Shangri-La Tourist Resort* with its ersatz Chinese architecture and a DC-3 fuselage converted into luxury suites. There are petroglyphs up Shigarthang lungma (*lungma* is Balti for 'tributary valley'), above the lake. This is an alternative to Satpara Lake for trekking the Deosai Plains (Kachura to Astor in four to six days).

### Deosai Plains National Park

The Deosai Plains are an immense, uninhabited, grassy plateau bordering Indian-administered Kashmir, about 50km south-west of Skardu. Nowhere lower than about 4000m, they're only accessible for about four months each year, and snowbound for the rest.

A track across the plains has become a popular jeep-trek route between Skardu and the Astor Valley, and in 1993 some 3630 sq km were declared a national park by the Chief Secretary of the Northern Areas, out of concern for its sub-alpine scrub, alpine meadows and a vulnerable population of Himalayan brown bear. The region also supports communities of endangered snow leopard and Indian wolf, plus Himalayan ibex, healthy populations of golden marmot and red fox, and unique snow trout.

Although the main worry is tourism, two other species are also putting pressure on Deosai's habitats – free-ranging yaks belonging to villages at the edges of the park, and soldiers of the Pakistan armed forces, patrolling the Line of Control in their 4WDs. There is also some illegal hunting of brown bear.

From July to September you can trek from Astor to Skardu in as little as a week (three days from Chilim to Satpara village), and at least in August you can hitch! One solo walker reported about 10 vehicles a day, mainly jeeps and tractors, most of whom offered rides. Intrepid mountain bikers have done Astor to Skardu in five days. Go prepared for mosquitoes, cold weather and sudden storms. A jeep can make the journey from Gilgit to Skardu via Astor, Chilim Gah and Deosai in 16 to 18 hours, with an overnight stop in Astor.

The park is still under review for the government's formal gazetting process, and visitors will find no evidence of park status yet. ■

**Fishing** The best trout fishing is said to be at a small lake and stream at Hosho, 2km west of the airport. Satpara Lake is OK but Kachura is better. A licence is US$2/day for foreigners, from roving wardens or from the Fisheries Office south of Skardu's Naya Bazaar. Fishing tackle can be hired from hotels at Satpara Lake, eg Rs 35/hour at Satpara Lake Inn (which also offers Rs 70 lessons). Trout season is mid-March to mid-October.

### Shigar

One of two routes from Skardu into the High Karakoram (the other is via Khapalu and Hushe), the lush, yawning Shigar Valley was once a separate kingdom. Shigar's original settlers may have come over the Karakoram from Yarkand in Xinjiang.

Shady Shigar village, where the Bauma Lungma empties into the Shigar River, is as far as most nontrekkers go. The main landmark is the former raja of Shigar's crumbling timber-and-stone palace. Royal descendants now live in the newer house in front. It's a five minute walk from the road, up the left side of the stream.

Along the Shigar Valley wall, down-river of Bauma Lungma, are recently excavated Buddhist ruins, including monastery foundations and rock inscriptions as early as the 5th century.

For huge views of the Shigar Valley, walk up Bauma Lungma for 20 minutes and double back up to the thumb of rock above the village. In 1840 Dogra troops crossed the 4900m Thalle La (pass) from Khapalu, destroying a fort on this ridge but sparing the palace.

**Places to Stay** Shigar village has a very pleasant *NAPWD Resthouse*, with good walk-in odds in May to June and September to October.

**Getting There & Away** The village is 32km (1½ hours by jeep) on a rough track from Skardu. Natco has a daily bus at 2 pm, for Rs 18. From 11 am to about 2 pm, cargo jeeps go from Hussaini Chowk and surrounding alleys for Rs 25-35.

### Khapalu

About 35km above Skardu the Indus River – locally called the Sind – is joined by the Shyok River (pronounced as one syllable, roughly 'shok'), flowing down from the Ladakh-Xinjiang border, its Hushe and

GILGIT REGION

Saltoro tributaries fingering the High Karakoram. The Shyok is the axis of Khapalu, biggest and richest of Baltistan's ancient kingdoms, and the scenery is on a mammoth scale.

The Shyok and Indus basins above their junction – embracing ancient Khapalu and four smaller principalities (Keris, Parkutta, Tolti and Kharmang) – now make up Ghanche District, created in 1989 with Khapalu village as headquarters. Development is on the way to bind the region closer to Pakistan, encourage tourism and supply the troops along the Line of Control. The road will soon be paved all the way to Khapalu village, 100km from Skardu.

Khapalu's Nurbakhshi Muslims are more open-hearted than the people of Skardu but they're still shy of westerners, and touchy about being photographed. Little English is spoken and even Urdu is a foreign language. 'One-pen-one-rupee' kids reveal the earlier passage of many trekking groups.

**Khapalu Village** The timber-and-stone houses and precision-made stone dry walls of Khapalu village climb up a wide alluvial fan beneath an arc of sheer granite walls. Painstaking irrigation has made it a shady, fertile oasis. As you climb, the icy peaks of the Masherbrum range rise on the other side of the valley. It's hard to imagine a more majestic setting near a public road anywhere in Pakistan.

A stony track climbs to the lower bazaar (with PCO, shops and a National Bank), a five minute walk. Half an hour up (continuing on foot) at a fork in the road is an elegant but run-down traditional-style house, where royal kin still live. Twenty minutes up the left fork is the polo ground, and uphill from that is the old royal palace, with a four storey balcony. If you get lost the local word for it is *Kar*, or try 'Raja-house'. To look inside, ask at the houses nearby.

**Chakhchun** Twenty minutes walk further up is Chakhchun village, with a mosque whose foundations were supposedly laid in the 16th century when the people embraced Islam. Unfortunately, non-Muslims may not enter this or other mosques. There are several more villages in Ganse Lungma, above Chakhchun.

**Hushe & Masherbrum Views** Those who would like to see the gorgeous massif of 7821m Masherbrum without trekking to it have only to walk on up the Shyok valley road. As the tributary Hushe Valley opens up, Masherbrum looms into view at its head, an unforgettable sight. It's a flat, hot 6km walk past Brok Lungma and Yuchung village to the best viewpoint, at a turn in the road. Surmo, 3km on, is about as far as foreigners can go toward the Siachen Glacier.

**Places to Stay & Eat** *Ghanche Inn* has gloomy doubles with squat loo for Rs 100, a small walled garden and a talented cook. It's on the Shyok valley road a 15 minute walk east of the bazaar turn off, although buses to Skardu do swing past it in the morning. Just before it are a renovated *NAPWD Resthouse* and yet another *PTDC Motel* under construction.

The *Khaplu Inn* in the lower bazaar has noisy doubles for Rs 200 with squat loo and cold shower, or Rs 150 without. On the track up to Chakhchun, an aching hour's walk from the road, is the *K-7 Hotel*, open from June to September with plain rooms for Rs 500 with western toilet and hot shower or Rs 200 without.

Food is mainly meat and rice.

**Getting There & Away** Buses from Natco in Skardu at 7 and 10 am and from Masherbrum at 7.30 am are Rs 56. From shops around the newsagent in Naya Bazaar, cargo jeeps depart Skardu from about 11 am for Rs 50-60 (the return trip with just passengers is cheaper). The 103km trip takes three hours by cargo jeep.

### ASTOR VALLEY & NANGA PARBAT
Strictly speaking, the Karakoram ends on the north side of the Indus River. On the other side is the western end of the Great Himalaya, crowned by 8125m Nanga Parbat,

JOHN KING

RICHARD I'ANSON

JULIA WILKINSON

GREG CAIRE

**Gilgit**

Top Left: Ready, steady, go! at Tarashing village, Astor Valley.
Top Right: Mosque at Skardu.

Bottom Left: Musical interlude.
Bottom Right: Rooftop accommodation in Shatial.

ROBERT MATZINGER

JOHN KING

JOHN KING

JOHN KING

**Gilgit**
Top : Home to roast!
Middle Left: Dassu village, Haramosh
  Valley.

Middle Right: View up the Hushe Valley, from
  Shyok River Valley near Khapalu.
Bottom: Dust flying at a polo match, Gilgit.

eighth highest mountain in the world and still growing. Its south (Rupal) face is a 4500m wall, too steep for snow to stick (its name is Kashmiri for 'Naked Mountain'). The north side steps down an incredible 7000m to the Indus.

Pre-Islamic traditions blame many of life's misfortunes on mountain fairies, and Nanga Parbat (or Diamar, 'DYA-mr', as it's known locally) is said to be a fairy citadel, topped by a crystal palace and guarded by snow serpents. The caprice of these spirits is manifest in the mountain itself, on which a great many climbers have died.

The track beside Nanga Parbat, up the Astor Valley and over the Burzil Pass, was an ancient caravan route, and it was the only link between British India and Gilgit until the Babusar Pass route was opened in 1892. The Indo-Pak Line of Control has closed the Burzil, but Astor is still the best way to get up close to the mountain. Until the dramatic track to Astor village was improved in 1987, jeeps regularly fell off it; now it's wider and safer, though only marginally more comfortable.

Astor Valley is about 75% Sunni and 25% Shia, the latter mainly in the upper tributaries.

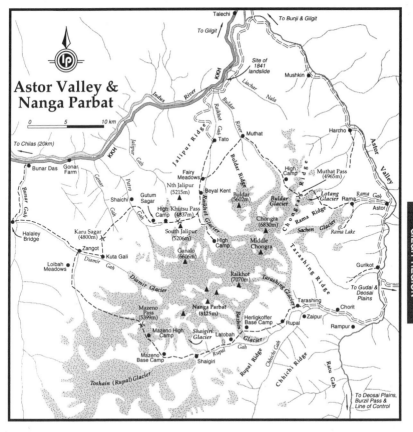

**GILGIT REGION**

Everyone speaks Shina and almost nobody speaks English. Some food is available in Astor but if you're going further, or camping, it's a good idea to bring your own.

### Jaglot to Astor Village

The spine-wrenching track from Jaglot to the mouth of the Astor valley passes through Bunji, once the maharajah of Kashmir's local garrison, now headquarters for the NLI. The lower valley is barren, slide-prone and oven-like in summer, but after Harcho it grows lovelier by the km.

**Astor** village is perched at 2450m on both sides of Rama Gah. The police (in the main bazaar) ask foreigners to register on arrival. At the top of the bazaar is the NAPWD Executive Engineer (☎ 11), where valley resthouses can be booked. A post office is across Rama Gah near the polo ground. For information on passenger jeeps, ask at the shop at the lowest fork of the main bazaar.

**Places to Stay & Eat** The *Saiful Muluk Inn* just upstream of Harcho has cheap beds and food. At Astor village, the *Dreamland Tourist Inn* at the top of the main bazaar does decent meals and a nice set of tea; around a small garden are Rs 50/bed dorms and Rs 200 doubles with squat loo and cold shower. Just down the hill we found the mid-range-looking *Kamran Hotel* under construction, with fine views. On the south side of Rama Gah are an *NAPWD Resthouse* (book it here or in Gilgit) and the run-down *Tourist Cottage*, with rooms for about Rs 60, charpois for Rs 20 and basic food.

### Rama Lake

Above Astor village is the steep and very beautiful Rama Gah, with scattered hamlets and thick pine and birch forest. A track starts from Astor bazaar. In a big meadow two to 2½ hours up, take the left-hand track and walk for an hour past the tree-line to Rama Lake, about 1 vertical km higher than Astor village, and considerably cooler in all seasons. From here you can see Rama Ridge, a minor shoulder of Nanga Parbat and the

Sachen Glacier (not to be confused with the Siachen in the High Karakoram).

**Places to Stay & Eat** A modest *NAPWD Resthouse* – and soon a not-so-modest *PTDC Motel* – are at the meadow. There is excellent camping here and at the lake. You can hire a jeep in Astor for the round trip to the lake for Rs 600-1000.

### Upper Astor Valley

Good walks start from up-valley villages including Gurikot (9km beyond Astor), Rampur and Tarashing. The track toward the Deosai Plains goes up Chilim Gah, just above Gurikot.

The track to Britain's old Burzil Pass route to Kashmir branches south up Ratu Gah, about 15km from Gurikot (Ratu Gah approaches the Line of Control and is therefore off limits). Here, as the jeep turns west, you may get your first views of Nanga Parbat's Rupal face. The track up Rupal Gah to Tarashing hardly seems wide enough for two pedestrians, let alone a jeep.

**Tarashing** is about 40km from Astor and 2850m high. Once you've caught your breath you can day-hike up the lateral moraine for a look at the dirty toe of Tarashing Glacier, or across the glacier and up Rupal Gah, or across Rupal Gah to Zaipur village, at the top of which are water channels on huge wooden towers said to be 400-500 years old.

For information on trekking around Nanga Parbat or across the Deosai Plains to/from Baltistan, see Lonely Planet's *Trekking in the Karakoram & Hindukush*.

**Places to Stay & Eat** Gurikot has two small serais. At Gudai, 15km up Chilim Gah, is an *NAPWD Resthouse*. At the end of the jeep track at Tarashing, the *Hotel Nanga Parbat* has a big garden and rooms with shared toilet and cold shower for Rs 300-500, depending on the view (some look right up at Nanga Parbat). Tarashing also has two small inns with rooms for Rs 100-150. Beyond Tarashing, bring a tent.

## Getting There & Away

From Gilgit's general bus stand, Rs 25 minibuses depart all day for Jaglot, from where frequent minibuses and passenger jeeps go to Astor for Rs 70. Vehicles occasionally go directly to Astor from the bus stand or the Diamer Hotel in Gilgit. Most return from Astor the next morning. By jeep, Astor is four to five hours from Gilgit.

Passenger jeeps run on from Astor, daily to Tarashing for about Rs 60, as well as up Chilim Gah to Gudai and beyond. You're unlikely to reach Tarashing in one day from Gilgit unless you hire your own jeep.

A jeep track also runs along the east bank of the Indus, opposite the KKH, from Raikhot Bridge into Astor Valley.

## GILGIT TO CHILAS
### Gilgit to Raikhot Bridge

Ten minutes south of the Skardu turn-off, say hello to the Indus River, one of the longest in the world; the KKH runs beside it for the next 340km, through Kohistan to Thakot.

Just below the confluence is the Parthab Bridge, on the old jeep (and pre-jeep) road to Skardu. Ten minutes on is **Jaglot** ('juh-GLOTE') bazaar, and just downstream is the bridge across the Indus toward Astor. Across the river is **Bunji**, once a garrison of the maharajah of Kashmir's army; above it is Matterhorn-like Mushkin peak.

From here, the closer you get to Nanga Parbat the more it hides behind its own lower reaches. Opposite **Talechi** is the deep Astor Valley, which winds around to Nanga Parbat's sheer south (Rupal) face.

Soon the gorge closes in, the vistas disappear and about 10 minutes drive south (or five minutes north of Raikhot Bridge), **Liachar Nala** enters the Indus across from the highway. In 1841 an earthquake caused an entire valley wall to collapse into the Indus here, damming it up and creating a lake that stretched nearly to Gilgit. When the dam broke, a wall of water roared down the canyon, washing away scores of villages and drowning thousands of people, including an entire Sikh army battalion camped at Attock, almost 500km downstream.

By now the Indus has turned west, deflected by Nanga Parbat. At a narrow spot in the gorge the KKH crosses **Raikhot Bridge**.

**Places to Stay & Eat** Jaglot bazaar is a corridor of grotty tea shops, serais and fruit and vegetable stands. Better to push on to Talechi, whose beautifully sited *NAPWD Resthouse* has a couple of Rs 150 doubles (book it through the Chief Engineer in Gilgit or the Executive Engineer in Chilas). Best to bring your own food.

### Fairy Meadows

Fairy Meadows is a lovely high plateau – isolated by a gruelling climb from the Indus – with level upon level of meadows and heart-stopping views up Nanga Parbat's north side, and north to Rakaposhi.

From the south side of Raikhot Bridge a private road has been driven up the mountain, originally with logging in mind. But subsequent plans for a meadows resort (the Shangri-La Motel by the bridge was to be a 'holding pen' for resort guests) got some backs up. Locals, through whose land the road runs, now offer their own expensive, monopoly jeep transport to Tato village, and have refused to maintain the road beyond that – simultaneously thwarting development at the meadows and getting a cut of whatever there is to be.

---

### In the Hall of the Mountain King

A good place to keep your eyes open on the road from Gilgit to Raikhot is 15 minutes south of Jaglot, 1½ hours from either Gilgit or Chilas, at Talechi ('TA-li-chee') village, the only place right on the KKH where both Rakaposhi and Nanga Parbat are visible. Along here are the best views of the largest number of snowy peaks anywhere on the KKH. From the north, the prominent ones are the Karakoram peaks of Rakaposhi (7790m, a sharp point above a broad white base), Dobani (6134m, a blunt pyramid) and Haramosh (7409m, a series of glaciated ridges) and the Himalayan massif of Nanga Parbat (8125m, eighth highest in the world). ■

To Tato it's a ferociously hot four hours on foot (locals make the climb at night) or an hour by jeep, with no water en route. An old footpath east of the jeep road, with a punishing six hours of switchbacks, has fallen into disuse and is now dangerous. Trekkers can go up the road without charge, although villagers are not uniformly warm-hearted. Tato kids are positively obnoxious if you don't have pens or sweets to distribute, and some will walk along with you and then ask for money for 'guiding' you.

From Tato you can only walk, three or four hours up to the meadows, 3200m above sea level and 2 vertical km above the river. Nights are cold there – nearly freezing by September. Above Fairy Meadows are numerous day hikes and more strenuous climbs, including six hours up the west side of the valley to an old expedition base camp at 4000m. Tato is the place to find a guide and/or porters for longer treks.

**Places to Stay & Eat** At Raikhot Bridge is the *Shangri-La Motel*, a notable rip-off. Police at the bridge have been variously described as very helpful and very unpleasant.

If you're walking up to the meadows, bring your own gear, food and water, or lots of cash to rent gear, buy food and pitch a tent. At the end of the road in Tato is the *Midway Inn* with charpois, tents and tent space, though most visitors buy a soft drink and move on. If you do camp here, beware the sticky fingers of some Tato kids.

Plans for a resort at Fairy Meadows have been abandoned, but locals have set up two camp sites. At Fairy Meadows is *Raikot Sarai*, with expensive tents and tent space, concrete toilet, food-tent and spring water. You can also rent tents, pads and stoves. A two hour walk above the meadows is a similar site at Beyal Kent.

**Getting There & Away** There's no public transport other than jumping off a KKH bus at the bridge. A hired jeep one way to Raikhot from Gilgit was Rs 1700 at the time of research.

### Raikhot Bridge to Chilas

Except for road-weeds, the river and a few bits of irrigated alluvium, the Indus Valley west of the bridge for 100km is 'a barren dewless country; the very river with its black water looks hot', in the words of the late-1880s *Imperial Gazetteer of India*. In a series of landslide zones beneath eroded sandstone cliffs, the KKH resembles the little make-believe roads that children make in dirt-piles.

Half an hour west of the bridge is a small tree-lined bazaar at **Gonar Farm**. Five minutes further (half an hour east of Chilas) is the village of **Bunar Das** (Bunar Plain), on a plateau below the Bunar Gah, the main access to Nanga Parbat's western (Diamar) face.

A jeep bridge spans the Indus just east of Chilas. Here, on both sides of the river, are the best known of the extraordinary rock inscriptions made by 2000 years of travellers through the Indus Valley and the Karakoram (see the boxed text The Petroglyphs at Chilas).

**Places to Stay & Eat** Gonar Farm has two small serais.

### CHILAS

Most visitors are here to look at the petroglyphs or to cross the Babusar Pass (see The Kaghan Valley in the Hazara chapter). There are few other reasons to stop in this sullen place. Western women especially may feel unwelcome.

Even after Kashmiri-British rule was imposed a century ago the Indus Valley west of Chilas was a hornets' nest of tiny republics, one in almost every side-valley, each loosely guided by a *jirga* (assembly) but effectively leaderless, all at war with one another and feuding internally. Though administratively lumped with Gilgit, Chilas and its neighbours are temperamentally more like Indus Kohistan, probably owing to a similar hostile environment and the same Sunni Muslim orthodoxy (their ancestors were forcibly converted centuries ago by Pathan crusaders, whereas hardly anyone north of Gilgit is Sunni).

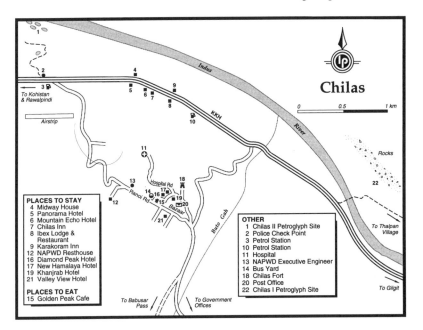

**Chilas**

0          0.5          1 km

PLACES TO STAY
4 Midway House
5 Panorama Hotel
6 Mountain Echo Hotel
7 Chilas Inn
8 Ibex Lodge & Restaurant
9 Karakoram Inn
12 NAPWD Resthouse
16 Diamond Peak Hotel
17 New Hamalaya Hotel
19 Khanjrab Hotel
21 Valley View Hotel

PLACES TO EAT
15 Golden Peak Cafe

OTHER
1 Chilas II Petroglyph Site
2 Police Check Point
3 Petrol Station
10 Petrol Station
11 Hospital
13 NAPWD Executive Engineer
14 Bus Yard
18 Chilas Fort
20 Post Office
22 Chilas I Petroglyph Site

The huge Chilas Fort was first garrisoned to protect British supply lines over the Babusar Pass, and beefed up after local tribes, nearly overran it in 1893. Now a police post, it has put a lid on Chilas, though not on the Darel and Tangir valleys to the west.

Chilasis are Shina-speakers, with some Pathan settlers speaking Pashto. Urdu and some English are also spoken.

### Orientation

Some hotels are on the KKH but the town is on a plateau above. You can flag a pickup for the 3km ride up to the bazaar from the police checkpoint, or walk up the Buto Gah road. The bazaar huddles by the fort, with a bus yard to one side. South of the bazaar a left fork drops to district offices and the right fork climbs toward Babusar Pass.

### Information

On the road to the bazaar is the NAPWD Executive Engineer (☎ 515), where rest-

houses in the area can be booked. The post office is opposite the fort. The police post *is* the fort. A district hospital is at the bottom of Hospital Rd.

### Places to Stay & Eat

On the KKH (and nearest the petroglyphs) are several places with plain, very overpriced but highly negotiable singles/doubles, western toilets, hot showers and adequate food – *Karakoram Inn* (Rs 400/500), *Chilas Inn* (Rs 500/550) and *Panorama Hotel* (Rs 580/780). Dozey *Mountain Echo Hotel* has doubles with squat loo and cold shower for Rs 250. *Ibex Lodge & Restaurant* asks Rs 200 for a filthy double that is worth no more than Rs 50.

Midway House is over the top at about Rs 1100/1400. Various 'restaurants' along the road are best avoided.

Up in the bazaar, two hotels – *New Hamalaya* and *Khanjrab* – have dirty, medieval doubles for Rs 80-120. The *Diamond Peak's*

GILGIT REGION

doubles with cold shower are Rs 150. You can spend Rs 150 far more enjoyably at the *NAPWD Resthouse*, but it's popular in summer. Otherwise the best value in the bazaar is the small *Valley View Hotel* (no view), where a single/double/triple with fan, air-con, squat loo and hot shower is Rs 300/350/400.

Other *NAPWD Resthouses* are at Gonar Farm, Jalipur (west of Chilas) and Gini (east of Chilas and off the highway) and there's a primitive one at Babusar village (the only one that closes in winter). All can be booked in Chilas.

### Getting There & Away

Minibuses run every few hours between the bus yard and Gilgit's general bus stand, for Rs 72. A minibus to Shatial is Rs 40. Local Datsuns will take you from the Chilas bus yard to the KKH for a few rupees, or on to Hodur, Thor or Shatial. Through buses to Rawalpindi pass about four hours after departing Gilgit.

**Babusar Pass & Kaghan Valley** A Natco 4WD pickup goes up to Babusar village from near the post office, early each morning in

---

### The Petroglyphs at Chilas

The ancient routes through the Karakoram are dotted with places where travellers pecked graffiti into the rocks: names, pictures or prayers for safe passage, merit in the afterlife or good luck on the next hunting trip. The desolation around Chilas must have moved many to special fervour, and several sites by the highway are rich with inscriptions on the 'desert-varnished' stones. One source estimates 30,000 separate petroglyphs.

Near the KKH checkpoint is a sign to the 'Chilas II' site. Just less than a km down a jeep track a huge rock is covered with hunting and battle scenes and Buddhist stupas. A common image is the long-horned ibex, ancient symbol of fertility and abundance, and an elusive trophy animal even now. On a rocky knoll facing the river are the oldest inscriptions, from the 1st century AD: scenes of conquest and stories of the Buddha's life.

Four km east beside the jeep bridge to Thalpan is the 'Chilas I' site, on both sides of the highway and the river. The most striking pictures are a large stupa with banners flying, close to the highway, and mythical animals, battle scenes, royal lineages and Buddhist tales across the river on dozens of rocks west of the track. The serene, 2000-year-old Buddha figures seem incongruous at this goatherds' crossing in the middle of nowhere.

Other petroglyphs are at Hodur, Thor and Shatial (see the Chilas to Shatial section); all can be reached by passenger pickups from Chilas. Take water: in summer the banks of the Indus are like an oven.

Half an hour east of Shatial (downstream of Chilas) a string of white markers is a reminder of a proposed dam across the Indus. This would permanently submerge and destroy these petroglyphs, which a UNESCO research team has identified as of great artistic and historical value.

Details of these and other sites are in two books you might find in Gilgit or Islamabad bookshops: Dr AH Dani's *Human Records on Karakorum Highway* and Dr Karl Jettmar's *Rockcarvings & Inscriptions in the Northern Areas of Pakistan*. Photographs, and a bibliography for those with academic interest, can be found on the World Wide Web at http://www.uni-heidelberg.de/institute/soust/adw/kara/welcome.html. ∎

ROBERT MATZINGER

summer only. You might be able to hire a jeep to Naran (in the Kaghan Valley) from the bus yard, but a surer way is to hire one in Gilgit. For information about crossing the Babusar Pass, see Kaghan Valley in the Hazara chapter.

## CHILAS TO SHATIAL

West of Chilas the Indus is flat and meandering. On the south side the Lesser Himalaya stretch 80km south toward the Punjab. On the north side are the Hindu Raj, the eastern arm of the Hindukush.

From **Hodur**, 20 minutes west of Chilas, take your last (or first) look at Nanga Parbat. Across the river, the remains of a 1000-year-old fort are on a ridge to the right of a ravine called Hodur Gah. The rocks below the fort are covered with old inscriptions. Twenty minutes on (or an hour east of Shatial) is **Thor** ('tore'), site of more inscriptions, below the bridge over Thor Gah.

Fifteen minutes west of Thor, the KKH crosses from the Northern Areas into the NWFP, passing a line drawn on a map by Sir Cyril Radcliffe in the feverish fortnight before Partition in 1947. This was the intended border between India and Pakistan, disarranged by the Gilgit Uprising. Ten minutes westward is another line, an ominous string of little white markers prefiguring 'Basha Dam', according to a sign; see the boxed text The Petroglyphs at Chilas.

**Shatial** was once the centre of a little republic, though from the road it's an ad hoc collection of cafes, minibuses and idle men. If you're using local transport you may have to change here. Stash your bags in a tea house and check out the petroglyphs east of the bazaar, near the bridge over the Indus. They include a detailed Buddhist tableau and lots of travellers' names. West of Shatial the landscape darkens as the Indus cuts a deep gorge into Kohistan.

### Places to Stay & Eat

Shatial bazaar has an ultra-basic inn with charpois, and a primitive *Forestry Resthouse*, booked with the District Forestry

Officer at Dasu or the Conservator of Forests in Abbottabad.

### Getting There & Away

From Shatial, Datsuns go upriver to Chilas (1½ hours) and minibuses down-river to Besham (five hours), all day. This is the transfer point for the Darel and Tangir valleys.

## DAREL & TANGIR

Two of the old unruly valley-states that have stayed unruly are Darel ('da-REL') and Tangir ('taan-GEER'), which meet the Indus across from Shatial. They voluntarily joined Pakistan only in 1952, and even today have the Northern Areas' worst reputation for lawlessness. 'Administration' from Chilas mostly means police garrisons to keep the customary blood feuds from boiling over.

Reports of gun battles between locals and police are common, and well-worn travellers' stories tell of theft and even rape. It's hard to separate fact from fiction but this clearly isn't a very safe place to go, and outsiders aren't warmly welcomed. It's a pity, because the valleys are said to be rich in natural beauty and archaeological remains. Darel was the site of some important Buddhist monasteries.

Oddly enough, despite their murderous reputation the valley males didn't always measure up to the standards of colonial machismo. One official wrote in 1907:

Their dislike for bloodshed is most marked: where amongst Pathans the disputants would betake themselves to their rifles, here they throw a few stones at each other or indulge in a biting match. If this does not settle matters, recourse is had to ... entertaining the community to dinner on alternate days.

### Places to Stay & Eat

*NAPWD Resthouses* at Tangir village and Gumari (the main village of Darel) can be booked in Chilas.

### Getting There & Away

You can hire a pickup at Shatial or a jeep at Chilas. Your first stop should be the Assistant Commissioner or the Chief of Police at Tangir or Gumari. Both are about 20km from Shatial.

# Indus Kohistan

Skirting the western end of the Himalaya at Nanga Parbat, the Indus River cuts a gorge so deep and narrow that some parts see only a few hours of sunlight in a day, and so inhospitable that even the caravan routes bypassed it. When the forerunner of the KKH was driven into the remote canyon in the early 1960s, highway engineers were offered hay to feed their jeeps! Kohistan, meaning 'land of mountains', refers to the expanse of sub-6000m peaks enclosing the upper Swat and Indus valleys. In administrative terms Indus Kohistan includes the Kohistan District and a stretch below Besham where the KKH briefly enters Swat District – both in the North-West Frontier Province (NWFP).

Its yawning, crumbling terrain made Indus Kohistan one of the most harrowing passages in Asia. The intrepid Chinese Buddhist pilgrim Fa Hsien, having already crossed most of China, the Tarim Basin and the Karakoram on foot, was awestruck. In 403 AD he wrote about the passage down the Indus from Darel to Swat:

> The road is difficult and broken, with steep crags and precipices in the way. The mountainside is like a stone wall 10,000 feet high. Looking down, the sight is confused and there is no sure foothold ... In old days men bored through the walls to make a way, and spread out ladders, of which there are 700 in all to pass. Having passed these, we proceed by a hanging rope bridge to cross the river.

Kohistanis live, literally and figuratively, in the shadow of their surroundings. Nanga Parbat in its slow upheaval has dealt them a steady stream of catastrophes. The worst in modern times were the floods following the 1841 landslide near Raikot Bridge (see Gilgit to Chilas in the previous chapter) and a massive earthquake at Pattan in 1974 that buried entire villages and killed more than 7000 people (and wrecked some 60km of the KKH).

The region's old nickname was Yaghistan,

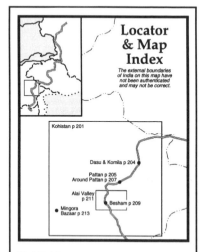

**Locator & Map Index**

The external boundaries of India on this map have not been authenticated and may not be correct.

Kohistan p 201

Dasu & Komila p 204

Pattan p 205
Around Pattan p 207

Alai Valley p 211

Besham p 209

Mingora Bazaar p 213

## Highlights

- The most dramatic, cliff-hugging stretches of the KKH
- The yawning gorge of the Indus River
- The beautiful and hospitable valleys of Swat and Alai

'Land of the Ungoverned'. Outlaws could hide here without fear of capture; tribal warfare and blood-feuds were commonplace. Stone watchtowers and fortified houses can still be seen in the older villages. The Sikhs, the British and then the Pakistanis left Kohistan more or less alone.

But in 1976, as the KKH was nearing completion, Pakistan took an interest in these semi-autonomous areas and a Kohistan District was created from them, partly at least to protect the Highway. The district government relies heavily on the police and the NWFP's Frontier Constabulary, whose large forts dot the valley. Away from the KKH, authority diminishes quickly.

Kohistan

Not surprisingly, travellers tend to rush through. The Highway bazaars are depressing even on a sunny day, and on the road, sometimes hundreds of metres above the thrashing Indus, you can empathise with Fa Hsien. And the setting seems to induce a kind of nihilistic abandon in bus drivers.

But this is one of the most dramatic of all Pakistan's mountain roads, and especially in the early morning when its side-canyons and corduroy hillsides are magnificent. As usual, the best is off the Highway, and while it would be madness to go off at random into the hills, there are some safe and beautiful detours. Out-

siders tend to be treated with reserve, though hospitality turns up everywhere.

Ironically, Indus Kohistan may not have a living river in it forever. Near Komila, Kayal and several other spots, signs identify future dam sites that could turn the narrow canyon into a chain of lakes (on the face of it a pretty stupid idea considering this is an earthquake zone).

### People

Kohistanis are an ethnic mishmash and the faces are as varied as those in the Gilgit bazaar.

INDUS KOHISTAN

**Transhumance**
In their harsh environment Shins eke out a living where others couldn't, by a strenuous hybrid of nomadic and sedentary lifestyles. Shepherds drive animals to high summer meadows in most south Asian mountain valleys, but here nearly *everyone* moves up and down, and many riverside villages are little more than places to wait out the winter.

A typical cycle takes villagers from the river to higher farmland (maize is the staple crop) in April-May, on to high pastures in early June and to higher pastures (as much as 3000m above the river) in July, then down starting in mid-September. ■

Most are thought to be Shins, descendants of invaders from the lower Indus Valley at least 1000 years ago. Pathans (Pashtuns), whose tribes straddle the Pakistan-Afghanistan border and who have ruled in lower Swat since the 15th century, expanded into Kohistan in the 18th and 19th centuries. Along the KKH they predominate around Besham.

Nearly everyone is Sunni Muslim, their forebears having been converted by Pathan missionaries from the 14th century onward. Five times a day you'll see men setting out their prayer mats wherever they are – in cornfields, motel courtyards, by the roadside; your own bus driver may stop at a local mosque.

Kohistani speech is a mixture of Shina, Pashto, Urdu and even Arabic. Pashto, the speech of the Pathans, is spoken around Besham and in the upper Kandia Valley. Beyond the Komila and Besham bazaars, there is little English spoken except by officials.

## SHATIAL TO DASU & KOMILA
West of Shatial, the Indus River abruptly turns south. Ten minutes south of the bend (40 minutes north of Dasu) is the confluence with the 80km-long **Kandia Valley**, a major Indus tributary. Until the 19th century, this was a prominent kingdom of Kohistan. The Kandia River runs parallel to the Indus for

almost a km behind a razor-sharp ridge before emerging, emerald-green.

North of Dasu, the road clings to increasingly vertical canyon walls, until in some places it's just an amazing notch in a sheer granite face. Highway workers became mountaineers here, and were often lowered on ropes to drill and set charges. Massive blasting loosened the mountains for several km up and down the valley. This particular stretch took a year to carve and cost more workers' lives per km than any other part of the KKH.

Strangely enough, across the river are broad, shallow slopes where a highway would have been much easier to build. In fact, that was the original plan. But villagers whose marginal landholdings were threatened put up such fierce resistance – sabotaging equipment, stealing supplies, harassing workers – that in the end the road was realigned.

### Places to Stay
About 15km north of Dasu at Barseen is a four-room *PTDC Motel* with doubles for Rs 550. Travellers say it's miserable, with a noisy generator, a problematic water supply etc, though you can apparently camp on the grounds for Rs 50.

**A Word of Caution**
Off the KKH, Indus Kohistan is fairly lawless and communities can be very suspicious of outsiders. Locals may advise you not to go into the hills alone; the police will advise you not to go at all, reciting stories of robbery, assault or rape. Many travellers do indeed find the vibes bad. On top of a reputation for anarchy, many local men have skewed ideas about western women.

If you plan to get more than a few hours off the KKH, especially between Shatial and Pattan, you should inform the local Chief of Police or the District Officer of the Frontier Constabulary. It's also worth paying a call on the Assistant Commissioner in Pattan or District Commissioner in Dasu, who might furnish introductions to local police chiefs, village elders and resthouse chowkidars, all of whom should help smooth your way. ■

**Cyclists' Notes, Indus Kohistan**
Cyclists, with obviously expensive gear, skin-tight clothing that may offend orthodox Muslims and a tendency to explore where others can't, are especially vulnerable in Indus Kohistan. There are unverified stories of assaults, though cyclists mostly report petty theft and stone-throwing kids, mainly south of Dasu.

At Dasu you can book C&W resthouses at Dasu, Pattan and Besham, and possibly at Sharkul (Chattar Plain) in Hazara, and Forestry resthouses at Shatial, Kayal Valley and Dubair Valley. Booking greatly improves your chances of getting in. Camping near police or army installations is not only comforting but pleasant: officers, most of them on long postings away from home, tend to be friendly and helpful.

Major climbs southbound: several short and nasty ones, eg south of Dasu. Major climbs northbound: several between Thakot and Dasu, some up to 7km long.

**Shatial to Dasu, about 60km** This stretch has no major climbs or descents. Shatial has a basic inn where some cyclists have been turned away, and a primitive resthouse with a sleepable veranda. Sumer Nala, about 30km down-river from Shatial, is a small truck stop with food and emergency charpois. PTDC has a pricey motel at Barseen, about 15km north of Dasu, but Dasu's hotels and C&W Resthouse are more pleasant. A few km north of Dasu is Afghan Afridi, a good restaurant with rooms at the back.

**Dasu to Besham, about 80km** The road climbs high on the canyon wall, with lots of bumpy ups and downs. Resthouses and basic food are at Kayal Valley, Pattan and Dubair Valley, respectively about 30, 40 and 60km south of Dasu. There are a few filthy inns with food on the KKH at Pattan. ∎

## DASU & KOMILA

A century ago, a fugitive from one side of the Indus only had to cross to the other side to be safe, and even 20 years ago towns like Dasu and Komila were worlds apart. Since being linked by the KKH bridge they have become a single extended town, the biggest between Chilas and Besham.

Dasu, headquarters of Kohistan District, has government offices and resthouses. Komila has the bazaar and regional transport. Opposite Komila, tiny Jalkot was once the main village of the area but has faded away since the KKH arrived.

## Information

Komila has a tiny upstairs post office. North of the bridge in Dasu are the police, District Commissioner, Frontier Constabulary and the office of the Executive Engineer of the NWFP Construction & Works (C&W) Department (☎ 25), where you can book C&W Resthouses here and at Pattan, Besham and possibly Sharkul (Chattar Plain). The District Forestry Officer (☎ 22), where you can book Forestry Resthouses here and at Shatial, Kayal, Sharakot (Palas

Valley) and Dubair, is 100m north of the petrol station in Dasu.

## Places to Stay & Eat

Decent budget accommodation and food on the Komila side are at the big green *Azim Hotel & Restaurant* and general store (☎ 31). Doubles/triples with toilet are Rs 60/80 and there are cheaper rooms with shared loo. The *Green Hills Hotel* is a little pricier. Other meat-and-chapatti cafes have charpois but aren't eager for western guests.

On the Dasu side, air-conditioned doubles with hot shower at the quiet *C&W Resthouse*, up a track north of the police station, are a bargain at Rs 250 (though some travellers were told Rs 500). The Kohistani cook is first-rate. Book it with the nearby Executive Engineer.

Doubles at the *Forestry Resthouse*, just over 1km north of the bridge, are overpriced at Rs 400.

A better deal is the cheerful *Indus Waves Hotel* next door, where a double with shared toilet is Rs 80, and a triple with attached bath is Rs 120. Some travellers recommend the cheap *Arafat Hotel* by the bridge.

**INDUS KOHISTAN**

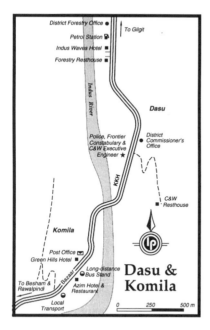

Map showing Dasu & Komila area with: District Forestry Office, To Gilgit, Petrol Station, Indus Waves Hotel, Forestry Resthouse, Indus River, Dasu, Police, Frontier Constabulary & C&W Executive Engineer, District Commissioner's Office, KKH, C&W Resthouse, Komila, Post Office, Green Hills Hotel, Long-distance Bus Stand, To Besham & Rawalpindi, Bazaar, Azim Hotel & Restaurant, Local Transport. Scale 0 250 500 m.

## Getting There & Away

Long-distance buses and minibuses use a wide space below the Azim Hotel in Komila, and may also stop at the petrol station or the Indus Waves Hotel in Dasu. Wagons to Pattan are Rs 20, and to Besham Rs 40. For Chilas, change at Shatial (Rs 30).

## Kandia Valley

This deep valley north of Dasu was an independent princely state until the 19th century, when Pathan influence and Sunni orthodoxy began percolating in from lower Swat. In 1939 Swat annexed it, but lost it in 1976 to Pakistan's new Kohistan District.

Kandia has a scattering of villages, the largest of which is Karang, 30km from the Indus.

From Gabrial, 65km in, a track crosses west to the Ushu River in upper Swat. From Sumi, near the head of the valley, another trek into Swat is a loop around 5918m Falaksair. However, multi-day trips should

*not* be attempted without a guide who is known in the valley, and without informing the authorities (see the boxed text A Word of Caution).

A long day trip is feasible by passenger Suzuki from Komila bazaar. Start early to allow enough time to get a ride back; Sumi is four hours from Komila.

**Getting There & Away** Catch regional transport in upper Komila bazaar. Suzukis go all day to Sumi in the Kandia Valley for Rs 40.

## DASU & KOMILA TO PATTAN

The pyramid peak south of Dasu is Lashgelash (3090m); soon saw-tooth Gunsher (4950m) looms south of it. In spring, or after rain, the dark gorge lined with white peaks is powerfully photogenic – and hair-raising: the crumbly walls slide regularly and the Indus looks miles away below. Across the river, houses cling to isolated, impossible slopes as if banished there.

## Kayal Valley

About 50 minutes south of Komila (20 minutes north of Pattan) the Highway slithers into a nala so narrow the traffic on the other side seems within reach. At the end, south of the bridge, a jeep road climbs 7km to Kayal village. Above that the valley divides and a track up the right fork continues for 15km to pastures at 3000m. Do not venture very far in without good local advice, as outsiders may not be warmly welcomed.

**Places to Stay & Eat** Just up a track north of the bridge is a *Forestry Resthouse*, with two doubles with cold shower for Rs 400; it can be booked at the District Forestry Officer in Dasu. The caretaker lives at the back of the resthouse. It would be easy to stay here for weeks. But the KKH shacks have only meat-and-chapatti and snacks, so bring your own food.

**Getting There & Away** Passenger Suzuki and Datsuns pass frequently between Pattan and Komila. Occasional passenger jeeps go to Kayal village from Pattan bazaar.

## PATTAN

Pattan ('PAH-tahn') sits in a fertile bowl where the Indus is joined by the Chowa Dara and Palas rivers. The Indus snakes through a cross-grain of ridgelines, making for multi-layered scenery and many tributaries.

This was the epicentre of the catastrophic earthquake of 1974 in which entire sections of valley wall collapsed, burying whole villages and killing thousands of people. A vast amount of relief money poured in, which accounts for the 'new' look of the place. There are no remaining ruins; arable land is too scarce (it comprises only 4% of the Kohistan District) and everything has been redeveloped. According to one government worker, the earthquake was followed by a noticeable upsurge in virtue among God-fearing locals, so that even today Pattan is a safer area for travel than, say, Dasu.

Pattan has some of the region's few remaining carved wooden grave markers, once common throughout Swat and Kohistan but now disappearing fast. Look out for their characteristic shape (like a four poster bed) by the side of the KKH, though better examples can be found down in the town itself.

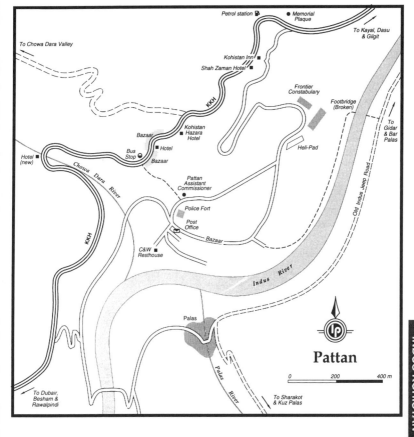

## Orientation

The village is far below the Highway. A link road descends from near a KKH memorial, but transport drops you almost a km south on a bluff above the village, from where you can short-cut straight down like everyone else.

## Information

The Assistant Commissioner is a good source of information on roads, villages and people in the upper valleys, especially Palas. His office, near the police fort, is a good place to stop before doing anything more than a day trip here (see the boxed text A Word of Caution).

## Chowa Dara Valley

The steep Chowa Dara ('CHO-wa da-RA') Valley makes a fine day hike, with channels and terraced fields, and hamlets every few km. A jeep road from the KKH north of the bus stop will eventually reach 15km (and climb 1400m) to Chowa Dara village at the head of the valley.

## Palas Valley

The canyon across the Indus from Pattan offers some strenuous day hiking and possible overnight stops. About 12km up a jeep road (less by a steep mule track) is Sharakot village.

Beyond it are the beautiful pastures of Kuz Palas (Lower Palas) with trails all the way to the Kaghan Valley.

Few foreigners visit this side of the Indus. The Assistant Commissioner has information on the road and the Forestry Resthouse at Sharakot, as well as advice on local protocol (eg paying a call on Sharakot elders would be a good idea). In any case you should call in at the Sharakot police post.

Cross the Indus on the road west from the Pattan bazaar. Occasional jeeps to Sharakot from the bazaar are around Rs 35. Bring your own food.

## Bar Palas

A longer jeep trip on the east side of the Indus is possible. About 15km north on the old road a track turns up into the Gidar ('guh-DAHR') Valley. It's 20km more up to Gidar village, above which are meadows beneath a glacier at Bar Palas (Upper Palas); see the boxed text Man & Nature.

Unscheduled cargo jeeps go from Pattan bazaar as far as Sichoy; any further and you will need to be self-sufficient, and ideally under the protection of the authorities, the police post at Paro and the tribal council.

## Places to Stay

Four basic truck stops on the KKH, the *Kohistan Hazara, Kohistan Inn, Shah Zaman* and one unnamed, offer equally grubby charpois for about Rs 40. The *Kohistan Inn* also has dirty doubles with attached loo for Rs 120. A new hotel is being built where the KKH crosses the Chowa Dara River.

A peaceful *C&W Resthouse* is on the

**Man & Nature**
The area above Bar Palas has been classified as a globally important area of pristine Himalayan temperate forest and is under the protection of the WWF-sponsored Himalayan Jungle Project. The region is home to the largest known population of the threatened western tragopan as well as brown bear, snow leopard, musk deer and Indian wolf.

Palas is also a very democratic place. Rich timber resources are legally classified as *guzara*, or communally owned land, and every man, woman and child enjoys an equal stake in 80% of all timber production, with community decisions taken by a tribal *jirga*, or council of village elders. ■

The threatened western tragopan

### Hospital

If you run into medical problems in Kohistan there is a small hospital in Pattan, run by a German team. So in case of emergency you can get treatment with understanding of western hygiene standards...

This clinic is built for the locals so please go there only in case of emergency. Be careful walking right in, you may upset cultural customs (ie not to enter the section of the other sex) which are taken VERY seriously in Kohistan (you may get shot if you, as a man, mistakenly enter the 'women only' section).

The clinic is not open all the time so you should ask around.

**Robert Matzinger**

banks of the Indus below the bazaar; comfortable doubles with hot shower are Rs 250. It's popular so book it, if you can, with the Executive Engineer in Dasu. The caretaker lives to the right of the gate.

*Forestry Resthouses* in the Kayal, Dubair and Palas valleys are within reach by Suzuki.

### Places to Eat

The chowkidar at the resthouse will fix a very basic meal at cost. You can get uninspir-

ing meat-and-dhal along the KKH or in the bazaar. Shops have biscuits and occasional fruit.

### Getting There & Away

The climb from the bazaar to through buses on the Highway is a killer and there is no regular transport. From the Highway, passenger Suzukis and Datsuns go to Dubair and Kayal Valley for Rs 10 and to Komila and Besham for Rs 20.

### PATTAN TO BESHAM

Across the Indus south of Pattan are several villages with stone watchtowers, reminders of the inter-valley warfare which was typical of pre-KKH days and is still common in the high country.

At **Jijal** (or Jajial), 20 minutes south of Pattan, the KKH crosses onto the Indian subcontinent, geologically speaking. The Himalaya and Karakoram were born some 50 million years ago in a cataclysmic slow-motion collision between a drifting Indian Plate and the Asian landmass.

The green rocks at Jijal were part of a chain of volcanic islands trapped against Asia, and the contorted white and grey material 100m

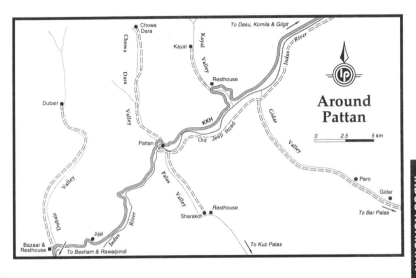

Around Pattan

south belongs to the subcontinent. See the Geology section in the Facts about the Region chapter.

The canyon walls are very prone to sliding here. Frontier Works Organisation crews in their tan overalls are a common sight, endlessly rebuilding the scarred road.

A few minutes south of Jijal a startling bright blue plume in the muddy Indus is actually its confluence with the clear Dubair River. Across the Indus are your last (or first) road views of permanent snow on the angular summits of the Lesser Himalaya.

### Dubair Valley
Half an hour south of Pattan (three-quarters of an hour north of Besham) is a rambling highway bazaar at Dubair ('doo-BARE') Valley. South of the bridge a jeep track climbs up beside a fast, clear stream, past terraced fields irrigated by wooden aqueducts and guarded by scare-crows with Chitrali hats.

The lower end of the valley is too cultivated and well trafficked for camping, but it makes a good day hike. Bar ('Upper') Dubair village is about 15km in, and a mule track reaches a further 20km to the valley head, though you should get local advice before going up there.

**Places to Stay & Eat** Just off the KKH is a peaceful *Forestry Resthouse* with two doubles, overpriced at Rs 400, which can be booked in Dasu (District Forestry Officer). The *Rest Point Inn*, overlooking the churning Dubair River in the centre of town, has a nice location and a decent restaurant but disappointing singles/doubles for Rs 100/130. The ragged Dubair bazaar has snacks, fruit and a couple of soft-drink stalls.

**Getting There & Away** Get off any Besham-Pattan transport. Passenger Datsuns go on up the canyon to Dubair village from opposite the Rest Point Inn.

### BESHAM
*Tel Area Code: 0941*
Besham ('beh-SHAAM' or 'beh-SHUM') is a long-distance transport junction about

midway between Rawalpindi and Gilgit, with a few tourist hotels, cheap serais, all-night shops and a main road choked with honking trucks and buses. This is no place to catch up on your sleep, but it's a base for visiting the Alai Valley, and pleasant Dubair Valley is not far away.

Besham is actually in Swat District, which reaches east to the Indus here. Swat, once a princely state like Hunza, was conquered during the 15th to 17th centuries by Pathans. Besham is now mostly a Pathan town, and the common speech is Pashto. Pathans call the Indus *Abaseen*, 'Father of Rivers'.

The forerunner of the KKH was the Indus Valley Road, meant to link the Northern Areas, not south to Hazara but west to Swat over the scenic Shangla Pass. Besham is still the junction for buses to Swat.

### Orientation
Nearly everything is right on the KKH. Most transport in every direction starts from near the fork to Swat, where the serais and tea houses are too.

### Information
For current information on road conditions and the surrounding valleys try the PTDC Motel (☎ 92), 2.5km south of town, accessible by local Suzuki for a few rupees (you may have to ask for it by its old name, the KDB Resthouse).

South of the bazaar are a post office, telephone exchange and the UBL and National banks. Further south is a police post. The District Hospital is down a side road near the Swat junction.

### Besham Qila
Some maps refer to Besham as Besham Qila, Pashto for Besham Fort. The former wali of Swat built a fortified villa here around 1945. It's now a private residence – probably for offspring of the old royal family – on the KKH, 400m north of the Swat junction. Besham Qila was one of three separate pre-KKH settlements that have since merged into modern Besham.

JOHN KING

BRADLEY MAYHEW

**Indus Kohistan**
Top: Pattan village on the Indus River.
Bottom: Dubair Valley, Kohistan.

BRADLEY MAYHEW

JOHN KING

JOHN KING

JOHN KING

**Indus Kohistan**

Top Left: Chattar Plain, Mansehra.
Top Right: Indus River, south of Dassu.

Bottom Left: Komila bazaar & KKH bridge.
Bottom Right: Fruit vendors, Mingora.

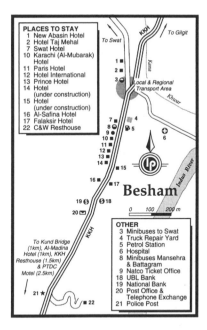

PLACES TO STAY
1  New Abasin Hotel
2  Hotel Taj Mehal
7  Swat Hotel
10  Karachi (Al-Mubarak) Hotel
11  Paris Hotel
12  Hotel International
13  Prince Hotel
14  Hotel (under construction)
15  Hotel (under construction)
16  Al-Safina Hotel
17  Falaksir Hotel
22  C&W Resthouse

Besham

OTHER
3  Minibuses to Swat
4  Truck Repair Yard
5  Petrol Station
6  Hospital
8  Minibuses Mansehra & Battagram
9  Natco Ticket Office
18  UBL Bank
19  National Bank
20  Post Office & Telephone Exchange
21  Police Post

## Fa Hsien's Crossing

The Chinese pilgrim Fa Hsien described a harrowing passage through Indus Kohistan, ending with 'a bridge of ropes, by which the river was crossed, its banks there being 80 paces apart'. In 1941 the Hungarian-English explorer Sir Aurel Stein concluded that the site of this bridge was near Kunshe village, south of Besham, where the Indus squeezes between vertical rock walls.

The spot is just below the Kund Bridge, up-river from the PTDC Motel.

## Kohistan Development Board (KDB) Road Marker

By the road south of town, below an obelisk honouring the KDB (which oversaw development of this area after the 1974 Pattan earthquake), a great stone marker includes the distances to Karachi, Kashgar, Beijing and other points. It's 20 minutes out, a few rupees on a Thakot-bound Suzuki; flagging a ride back is easy.

## Dubair Valley

This long valley, three-quarters of an hour north of Besham, has a peaceful resthouse. See the Pattan to Besham section earlier in this chapter.

## Places to Stay – bottom end

Serais near the Swat junction have grotty doubles for around Rs 50 and charpois in the open for less. Two that welcome foreigners are the *Swat Hotel* and the *Karachi (Al-Mubarak) Hotel*.

The *Prince Hotel* (☎ 56) has basic, good-value rooms with loo and shower for Rs 70/100, but be aware that your room curtains become transparent at night. The *Hotel International* (☎ 65), next door, and the nearby *Al-Safina* and *Falaksir* are marginally cheaper but less friendly. The Falaksir also has pricier carpeted rooms for Rs 100/200. Too far to walk is the *Al-Madina Hotel*, 1.5km south of the bazaar.

The friendly *New Abasin Hotel* (☎ 38) just north of the Swat junction has plain, clean rooms with loo and cold shower for around Rs 100/150 (but with upper windows that can act like mirrors to the hallway outside). It also boasts an in-house 'flesh system'. The *Hotel Taj Mehal* next door is cheaper and rougher at the edges, with some comfortable rooms on the top floor. At the time of writing there were several new hotels being built opposite the Prince Hotel. Prices seem to vary a lot with the season. All but the serais have generator electricity.

## Places to Stay – middle

A five minute walk down a track near the police post, the quiet, comfortable *C&W Resthouse* has nice doubles for Rs 250, but it can only be booked with the Executive Engineer in Dasu (and not at the C&W office next door!). The *Hotel Paris & Restaurant* (☎ 310) has doubles for Rs 200-500, but be prepared to haggle.

## Places to Stay – top end

The *PTDC Motel* (☎ 98) has clean bed linen, tiled bathrooms and a great location beside the Indus, 3km south of town. But it also has poor food and high prices (eg doubles for Rs 1000). Similarly priced imitators include the next-door *Besham Cottage* and the *KKH Resthouse*, 1.5km south of Besham, run by a PTDC waiter.

### Places to Eat
The serais have cheap meat, vegetables and omelettes, and the *Swat Hotel* has good chapli kebabs. In the morning, try deep-fried puri pastry with sweet orange halwa. The best hotel restaurants are probably at the *Taj Mehal, Paris* and *New Abasin*. The *Prince Hotel* will cook up whatever you give them. Shop supplies here are the best in Indus Kohistan.

### Getting There & Away
**Rawalpindi to Gilgit** Natco and Mashabrum Tours buses stop every few hours by the Swat Hotel but don't always have empty seats. Buy Natco tickets from the office next door: about Rs 135 for Rawalpindi or Rs 180 for Gilgit (more for 'deluxe' or 'air-con deluxe' buses). Sargin and Hameed minibuses passing through are likely to be full. Unscheduled minibuses run to Gilgit, leaving when they're full; ask at the Swat Hotel or Swat junction.

**Mansehra/Battagram** Minibuses go frequently from beside the Swat Hotel for about Rs 30/40.

**Swat** Minibuses leave for Mingora (Rs 40) from just south of the Hotel Taj Mehal. Change at Khwazakhela (Rs 35) for upper Swat.

**North-Bound Local** Suzukis, Datsuns and minibuses leave from Swat junction when they're full, for Pattan (Rs 20) and Dasu (Rs 40).

## ALAI VALLEY
The 100,000 or so people of the beautiful Alai ('ah-LYE') Valley are Pathans whose forebears were probably driven out of Swat in the 16th century. They had their own ruler, or *nawab*, and were mostly left alone until

the late 1970s, when the area was brought under NWFP control (enforced from the huge Frontier Constabulary stockade in the middle of the valley) and Nawab Ayub Khan was demoted to a parliamentary delegate.

In spite of the Pathans' love of independence and the fact that everyone here is armed to the teeth, the change apparently came without bloodshed. In fact Ayub Khan (who lives in the village of Biarai) remains the valley's effective leader.

Though surprised to see foreigners, people are instinctively hospitable. Try *asalaam aleikum* and a few Pashto words (see the Pashto section in the language chapter). If you show your respect for their Sunni orthodoxy – particularly by dressing modestly – you may enjoy some legendary Pathan hospitality. Only the present generation (and mainly boys) are learning English; if you need a translator, watch for schoolboys in their berets.

You get to Alai Valley from Thakot ('ta-KOTE'), on a road so lofty that near the top you can see 20km of the Indus in one sweep – reason enough to go, with the Alai Valley as a bonus, lush with maize, rice terraces and orchards rising to pine-clad mountains. The optimal visit is probably a long day trip from Besham, but a back-up resthouse booking is a good idea.

Down in Besham people may advise you to avoid Alai Valley, or at least to register with the police when you get there. The police may ask you to accept an escort – sound advice in many parts of Indus Kohistan but inappropriate for a respectful visitor here.

The valley is cool, even in summer, so take an extra layer if you plan to stay the night. From November to April it's very cold, with snow by December.

### Orientation & Information
The 29km Thakot to Alai Valley road rises more than one vertical km. A single hamlet, Kanai, is on the way. From the end of the bus line at Karg, walk 0.5km back to the pass for good Indus views. A long way down-river

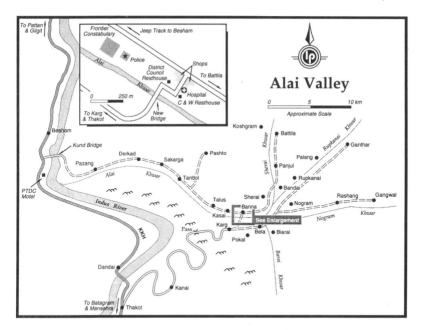

you can see Thakot bridge, and above it flat-topped Pir Sar (2160).

At the east end of Karg, fork left to the main village of Banna across the Alai River, with a red-roofed District Council Resthouse, C&W Resthouse and a small hospital. Left from Banna is the police post, Frontier Constabulary fort and a jeep track running 30km down-valley directly to Besham.

### Things to See & Do

The road from Banna up Sherai Khwar *(khwar* is Pashto for river or canyon) offers the best up-valley views. The right fork at Karg eventually takes you into Rupkanai Khwar, at the head of which is Sukai Peak. At the first bridge, 3 to 4km from Karg, look up toward Biarai, which locals consider the valley's prettiest village.

Choar is a vast alpine meadow area, as big as Alai Valley itself, one or two days walk (one way) up either the Rupkanai or Nogram khwar. It's accessible only from May to

August, when herds are driven up to it. You can camp there, even trek across to the Kaghan Valley, but a local guide is essential; try asking at Pokal village.

### Places to Stay & Eat

There are two resthouses and a couple of basic restaurants/tea shops but no hotels. The *C&W Resthouse* in Banna, with doubles for Rs 150, is under the jurisdiction of the Executive Engineer in Batagram (see the Batagram section in the Hazara chapter) but you might get help from PTDC or the Executive Engineer in Besham.

Arrange meals with the chowkidar, or bring your own food. There are also *Forestry Resthouses* here and up Nogram Khwar at Gangwal.

### Getting There & Away

Alai Valley is actually in Mansehra District, not Kohistan, but its road access is from the Indus.

Occasional cargo jeeps make the two hour trip up the track from Kund Bridge, south of Besham, but there's no passenger service that way yet.

Until there is, you must go the long way via Thakot, 28km south of Besham on the KKH and Rs 10 on a Suzuki or minibus. From there regular Datsun pickups and minibuses climb to Karg every hour or so, a two to three hour trip for Rs 25. You can hire a Datsun for about Rs 300 one way.

### Getting Around
The occasional cargo jeep will take you to Alai Valley's upper villages for a few rupees.

### SWAT
*Tel Area Code: 0536*
The Swat Valley parallels the Indus to the west. The upper end (see the Indus Kohistan map) is known for its rough natural beauty and deodar-forested, snow-capped peaks, and for excellent trekking, fishing and winter skiing. The people are mainly Pathans, except in the extreme north, called Swat Kohistan, where they are Kohistanis.

Southern Swat has been a civilised place for at least 35 centuries. It was the northernmost end of the Buddhist empires of Gandhara, and probably the birthplace of Vajrayana, or Tantric, Buddhism which, in the 7th century, took root in Ladakh and Tibet. A wealth of ruined stupas, monasteries and non-Buddhist sites are open to the public, and the Swat museum has artefacts dating from the 2nd century BC.

The year-round passage from Besham, three hours over the 2134m Shangla Pass, is a fine trip in itself. This was the ancient route from the Indus Valley to Peshawar and the plains. In fact, if you're bound for Peshawar, Swat is quicker and more interesting than going via Rawalpindi.

### Places to Stay
*Forestry Resthouses* at Alpurai and Yakhtangai on the east side of the Shangla Pass, and another near the summit, can be booked with the Conservator of Forests in Saidu Sharif or District Forestry Officer in Mingora.

### Mingora & Saidu Sharif
Swat's traditional seat of government is Saidu Sharif, while its sister city, Mingora, is mainly a market town and long-distance transport hub. This is the most urbanised centre in the northern mountains, and its noise, pollution and manic pace will come as a shock if you've just come down from the Northern Areas.

**Orientation** Mingora is on the south bank of the Swat River beside the main Swat Valley road.

Saidu Sharif's Swat Museum is about 1km south of the Mingora bazaar and a PTDC office and hotel are just over 1km further. The bus station is on the Grand Trunk (GT) Road, to the east of Sohrab Chowk – the main accommodation centre. The airport is about 4km north-west of Mingora.

**Information** The helpful PTDC office (☎ 711205), at the PTDC Hotel in Saidu Sharif, has information on hotels, transport, local archeology, the museum and the upper valley. Several banks at Mingora's Bank Square will do foreign exchange. The Mingora post office is hidden to the south-west of Green Chowk; in Saidu Sharif it's on the main road, south of the Swat Serena Hotel.

**Museum & Buddhist Sites in the City** The Swat Museum is stuffed with artefacts from Swat's pre-Buddhist and Buddhist sites.

Several excavations are right in Saidu Sharif. Butkara No 1, 1km east of the museum and centred on an enormous 3rd century stupa, has yielded one of Swat's richest harvests of artefacts.

The remains of another large stupa and monastery are behind Central Hospital.

**Nearby Sites** The most interesting site near Saidu Sharif is to the south at Udegram, with remains of the Buddhist town of Ora (defeated by Alexander the Great in the 4th century BC), the mountainside citadel of the region's last Hindu raja and a mosque from the time of Mahmud of Ghazni.

There is a serene 7th century Buddha

carved on a rockface north of Mingora at Jehanabad.

**Places to Stay** There are dozens of hotels, mostly in Mingora. Three noisy bottom-end places are opposite the general bus stand. Marginally quieter hotels are nearby on the GT Rd – the *Shams* and *Salatin* have singles/doubles for around Rs 50/100; the *Erum* and *Diamond* are double this. All have pricier rooms with hot showers. The friendly, quiet *Rainbow Hotel*, off New Rd, has good-value doubles for Rs 150.

For a decent mid-range place in the centre try the *Zeeshan Hotel*, with deluxe rooms for Rs 300/400, or the *Swat View Hotel*, with air-con rooms for Rs 450/550. Both also offer cheaper rooms.

At the top end are the centrally located *Pameer Hotel* on GT Rd (Rs 1000/1200) and Saidu Sharif's luxurious *Swat Serena Hotel* at Rs 1523/2050 and up. The Serena's food is 1st class.

**Places to Eat**
The best cheap meal in town is at the clean, interesting-looking *Cafe Kehkeshan* on Madyan Road. It doesn't have an English sign but it's left of the Cafe Anwar, which does. Fill up for Rs 70 on kebabs, barbecue or kadahi (braised) chicken and rice. The *Nishat Restaurant* at Nishat Chowk has delicious kadahi lamb chops, a 'half kilo' for Rs 35; out the front you can buy fresh yoghurt and lassi all day for a few rupees.

The uninspired but clean *Marghazar Restaurant* serves Pakistani standards; it's just west of the general bus stand. Or try one of the hundreds of Pashtun eateries all over town – some cleaner than others – serving chicken, kebabs, curries and dhal. Good but pricey (Rs 150 to Rs 250) hotel food includes the *Pameer Hotel's* western and Pakistani dishes, and the buffet at the Serena's *Suvastu Restaurant*.

Seasonal fruit vendors are everywhere, especially trying to out-shout one another at Green Chowk. There's a wholesale vegetable market about 200m north of People Chowk. Sweet tooths can get good kheer

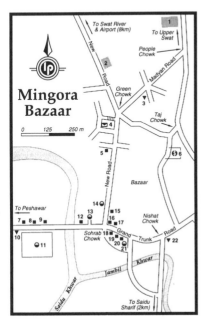

**PLACES TO STAY**
   5   Rainbow Hotel
   7   Meezan Hotel
   8   Taj Mahal Hotel
   9   National Hotel
  12   Zeeshan Hotel
  15   Swat View Hotel
  16   Hotel Shams
  17   Erum Hotel
  18   Diamond Hotel
  19   Pameer Hotel
  20   Salatin Hotel

**PLACES TO EAT**
   1   Vegetable Market
   3   Cafe Kehkeshan
  10   Marghazar Restaurant
  22   Nishat Restaurant

**OTHER**
   2   City Bus Stand
   4   Post Office
   6   Bank Square
  11   General Bus Stand
  13   Suburban Transport
  14   Taxi Yard
  21   Suzuki Yard (to Saidu Sharif)

INDUS KOHISTAN

from a shop on GT Road opposite the Salatin Hotel.

**Getting There & Away** The general bus stand is on the GT Rd in Mingora, though some minibuses from Besham may use the city bus stand on New Rd. Transport is plentiful from Mingora on to Peshawar (three hours) and Rawalpindi (five hours). From May to September, PTDC runs a daily aircon Coaster between Rawalpindi and Saidu Sharif, for Rs 140.

PIA (☎ 4639) has an office in Saidu Sharif and flies daily to Islamabad (Rs 740) and Peshawar (Rs 390).

**Getting Around** Passenger Suzukis ply between Mingora bazaar and Saidu Sharif Rd for a few rupees, and there are many motor-rickshaws. There may be occasional buses to the airport from the city bus stand, though the easiest airport transport is to hire a Suzuki for about Rs 50.

### Upper Swat

**Miandam** is a tourist resort at 1820m, an hour's drive north of Mingora and 10km up a side-valley. **Madyan**, by the Swat River 1¼ hours from Mingora, was a hippie haven in the 1960s and 1970s and is still a fine place to relax. Just north of it is **Bahrain**, a good place to shop for Swat's famous carved furniture. At 2070m and 100km from Mingora on a gradually disintegrating road is the glum Kohistani village of **Kalam**, centre of an independent state in the 19th century, but now overwhelmed by an incredible 100-plus tourist hotels.

Beyond Kalam, up the heavily forested Utrot and Ushu valleys, is legendary trout fishing and world-class trekking, but although new hotels continue to spring up like weeds, the area is not safe to trek without a trustworthy (and armed) local guide.

About 25km up the Ushu Valley is Lake Mahodand and views of Swat's highest peak, Falaksair (5918m).

**Places to Stay** In upper Swat, hotel prices are *highly* seasonal, with absurd bargains in

the off-season. Camping is safe only as far north as Madyan.

**Miandam** Doubles at the *Nizara* and *Karashma* hotels start at about Rs 150. At the *Evergreen* they're Rs 300 and up.

**Madyan** The best choice is *Caravans Guesthouse*, where rooms with shared hot shower are about Rs 75/bed. For cheap rope-beds in a village house, ask at Muambar Khan's shop. The friendly *Hunza Guest House* at the north end of town is Rs 60/100.

**Bahrain** Hot-water doubles start about Rs 150 at the overpriced *Abshar* and *Jabees* hotels and about Rs 250-300 at the better-value *Deluxe Hotel* and *Dim Sum*.

**Kalam** The prominent cold-water cheapo in the bazaar is the *Khalid Hotel* with doubles from Rs 150. Decent mid-range places include the *Shangrilla* and *Tariq* north of the bazaar, *King's Valley* in the centre and *Panorama* and *Hill Top* above town, all offering doubles for around Rs 300. Best at the top end (Rs 500/double) are the *Heaven Breeze*, *Manano Inn*, *Pameer Hotel* and *Motel Sangam*.

**Ushu** The *Ushu Hotel* has doubles for Rs 400 and up in mid-summer. There are resthouses at Ushu, Utrot and Gabrial.

**Getting There & Away** Mingora's general bus stand has plentiful up-valley transport; Madyan is Rs 15, Kalam Rs 30. To go directly from the KKH to upper Swat, change at Khwazakhela.

Buses go round the clock to Rawalpindi for Rs 50.

## BESHAM TO THAKOT

Forty minutes south of Besham the KKH crosses the Indus on an elegant suspension bridge decorated with stone lions. In 1976 a lively party was held here, with Pakistani and Chinese music and dance, to open the bridge and celebrate the completion of the Indus Valley Road. On either side are seedy roadside bazaars, **Dandai** on the west and

**Thakot** on the east. Dandai also has the basic *Hotel Sapari.*

This is the southernmost of the Chinese bridges, and in many respects the real southern end of the KKH is at Thakot, not at the Havelian railhead.

The Highway has run beside one or another branch of the Indus River since the first trickle at the Khunjerab. A few km from here it leaves the wide and heavy 'Father of Rivers' behind, and soon climbs down out of the mountains.

# Hazara

Below Thakot the KKH leaves the Indus Valley, climbs briefly and then descends through progressively gentler countryside to the upland plateau of Rawalpindi and Islamabad. This is a region of forested mountains below 4000m, with a series of broad, fertile valleys up its middle. Ease of travel through these valleys has for centuries made this a gateway from the south into the mountains, towards Kashmir and Gilgit.

The region's historical name is Hazara. Its natural boundaries are the Indus River on the west, the Margalla and Murree hills on the south and east, and the peaks of the Lesser Himalaya to the north. In administrative terms it includes the Abbottabad and Mansehra districts of the North-West Frontier Province (NWFP).

If you're south-bound, Hazara is a way to ease back into civilisation, though it may feel like you've left the real KKH behind – no more Chinese bridges, no more outlaws, no more fickle, harrowing high road. If you're north-bound, Hazara will be your first escape from the thick air of the Punjab.

### History

As the strength of the Moghul Empire waned in the 18th century the region was for a time under the control of various Afghan chieftains. One of them in 1799 granted the governorship of Lahore to Ranjit Singh, a Sikh warlord from the Punjab. Ranjit expanded his domain into a small empire that by the time of his death in 1839 included most of the Punjab, Kashmir, Hazara and Peshawar.

An early treaty with the British had barred

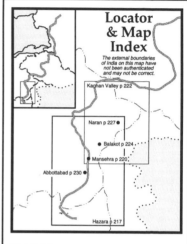

## Locator & Map Index

The external boundaries of India on this map have not been authenticated and may not be correct.

Kaghan Valley p 222

Naran p 227 ●

● Balakot p 224

Mansehra p 220

Abbottabad p 230 ●

Hazara p 217

### Highlights

- The rugged grandeur of the Kaghan Valley
- Sublime Lake Saiful Mulk, home of mountain spirits
- Ashoka's 3rd century edicts, carved into rocks at Mansehra
- The stately elegance and pine-clad hills of Abbottabad Cantonment

his expansion south-east, but in 1845 this was violated by the regent who succeeded him. Following the short and bloody Sikh Wars of 1846 and 1849 the British annexed the entire state, including Hazara. At Partition in 1947, Hazara's Sikhs fled to India. Many Hazara and Punjab towns still have buildings from this time, including fortifications from before the Sikh Wars and *gurdwaras* (temples) built in this century. Some towns have names from this period: Haripur and Mansehra, for example, were strongholds of Hari Singh and Man Singh, two of Ranjit's governors-general.

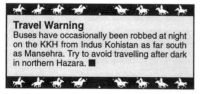

**Travel Warning**
Buses have occasionally been robbed at night on the KKH from Indus Kohistan as far south as Mansehra. Try to avoid travelling after dark in northern Hazara. ■

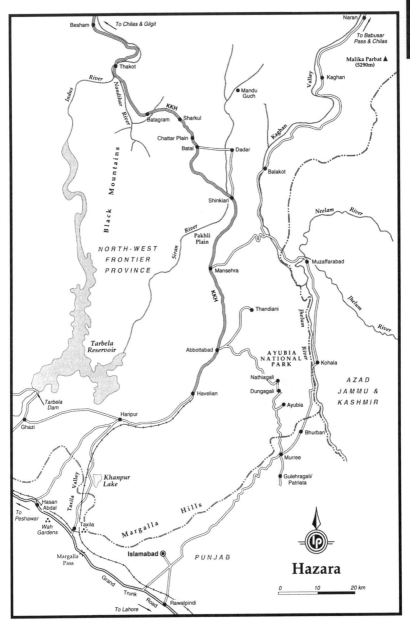

# Hazara

0    10    20 km

## BATAGRAM

The Pathan village of Batagram, straddling the Nandihar River 20km above the Indus, has little to offer but picturesque walks in the fields, and some hard-to-find Buddhist ruins in the hills near Pishora. Little English is spoken.

Across the Nandihar River, 15 minutes north on the KKH, is the village of Kotgala, tarted up like an amusement park. Local people say the gaudy paint-jobs are by villagers showing off fat remittances from overseas work.

Further north watch for the 'cable cars' (some of them just rickety seats suspended from a single cable) that connect villages on the west side of the river to the KKH. For a cheap (Rs 2) thrill, try one yourself.

### Pishora & Kala Tassa

Archeological researchers say there are Buddhist ruins by a spring near Pishora village, 8km north of Batagram, though you would need good local help to find them. In the same area, Kala Tassa, there are petroglyphs depicting hunters, animals and a Buddhist stupa beneath a rock overhang. The writing refers to a monastery in the time of a Kushan king of the 1st and 2nd century AD.

It's not a leisurely trip, but a 2km climb into a steep ravine just south of the village, offers fine views of the Nandihar River Valley. You will need to ask someone in the village for help to show you the way. Catch a Suzuki to Pishora from near the Shangri-La Hotel in Batagram. There is also a 6km track to the ridge above Kala Tassa, starting at the petrol pump at the north end of Batagram.

### Places to Stay & Eat

The *Shangri-La Hotel*, by the bus stop north of the bridge, has damp doubles for Rs 60 and up. Across the bridge, the *Tarand Hotel*, 200m off the KKH up Kucheri Rd, is about the same. The *Spogmay Hotel*, in main bazaar, has doubles for Rs 70. The quieter *Al-Fakhar Hotel*, on the KKH 500m south of the bridge, is a few rupees more and a long climb. All have restaurants, and there are street-side cafes and fruit vendors in the area.

### Privatising the Resthouses

NWFP's Sarhad Tourism plans to turn all of the province's government resthouses over to private ownership. The process will take years, though some resthouses, especially in Swat and the Kaghan Valley, may go private (and upmarket) during the life of this edition. ■

### Getting There & Away

There is a bus yard about 200m south of the bridge, from which minibuses go all day to Besham (1½ hours) and Mansehra (two hours) for about Rs 20. You can catch a long-distance bus by the Shangri-La Hotel, if it stops.

## BATAGRAM TO MANSEHRA

South from Batagram the Highway climbs steeply through pine plantations, out of the Nandihar River basin. Dipping for a while into the picturesque bowl called **Chattar Plain** (after Chattar Singh, yet another Sikh general), it then enters the basin of the Siran River. The land rises once more and then flattens as you descend, through cornfields and the precision terracing of rice paddies, into the Pakhli Plain surrounding Mansehra. Half an hour south of Chattar Plain (45 minutes north of Mansehra) is the village of **Shinkiari**. A few minibuses from Mansehra continue from here up the picturesque Siran River Valley to pine-scented **Dadar**. You can walk over the mountains into the Kaghan Valley in a few days – from Shinkiari to Balakot, or from Dadar to Balakot/Sharan via Mandu Guch. But the hills still harbour a few bears and wild cats (and outlaws, according to some), so a local guide is a good idea. Pakistan Tourist Development Corporation (PTDC) in Abbottabad is a good source of information.

### Places to Stay

Dadar has a *Forestry Resthouse* with doubles for Rs 200, booked with the Conservator of Forests in Abbottabad. There is also a *Forestry Hut* on the trek from Dadar to Sharan;

## Cyclists' Notes, Hazara

The KKH is wide and paved here, but from Mansehra south, traffic is very heavy and drivers are reckless. Major climbs southbound: Thakot to Sharkul, above Chattar Plain. Major climbs northbound: Havelian to Abbottabad, Mansehra to Chattar Plain.

Separate notes for the Kaghan Valley and Babusar Pass are in the Kaghan Valley section of this chapter. For alternative routes down to Rawalpindi, see the Cyclists' Notes for the Rawalpindi & Islamabad chapter.

**Besham to Chattar Plain, about 70km** As the KKH climbs out of the Indus Valley at Thakot, 28km south of Besham, the road is very vulnerable to slides. Batagram is about 20km up from Thakot. The road climbs for 16km beyond this to a 1670m pass at Sharkul, with two pricey hotels and a C&W Resthouse (book it at Dasu, Besham or Mansehra), then drops for several km into Chattar Plain.

**Chattar Plain to Mansehra, about 50km** It's downhill most of the way to Mansehra. About 20km from Chattar Plain and just north of Shinkiari is a tourist restaurant called Jangal Mangal. There is cheap food along the road south of Shinkiari. An alternative route is on the back road via Batal village and Dadar.

**Mansehra to Hasan Abdal, about 100km** From Mansehra it's about 30km to Abbottabad, with an overall rise of about 200m. A Pakistan Youth Hostel is north of Abbottabad at Mandian. In the 15km from Abbottabad to Havelian the KKH plunges almost 500m. South of Havelian the road is flat for 60km to Hasan Abdal. An alternative route from Haripur is a rough road directly to Taxila, via Khanpur Lake. Taxila bazaar is horribly congested. ■

ask the District Forestry Officer in Mansehra.

There's a fine *NWFP Construction & Works (C&W) Department Resthouse* at Sharkul, in the woods above Chattar Plain, with doubles for Rs 250; it is booked with the C&W Executive Engineer in Mansehra. Just next door is *Green's* (☎ (0987) 36674) with doubles starting from Rs 700. The PTDC-owned *Affaq Hotel* is further up the hill, with doubles for about Rs 500.

## MANSEHRA
### Tel Area Code: 0987

Tourists don't pay much attention to Mansehra except to get out and squint at three big rocks on the northern outskirts, on which the Mauryan king Ashoka inscribed a set of edicts over 2200 years ago. But the town itself, on high ground (975m) in the fertile Pakhli Plain, is an interesting place too, with traces of its history as a Sikh garrison town in the early 18th century. It's also a good place for people-watching, with a rich mix of Pathans (Pashtuns), Punjabis, Kashmiris and Afghans. The Afghan men stand out because of their stature and their big, loosely wrapped turbans, and the women (when not veiled) because of their beauty and their bright and elaborate clothing. The most common language is Pashto, with some Hindko Punjabi (similar to Urdu). Mansehra is a major transportation junction for Rawalpindi, Azad Jammu and Kashmir, the Kaghan and Swat valleys, and the KKH.

### Orientation

The KKH goes around Mansehra but the local roads come through. The three main streets, named for their destinations – Abbottabad, Shinkiari village and Kashmir – converge on the bridge in the middle of town. Most buses use the general bus stand 1.5km north of town, though some local minibuses use the old GTS stand south of the bridge. Through buses will often drop you on the KKH near the Ashoka Rocks, a 1km walk to the bazaar on Shinkiari Rd.

### Information

The telephone exchange and post office are a fair way out on Kashmir Rd. No banks here will change money; if you're broke, spend your last Rs 7 on the bus to Abbottabad and do it there.

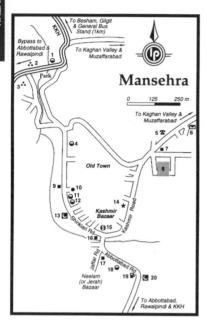

**Mansehra**

To Besham, Gilgit & General Bus Stand (1km)
Bypass to Abbottabad & Rawalpindi
To Kaghan Valley & Muzaffarabad
Park
To Kaghan Valley & Muzaffarabad
Old Town
Kashmir Bazaar
Shinkiari Rd
Kashmir Road
Jaffar Rd
Abbottabad Rd
Neelam (or Jerah) Bazaar
To Abbottabad, Rawalpindi & KKH

0   125   250 m

**PLACES TO STAY**
7    Parbat Hotel
9    Errum Hotel
16   Zam Zam Hotel
17   Taj Mahal Hotel

**OTHER**
1    Bus Stop (Through Buses)
2    Ashoka Rocks
3    Ashoka Rocks
4    Suzuki Stand
5    Telephone Exchange
6    Post Office
8    Sikh Fort
10   Cinema
11   Suzuki Stand
12   Suzukis to Bus Station
13   Mosque
14   Police Station (former Sikh Temple)
15   National Bank
18   Local Minibus Stand
19   Petrol Station
20   Mosque

### Ashoka Rocks

Mansehra's tourist attraction is on the north side of town – three granite boulders on which 14 edicts were engraved by order of the Mauryan king Ashoka in the 3rd century BC. Appalled by the suffering his military campaigns caused, Ashoka became interested in Buddhism and tried to dictate a new morality based on piety, moderation, tolerance and respect for life. He was greatly revered but his reforms (and his empire) didn't last much longer than he did. The inscriptions have done better, but they too are fading away; the ancient Kharoshthi script is now almost impossible to see.

### Former Sikh Temple

Up Kashmir Rd is a gaudy three storey building, a pastiche of colours and styles. Built in 1937 as a Sikh gurdwara, it's now the police station. The interior hasn't been altered much either, and they might let you in for a look.

### Sikh Fort

Up an alley 300m past the police station is a fort, built in the early 19th century by Sikh governor-general Man Singh (after whom Mansehra is named) and rebuilt by the British in 1857 after the annexation of the Sikh state. It now houses government offices and a jail. A few traces of the original mud-and-rock structure can be seen inside.

Further up the side street, under pine, eucalyptus and maple trees, are old British garrison buildings, district courts and the homes of government officials.

### Bazaars

Shinkiari Rd and Kashmir Rd curve round a hill in the middle of town, and Kashmir Bazaar sprawls across the top. It's a warren of shops and homes, its narrow lanes in semi-permanent shadow. Across the bridge along Jaffar Rd is the smaller, older Neelam (or Jerah) Bazaar, with spice vendors and confectioners.

### Hill Walking

If you're feeling active, there are some good hill walks, with views of the Pakhli Plain and the Black Mountains, starting about 2km out Kashmir Rd.

## Places to Stay

The friendly but basic *Taj Mahal* is the best of a bunch of cheapos near the local minibus stand. Room rates range from Rs 60 to Rs 120 depending on the amount of dirt in the room. The pleasant *Zam Zam Hotel* (☎ 2127) has small singles/doubles with communal cold shower for Rs 60/70 (Rs 100/130 with a loo). It's hidden off Shinkiari Rd 50m west of the bridge.

The *Errum Hotel* (☎ 36848), further up Shinkiari Rd, has quiet, clean doubles with toilet and shower for Rs 350, good-value singles for Rs 150, and a rooftop patio. On Kashmir Rd, beyond the fort, the newish *Parbat Hotel* (☎ 36579) has ugly but clean rooms with attached shower for Rs 100/200.

## Places to Eat

Food along Abbottabad Rd is cheap and good. Little cafes serve braised mutton, chapli kebabs, qeema (mince), omelettes and thick northern-style noodle soup. There are enough vegetable and fruit stalls to keep vegetarians going. Finish off a meal with home-made ice cream from near the Erum Hotel.

The best (and cleanest) restaurants are in the hotels. As one of its highway signs says, the *Zam Zam*'s food is 'very cheap and testy'.

## Getting There & Away

A local minibus stand on Abbottabad Rd has departures for Abbottabad, Haripur and Rawalpindi only; Hi-Aces and Coasters to/from Rawalpindi via Abbottabad are Rs 35/40 and take three hours.

For other destinations take a Rs 2 Suzuki from Shinkiari Rd to the chaotic general bus stand, 1.5km north of town on the KKH. Some operators have schedules but most go when they're full; buy tickets on board or at makeshift desks nearby.

**Abbottabad** Both stands have departures all day for Rs 7.

**Besham** Minibuses go infrequently from the general bus stand for about Rs 35 and take 3½ hours. Otherwise take one of the fre-quent minibuses to Batagram and change or, alternatively, flag down a through bus.

**Gilgit** There's no direct service. Natco and Mashabrum Tours make tea stops at the Murtazar Hotel, 300m north of the general bus stand, just past the PSO petrol station, but space can be tight. The alternative is to take a minibus to Besham, where there are local and direct options to Gilgit.

**Kaghan Valley** Wagons from the general bus stand go to Balakot for Rs 15, sometimes as far as Naran for Rs 65. Buses are much slower.

**Muzaffarabad** Minibuses take two hours and leave from the general bus stand all day for Rs 20.

**Rawalpindi** Minibuses go from the general bus stand to Saddar Bazaar all day, and buses go to Pir Wadhai bus stand hourly. The trip takes three to 3½ hours and costs about Rs 40. The Abbottabad Rd stand has minibuses to Liaquat Chowk for slightly less. A slow, scenic alternative is to catch a bus from Abbottabad via the hill-station towns around Murree, though this takes twice as long.

## THE KAGHAN VALLEY

Embraced by forested peaks of the Lesser Himalaya and drained by the Kunhar River, this 160km-long valley is one of Pakistan's most popular holiday spots. For all its accessibility and rugged beauty, however, it's surprisingly undeveloped.

At its head is 4175m Babusar Pass over to the Indus Valley at Chilas. In 1892 the British opened a supply line across the pass, one of only two links to Gilgit from the outside world. After Partition the Babusar Pass was Pakistan's only reliable overland route to the Northern Areas until the KKH was built. For about six weeks each summer a jeep road over the pass is a challenging alternative to the KKH between Chilas and Mansehra.

The valley has photogenic treks of all sizes, and the Kunhar River from Naran to Kaghan is open for white-water rafting.

HAZARA

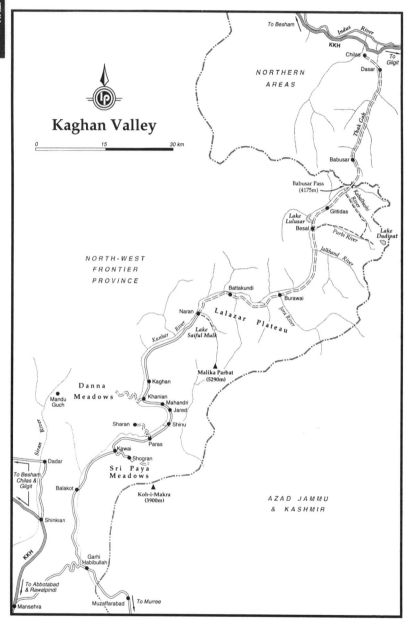

# Kaghan Valley

0    15    30 km

**Cyclists' Notes, Kaghan Valley & Babusar Pass**
The road north from Balakot averages about 20m climb per km, steeper near the Babusar Pass. Some who have cycled over the 4175m pass say it's only sensible on a lightly loaded mountain bike, and only if you're in very good shape. Food from Naran to Chilas is very basic – dhal, chapatti, sometimes rice.

**Mansehra to Balakot, about 50km** The road is hilly and twisting, and drivers are reckless. Garhi Habibullah, the junction for the road to/from Muzaffarabad, has food stalls and at least one simple charpoi hotel.

**Balakot to Naran, 84km** The road is more or less paved for 62km to Kaghan, then gravelled for 22km to Naran. The stretch to Kaghan has cheap hotels at Mahindri and Khanian. From Kawai, 24km from Balakot, a steep, mostly paved road climbs 1300m in 8km to Shogran. From Paras, 30km from Balakot, a jeep track climbs 15-20km to Sharan, with a youth hostel and resthouse.

**Naran to Babusar Pass, about 70km** Above Naran the track grows steeper and gets worse. Battakundi, 16km beyond Naran, has a resthouse, a Forestry hut, a collapsing youth hostel and a cheap cafe. At Burawai, 15km on, is a resthouse and charpoi hotel. You can camp safely from Naran to Lulusar, but Kohistani villages beyond that have stone-throwing kids, and camping is not advisable from there to Chilas. The pass is about 35km past Burawai, and the track over it is awful.

**Babusar Pass to Chilas, 52km** Babusar village, with a primitive resthouse and a few cheap inns and shops, is 13 very rocky km north of the pass. There is a rutty jeep track for 39km from there to Chilas. ■

The valley population consists of a string of villages along the river (Hindko-speaking up to Gittidas, Kohistani from there), plus a biannual migration of Gujars, the 'cowboys' of northern Pakistan (see the boxed text The Gujars in the Facts about the Region chapter).

### Orientation
Balakot is 50km from Mansehra on a snakey paved road. The valley road is more or less paved up to Kaghan village, 62km from Balakot, and gravelled to Naran, 22km further on. From Naran to Babusar Pass it's 70km of gradually deteriorating jeep track. Regular buses and passenger pickups go up and down the valley, and jeeps and other vehicles can be hired in Balakot or Naran, with rates dropping in the off-season.

### Information
Change money in Abbottabad; no banks in the valley will do it.

### When to Go
By May, Shogran and Naran are accessible by 4WD. Hotel prices and occupancy are low at this time but many of the prime scenic attractions are still under snow. Tourist season begins in earnest in June. The monsoon brings rain and delays in July and August but up-valley travel is possible; in fact, mid-July to August is the only reliable time for a jeep crossing of the Babusar Pass. Fine weather returns in September. In October, the upper valley again becomes 4WD-only. From late November to early April snow blocks the road beyond Kaghan, and upper villages are mostly deserted. Conditions vary widely from year to year.

### Places to Stay
Hotels overflow in tourist season, but in May and in September-October they'll fall all over themselves for your business and you can negotiate some real bargains. Few hotels offer single rates in season. There are several *Pakistan Youth Hostels*, but they tend to be run down, packed with Pakistani students in summer and closed the rest of the time.

A few *Government Resthouses* are available on the rare occasions officials aren't using them. Some *Forestry Resthouses* can be booked with the Kaghan Valley Project Director in Abbottabad (☎ 0992-2893), but the best ones can only be booked in

Peshawar (☎ 091-217025). The same is true of most of the *C&W Resthouses*, though many of these are due for privatisation in the next few years.

## Balakot
### Tel Area Code: 0985

Balakot (982m) looks better from a distance than up close. Aside from a small bazaar there's little of interest except information and transport. Heavy monsoon flooding in 1992 swept away parts of the town, including the Syed Ahmad Shaheed Mosque and the Youth Hostel.

### Orientation & Information
PTDC, at the south end of town, can arrange jeeps and has information on weather, road conditions and jeep availability in the upper valley. The police, main post office, telephone exchange and hospital are a short walk south of PTDC, and there is a post office franchise opposite the Balakot Hotel.

### Places to Stay – bottom end
The *Mashriq Hotel* is the cheapest in town, but vastly overpriced like the rest; a barren double without loo is about Rs 125. On the main road some serais have charpois in open rooms, but they aren't interested in foreigners.

### Places to Stay – middle
The *Balakot Hotel*, *Koh-i-Toor Hotel* (☎ 210163) and Paradise Inn all have dull but clean and carpeted rooms with hot water for about Rs 300. The *Taj Mahal Hotel* (☎ 210321) has comfortable rooms with TV for Rs 600; upstairs rooms are much nicer for the same price.

### Places to Stay – top end
A double at the *PTDC Motel* (☎ 210208) is a non-negotiable Rs 590. Balakot's top hotel is the *Pine Park* (☎ 210533), perched on the ridge above town. Rooms in the new building cost Rs 800/1000 and the views are great; rooms in the old block are half the price. In between the two is the *Hotel Gate Way* (☎ 210591), a good compromise with rooms from Rs 600 to Rs 800.

### Getting There & Away
The general bus stand and jeep lot are opposite the Mashriq Hotel.

Buses, minibuses and cargo jeeps go up to Kaghan (Rs 35) and Naran (Rs 50) all day in summer; out of season you may have to take a jeep to Naran (Rs 100) or transfer to one in Kaghan. Buses go at least to Kaghan.

Buses and minibuses go to Mansehra every hour until mid-afternoon from the general bus stand, for about Rs 15. For Muzaffarabad, take a bus or Suzuki for Rs 7 from the general bus stand to Garhi Habibullah ('ha-BEE-bu-la') and catch a Mansehra to Muzaffarabad bus.

*Rental* You can hire a Suzuki for a day trip or a jeep for longer. Some PTDC jeep rates are: Shogran, Rs 700 return with a few hours there; Naran, Rs 900 one way; Naran one way via Shogran, Rs 1200. A full Suzuki is cheaper per person but drivers are less reliable in the face of problems, and dislike waiting around while you enjoy the view. For trips beyond Naran you can hire a private jeep there.

**Balakot**

Map labels: Mosque & School; General Bus Stand; Jeep Lot; Paradise Inn; Petrol Station; To Naran & Upper Kaghan Valley; Pine Park Hotel; Mashriq Hotel; Taj Mahal Hotel; Post Office; Balakot Hotel & Restaurant; Koh-i-Toor Hotel; Hotel Gate Way; Balakot Bridge; Brewi Bazaar; New Mosque; River Kunhar; Passenger Bridge (Under Repair); PTDC Motel & Tourist Information Centre; Petrol Station; Police; Civil Hospital; Telephone Exchange; (Main) Post Office; To Mansehra, Muzaffarabad & KKH; 0  150  300 m

## Shogran & Kawai

At Kawai, a stomach-churning hour north of Balakot by pickup, a jeep track climbs steeply for 8km onto the Shogran Plateau. With views down to a carpet of forest and up to majestic peaks – including 5290m Malika Parbat (Queen of Mountains), tallest in the Kaghan Valley, and brooding Koh-i-Makra (Spider Mountain) – this is a great place to walk the soles off your boots or snooze away a few days. A good place to head for is the small lake and beautiful meadows of Sri Paya, 9km beyond Shogran up a rough jeep track.

**Places to Stay – Shogran** New hotels are sprouting like weeds. The first and last you come to are the *Tourist Inn* and *Hilltop*, both with clean rooms and fine views for Rs 400. A good option at half the price is the *Shogran Hotel*. The *Faisal* and *Punjab Hazara* are crummy and overpriced. By contrast the top end *Pine Park* (☎ (0985) 410333) is opulent and almost worth the Rs 1600 tag. Rooms in the tourist block are cheaper at Rs 600 but not especially good value. The older of two *Forestry Resthouses* can be booked from Abbottabad, as can the basic *resthouse* in Sri Paya. To beat the crowds, pitch a tent in higher pastures, two to three hours up.

**Places to Stay – Kawai** *Tourist Inn* (☎ (0985) 410022) has good value singles/ doubles for Rs 150/200. The *Punjab Hotel* is really a restaurant but with a few rooms around the back for Rs 100 and charpois for Rs 50. The plush *Faisal* is Rs 1000 for a double. There is also a *C&W Resthouse*, booked with the C&W Executive Engineer (☎ (0987) 2710) in Mansehra.

**Getting There & Away** A passenger pickup is about Rs 15 from Balakot to Kawai. From here special jeeps cost Rs 200 up to Shogran, though you can normally get a cheaper ride if you're patient. Special jeeps from Shogran to Sri Paya cost about Rs 500.

## Sharan

At Paras ('pa-RAHS'), about 10km north of Kawai, a rough track crosses the river and climbs about 15km to Sharan, in the middle of nowhere at 2400m. From there you can hike through the forest, or trek overnight across to the Siran Valley, north of Mansehra (a local guide will help you find the trail and avoid the occasional bear or wild cat). A special jeep from Paras to Sharan costs around Rs 500.

**Places to Stay** Sharan's *Pakistan Youth Hostel* was under repair at the time of writing. You may be able to book the *Forestry Resthouse* from Abbottabad. Paras has the cheap and cheerful *Green View Hotel*.

## Jared

The NWFP government operates a 'handi-crafts development centre' at Jared ('ja-RED'), two hours from Balakot. State-run and private shops sell traditional-style carved furniture, hand-made woollen shawls and other work.

**Places to Stay** Just past Jared at Mahandri is the basic *Bismillah Hotel* and a *Forestry Resthouse*, booked with the Kaghan Valley Forestry Project Director in Abbottabad.

## Khanian

This undeveloped village at an attractive turn of the Kunhar River offers a quiet, cheap place to stay if the hordes of tourists are getting to you. From Khanian a 10km jeep track winds up the hillside to picturesque Danna Meadows.

**Places to Stay** Bottom-end hotels include the *Yasir* and *Khanian*. The *Pine Park Hotel* has rooms from Rs 400/600.

## Kaghan

This is a dreary place whose only advantage is that it's usually open year-round and so makes a base for winter trips. Any other time, move on to Naran if you can.

**Places to Stay** There are a few bottom-end local hotels. The huge *Lalazar Hotel* (☎ 22) has bare doubles for Rs 100-300. The equally bloated *Vershigoom Hotel* (☎ 12) has neglected rooms for Rs 75/150 (the room they tried to give us had a big turd in the middle of the bathroom). The *Siachin* is probably the best of a poor bunch, with a couple of clean carpeted rooms for Rs 100/200. There are several basic doss houses including the *Bismillah, Green View* and *Nashaman*. A VIP *Forestry Resthouse* can only be booked in Peshawar.

**Getting There & Away** From Balakot, a Datsun is Rs 35, and there are frequent departures. Jeeps to Naran take an hour and cost Rs 50.

### Naran

At 2400m, Naran is the summertime base for exploring the valley. Just a one-road bazaar full of hotels, it's a beehive in tourist season, choked with jeeps and minibuses. The most popular destination from here is picture-postcard Lake Saiful Mulk.

Hotels are packed in summer (Naran visitors sometimes have to stay in Kaghan), but in October hotels may ask less than a *fifth* of the summer price. From December to April, snow shuts Naran down.

**Information** PTDC has guides for hire and can help you negotiate jeep rates. Fishing licences (Rs 50) are sold at the Fisheries Office, near the road on the track to Lake Saiful Mulk. The only equipment for rent is tackle in some shops during fishing season. The post office is to the south of town in the bazaar.

**Places to Stay – bottom end** By the road, several km south of town, is a *Pakistan Youth Hostel*, in a state of disrepair. Some mid-range places may let you pitch a tent and use their water and toilets for a small fee (though PTDC won't). The *Sarhad, Zam Zam, Pakistan, Shalimar* and *Snow View*, to the north of town, all have basic rooms for about Rs 150.

The *Zero Point* and *Park View* hotels are better but more expensive; all will charge more if the traffic will bear it. If these are full

try the *Saiful Mulk, Mehran* or *Punjab* in the north of town or the *Shrubland (Sadiq)* in the south.

**Places to Stay – middle** The monster *Lalazar* (☎ 1) has doubles from Rs 200. *Dreamland* (☎ 19), fitted out like a surreal Austrian chalet, is pretty good value for Rs 400 a double, as is the nearby *Mount View* (☎ 30). Both are down a side road from the Lalazar. Further south the *Balakot Hotel* (☎ 29) has clean carpeted doubles for Rs 300. Naran has two *C&W Resthouses*, booked in Peshawar, and two *Forestry Resthouses*; the older one can be booked with Abbottabad PTDC.

**Places to Stay – top end**. In the southern end of town the *Daricha Gul* (☎ 36) and *Kunhar* have nice doubles for about Rs 500. The *Naran* and better *New Park Hotel* (☎ 23) have balconies and decent rooms from Rs 400. The *PTDC Motel* complex (☎ 2) has doubles with shared loo for Rs 400 and deluxe doubles with bath from Rs 1200. You should book this through Islamabad or Rawalpindi PTDC in peak season.

A rash of plush top-end hotels is slowly spreading up the road to Saiful Mulk.

**Places to Eat** All but the cheapest hotels have restaurants with basic meat, dhal and chapattis.

**Getting There & Away** Buses to/from Balakot are about Rs 30, and minibuses about Rs 50; they go every hour or two. Outside July, August and September you may have to take a 4WD to Kaghan (Rs 50) and change, or hire a jeep. Naran PTDC has no jeeps for hire but they'll help you bargain with greedy local drivers.

### Lake Saiful Mulk & Other Walks

Lake Saiful Mulk is a two to three hour uphill walk from Naran; the path starts just above the bazaar. Alternatively, you can hire horses along the trail for Rs 200 return. At 3200m, surrounded by moody, snowy mountains, the lake is said to be inhabited by mountain

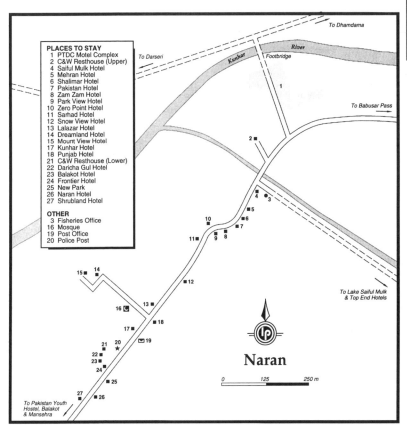

PLACES TO STAY
1 PTDC Motel Complex
2 C&W Resthouse (Upper)
4 Saiful Mulk Hotel
5 Mehran Hotel
6 Shalimar Hotel
7 Pakistan Hotel
8 Zam Zam Hotel
9 Park View Hotel
10 Zero Point Hotel
11 Sarhad Hotel
12 Snow View Hotel
13 Lalazar Hotel
14 Dreamland Hotel
15 Mount View Hotel
17 Kunhar Hotel
18 Punjab Hotel
21 C&W Resthouse (Lower)
22 Daricha Gul Hotel
23 Balakot Hotel
24 Frontier Hotel
25 New Park
26 Naran Hotel
27 Shrubland Hotel

OTHER
3 Fisheries Office
16 Mosque
19 Post Office
20 Police Post

To Dhamdama
Kunhar River
Footbridge
To Darseri
To Babusar Pass
To Lake Saiful Mulk
& Top End Hotels

Naran

To Pakistan Youth
Hostel, Balakot
& Mansehra

0      125      250 m

spirits. Legend has it that in ancient times a mortal, Prince Saiful Mulk, fell in love with one and married her.

The best way to enjoy it to yourself is to camp. A *Forestry Resthouse* at the lake can be booked in Abbottabad or you could sleep on the porch if you have a warm bag.

The *Lalazar Hotel* has a cottage with doubles for Rs 700 – book in Naran. There's no electricity.

A further day's walking takes you to the edge of the Lalazar Plateau (though this is more easily reached from Battakundi). A *Water & Power Development Administra-*

*tion (WAPDA) Hut* at Lalazar is booked with WAPDA in Abbottabad, though the *chowkidar* may let you stay if you just turn up. You can make a day trip by jeep from Naran to Saiful Mulk for Rs 400-600 or to Lalazar for Rs 600.

Local people suggest other walks across the Kunhar River from Naran. Cross the footbridge by PTDC. Turning left, you can walk to Darseri village opposite Naran. If instead you turn right, it's 3km to Dhamdama village. Or you can climb right up the hill in front of you, an all-day outing, for excellent views.

## Babusar Pass

The Kaghan Valley's most dramatic scenery is beyond Naran. Travel is by 4WD, pony, mountain bike or foot. At **Battakundi**, 16km up the valley, you can detour 5km up to summer pastures on Lalazar Plateau (see the preceding section). Battakundi has a *Forestry Hut*, booked with the District Forestry Officer in Balakot, and a *Pakistan Youth Hostel* which is in a state of collapse. There are *resthouses* here and 15km up-valley at **Burawai**. There is basic charpoi accommodation at Battakundi and Besal.

The road degenerates to a barely 'jeepable' track 20km beyond Burawai, at **Besal** ('BEH-sal'). From there you may detour about 15km east up to beautiful, green **Lake Dudipat**, or stay on the main track about 3km to **Lake Lulusar**, the biggest natural lake in Hazara and the source of the Kunhar River.

**Gittidas**, about 6km north of Lake Lulusar, is the southernmost Kohistani village in the region, and apparently not a friendly place to stay the night without a guide from the area. From there it's about 8km to 'Babusar top' (4175m). If the weather is clear you can walk about a km east from the summit for views of the Kaghan Valley behind you and Nanga Parbat to the east. **Babusar village** is 13km north of the pass on the track, or about half that far on a short-cut footpath. In summer there are a few shops and serais open, and a spartan *Northern Areas Public Works Department (NAPWD) Resthouse* with two doubles at Rs 150 (coming from the north, book it at Chilas NAPWD). Folks are not very hospitable along here, so camping is not recommended.

It's 39km from Babusar village to **Chilas** on a rutty jeep track. Northern Areas Transport Company (Natco) 4WD cargo pickups make this trip daily in summer.

**Getting There & Away** A small 4WD jeep can manage the narrow, rocky track over the pass in July and August, though even then monsoon rains make it problematic. One-way jeep rental from Naran to Babusar/ Chilas at the time of writing was Rs 1500/2400. The pass is also feasible as a day

trip from Naran and back, for about Rs 2000. Cargo jeeps sometimes go up as far as Besal.

On foot, give yourself at least a week from Naran to Babusar village, which allows for some side-trips. It may be possible to trek across as early as mid-June (though you'll still find snow) and until early October (though most villagers will be gone for the winter by then). Snow normally begins in November. A local guide might be helpful, especially in the Kohistan region from Gittidas to Babusar, as not everyone is friendly en route.

Any way you do it, get some local advice before crossing the pass. PTDC is a good source in Naran; in Chilas try field officers at the NAPWD office, or Natco drivers on the Babusar village run. Naran to Chilas is 130km.

Allow for wide variations in the seasonal changes noted in this chapter.

## ABBOTTABAD
*Tel Area Code: 05921*

Abbottabad ('AB-it-uh-bahd') is the headquarters of NWFP's Hazara Division and its biggest town. Named after James Abbott, a British officer in the Sikh Wars and Hazara's first deputy commissioner, it was established as a British military cantonment in the 1850s.

Its continuing military importance (home to the Pakistan Military Academy at nearby Kakul and to several frontier regiments) has preserved some colonial-era flavour. Shady gardens and clean streets seem lifted from the 19th century, and it's not unusual to hear church bells or a military band. There is a robust old bazaar beside the cantonment. At 1220m, Abbottabad has a cool climate, and one of Pakistan's finest hill-station retreats is an hour away at Thandiani.

The town has a sizeable Christian minority and three active churches. Abbottabad's Muslims are mostly Sunni, with large numbers of Shias and some Ismailis. The language of the region is Hindko Punjabi, but English and Urdu are spoken.

## Orientation

North of the general bus stand is a roundabout, Fowara Chowk. Down the right fork is The Mall (or Mansehra Rd). The left fork is Jinnah Rd, the town's axis, running past the bazaar and cantonment and rejoining The Mall. From either end roads climb toward Shimla Peak.

## Information

PTDC (☎ 34399), across from Cantonment Park, is open from 9 am to 3 pm daily, except closed Sunday and Friday afternoon. The Foreigners' Registration Office (FRO) is at the Senior Superintendent of Police (SSP) office by the district courts, south of Kucheri Rd.

To book Forestry Resthouses at Thandiani, Dadar or the Kaghan Valley, see the Conservator of Forests (☎ 30728) or the Forestry Project Director (☎ 30893), both in a compound on Jail Rd. PTDC may be able to help with some Kaghan Valley resthouses.

The post office is at the corner of Club and Central Rds. Overseas calls can be placed from the telegraph office on Pine View Rd.

The main office of National Bank (near the courts) and the Pine View Rd office of UBL Bank will do foreign exchange. If you're going to the Kaghan Valley, change money here, as no banks in the valley do foreign exchange.

There is a police post on Jinnah Rd near the bazaar. The small Cantonment General Hospital is on Pine View Rd and the big District Headquarters Teaching Hospital is on Id Gah Rd east of The Mall.

## Abbottabad Town

Abbottabad's historical heart is the cantonment, with its orderly streets, European architecture and grand parade ground. St Luke's Church, opposite Cantonment Public Park, is as old as the town. A melancholy Christian cemetery is 500m up Circular (or Sabir Sharif) Rd. Abbottabad's other persona is the bazaar, 10 square blocks of crumbling colonial architecture, full of noise and the smells of incense and lime. In Gurdwara Bazaar, beneath the arch off Jinnah Rd, is a former Sikh gurdwara (temple) built in 1943, abandoned at Partition and now used as municipal offices.

## Shimla Peak

The hills cradling Abbottabad are Shimla peak to the north-west and Sarban peak to the south.

Shimla's cool, piney summit is full of trails with fine panoramas of the town and its surroundings. You can walk up (3 steep km) or take a Rs 3 passenger Suzuki from upper Pine View Rd; ask for *Shimla Pahari* ('pah-REE').

## Ilyasi Mosque

Near Nawan Sheher village, 5km east on the Murree road, is this striking mosque, which includes a complex of spring-fed bathhouses and pools. A small bazaar has tea shops and cafes. Catch a Rs 3 Suzuki to Nawan Sheher from Id Gah Rd.

## Places to Stay

**Bottom End** A *Pakistan Youth Hostel*, north of Abbottabad at Mandian, is quite isolated unless you're cycling or driving. Take a Rs 4 Suzuki to Mandian from Id Gah Rd. At the end of the line turn left at the 'Ayub Medical College' sign, go 700m to a T-junction, and then left for 300m.

The *Bolan Hotel* (☎ 34395) near the general bus stand has worn-out but acceptable singles/doubles with loo and hot shower from Rs 80/150. The nearby *Park Hotel* and the miserable *Marhaba, Mount View* and *Asia* hotels on Id Gah Rd are only for the desperate.

North on Jinnah Rd, the old-style *Cantt View* is cheap and clean at Rs 100/150, if you ignore the hideous decor. The nearby *Pineview* is a fine tea house but a poor hotel. Hotels in the same range on The Mall include the *Faisal* and *Zarbat*, neither of them interested in foreigners, and the friendlier *Falcon* (☎ 4169), with clean but noisy rooms for Rs 100/200.

**Middle** At Fowara Chowk the *Ramlina Hotel* (☎ 34431) has comfortable singles/doubles from Rs 150/250 and is convenient for onward transport. The grandiose but neglected *Al-Zahra* (☎ 30155) behind it is Rs 175/200. The *Kohisar* on Jinnah Rd is a

HAZARA

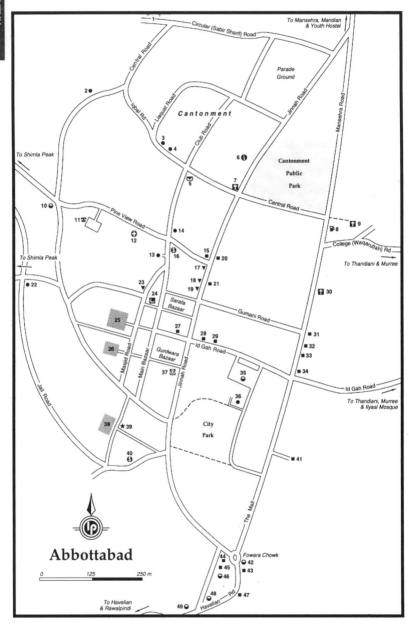

To Mansehra, Mandian
& Youth Hostel

Circular (Sabir Sharif) Road

Central Road

Parade
Ground

Iqbal Rd

Liaquat Road

Cantonment

Jinnah Road

Mansehra Road

Club Road

To Shimla Peak

3
4

6

Cantonment

Public

Park

5

7

Central Road

10

Pine View Road

11

12

14

8    9

College (Waqarullah) Rd

To Shimla Peak

13    16

15    20

To Thandiani & Murree

22

17

18    21

19

30

23

24

Sarafa
Bazaar

Gumani Road

Masjid Road

Main Bazaar

25

27

28    29

31

26

Gurdwara
Bazaar

Id Gah Road

32

33

Jinnah Road

37

35

34

Jail Road

38    39

36

Id Gah Road

To Thandiani, Murree
& Ilyasi Mosque

40

City

Park

41

The Mall

Abbottabad

0        125        250 m

Fowara Chowk

44    42

45    43

46

48    47

To Havelian
& Rawalpindi

49    Havelian Rd

| | PLACES TO STAY | 23 | Iqbal Restaurant | 13 | Cinema |
|---|---|---|---|---|---|
| 15 | Cantt View Hotel | 25 | Vegetable Market | 14 | Variety Book Stall |
| 20 | Pineview Hotel | 26 | Vegetable Market | 16 | UBL Bank |
| 21 | Hotel Kohisar | | | 22 | Conservator of |
| 27 | Marhaba Hotel | | **OTHER** | | Forests |
| 28 | Asia Hotel | 1 | Christian Cemetery | 24 | Mosque |
| 29 | Mount View Hotel | 2 | C&W Executive | 30 | Catholic Church |
| 31 | Zarbat Hotel | | Engineer | 35 | Regional Bus Yard |
| 32 | Falcon Hotel | 3 | Public Library | 36 | City Hall |
| 33 | Faisal Hotel | 4 | Commissioner's | 37 | Old Sikh Temple |
| 34 | Sarban Hotel | | Office | 38 | District Courts |
| 41 | Springfield Hotel | 5 | Post Office | 39 | Senior |
| 43 | Bolan Hotel | 6 | PTDC Tourist | | Superintendent of |
| 44 | Ramlina Hotel | | Information Centre | | Police (SSP) |
| 45 | Al-Zahra Hotel | 7 | St Luke's Church | 40 | National Bank |
| 47 | Park Hotel | 8 | Petrol Station | 42 | Coasters to |
| | | 9 | Presbyterian Church | | Rawalpindi |
| | **PLACES TO EAT** | 10 | Shimla Peak Suzuki | 46 | Coasters to |
| 17 | Wood Lock | | Yard | | Rawalpindi |
| | Restaurant | 11 | Telegraph Office | 48 | Taxi Stand |
| 18 | New Friends Cafe | 12 | Cantonment | 49 | General Bus |
| 19 | Rainbow Cafe | | General Hospital | | Stand |

good choice with clean rooms for Rs 150/300 and a pleasant terrace; reception is in the Wood Lock Restaurant opposite. Prices tend to drop in the off-season.

**Top End** On The Mall, doubles at the *Springfield Hotel* (☎ 34397) start from Rs 450 and at the *Sarban Hotel* (☎ 30167) from Rs 500.

### Places to Eat
The *Rainbow Cafe, New Friends Cafe* and *Wood Lock Restaurant* on Jinnah Rd serve curries, braised meat, rice and vegetables in fairly clean surroundings, as do several restaurants around the general bus stand. In the bazaar the *Iqbal Restaurant* has an elegant interior but so-so food, and always seems to be full of Pathans mesmerised by MTV.

### Things to Buy
The best of several neighbouring bookshops is Variety Book Stall, south of the post office, with foreign magazines, novels and postcards.

Hazara embroidery is a local speciality. Good deals on shawls and other items are in small shops in the bazaar.

### Getting There & Away
The general bus stand has buses and Hi-Aces to Mansehra (Rs 7) and Rawalpindi. More comfortable Coasters go to Rawalpindi (Rs 35) from Hazara Flying Coach (☎ 32211), in front of the Al-Zahra Hotel, and from beside the Bolan Hotel – all via Havelian in two to three hours.

A slow, scenic alternative route to Rawalpindi is via Murree (see the Rawalpindi & Islamabad chapter). Buses go to Murree all day for Rs 25, a five hour trip. For upcountry travel to Kohistan or Kaghan, there are more options from Mansehra.

The bus yard for regional trips (eg Thandiani) is down an alley east of the Mount View Hotel on Id Gah Rd.

### Getting Around
Regional passenger Suzukis clog Id Gah Rd and run up and down The Mall all day. There is a taxi stand opposite the general bus stand.

### THANDIANI
Thandiani ('tahn-dee-AH-nee'), a series of 2700m forested ridges north-east of Abbottabad, is the northernmost of the hill-station retreats called the Galis (the others are described in the Rawalpindi & Islamabad chapter). The air is cool and clean, development is minimal and there are fine views east across the Pir Panjal Range and north even

to Nanga Parbat in clear weather. *Thandiani* means 'cool place', so bring an extra layer or two. It's possible as a long day trip.

### Places to Stay & Eat

To stay cheaply, bring a tent. The little *Far Pavilions Hotel* at the bus terminus has two doubles for Rs 400 and some two or four-person tents for about Rs 300, which you can book through the Sarban Hotel in Abbottabad. A cafe and snack shops are open in summer. There is a *C&W Resthouse* 1km south, by the TV tower, where a double with bath is Rs 250. Theoretically you can only book it in Peshawar (Secretary, Construction & Works, (☎ (091) 279815) but travellers report booking it with the Executive Engineer in Abbottabad. One km further, a *Forestry Resthouse* has doubles for Rs 400, booked with the Conservator of Forests in Abbottabad.

### Getting There & Away

Thandiani is an hour's ride on a winding road beside the Kalapani River, through terraced fields and pine and deodar forest. A Datsun, Suzuki or Hi-Ace is Rs 15, and a bus is Rs 10, from the back of Abbottabad's regional bus yard. Departures are frequent until mid-afternoon.

### HAVELIAN

This dusty, nondescript market town and railhead has only one claim to fame: it's the official southern end of the KKH, 790km from the Chinese border and 1200km from Kashgar. No signs announce it, and in fact there was already a road through to Abbottabad before the KKH was even an idea.

But there is a kind of geographical boundary here. The road falls out of the hills to the banks of the Dor River beside Havelian. Southward, road and railway proceed almost horizontally to Rawalpindi. This certainly feels like the southern end of the mountains. There's no reason to stop here unless you want to carry on to Rawalpindi by rail.

### Places to Stay & Eat

The *Indus Hotel* has cheap rooms and a little cafe. Nobody speaks much English.

### Getting There & Away

Creaky trains go each morning and each evening to/from Rawalpindi for Rs 22, taking three hours. If you've come from Rawalpindi on the train, you may find a bus waiting at the station, which takes half an hour to Abbottabad or an hour to Mansehra for a few rupees. Or walk to the fork, keep right, and at the end of the bazaar you'll find more buses, leaving about every 30 minutes. Buses to Rawalpindi stop at the petrol station down the left fork.

### HAVELIAN TO THE GRAND TRUNK ROAD

From Havelian southward it's flat and warm. Half an hour away is **Haripur**, once the centre of Hazara. It was founded in 1822 as the headquarters of the Sikh General Hari Singh, after whom it's named. In 1853 its administrative functions were all moved to Abbottabad and now it's just a big market town. From Haripur the road crosses the wide, sandy **Taxila Valley**. It's odd to reflect that this quiet plain was for almost five centuries a world centre of Buddhist philosophy and art, the Buddhist 'Holy Land'. Taxila was the cultural capital of the Mauryan and Kushan empires – from the 3rd century BC to the 3rd century AD – and the valley still has abundant evidence of this extraordinary period, at archeological sites and in a fine museum. This makes a worthwhile one or two day trip from Rawalpindi (see the Taxila section in the Rawalpindi & Islamabad chapter).

At Taxila town or at Hasan Abdal (there are several routes from Haripur) you arrive at the **Grand Trunk Road**, the old axis of the Moghul Empire and the British Raj – Rudyard Kipling's 'broad, smiling river of life' that once ran 2500km from Kabul to Calcutta. Now the 'GT Road' is a thunderous stream of chrome-plated trucks and buses, and the Karakoram Highway seems pretty far away.

# Rawalpindi & Islamabad

*Pop: Rawalpindi 800,000, Islamabad 350,000*
*Tel Area Code: 051*

This is the business end of the KKH. Coming or going, you're likely to pass through but not to linger. But there's plenty to do while waiting for your visa, trekking permit or plane out.

Rawalpindi came into its own after the Sikh Wars of the 1840s, as the largest cantonment in Asia (cantonments were the tidy residential-military-administrative enclaves built next to major British colonial towns). Astride the Grand Trunk Road, Rawalpindi 'Cantt' is today the Pakistan Army HQ. Islamabad may be the capital, but in a country that has been ruled by the military for most of its life, 'Pindi is still the centre.

By contrast, where Islamabad stands there was nothing 40 years ago. Karachi being too far from everything, it was decided in the 1950s to build a new capital near Rawalpindi and the summer hill stations. To avoid urban chaos and decay, architect-planner Konstantinos Doxiades' idea was to let it grow in only one direction, sector by sector across a grid, each sector having its own residences, shops and parks. Construction began in 1961 and will go on for decades.

Subdued and suburban, Islamabad couldn't be less like Rawalpindi. So far only half a dozen sectors are done, but in the long term they'll swallow up 'Pindi itself. Until then, jokers will tell you that the best thing about the capital is that it's only 15km from Pakistan.

## Orientation

The two cities, 15km apart, are effectively a single mega-town with bazaars at one end and bureaucrats at the other. Buses between them are tedious but straightforward. If you're only here for the paperwork you can stay cheaply at Aabpara or Sitara in Islamabad. The rest of Islamabad is expensive, spread out and fairly boring. In Rawalpindi,

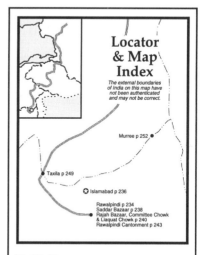

Locator & Map Index

The external boundaries of India on this map have not been authenticated and may not be correct.

Murree p 252

Taxila p 249

Islamabad p 236

Rawalpindi p 234
Saddar Bazaar p 238
Rajah Bazaar, Committee Chowk
& Liaquat Chowk p 240
Rawalpindi Cantonment p 243

### Highlights

- The colonial hill stations of Murree and the Galis
- Graeco-Buddhist sculpture and millennia-spanning excavations at Taxila
- The 'shrine city' of Hasan Abdal
- Shah Faisal, Asia's biggest (and richest) mosque

Saddar Bazaar is the sensible choice, with cheap hotels and transport to everywhere.

**Rawalpindi** The axes are Murree Rd and The Mall (also called Shahrah-i-Quaid-i-Azam). The cheaper hotels are in Saddar and Rajah bazaars and along Murree Rd at Liaquat ('LYAH-kut') Chowk and Committee Chowk. The railway station is in Saddar, the Pir Wadhai bus stand is north-west of town and the airport is to the north-east.

South of Saddar, the Cantonment has top-end hotels and traces of colonial life. At Rajah, the biggest bazaar, six-way Fowara

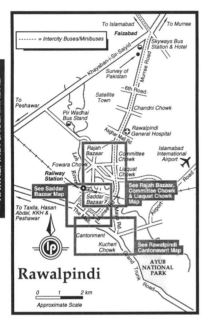

Rawalpindi

Karachi Company (G-9) and Peshawar Mor (G-8/1) in the west of the city. Between the Fs and Gs is a commercial belt called the Blue Area. Federal offices (Parliament, the president's and prime minister's houses, and ministries in the Secretariat) and most foreign embassies are on the east side of the city.

**Maps** The Survey of Pakistan office, on Murree Rd in Faizabad, sells a range of good maps, including a detailed but dated *Islamabad & Rawalpindi Guide Map*. Pakistan Tourism Development Corporation (PTDC) has a useful map of Islamabad. A better one, published by Pakistan Views and Tourism System, is hard to find.

### Information

**Tourist Offices** In Rawalpindi, PTDC has a marginally useful information office (☎ 517073), open 9 am to 4 pm, closed Sunday and Friday afternoon, at Flashman's Hotel, Saddar Bazaar. The Tourist Development Corporation of the Punjab (TDCP) (☎ 565824), at 44 Mall Plaza (corner of Kashmir Rd and The Mall) in Saddar Bazaar, has a few brochures, plus daily buses to Lahore.

A more helpful one is in Islamabad at the Ministry of Tourism (☎ 920 2766) in Jinnah Market. This is also the starting point for trekking permits (see Activities in the Facts

Chowk has 'spoke' roads to Saddar, Pir Wadhai and Murree Rd. The city's growing end is Satellite Town, touching Islamabad at the local transport junction of Faizabad.

**Islamabad** Islamabad has no axis or centre. Each sector, built around a commercial area, or *markaz*, has a letter-number designation (eg F-7), with quarters numbered clockwise (eg F-7/1 in the south-west corner, F-7/2 north-west corner). These Orwellian coordinates also have names; F and G are Shalimar and Ramna, so F-7 is also Shalimar-7, and so on. Numbered streets run within sectors, while avenues and *khayabans* (meaning avenue or boulevard) run between sectors.

But as a practical matter sectors are called by the names of their markets. The main ones, in sequence on the bus line, are Aabpara ('AH-pa-ra') (south-west G-6), Melody or Civic Centre (G-6), Super Market (F-6), Jinnah or Jinnah Super (F-7) and Ayub Market (F-8). Other important landmarks are

---

### Cyclists' Notes, Rawalpindi & Islamabad

The flat 50km or so from Hasan Abdal to Rawalpindi is via the Grand Trunk Road, a high-speed divided highway that is neither enjoyable nor very safe for cyclists.

Alternative routes to Rawalpindi are a very hilly 200km from Mansehra via Gahri Habibullah, Muzaffarabad and Kohala, and a steep and hilly 130km or so from Abbottabad via Murree. The northbound trip via the Galis includes an all-day uphill slog to Nathiagali (2500m), punishing at lower elevations in summer heat and humidity. The Galis are among the driest areas near the KKH (though there's bottled water and soft drinks for sale along the way). ■

for the Visitor chapter). A third office is on Aga Khan Rd in Super Market (F-6 markaz).

**Foreign Embassies** Most embassies are in the Diplomatic Enclave (G-5) at the east end of Islamabad. From Aabpara, Suzukis to Quaid-i-Azam University pass the American, Chinese, Russian, French and Australian embassies. Minibus Nos 3 and 120 to Bari Imam (Nurpur Shahan village) pass near the Canadian, Iranian, Indian, German and British embassies.

Afghanistan
    House 8, St 90, G-6/3 (☎ 824505)
Australia
    Diplomatic Enclave (☎ 279223)
Canada
    Diplomatic Enclave (☎ 279100)
China
    Diplomatic Enclave (☎ 279600, visa office)
France
    Ataturk Ave, Diplomatic Enclave (☎ 278730)

Germany
    Diplomatic Enclave (☎ 223516)
India
    Diplomatic Enclave (☎ 272676, visa office)
Iran
    House 222-238, St 2, G-5/1 (☎ 276270)
Kazakhstan
    House 2, St 4, F-8/3 (☎ 262924)
The Netherlands
    2nd Floor, PIA Building, Blue Area (☎ 279510)
New Zealand
    (go to the British High Commission)
Russia
    Diplomatic Enclave (☎ 278670)
UK (British High Commission)
    Diplomatic Enclave (☎ 822131; fax 823439)
USA
    Diplomatic Enclave (☎ 826161; fax 214222)
Uzbekistan
    House 6, St 29, F-7-1 (☎ 820779)

**Foreigners' Registration** If you register here, do it in the city where your hotel is (see the Foreigners' Registration section in the

### Visa Extension, Replacement or Modification
Islamabad is the only place in Pakistan to extend a visa, upgrade a transit visa or deal with expired visas and lost documents. You can also get an extra entry on your visa here (see Re-entry Visa). Following are the procedures in effect at the time of research, but don't be surprised if they've changed by the time you read this!

For the extension or replacement of anything other than a tourist visa – for example, a transit or business visa – or any visa that has expired, you must first get a Certificate of No Objection from the Interior Ministry, Block R, Civil Secretariat.

For a tourist visa, start at the Regional Passport Office at Peshawar Mor (G-8/4). Submit the form and (if applicable) a photocopy of your passport data pages and Pakistan visa. A one month extension is usually granted, to a maximum of three months. There's no charge. The office accepts applications from 9 am to noon Monday to Saturday, except only to 11 am on Friday. Your new/extended visa is ready the next morning, though if they're not busy you might get it the same day, after 2.30 pm.

Then go to the Foreigners' Registration Office (FRO) in Islamabad or Rawalpindi (depending on where you're staying) and register – just as if you were staying over 30 days, but even if you aren't (see Registration in the Facts for the Visitor chapter). They will give you a Certificate of Registration (Form B) and a Residential Permit. There's no fee. FROs usually close at 4 pm.

**Re-Entry Visa** If you decide while in Pakistan to depart the country and then return (eg from Sost up to Kashgar and back) and don't have a multiple-entry Pakistan visa, you can get a re-entry visa stamped in your passport.

If you have not already done so, register at the FRO and get a Certificate of Registration (Form B) and Residential Permit (see Registration in the Facts for the Visitor chapter). Take these to the Regional Passport Office at Peshawar Mor, with a photocopy of the data pages of your passport and two passport-size photos. The cost for a re-entry visa depends on your nationality, eg at the time of research a single re-entry was Rs 2244 for British citizens, Rs 620 for Americans and Rs 709 for Australians. You pay the fee at any National Bank branch (there is one nearby in G-9/2), which gives you a confirmation receipt for the Passport Office.

Note that you'd still have to get a new Certificate of Registration and Residential Permit on your return from China. ■

RAWALPINDI & ISLAMABAD

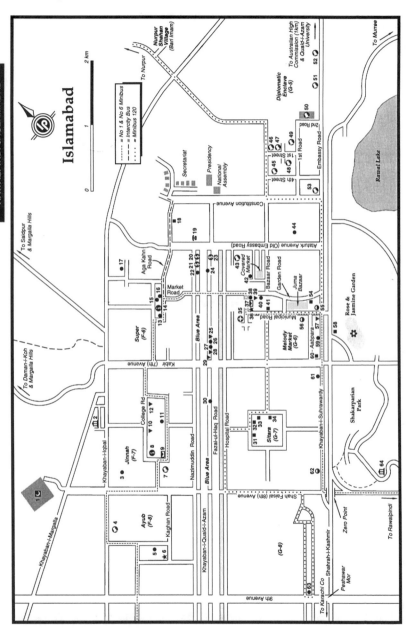

Islamabad

- - - = No 1 & No 6 Minibus
——— = Intercity Bus
········ = Minibus 120

## PLACES TO STAY

18  Marriott
31  Blue Sky Hotel
32  Sitara Hotel
33  Al Hujurat Hotel
34  Simara Hotel
41  Holiday Inn
54  Pakistan Youth
    Hostel
58  Tourist Campsite
60  Ambassador Hotel

## PLACES TO EAT

10  Kabul Restaurant &
    Afghan Bakery
12  Pappasalli's Italian
    Restaurant
25  Village Restaurant
28  Shop 67
29  Omar Khayam
    Restaurant
39  French Bakery
57  Kamran Restaurant

## OTHER

1  Shah Faisal Mosque
2  Islamabad Museum
3  Alliance Française
4  Kazak Embassy
5  Foreigners'
   Registration Office
6  Police Station
7  Uzbek Embassy
8  Ministry of Tourism
   & PTDC Tourist
   Information Centre
9  International Mail
   Office
11  Book Fair
13  Vanguard Bookstore
14  PTDC Tourist
    Information Centre
15  Agfa Rapeed
16  Mr Books
17  London Book
    Company
19  Central Telegraph
    Office
20  American Express
21  Bank of America
22  American Centre
23  Société Générale
24  Shaheen Air
26  Aero Asia & Bhoja
    Air
27  PIA Booking Office
    & Dutch Embassy
30  Asian Study Group
35  Capital Hospital
36  Police Station
37  General Post Office
    (GPO)
38  Pakistan Railways
    Booking Office
40  British Council
    Library
42  World Conservation
    Union (IUCN) &
    SDNP
43  Afghan Embassy
44  US Consular
    Office
45  German Embassy
46  Canadian High
    Commission
47  Iranian Embassy
48  Indian High
    Commission
49  British High
    Commission
50  US Embassy
51  Chinese Embassy
52  Russian Embassy
53  French Embassy
55  Minibus/Suzukis to
    Diplomatic
    Enclave
56  Minibuses to Sitara
    & Peshawar Mor
59  Travel Walji's
61  Capital
    Development
    Authority (CDA)
62  Bus Stop
63  Passport Office
64  Lok Virsa Museum

**RAWALPINDI & ISLAMABAD**

Facts for the Visitor chapter). Rawalpindi's Foreigners' Registration Office (FRO) is in the Civil Courts beside the Senior Superintendent of Police (SSP). Catch an airport Suzuki on Adamjee Rd and get off just past Kucheri Chowk (see the Rawalpindi Cantonment map). The Islamabad FRO is by the SSP in Ayub Market. The FROs are open from 9 am to 4 pm Monday to Saturday, and 9 am to noon on Sunday.

**Police** Saddar Bazaar police station (☎ 564760) is on Police Station Rd near the railway. Pir Wadhai has a police post (☎ 863787) at the bus station.

In Islamabad there are stations in Melody Market and in south-west Ayub Market. Police emergency numbers are ☎ 823333, 810222 and 15.

**Money** Most banks in Saddar Bazaar do foreign exchange. In Rajah Bazaar try Habib's City branch in Bara Bazaar. In Islamabad, go to UBL beside the Holiday Inn or National Bank behind it.

American Express on Murree Rd and in the Blue Area can also arrange cash from Amex cards. They're open from 9 am to 1.30 pm Monday to Thursday, and to 11.30 am Friday. Bank of America (☎ 828801), near American Express in the Blue Area, can arrange cash from major credit cards at 2% commission. Other foreign banks in the area are Citibank and Grindlays in Saddar Bazaar and Société Générale in Islamabad's Blue Area.

Moneychangers are grouped around the corner of Kashmir Rd and The Mall in Saddar, and in the Blue Area. They keep longer hours than banks, offer better rates and will often change travellers cheques.

**Post & Communications** The Rawalpindi general post office (GPO) is on Kashmir Rd

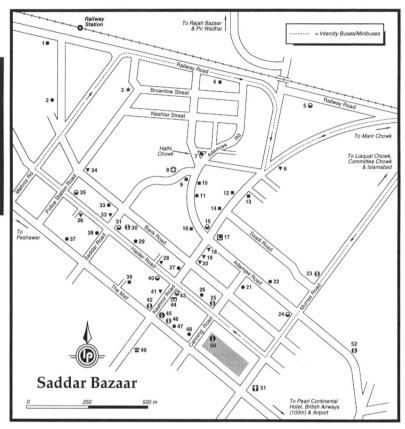

Saddar Bazaar

in Saddar Bazaar; the poste restante is in the rear building. It's closed Sunday. American Express card-holders can have mail sent to the Rawalpindi American Express office. For overseas calls, cables, telex and fax, the central telegraph office (☎ 580276) is on Kashmir Rd south of The Mall, and is open 24 hours. Email can be sent from Pearl Continental Hotel's business centre in Rawalpindi cantonment.

The Islamabad GPO is at the north end of Melody Market, and there's an international mail branch in Jinnah, both closed Sunday. The Islamabad telegraph office (☎ 821579)

is on Ataturk Ave, close to the eastern end of the Blue Area, and is also open 24 hours. Email can be sent from Sustainable Development Networking Programme (SDNP) (☎ 270684), House 26, St 87, G-6/3 Islamabad.

**Travel Agencies** Some recommended agencies are:

American Express Travel Service, American Express, Murree Rd, Rawalpindi (☎ 586773, 566001); 1-E Ali Plaza, Blue Area, Islamabad (☎ 212425)

Shakil Express, Haider Rd between Canning & Kashmir Rds, Saddar Bazaar, Rawalpindi

## PLACES TO STAY
4 Bolan Hotel
7 Al-Azam Hotel
9 Venus Hotel
10 Hotel Shah Taj
11 Hotel Lalazar
12 Khyaban Hotel
13 New Kamran Hotel
14 Marhaba Hotel
16 Al-Falah Hotel
22 Paradise Inn
39 Golden Grill Hotel
47 Kashmirwala's Hotel

## PLACES TO EAT
6 Jahangir Inn
18 Anwar Cafe
19 Burger Express
20 Bakery
28 Data Restaurant
32 Bakery
34 Chung Po Chinese Restaurant
36 Mei Kong Chinese Restaurant
41 Mehr Ali Restaurant

## OTHER
1 Railway Commercial Department
2 Railway Booking Office
3 Police Station
5 Minibuses to Murree & Taxila
8 Cantonment General Hospital
15 Suzukis to Rajah Bazaar
17 Mosque
21 Rohtas Travel Agency
23 American Express
24 Suzukis to Airport
25 Grindlays Bank
26 Shakil Express Travel Agency
27 Old Book Bank
29 Ciroz Cinema
30 National Bank
31 Coasters to Abbotabad & Mansehra
33 Variety Book Store

35 Minibuses to Abbottabad & Mansehra
37 PIA Booking Office
38 Book Centre
40 Bus to Taxila, Wah & Hasan Abdal
42 Habib Bank, Cantt Branch
43 Minibus Nos 1 & 6 to Islamabad
44 General Post Office (GPO)
45 Tourist Development Corporation of the Punjab (TDCP)
46 Moneychangers
48 Bhatti Studio
49 Central Telegraph Office
50 PTDC Tourist Information Centre & Flashman's Hotel
51 St Paul's Church
52 Citibank

Rohtas Travel Consultants Rawalpindi office (☎ 563224, 566434), 60-A/5 Khan Chambers, Canning Rd, Saddar Bazaar, Rawalpindi; 2 Kashmir Plaza, Blue Area, Islamabad (☎ 818971, 820271)

Travel Walji's (☎ 270745, 270757), 10 Khayaban-i-Suhrawardy, Aabpara, Islamabad

**Libraries** The American Centre (☎ 824051) in the Blue Area has a posh library of periodicals, videotapes and US Information Service propaganda. The British Council Library (☎ 829041) in Melody Market, Islamabad, has week-old British papers. Alliance Française (☎ 822176) is at House 15, St 18, F-7/2 Islamabad.

The Asian Study Group (☎ 815891), 80-West, Blue Area, was started in 1973 to help expatriate residents get acquainted with the area. They have programmes on history, art and so on, a tiny but well-thumbed library and a file of hand-drawn maps of local trails, available for photocopying at your expense. Strictly speaking you need to be invited by a member to get in.

**Medical Services** In an emergency you

might first want to call your embassy. Hospitals in Rawalpindi open to foreigners include Rawalpindi General (☎ 847761), Murree Rd at Ashgar Mall Rd; and Cantonment General (☎ 562216), Saddar Rd in Saddar Bazaar. In Islamabad, Shifa International (☎ 252509) in H-8/4 is said to be the best; others include Capital (☎ 825691), a few blocks west of the GPO; and the Government Poly Clinic, both in Melody (G-6), just south of the Blue Area.

**Luggage Storage** The railway station left-luggage room, open seven days a week, will store baggage at Rs 3 per piece per day.

### Things to See & Do – Rawalpindi
**Rajah Bazaar** The biggest of Rawalpindi's bazaars, Rajah is a kaleidoscope of people and markets spreading in every direction from Fowara Chowk. Dotted around are crumbling stone towers marking old Hindu temples. Get there by Suzuki from Kashmir Rd in Saddar or from Committee Chowk. For some of the bigger markets (in this and

RAWALPINDI & ISLAMABAD

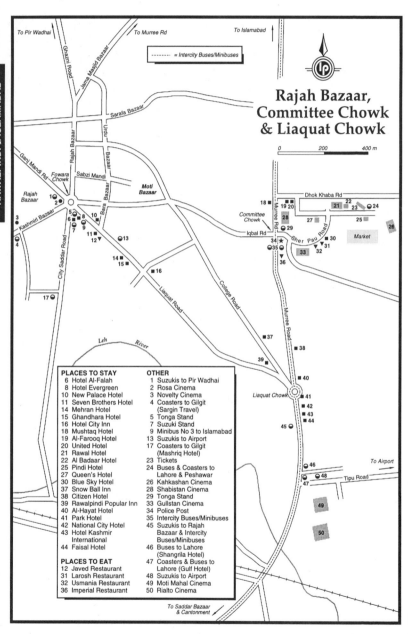

# Rajah Bazaar, Committee Chowk & Liaquat Chowk

-------- = Intercity Buses/Minibuses

**PLACES TO STAY**
6 Hotel Al-Falah
8 Hotel Evergreen
10 New Palace Hotel
11 Seven Brothers Hotel
14 Mehran Hotel
15 Ghandhara Hotel
16 Hotel City Inn
18 Mushtaq Hotel
19 Al-Farooq Hotel
20 United Hotel
21 Rawal Hotel
22 Al Badaar Hotel
25 Pindi Hotel
27 Queen's Hotel
30 Blue Sky Hotel
37 Snow Ball Inn
38 Citizen Hotel
39 Rawalpindi Popular Inn
40 Al-Hayat Hotel
41 Park Hotel
42 National City Hotel
43 Hotel Kashmir International
44 Faisal Hotel

**PLACES TO EAT**
12 Javed Restaurant
31 Larosh Restaurant
32 Usmania Restaurant
36 Imperial Restaurant

**OTHER**
1 Suzukis to Pir Wadhai
2 Rosa Cinema
3 Novelty Cinema
4 Coasters to Gilgit (Sargin Travel)
5 Tonga Stand
7 Suzuki Stand
9 Minibus No 3 to Islamabad
13 Suzukis to Airport
17 Coasters to Gilgit (Mashriq Hotel)
23 Tickets
24 Buses & Coasters to Lahore & Peshawar
26 Kahkashan Cinema
28 Shabistan Cinema
29 Tonga Stand
33 Gullstan Cinema
34 Police Post
35 Intercity Buses/Minibuses
45 Suzukis to Rajah Bazaar & Intercity Buses/Minibuses
46 Buses to Lahore (Shangrila Hotel)
47 Coasters & Buses to Lahore (Gulf Hotel)
48 Suzukis to Airport
49 Moti Mahal Cinema
50 Rialto Cinema

ROBERT MATZINGER

JOHN KING

ROBERT MATZINGER

**Rawalpindi**
Top: After the KKH, the roads are a little busier in Rawalpindi.
Left: Showbiz, Rajah Bazaar.
Right: Picture wall, Saddar Bazaar.

## Rawalpindi

Everyday bazaar scenes from Rawalpindi.

other bazaars) see the Things to Buy section later in this chapter.

**Ayub National Park** Named after General Ayub Khan, the first of Pakistan's martial law administrators, this staid park lies south of the Cantonment and has 900 hectares of paths, gardens and lakes. Get off an airport Suzuki at Kuchaheri Chowk and take the right fork for about 1km.

**Army Museum** If you're interested in matters military, there's an Army Museum in the Cantonment, on Iftikhar Rd, 1½ blocks south of the Pearl Continental Hotel. Summer hours are 8 am to noon and 5.30 to 7 pm; winter hours are 9 am to 3 pm.

### Things to See & Do – Islamabad
**Shakarparian Park** Shakarparian Park, in the urban wilderness south of Islamabad, has sculpted gardens, an arboretum with trees planted by heads of state from around the world, and panoramas of both cities from its east viewpoint. Down below is the 20-hectare Rose & Jasmine Garden, site of several annual flower shows.

On Garden Rd is **Lok Virsa**, the National Institute of Folk & Traditional Heritage (☎ 812675, 823883), with a first-rate ethnographic museum including traditional handicrafts, the best of which are the textiles and carved wood. It's open from 9 am to 1 pm and 2 to 5 pm, closed Friday and Monday. Next door is a book and tape library and a bookshop, open from 9 am to 3 pm daily except Friday.

There's no public transport. The cheapest way is to get off the bus at the Zero Point stop, where a path climbs 20 minutes up the hill. For Lok Virsa you can walk on over the hill. From the bus stop, cross the road, bear right and enter the woods on a path where an approach road joins the Rawalpindi road, a 15 minute walk. A taxi from Aabpara is about Rs 40.

**Shah Faisal Mosque** This incredibly opulent, marble-faced mosque is said to be Asia's biggest, with room for 100,000 worshippers. Most of the US$50 million it cost was a gift from King Faisal of Saudi Arabia. The late President Zia ul-Haq is buried in the grounds. Get off an intercity bus at 8th Ave.

Shah Faisal Mosque, with room for 100,000 worshippers, is the biggest in Asia.

**Islamabad Museum** Just south-east of the mosque, the new Islamabad Museum (☎ 223826), House 41, St 3, E-7, features a good selection of archeological finds from throughout Pakistan. Opening times are 9.30 am to 4.30 pm, daily except Wednesday.

**Daman-i-Koh & Saidpur** Daman-i-Koh ('DAH-ma-ni-ko') is a picnic spot in the Margalla Hills with great views over Islamabad and, on clear days, south to the Salt Range. Get off the intercity bus at 7th Ave and catch a Suzuki at Khayaban-i-Iqbal, or walk up the nearby path. Just east is a 1km road to Saidpur, a village famous for pottery shops and workshops.

**Nurpur Shahan & Bari Imam Shrine** North of the Diplomatic Enclave at Nurpur Shahan village is a shrine to Shah Abdul Latif Kazmi, also known as Bari Shah Latif, or 'Bari Imam', a 17th century Sufi mystic and Islamabad's unofficial patron saint. Thursday evening is quite festive, with pilgrims and trance-like *qawwali* music, and in the first week of May the carnival-like *urs* (death anniversary) of Bari Shah Latif is celebrated here. Minibus No 3 goes from Rajah Bazaar via Aabpara; No 120 goes there from Karachi Company, via Sitara Market and Aabpara.

**Margalla Hills National Park** The hills north of Islamabad are full of hiking trails and resthouses. These are described in the Capital Development Authority's (CDA) map-brochure, *Trekking in the Margalla Hills*, available from CDA's public relations office, Room 121 (☎ 828301), on Khayaban-i-Suhrawardy west of Aabpara. *Hiking Around Islamabad*, a more detailed walking guide, is available from most bookshops. One trail starts from behind the Shah Faisal Mosque.

### Places to Stay – bottom end
**Saddar Bazaar (Rawalpindi)** The *Venus, Lalazar* and *Shah Taj* hotels on Adamjee Rd and the grim *Bolan Hotel* on Railway Rd have noisy singles/doubles with part-time hot water for about Rs 80/110. Others along Railway Rd don't take foreigners. The friendly *Al-Azam Hotel* (☎ 565901), on Adamjee Rd, has decent top floor rooms with shower and balcony for Rs 90/160; the *Al-Falah Hotel* nearby has similar rates.

**Liaquat Chowk (Rawalpindi)** The friendly *Rawalpindi Popular Inn* (☎ 531884) is well set up for backpackers with dormitory beds for Rs 75, a laundry service, international telephone and snack bar. Singles/doubles with shared bath cost Rs 100/150, rooms with private bath are Rs 125/200. Rooms at the nearby *Snow Ball Inn* and *Citizen Hotel* are tatty but clean at Rs 130/180.

**Rajah Bazaar (Rawalpindi)** Most cheap hotels are reluctant to take foreigners. The friendly *Hotel Al-Falah* (☎ 553206), behind the tonga stand at Fowara Chowk, has pretty basic singles/doubles for about Rs 90/140 and great views from the roof. The *Hotel Evergreen* next door has similar rates. On Liaquat Rd, the *Seven Brothers Hotel* (☎ 551112) has acceptable rooms for Rs 140/220.

**Pir Wadhai (Rawalpindi)** Hotels here are sleazy and not keen on foreigners, but in a pinch try the grotty *Al-Medina Hotel* at the west end.

**Islamabad** Cheapest of all is the down-and-out *Tourist Campsite* near Aabpara – hardly a 'family' camp site, but good for those on a tight budget, or overlanders with their own transport. A tent platform or space in a concrete 'bungalow' (no beds) is Rs 15, a spot on the ground is Rs 8 with a tent or Rs 3 without, and parking is Rs 5/10 for a car/bus. Locked storage is available. The maximum stay is two weeks.

Nearby, on Garden Rd, is a *Pakistan Youth Hostel* (☎ 826899) with dozens of four-bed rooms, communal toilets and cold showers – but no cooking facilities and no camping. Beds are Rs 45 for HI/IYHF card-holders. Nonmembers are supposed to be able to join on the spot, though some travellers complain of obstructive management. It's popular with

Pakistani students in summer when the maximum stay may be three days.

### Places to Stay – middle

**Saddar Bazaar (Rawalpindi)** On Kashmir Rd the *New Kamran Hotel* (☎ 582040) has good service and clean doubles/triples with hot shower for Rs 200/250. Opposite is the slightly pricier *Khyaban Hotel*. On The Mall the *Golden Grill Hotel* (☎ 512842) has dark singles/doubles with clean bathrooms for Rs 250/350, and more cheerful ones for Rs 350/445.

The *Paradise Inn* (☎ 568594) on Adamjee Rd has comfortable but overpriced singles/doubles for Rs 480/600, or Rs 720/900 and up with TV and air-conditioning.

**Liaquat Chowk (Rawalpindi)** The *Park Hotel* (☎ 73284) on Murree Rd is an old-fashioned building with air-con doubles with TV for Rs 540-693; spacious rooms at the side are good value from Rs 260. The *Hotel*

*Kashmir International* (☎ 500495) has decent rooms for Rs 250/350 with TV; the next door *National City* is pricier but no better. The *Shangrila* and *Gulf* are noisy into the night because of the bus stands outside.

**Rajah Bazaar (Rawalpindi)** A five minute walk from Fowara Chowk, along Liaquat Rd, are the *Antepara* and *Ghandhara* hotels, offering small but comfortable singles/doubles with TV for Rs 250/350, or deluxe rooms for Rs 450/550. Next door the *Mehran* has cheaper windowless rooms for Rs 150/200. Best value is probably the friendly *Hotel City Inn* (☎ 530218), further along, with clean rooms for Rs 130/200.

**Committee Chowk (Rawalpindi)** Recommended is the *Pindi Hotel* (☎ 558809) next to the bus station, with clean, spacious rooms for Rs 175/250. The *Mushtaq Hotel* (☎ 553998) on Murree Rd, and the nearby *Al-Farooq* (☎ 556200), have comfortable

RAWALPINDI & ISLAMABAD

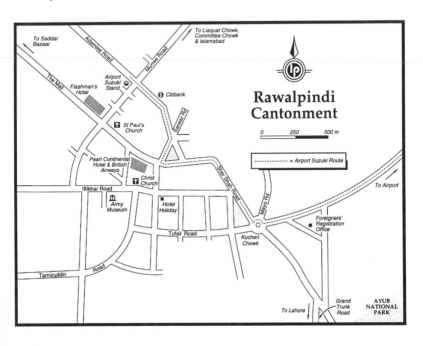

doubles for about Rs 450. Pricier air-conditioned options include the *United* and *Blue Sky* hotels, for about Rs 650/750, or the three-star *Al Baddar*.

**Islamabad** Sitara (G-7) Market has the capital's best selection of cheap hotels. To get there from Aabpara take minibus No 105 or 120. The *Al Hujurat* (☎ 828374), *Simara* (☎ 811134) and *Blue Sky* (☎ 275546) hotels are all clean, bright and good value at about Rs 200/250 for a single/double. The *Sitara Hotel* is cheaper but run down.

### Places to Stay – top end
**Rawalpindi** *Kashmirwala's* (☎ 583186), on The Mall, is a good choice with comfortable air-con rooms, satellite TV and a good location for Rs 1205/1446. In the cantonment, the *Hotel Holiday* (☎ 568068), on Iftikhar Rd behind State Bank of Pakistan, is a step up at Rs 1440/1920. Many rate PTDC's *Flashman's Hotel* (☎ 581480) a bad deal, with shabby doubles for Rs 1680 and up. The *Pearl Continental* (☎ 566011) is Rawalpindi's primo hotel; for the price of a night there you could stay in the bazaar for a month.

**Islamabad** Best value are various private guesthouses in residential backstreets. Singles/doubles range from Rs 600/700 to Rs 1000/1200 and normally include breakfast and a free airport pickup; telephone in advance. These include:

*Decent Accommodators* (☎ 815275), House 2, St 15, F-7/2
*Host Inn Guest House* (☎ 856621), Kaghan Rd, F-8 markaz
*Pearl House* (☎ 822108), 22A College Rd, F-7/2
*Services Guest House* (☎ 826271), 54 Bazaar Rd, G-6/4
*Shelton House* (☎ 856428), House 11, Kaghan Rd, F-8/3
*Su Casa House* (☎ 825578), House 3, St 20, F-7/2
*VIP Accommodators* (☎ 815144), House 18, St 30, F-6/1

The *Ambassador Hotel* (☎ 824011) in Aabpara is good value at Rs 810/990. Bigwigs stay at the *Holiday Inn* (☎ 827311)

in Melody Market or the *Marriott* (☎ 826121) near the Secretariat.

### Places to Eat
**Quick & Cheap** Quick-service stalls are plentiful around markets and transport stops. Typical items are samosas, pulau, tikkas and shami kebabs.

**Saddar Bazaar (Rawalpindi)** Two recommended cheapos with good Pakistani dishes are *Data Restaurant* in an alley off Haider Rd and the busy *Anwar Cafe*, opposite the mosque on Adamjee Rd. *Jahangir Inn* at the north end of Kashmir Rd has some of Pakistan's best chicken karahi; a half chicken costs Rs 80. *Mehr Ali Restaurant*, opposite the GPO, has good grilled meats. Two Chinese restaurants – *Mei Kong* off Haider Rd and *Chung Po* on Bank Rd – are overpriced and mediocre. Fast-food places with hot sandwiches, French fries etc are everywhere – eg *Burger Express* on Kashmir Rd. A Pakistani-style breakfast of tea, yoghurt, cholla (spicy chickpeas), fried paratha bread or halwa puri pastry is available outside the *Anwar Cafe* until mid-morning.

If you've developed a craving for a banana split or a good cup of coffee, you'll find it at the *Pearl Continental Hotel* in the cantonment.

**Rajah Bazaar (Rawalpindi)**. The *Seven Brothers Hotel* has good views and average food. *Javed*, next door, has pretty good meat dishes.

**Committee Chowk (Rawalpindi)** Travellers give *Mushtaq Hotel* good marks for food. *Usmania Restaurant* isn't cheap but the Pakistani dishes are varied and good; eat well for Rs 100. Almost as good is *Larosh Restaurant* next door. The *Imperial Restaurant* on Murree Rd has cheaper Pakistani staples.

**Islamabad** Aabpara and Melody Market have kebab stands and cafes with cheap curries and shami kebabs. Pakistani items at

Aabpara's *Kamran Restaurant* are not too pricey. At the fantastic *French Bakery* in Melody Market you can ruin your budget with brownies, banana bread, pizza and imported cheese.

Expats say *Omar Khayam* Iranian restaurant, on Khayaban-i-Quaid-i-Azam in the Blue Area, is very good; it's open from 7 pm. Just round the corner is the hip *Shop 67* with cheap buffet-style Pakistani food. Also nearby, on Fazal-ul-Haq Rd, the *Village Restaurant* is worth a try for its unusual Pakistani dishes, vegetable thalis (a thali is a sectioned tray of many small dishes) and sizzling steaks for Rs 120.

Super and Jinnah markets are full of fast-food cafes. Jinnah also has some good restaurants, including the *Kabul Restaurant* and *Afghan Bakery* at the west end of the market and pricey *Pappasalli's Italian Restaurant* at the east end.

### Alcohol

In unmarked lounges or backrooms in top-end hotels (Pearl, Flashman's, Marriott, Holiday Inn) you can sign a form saying you aren't a Muslim, pay a fee and get a one-day permit allowing you to buy spirits or lager brewed in Pakistan for non-Muslims.

You can get a longer-term liquor permit, as foreign residents do, from the Excise & Tax Office, beside the FRO in either city, and then buy the goodies from storerooms hidden around the side of the Marriott or Flashman's. The Rawalpindi permit is supposedly good throughout Pakistan, though along the KKH you won't find anything to buy with it.

### Entertainment

The Australian Club (☎ 822115) at the Australian embassy has a social night for all Australian visitors (and guests by permission) on *most* Thursdays from 4.30 to 7.30 pm; bring your passport. On Wednesday evenings the Canadian Club on Embassy Rd admits Canadian visitors who are guests of members. The Ciroz Cinema in Saddar Bazaar shows western films.

### Things to Buy

**General Supplies** For western-style supplies and fast food, toiletries and tampons, go to the shops in Jinnah or Super markets.

**Books** In Rawalpindi, the Book Centre (☎ 565234) on Saddar Rd has maps, overseas periodicals, used books and lots of French and English Lonely Planet titles. Variety Books, on Bank Rd, has one of the best selections of Pakistani reprints. For cheap secondhand books and western magazines try the Old Book Bank, just off Kashmir Rd, or the huge book market that fills the streets of Saddar every Sunday.

In Islamabad, the good London Book Company (☎ 823852) has a big Pakistan section, maps, periodicals and used books. To get there from Super Market, walk north on 14th St and turn right at 10th St to Kohsar Market. Mr Books and Vanguard Books in Super Market have a good selection including overseas newspapers. At the Old Book Fair, behind Mr Books, you can trade two of your secondhand books for one of theirs.

Book Fair in Jinnah Market is also good and there are more secondhand bookstalls nearby. The Lok Virsa Bookstore (see the Shakarparian Park section earlier) has books on Pakistani folk art and history and tapes of folk music.

**Film** A good place for film and processing is Bhatti Studio (☎ 568771) on Canning Rd in Saddar Bazaar. Agfa Rapeed (☎ 821041) in Super Market, Islamabad, can process slide film in two hours.

**Handicrafts** Juma Bazaar, Islamambad, the block between Municipal and Garden Rds in Aabpara, comes to life on Friday as a huge handicrafts market with carpets, leather, jewellery, clothing and Afghan curios. It may soon shift to Sunday, so check first.

Tourist and Government Handicraft Shops – on The Mall and nearby Canning Rd (Saddar Bazaar), and in the Blue Area and Super Market (Islamabad), and in top-end hotel arcades – have marked-up carpets, brasswork, jewellery, Kashmiri shawls,

RAWALPINDI & ISLAMABAD

carving and antiques. If you prefer hunting in the bazaars, following are some prominent markets. You can knock a third off a merchant's opening price if you're firm and friendly about it.

Pottery – try Bara Bazaar (Rajah Bazaar), Faizabad Bazaar (north end of Rawalpindi) or Saidpur village.

Jewellery & Brasswork – try Sarafa Bazaar (Rajah Bazaar) or Murree Rd around Asghar Mall Rd

Clothing & Tailors – these are all over Rajah and Saddar bazaars; off-the-shelf shalwar qamiz start about Rs 350

Spices – the main spice area is between Rajah Bazaar and Ganj Mandi Rd

Fruit & Vegetables – go to the Sabzi Mandi ('vegetable market') in Rajah Bazaar or the stalls at the western end of Haider Rd, Saddar Bazaar

### Getting There & Away – Air
PIA's Rawalpindi booking office (☎ 567011 for Northern Areas; ☎ 568071 for other destinations) is on The Mall, Saddar Bazaar. The Islamabad office (☎ 815041) is in the Blue Area at 7th Ave. Both are open seven days a week and accept Visa cards and travellers cheques. Aero Asia (☎ 823072) and Bhoja Air (☎ 828123) have offices near one another in the Blue Area; in Rawalpindi it's easier to book them through a travel agent.

**Gilgit & Skardu** These flights must be booked at the Northern Areas desk, around the side of PIA's Rawalpindi office. Competition can be stiff; see the Getting Around chapter, especially the boxed text Booking a Northern Areas Flight.

**Air Safari** For information on PIA's weekly 'sightseeing' flights over the Karakoram, see the boxed text PIA Air Safari in the Getting Around chapter,

**Other Pakistan Destinations** PIA has multiple direct connections every day with Karachi, Lahore, Peshawar and Saidu Sharif (Swat), and almost every day with Faisalabad and Quetta. Aero Asia has four a day with Karachi and Bhoja Air, two a day with Karachi via Lahore. At the time of research the cheapest flight *to* Karachi was

Aero Asia's 1.30 am 'Special Night Coach', for about 25% off the daytime fare. Those truly strapped for cash can save more by bussing to Lahore and catching a night-coach flight from there to Karachi.

**International Flights** Only PIA, Aero Asia, British Airways, Saudia and Xinjiang Airways have direct Islamabad connections. These and other carriers have booking offices along The Mall, in the Blue Area or in top-end hotels (see the boxed text Pakistan Booking Numbers in the Getting There & Away chapter), but you'll do better through a good travel agent.

### Getting There & Away – Bus
The most convenient long-distance transport goes to/from Committee Chowk, Liaquat Chowk (on Murree Rd) and Saddar Bazaar. Pir Wadhai general bus stand is inconveniently situated in north-west Rawalpindi. Between there and Kashmir Rd in Saddar Bazaar, passenger Suzukis cost a few rupees and take 25 to 50 minutes with a change at Fowara Chowk in Rajah Bazaar. The cheapest way from Pir Wadhai to Islamabad is by minibus No 121, or by bus with a change at Faizabad.

**Lahore** TDCP (☎ 564824) runs three daily air-conditioned coaches from the corner of Kashmir Rd and The Mall; they're Rs 110 and can be booked ahead. New Khan Road Runners at Committee Chowk and New Flying Coach from behind the Shangrila and Gulf Hotels in Liaquat Chowk have hourly departures for around Rs 100. Skyways (☎ 456116) in Faizabad and Citylinkers in Islamabad (F-8 markaz) have half-hourly departures (Rs 110, five hours).

**Abbottabad & Mansehra** Best are Hi-Ace/Coaster minibuses from Haider Rd in Saddar, Rs 35/40 to Mansehra, via Abbottabad. Buses go from Pir Wadhai all day for about the same price.

**Swat** From May to September, PTDC runs a daily air-con Coaster from Flashman's

Hotel in Rawalpindi to Saidu Sharif, for Rs 140.

**Gilgit** Natco goes from Pir Wadhai every few hours in summer. The 9 am and 3 pm 'air-con deluxe' buses are Rs 370, the 11 am and 1, 5 and 8 pm 'deluxe' buses are Rs 320, and the 4 am and 11 pm normal services are Rs 276. A 50% student discount is available on all but air-con deluxe. Mashabrum Tours (☎ 863595) has daily buses from Pir Wadhai for Rs 300 at 2, 6 and 9 pm; the 'office' is a man in a chair near the waiting area. These buses cannot be booked ahead.

Hameed Travel runs Coasters at 3 pm from the Mashriq Hotel (☎ 73387) south of Fowara Chowk, for Rs 380, for which you can book ahead. Nearby Sargin Travel (☎ 531776) runs the same service departing an hour later. The trip takes 14 to 17 hours, punctuated by numerous police checkposts where foreigners must troop out and sign the register. Departure times and fares may vary with the season. All vehicles go with two drivers.

Sit on the right for the overall best views, unless you suffer from vertigo!

### Getting There & Away – Train

The Pakistan Railways booking and information office (☎ 920 7474) is at Melody Market in Islamabad; it's open from 8.30 am to 4.30 pm daily. A less user-friendly booking office is 300m south of the railway station in Saddar Bazaar. For student and tourist discounts, go first to the pink Commercial Department building directly opposite the main station. A letter from PTDC is not necessary.

You can ride to Havelian, the KKH's official southern end, in an ancient 2nd class carriage on a lightly used spur from Taxila. There are two trains a day and the three hour ride is Rs 22. For other destinations, and information on discounts, see the Getting There & Away chapter.

### Getting Around
**To/From the Airport** Suzukis to the airport go from Adamjee Rd in Saddar Bazaar and

from Fowara Chowk in Rajah Bazaar via Liaquat Chowk. They're Rs 5 and take under half an hour in normal traffic.

To catch one *from* the airport, go out the gate and turn right. Those to Rajah Bazaar are near a petrol station on the left, about 100m up; those to Saddar Bazaar are 100m further at a fork on the right. For Islamabad, take a Rajah Bazaar Suzuki and change at Liaquat Chowk.

There's no bus service. A taxi is about Rs 50 to Rawalpindi, or Rs 90 to Islamabad, and almost double that at night.

**Intercity Transport** Numbered minibuses are the quickest. Nos 1 and 6 from Haider Rd in Saddam Bazaar go via Aabpara to Super Market, then east to the Secretariat, for under Rs 10. For about the same price, gaudy Bedford buses link Saddar Bazaar (Haider Rd), the railway station, Murree Rd, Aabpara and Islamabad's markets in a tedious line (see the Islamabad and Saddar Bazaar maps); Saddar to Super Market takes one to 1½ hours. All go via Liaquat and Committee chowks.

Black-and-yellow taxis have meters but most are 'broken', so fix a price before you get in; Rawalpindi to Islamabad is at least Rs 100.

**Intracity Transport** In Rawalpindi, fixed-route Suzukis are a few rupees. Snarling motor-rickshaws are not much cheaper than taxis and a lot less comfortable. Horse-drawn tongas are a relaxing way to get to/from Rajah; some are fixed-fare, some for hire.

In Islamabad, minibus No 105 links Karachi Company (G-9), the Passport Office (Peshawar Mor), Sitara Market, Melody Market and Aabpara. No 120 follows the same route and continues to Nurpur Shahan Village via the French and Canadian Embassies. Coasters run up and down the Blue Area along Fazal-ul-Haq Rd.

**Car Rental** A reliable place to rent a car, minibus or 4WD at reasonable prices is Voyager, at 2-37 Sethi Plaza, Fazal-ul-Haq Rd, Blue Area, Islamabad (☎ 818855,

276073; fax 817812); and 19 Shalimar Plaza, Aziz Bhatti Rd, Rawalpindi (☎ 520590, 563901).

# Around Rawalpindi & Islamabad

## MARGALLA PASS
Twenty minutes from Rawalpindi the Grand Trunk Road crosses the low Margalla Pass. At the top is a monument to John Nicholson, a British soldier-administrator who at age 25 led Pathan (Pashtun) tribesmen against the Sikhs here in 1848, and died a hero at the Siege of Delhi in 1857.

On the far (west) side is a tiny surviving stretch of the original Grand Trunk Rd, built in the 16th century by an Afghan ruler named Sher Shah Suri.

## TAXILA
### Tel Area Code: 0596
The Peshawar Plain, known historically as Gandhara, has attracted invaders since the 6th century BC when the Achaemenians built a city called Takshasila here. In 326 BC, Alexander the Great rested at Takshasila – he called it Taxila – in his drive toward India. Half a century later, the Mauryan Emperor Ashoka, a patron of Buddhism, built a university at Taxila to which pilgrims and scholars came from all over Asia. After about 180 BC, Bactrian Greeks moved in, and later Scythians and Parthians.

In the 1st century AD, the Kushans built their own city. Until the 3rd century this was the cultured capital of an empire stretching across the subcontinent and into Central Asia, the place from which Buddhism spread into China, and the birthplace of a striking fusion of Greek and Indian art. The city fell into obscurity after it was destroyed by White Huns in the 5th century.

The various excavations at Taxila are open to the public, along with many smaller sites over a 25 sq km area. Tools and ornaments, temple friezes and Buddha figures with Mediterranean faces are on display in the excellent Taxila Museum. A long day of walking from the museum should include Sirkap, Jandial Temple and Dharmarajika stupa, though two days would be better.

'No Photographs' signs at various sites serve no useful purpose except as the basis for a few rupees to the caretakers to 'let' you snap away.

### Taxila Museum & Information Centre
This excellent museum is open daily (except the first Monday of each month) from 8.30 am to 12.30 pm and 2.30 to 5.30 pm in summer, and 9 am to 4 pm in winter. Museum guards have been known to close the coin room in order to squeeze some baksheesh from tourists. The information centre (☎ 2344) at the PTDC Motel, opposite the museum, has some useful books for sale.

### Excavations
**Bhir Mound** This Achaemenian site from the 6th to 2nd centuries BC is mostly unexcavated

Buddhisattua Maitreya, one of the exhibits at the Taxila Museum.

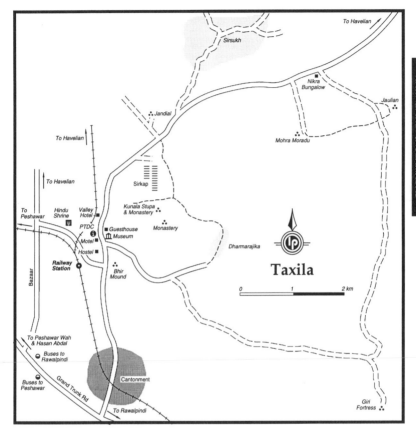

mound, 300m from the museum. What has been excavated shows twisting streets and tiny stone houses or shops. This is where Alexander the Great would have rested in 326 BC.

**Sirkap** The Bactrians began 'their' Taxila, an orderly walled city, in the 2nd century BC. It was later adapted by Scythians and Parthians; in fact most of what you can see is Parthian. Along 0.5km of the wide main street are foundations of houses, stupas and a Buddhist temple; at the south end were wealthier homes. South of the town are Kunala Stupa,

named for Emperor Ashoka's son, and the remains of two Kushan-era monasteries.

**Jandial** Near the road just north of Sirkap are the ruins of a classical Greek temple, a rather haunting place with Ionic columns in front and the base of what may have been a Zoroastrian tower in the rear.

**Dharmarajika** Within the huge Dharmarajika stupa, 3km east of the museum, is an original, smaller stupa built by Ashoka, possibly to house ashes of the Buddha. Around it are the bases of statues and small votive stupas and the remains of a monastery complex.

**Sirsukh** Little of the Kushan city, started in the 1st century AD, has been excavated, and there isn't much to see.

**Mohra Moradu** In a hollow about 5km north-east of the museum and 1km off the road is the isolated Mohra Moradu monastery, dating from the 3rd to 5th centuries. In one monk's cell is a small complete stupa.

**Jaulian** At this site, on a hill east of Mohra Moradu, the stupas are gone but the courtyard and foundations are in good condition. In a security enclosure are the bases of several 5th century votive stupas, ornamented with Buddhas and other figures. Other stupa bases have equally vivid carvings.

East of the courtyard is a monastery with dozens of closet-sized meditation cells. The caretaker may offer a garbled commentary and then hover for baksheesh.

### Places to Stay
Near the museum is a dilapidated *Pakistan Youth Hostel*. On the museum grounds is a deluxe *guesthouse*; both this and the *Nikra Bungalow*, near the Jaulian turn-off, must be booked through the museum (☎ 0596-2495). The *PTDC Motel*'s doubles are Rs 400/600 with/without air-con. Rooms at the antiseptic *Valley Hotel* are acceptable but overpriced at Rs 280.

### Getting There & Away
From Rawalpindi, Taxila is half an hour from Haider Rd by bus or from Railway Rd by minibus, but the slower train ride (Rs 6) is far more pleasant. From the permanently congested Taxila Bazaar, buses, Suzukis and tongas pass Taxila cantonment railway station en route to the museum. Returning to Rawalpindi, check whether your vehicle is going to Saddar, Rajah or Pir Wadhai. Some Saddar-bound minibuses start from Taxila Bazaar.

### Getting Around
Some buses and Suzukis from Taxila Bazaar go on up the road past Sirsukh, Mohra Moradu and Jaulian, or you can hire one of the tongas lurking around the museum.

## WAH GARDENS
West of Taxila is the site of a Moghul camp developed by Emperor Akbar into a pleasure-ground of pools and gardens. It's gone to seed but the rows of ancient cypress and plane trees, the empty canals and run-down pavilions are still stately. Unfortunately, Wah town is the site of a Pakistan Ordnance Factory too, and the peace is frequently shattered by explosions from across the highway. This makes a good addition to Taxila but is dubious as a day trip on its own.

### Getting There & Away
Get on any bus going west on the Grand Trunk Road and ask for Wah Gardens (not just Wah). Some go directly from Haider Rd in Rawalpindi. Fifteen minutes beyond Taxila a 'Mughal Garden Wah' sign marks a road on the south side of the highway. The gardens are a 10 minute walk down this road.

## HASAN ABDAL
This town on the Grand Trunk Road is a city of shrines. Pilgrims have been visiting since the 7th century when it was a Buddhist holy place. On a hill east of the village is a *ziarat* (shrine) to Baba Wali Kandahari, a 15th century Sufi preacher. Sikhs still come from India to Panja Sahib, a shrine to Baba Wali's contemporary Guru Nanak, founder of Sikhism – especially in mid-April for the Baisakhi festival (see Public Holidays & Special Events in the Facts for the Visitor chapter). Also in the old walled town are abandoned Hindu temples and several Moghul tombs.

### Orientation & Information
From the highway, walk 150m to a fork, bearing right past a post office and a playing field, and 0.5km to another fork. Panja Sahib is left and around the corner; the Moghul tombs are to the right. Beyond the playing

field a path climbs for an hour to Baba Wali's ziarat.

### Panja Sahib

You may not be allowed into the yellow and white gurdwara. A central temple is surrounded by pools and shade trees, and around that several storeys of rooms, probably a pilgrims' hostel.

### Moghul Tombs

The first tomb, built by a Punjab governor for himself, was commandeered by Emperor Akbar for a couple of his own court favourites. Beyond this, in a tiny garden, is the tombstone of one Lala Rukh.

### Baba Wali

The hilltop has an undramatic 360° view that includes Wah Gardens below, and on a clear day Taxila and the Margalla Pass.

### Getting There & Away

From Rawalpindi, Hasan Abdal is 20 minutes beyond Taxila by bus (from Haider Rd) or minibus (from Railway Rd).

## MURREE & THE GALIS

A few hours north of Islamabad is a maze of cool, forested ridges. As in other hilly bits of colonial India, the British developed many villages as 'hill stations' – beat-the-heat resorts for bureaucrats and army officers. In summer, the entire Punjab administration moved up to Murree, and anyone who was anyone had a villa at Nathiagali or one of the other hamlets whose names mostly end in *gali* (Hindko Punjabi for 'pass').

All still show the colonial imprint: prim bungalows, guesthouses and churches on the heights, roads and noisy bazaars below. Nowadays they bulge with middle-class Punjabi tourists all summer and on winter weekends. Summer season is May to September, and demand is heaviest in July and August. There seems to be no limit to summer hotel prices, but out of season you can strike good bargains. Youth hostels at Khanspur and Bhurban are open to HI

members but are also beloved by Pakistani students.

For a regional map of the area, see the Hazara chapter introduction.

### Murree

Murree sits high above its surroundings so the views are impressive, but there's little to do but stroll around or shop. A faint colonial aroma lingers along The Mall but it's pretty modern and touristy now.

**Orientation** Climb Cart Rd from the general bus stand. Past the Blue Pines Hotel, shortcut up through a small bazaar to The Mall. British-era Murree rambles for 4km along the ridge-top.

The downhill transport junctions of Sunny Bank, Kuldana Chowk and Jhikagali are effectively suburbs of Murree.

**Information** The best source for tourist information is TDCP, with an office (☎ 411050) below the Blue Pines Hotel on Cart Rd and a kiosk (☎ 410730) on The Mall. No banks do foreign exchange.

**Walks** From Pindi Point you can look out toward the Punjab or ride a chairlift 3km down to the road and back for Rs 60. Kashmir Point (the highest place in Murree, 2260m) looks out beyond the Pir Panjal Range into Kashmir. From Bank Rd, a trail descends for an hour through woods to the Kuldana to Jhikagali road; a branch goes to Kuldana Chowk. Return on the trail or by any minibus to Sunny Bank or the general bus stand.

**Places to Stay** Even the cheap hotels, eg the *Al-Nadeem* by the general bus stand and the *Rahman* and *New Murree Grand* on The Mall, want at least Rs 150 for a double in summer, though few are worth even Rs 50, their approximate off-season price.

Decent hotels asking Rs 300 to Rs 400 for a double in summer are the *Tanveer, Chambers* and *Murree International* on Cart Rd and the better value *Al Qamar*, further up the hill on the other side of town. The *Blue Pines*

RAWALPINDI & ISLAMABAD

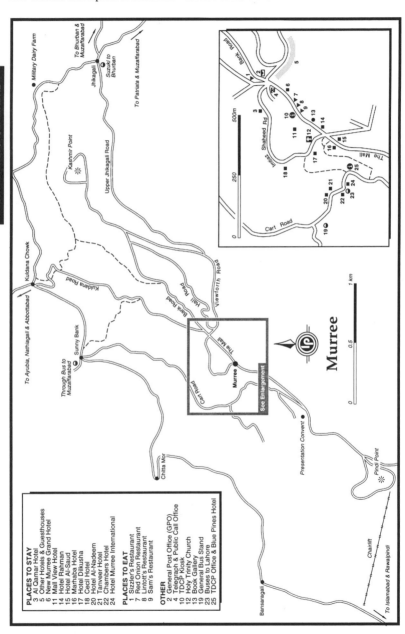

**Murree**

To Bhurban & Muzaffarabad

Military Dairy Farm

Jhikagali

Suzuki to Bhurban

To Patriata & Muzaffarabad

Kashmir Point

Upper Jhikagali Road

Kuldana Chowk

To Ayubia, Nathiagali & Abbottabad

Kuldana Road

Sunny Bank

Bank Road

Hall Road

Viewforth Road

Through Bus to Muzaffarabad

Chitta Mor

See Enlargement

Cart Road

Presentation Convent

Pindi Point

Bansaragali

Chairlift

To Islamabad & Rawalpindi

Bank Road

Shaheed Rd

Imtiaz Rd

The Mall

Cart Road

500m

250

0

0     0.5     1 km

**PLACES TO STAY**
3  Al Qamar Hotel
5  Other Hotels & Guesthouses
6  New Murree Grand Hotel
11 Mall View Hotel
14 Hotel Rahman
15 Hotel Al-Saud
16 Marhaba Hotel
17 Hotel Dilkusha
18 Cecil Hotel
20 Hotel Al-Nadeem
21 Tanveer Hotel
22 Chambers Hotel
24 Hotel Murree International

**PLACES TO EAT**
7  Sizzler's Restaurant
8  Red Onion Restaurant
8  Lintott's Restaurant
9  Sam's Restaurant

**OTHER**
2  General Post Office (GPO)
4  Telegraph & Public Call Office
10 TDCP Kiosk
12 Holy Trinity Church
13 Book Gallery
19 General Bus Stand
23 Buses to Lahore
25 TDCP Office & Blue Pines Hotel

*Hotel* has doubles for Rs 300 and up. Most of Murree's 50-plus hotels seem to be top end. The *Dilkusha* wanted Rs 400 for a double in the *off*-season. The centrally located *Marhaba* is in the same range. Doubles at PTDC's *Cecil Hotel* are ridiculous at over Rs 1700 but the grand old building and the views from the garden are worth a look.

**Places to Eat** Cafes along Cart Rd have cheap curries, braised chicken, qeema and vegetables. The Mall has fast-food shops and several clean restaurants with identical Pakistani-Chinese-western menus – *Sam's, Lintott's, Red Onion* and *Sizzler's*. The *Marhaba Hotel*'s restaurant is good for breakfast.

**Getting There & Away** Minibuses go to Murree all day from Railway Rd in Rawalpindi and take about two hours, for Rs 25. Dawdling buses go from Pir Wadhai and Faizabad for less. Several buses a day run between the general bus stand and Abbottabad, five hours away.

### Bhurban
Besides the scenery, Bhurban has a nine-hole military golf course, a *Pearl Continental Hotel* and a *Pakistan Youth Hostel*. It's 15km north-east of Murree, via Suzukis from the general bus stand and Jhikagali.

### Patriata
TDCP runs a Rs 100 chairlift and cable car from Gulehragli, 17km from Murree, to the top of 2300m Patriata Peak. Suzuki-wallahs call the place 'New Murree' and charge Rs 15 from Murree bus stand.

### Ayubia
Named for Ayub Khan, Pakistan's military ruler from 1958 to 1969, Ayubia is a resort area and national park encompassing the hamlets of Khairagali, Changlagali, Kuzagali, Ghora Dhaka and Khanspur. At Ghora Dhaka, five minutes drive off the main road, are a few elegant houses, a modest bazaar and a cable car up the mountainside. Khanspur is 3km further along this spur road.

At Ghora Dhaka are the mid-range *Summer Inn*, the old *Ayubia Palace Hotel* and PTDC's *Ayubia Motel*. Khanspur has the small *Kashmir View Hotel* and a *Pakistan Youth Hostel*. There are minibuses direct to Ghora Dhaka from Murree's general bus stand.

### Nathiagali
At 2500m, Nathiagali ('naht-YA-ga-li') is the prettiest and most popular of the gali resorts. From the main road it's a 10 minute climb on a link-road to an old wooden church. From there it's three hours up 2891m Miranjani peak, with views across the Pir Panjal range into Kashmir.

A similar climb is up 2817m Mukshpuri peak behind Dungagali, which is an hour's walk down the road or the ridge from Nathiagali. It's a day's walk from Nathiagali down to Ghora Dhaka.

**Places to Stay** On the road are some cheapos with grotty doubles for Rs 50 to Rs 80. Hotels with views and hot-water doubles for Rs 150 to Rs 300 include the *Skyways, Bismillah* and *Kamran*. Up on the ridge are half a dozen more expensive hotels. In Dungagali is the pricey *Mukshpuri Hotel* (☎ 868287) or the cheaper *Green Vally* (sic).

**Getting There & Away** Murree to Abbottabad buses stop at many of the galis. Nathiagali is midway between, 1½ to two hours from each, and under Rs 15 either way. A few buses and minibuses go direct from Nathiagali to Murree early in the morning, otherwise you must change at Ayubia.

# Language

Travelling down the KKH is like passing through half a dozen tiny countries. Every few hundred km you find not just another dialect but a new language. In addition to the two 'national' languages of Urdu and Mandarin Chinese, there are at least seven other common tongues, from three different linguistic families. Persian is also understood to some extent throughout the region.

You can get by with some basic Urdu and Chinese, especially in official situations. However, neither is native to Xinjiang or the Northern Areas and they're often used grudgingly. But even the most garbled attempts at local speech can reward you out of all proportion to what you're actually trying to say.

The prominent local languages are Uyghur (Kashgar, Tarim Basin); Wakhi (Tashkurghan, Gojal); Burushashki (Hunza); Shina (lower Hunza, Gilgit, Punial, Astor, Chilas); Kohistani (Indus Kohistan); Pashto (Besham, Swat and northern Hazara); and Khowar or Chitrali (Ishkoman, Yasin, Ghizar and Chitral). Included here are common words and phrases in these as well as Urdu and Chinese, plus a few phrases of Balti, the speech of Baltistan.

English is rarely used in western Xinjiang, except by a few educated officials. It's common in larger towns of the Northern Areas and widespread in Rawalpindi and Islamabad. The entire top echelon of the Pakistani civil service speaks English, so if you can't make yourself understood anywhere else, try a government or police official.

If you really want to make the most of your trip, get hold of the Lonely Planet *Central Asia phrasebook*, which includes all the languages of the region, communication and cultural tips.

## Writing

The written characters for numbers and for 'men' and 'women' might come in handy.

|    | Chinese | Urdu |
|----|---------|------|
| 1  | 一      | ۱    |
| 2  | 二      | ۲    |
| 3  | 三      | ۳    |
| 4  | 四      | ۴    |
| 5  | 五      | ۵    |
| 6  | 六      | ۶    |
| 7  | 七      | ۷    |
| 8  | 八      | ۸    |
| 9  | 九      | ۹    |
| 10 | 十      | ۱۰   |

|         | Man | Woman |
|---------|-----|-------|
| Chinese | 男  | 女    |
| Uyghur  | ەر  | ایال  |
| Urdu    | مرد | خاتون |

## Urdu

Urdu is the 'national language' of Pakistan, although fewer than 10% of Pakistanis speak it as a first language. It sounds much like Hindi, the speech of north India, but is written in a modified Arabic script.

Urdu is an acquisitive language, swallowing whole phrases verbatim from Persian, Arabic, English, wherever. You'll have no trouble with *plet, machiz* and even the word for you, the foreigner, *angrez* (no matter where you're from).

A more detailed guide to grammar, pronunciation and phrases is Lonely Planet's *Hindi & Urdu phrasebook*. The home-grown *Teach Yourself Urdu in Two Months* (Noor Publishing House, Karachi) is available in Pakistani bookshops.

## Pronunciation

Most Urdu vowels have more than one sound, which in some English transliterations are distinguished with diacritical marks (eg a bar over long forms of *a, i* and *u*). These aren't used here, but you're fairly safe with the following sounds: **a** like 'a' in 'father', **e** like 'e' in 'bet', **i** like 'ee' in 'beet', **o** between 'oh' and 'aw', **u** like 'u' in 'put'. The use of **ā**, **eng**, **ō** and **ung** for nasal vowels, spoken with the nose open, are used in this book.

The combined consonants **th** are pronounced not as in English but separately – 't' with a light exhalation at the end (as in 'fathead'); similarly for **chh** and **dh**. But **sh**, **ch**, **gh**, **kh** and **zh** are not aspirated in this way. Pronounce **g** as in 'go' not 'gin', and **r** with a snap of the tongue.

## Questions

Roughly speaking, you can make a phrase into a question with a simple inflexion of your voice, or by adding 'is it?' *(heh?).*

## Postpositions

These are like prepositions except that they go after the word. For example, 'the bus to Passu' is *passu-ko bus*; 'in the hotel' is *hotel-me*; 'John's wife' is *jan-ki bivi*.

| | |
|---|---|
| to | *-ko* |
| from | *-seh* |
| in | *-me* |
| belonging to | *-ka* (m) or *-ki* (f) |

---

**Achhah**
The word for 'good' *(achhah)* is Urdu's all-purpose expression. Depending on context and tone of voice it can also mean 'as you wish', 'I understand', 'I agree', 'right', 'really?' and more. ■

---

## Adjectives

| | |
|---|---|
| bad | *kharab* |
| first-rate | *pakka* |
| inferior | *kacha* |
| hot/cold | *garam/thanda* |
| expensive/cheap | *mahenga/sasta* |
| clean/dirty | *saaf/gandah* |
| left/right | *bayā/dayā* |
| near/far | *nazdik/dur* |
| beautiful | *khubsurut* |
| delicious | *laziz* |
| happy | *khush* |
| hungry | *bukha* |
| ill | *bimar* |
| late | *der* |
| and/more | *or* |
| one more/another | *ek or* |
| this/that | *yeh/woh* |
| here/there | *yahā/wahā* |
| both | *dono* |
| another (bus) | *dusri (bus)* |
| next (bus) | *agli dusri (bus)* |
| finished | *khatam* |

---

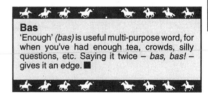

**Bas**
'Enough' *(bas)* is useful multi-purpose word, for when you've had enough tea, crowds, silly questions, etc. Saying it twice – *bas, bas!* – gives it an edge. ■

---

## Adverbs

| | |
|---|---|
| very much/very | *bohut* |
| a little | *thora* |
| back/return | *wapas* |

## Pronouns

| | |
|---|---|
| I/we | *me/ham* |
| you (polite) | *ap* |
| he/she/they | *yeh* |

Possessive pronouns are as follows for masculine objects; for feminine ones they end in *-i* not *-a*.

| | |
|---|---|
| my/our | *mera/hamara* |
| yours (polite) | *apka* |
| his/hers/theirs | *inka* |

## People

| | |
|---|---|
| man | *admi* |
| woman | *aoraat* |
| father/mother | *abba/amma* |
| husband/wife | *shohar/bivi* |
| brother/sister | *bhai/behn* |
| friend | *dost* |
| respected sir | *babu* |

## Greetings

| | |
|---|---|
| Sir/Madam | *jenab/begum* |
| How are you? | *kya hal heh?* |
| Fine/OK. | *teek heh* |
| Goodbye (God be with you). | *khuda hafiz* |
| See you again. | *pir melengeh* |

---

**Asalaam Aleikum**

The nice thing about this general Muslim (Arabic) greeting, which means 'Peace be with you' – and is sometimes used for departures too – is that it can help break the ice in any situation. The reply to an older or respected person is to repeat the phrase; to anyone else, it's *wa aleikum salaam* ('and with you too'). ■

---

## Accommodation

| | |
|---|---|
| bedding | *beestar* |
| caretaker | *chowkidar* (CHO-kee-dar) |
| key | *chabi* |
| room | *kamra* |
| rope bed | *charpoi* |
| toilet | *pakhana/latrin* |
| woman's | *zanana* |
| men's | *mardana* |
| travellers' inn | *serai /musafir khana* |
| water heater | *gizar* |

## Food

| | |
|---|---|
| food | *khana* |
| bread | *roti* |
| fried bread | *paratha* |
| tandoori rounds | *nan/tandoori roti* |
| sliced bread | *dabl roti* |
| unleavened flat-bread | *chapatti* |
| butter | *makhan* |
| cheese | *panir* |

| | |
|---|---|
| chillies | *mirch* |
| without chillies | *mirch kay baghair* |
| egg | *anda* |
| (boiled) egg | *(ubla) anda* |
| fried egg | *anda frai* |
| fish | *machli* |
| fruit | *phal* |
| apple | *seb* |
| apricot | *khubani* |
| banana | *kela* |
| mango | *aam* |
| meat | *gosht* |
| beef | *gay-ka gosht* |
| chicken | *murgi* |
| mutton | *bakri ka gosht/ chota ghosht* |
| rice | *chawal* |
| fried rice | *pulau* |
| plain rice | *sadha chawal* |
| salt | *namak* (NUM-uk) |
| spices | *masala* |
| sugar | *chini* |
| vegetable | *sabzi* |
| cabbage | *gobhi* |
| carrot | *gazhar* |
| lentils | *dhal* |
| okra | *bhindi* |
| peas | *matar* |
| potato | *alu* |
| spinach | *palak* |
| yoghurt | *dahi* |

| | |
|---|---|
| fork | *kanta* |
| knife | *chhuri* |
| spoon | *chammach/chamcha* |
| small spoon | *chamchi* |
| glass | *geelas* |
| plate | *plet* |
| I only eat vegetables. | *main sirif sabzi khata hung* |

## Drink

| | |
|---|---|
| milk | *dudh* |
| soft drink | *botal* |
| tea | *chai* |
| milky tea | *dudh wali chai* |
| green tea | *sabz-chai* |
| Pathan-style green tea | *khawa* |
| water | *pani* |
| boiled water | *ubla pani* |

LANGUAGE

## Some Useful Words

| | |
|---|---|
| candle | *mombatti* |
| cobbler | *mochi* |
| guide | *rasta* |
| hospital | *shifa khana* |
| hot spring | *garam chashma* |
| jeep | *gari* (ga-REE) |
| luggage | *saman* (sa-MAHN) |
| map | *naksha* |
| mosque | *masjid* |
| mountain | *pahar* |
| small mountain | *pahari* |
| river | *nadi* |
| tributary valley | *nala* |
| shop | *dukan* |
| soap | *sabun* |
| tailor | *darzi* |
| Karakoram Highway | *shahrah-i-karakoram* |
| Silk Road | *shahrah-i-resham* |

## Some Useful Phrases

| | |
|---|---|
| Thank you. | *shukria* |
| Special thanks/ Please. (literally 'your kindness') | *mehrbani* |
| Excuse me (polite) | *maf kijiyeh* |
| No problem. | *koi bat nai* |
| Yes./No. | *hā/nai* |
| Do you speak English? | *ap inglish bolteh heh?* |
| I don't understand. | *me nāi samaja (m)/ samji (f)* |
| I can't read Urdu. | *me urdu nāi parsakta* |
| Of course. | *bilkul* |
| What's your name? | *apka nam kya heh?* |
| My name is (John). | *mera nam (jan) heh* |
| What's the name of this place? | *ees jaga-ka nam kya heh?* |
| Where are you going? | *ap kahā jateh he?* |
| Is there a (Gilgit) bus today? | *kya (gilgit)-ko bus aj heh?* |
| What time is it going? | *kitna bajeh jaegi?* |
| Where is (the GPO)? | *(gpo) kidr heh?* |
| Is it far? | *kitni dur heh?* |

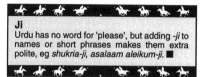

**Ji**
Urdu has no word for 'please', but adding *-ji* to names or short phrases makes them extra polite, eg *shukria-ji, asalaam aleikum-ji.* ∎

| | |
|---|---|
| Where are you from? (where is your house?) | *apka ghar kidr heh?* |
| I'm from America. | *mera ghar amrika-me heh* |
| Do you have (food)? | *apka pas (khana) heh?* |
| Is there (hot water)? | *kya (garam pani) heh?* |
| What do you want? | *ap kya chahteh he?* |
| I (don't) want tea. | *muje chai (nāi) chahyeh* |
| How much does this cost? | *kitna rupia?/ kitna paisa?* |
| too expensive | *bohit mahenga heh* |
| He is my husband. | *yeh mera shawarh heh* |
| She is my wife. | *yeh meri bivi heh* |
| God willing. | *inshallah* |
| Hurry! | *jaldi karo!* |
| Stop! | *rukia!* |

## Time

| | |
|---|---|
| When? (date) | *kab?* |
| When? (time) | *kitna bajeh?* |
| What time is it? | *kitna bajeh heh?* |
| How long? | *kitna vakt?* |
| today | *aj* |
| tomorrow/yesterday (according to context) | *kal* |
| day after tomorrow/ before yesterday | *parsō* |
| now | *ab* |
| immediately | *abhi* |
| (three) o'clock | *(teen) bajeh* |
| half-past (eight) | *sarreh-(aht) bajeh* |
| am | *suba* |
| pm | *dopehar/sham* |
| hour | *ganta* |
| day | *din* |
| month | *mahina* |
| year | *sal* |

LANGUAGE

| (five years) ago | *(panj sal) pehleh* |
| next (year) | *agleh (sal)* |

## Numbers

Urdu number-words don't have the regularity of English, so try to do things in round numbers! Don't confuse 25 and 50, or 7 and 60. To add ½ to a number (except 1 or 2) precede it with *sarreh* (eg 3½ is *sarrehteen)*; this is common with prices and time.

*Lakh* (hundred thousand) and *kror* (10 million) are used for big numbers. Once into the thousands, large written numbers have commas every two places, not three.

| | |
|---|---|
| 1 | *ek* |
| 1½ | *derh* |
| 2 | *doh* |
| 2½ | *dhai* |
| 3 | *teen* |
| 4 | *char* |
| 5 | *panch* |
| 6 | *chay* |
| 7 | *saht* |
| 8 | *aath* |
| 9 | *nau* |
| 10 | *das* |
| 11 | *gyara* |
| 12 | *bara* |
| 13 | *tera* |
| 14 | *chauda* |
| 15 | *pandra* |
| 16 | *sola* |
| 17 | *satra* |
| 18 | *atthara* |
| 19 | *unnis* |
| 20 | *bees* |
| 25 | *pachees* |
| 30 | *tees* |
| 35 | *pantees* |
| 40 | *chalees* |
| 45 | *pantalees* |
| 50 | *pachaas* |
| 60 | *sath* |
| 70 | *sattar* |
| 80 | *assi* |
| 90 | *navveh* |
| 100 | *sau* |
| 1000 | *hazar* |

| | |
|---|---|
| 100,000 | *lakh* |
| (Pakistanis write 1,00,000) | |
| 10,000,000 | *kror* |
| (Pakistanis write 1,00,00,000) | |

# Mandarin Chinese

Mandarin (or *putonghua*, 'people's speech') is China's official language, the dialect of Beijing and the speech of bureaucrats. Basic spoken Mandarin is surprisingly easy: no conjugations, no declensions, word order like English – just string them together. The hard parts are pronunciation and tones.

## Pronunciation

Mainland China's official Romanised 'alphabet' of Chinese sounds is called Pinyin. It's very streamlined, but the sounds aren't always self-evident. The letters that don't sound quite like English are as follows:

**Consonants q** (flat 'ch'); **x** (flat 'sh'); **zh** ('j'); **z** ('dz'); **c** ('ts'); **r** (tongue rolled back, almost 'z').

**Vowels a** ('ah'); **er** ('ar', American pronunciation); **ui** ('oi' or 'wei'); **iu** ('yoh'); **ao** ('ow' as in 'now'); **ou** ('ow' as in 'low'); **e** ('uh' after consonants); **ian** ('yen'); **ong** ('oong'); **u** ('oo', or sometimes like 'ü': say 'ee' with your mouth rounded as if to say 'oo').

## Tones

A given sound has many meanings depending on how it's 'sung'. But with common phrases you can get away without tones because the Chinese try hard to figure out what you mean. Syllables aren't stressed strongly.

## Negation

Adjectives and present-tense verbs are negated by preceding them with *bu*, or occasionally *mei* (as in the all-too-familiar *mei you*, 'we don't have any').

## Questions

A phrase becomes a question if you add *ma* to the end of it (you understand, *ni dong*; do you understand? *ni dong ma?*). Or you can make a question by juxtaposing positive and negative forms (Do you want it?, 'want-not-want?' *yao bu yao?*; Do you have it? *you mei you?*; OK?, 'good-not-good?' *hao bu hao?*).

## Books

Be sure your phrasebook or dictionary uses Pinyin, not earlier Romanisations which are even more confusing. It helps if it has Chinese characters too, for showing to Chinese who speak other dialects. Lonely Planet's *Mandarin Chinese phrasebook* has Chinese characters, tones, Pinyin and useful word-lists.

## Adjectives

| | |
|---|---|
| very | *hen* (hun) |
| good/bad | *hao/huai* |
| beautiful | *hao-kan* |
| delicious | *hao-chi* (how-chr) |
| happy | *gaoxing* (gow-sheeng) |
| expensive | *gui* (gway) |
| cheap | *pianyi* (pyen-yee) |
| left/right | *zuo/you* |
| open (for travel) | *kaifang* (kye-fung) |
| broken | *huai-le* (hwy-luh) |
| here/there | *zhe-li/na-li* |

## Verbs

| | |
|---|---|
| buy | *mai* |
| go | *qu* (chü) |
| live/reside | *shenhuo* (shun-hwoh) |
| work | *gongzuo* (goong-zwoh) |
| like | *xihuan* (shee-hwan) |

## Prepositions

| | |
|---|---|
| from | *cong* (tsoong) |
| to | *dao* |
| in/on/at | *zai* |

## Pronouns

| | |
|---|---|
| I/we | *wo/women* (woh-mun) |
| you (sg/pl) | *ni/nimen* |
| he/she/it/they | *ta/tamen* |

**Possessive Form** Add *-de* (duh); 'our' is *nimen-de* and so on.

## People

| | |
|---|---|
| person | *ren* (run) |
| father/mother (inf) | *baba/mama* |
| husband | *zhangfu* (jahng-fu) |
| wife | *qizi* (chee-dzih) |
| son | *erzi* (ar-dzih) |
| daughter | *nuer* (nu-ar) |
| friend | *pengyou* (pung-yo) |
| foreigner | *waiguoren* |
| student | *xuesheng* (shway-shung) |
| tourist | *luyouzhe* (lü-yo-dzih) |

## Countries

| | |
|---|---|
| Australia | *ao-da-li-ya* |
| Canada | *jia-na-da* |
| China | *zhongguo* (joong-gwoh) |
| England | *yingguo* |
| Hong Kong | *xiang-gang* |
| New Zealand | *xing-xi-lan* |
| Pakistan | *ba-ji-si-tan* |
| the USA | *meiguo* |

## Accommodation

| | |
|---|---|
| dormitory | *sushe* (su-shuh) |
| double room | *shuang ren fangjian* |
| guesthouse | *binguan* |
| hotel, cheaper | *lüguan* (lü-gwahn) |
| key | *yaoshi* (yow-shr) |
| shower | *linyu* (leen-yü) |
| single room | *dan-ren fangjian* |
| telephone | *dianhua* (dyen-hwa) |
| toilet | *cesuo* (tsuh-swoh) |

## Around Town

| | |
|---|---|
| airmail | *hang-kong* |
| bank | *yinhang* |
| hospital | *yiyuan* |
| post office | *you-ju* (yoh-jü) |
| Public Security Bureau | *gong-an ju* |
| stamp | *you-piao* |

## Getting Around

| | |
|---|---|
| airport | *feiji chang* |
| bicycle | *zixingche* (dzih-sheeng-chuh) |
| bus | *qiche* (chee-chuh) |
| bus station | *qiche zhan* |
| ticket to (Ghez) | *dao (ghez) de piao* |
| train station | *huoche zhan* |
| truck | *dakache* |

## Food

| | |
|---|---|
| chopsticks | *kuaizi* (kwy-dzih) |
| restaurant | *fanguar* |
| menu | *caidan* (tsy-dahn) |
| bill/check | *maidan* |
| beef | *niu rou* |
| bread | *mianbao* |
| cake | *dangao* |
| chicken | *ji rou* |
| egg | *jidan* |
| boiled | *zhu* ... (ju) |
| fried | *jian* ... (jyen) |
| fried noodles | *chaomian* |
| green vegetable | *qingcai* (cheeng-tsy) |
| hot chillies | *lajiao* |
| melon | *gua* |
| MSG | *wei-jin* |
| mutton | *yang rou* (roe) |
| rice | *fan* |
| steamed rice | *mifan* |
| fried rice | *chaofan* |
| rice porridge | *shi fan* |
| salt | *yan* |
| soup | *tang* (high tone) |
| sugar | *tang* (rising tone) |

## Drink

| | |
|---|---|
| beer | *pijiu* (pee-joh) |
| boiling water | *kai shui* (ky-shway) |
| milk | *niu nai* |
| tea | *cha* |
| a pot of tea | *yi-hu cha* |
| white spirits | *baijiu* |
| wine | *putaojiu* |

## Some Useful Words

| | |
|---|---|
| home-place | *jia* |
| Silk Road | *sichou zhi lu* |

| | |
|---|---|
| Karakoram Highway | *zhong-pa gong lu* |
| Uyghur language | *weizuhua* |
| money | *qian (chyen)* |
| RMB | *renminbi* |
| US dollar | *meiyuan* |
| Hong Kong dollar | *gangbi* |
| map | *ditu* |
| toilet paper | *weisheng zhi* (way-shung jr) |

## Some Useful Phrases

| | |
|---|---|
| Hello ('are you well?'). | *ni hao* |
| Goodbye. | *zaijian* |
| Thank you. | *xiexie* |
| Please. | *qing* |
| Excuse me. | *dui bu qi* (dway-bu-chee) |
| Yes. ('you are correct') | *dui* (dway) |
| No. | *bu dui/bu shi* |
| Where is (the toilet)? | *(cesuo) zai na li?* |
| Do you have (hot water)? | *(kai shui), you mei you?* |
| I (don't) have rice. | *wo (mei) you fan* |
| I (don't) want tea. | *wo (bu) yao cha* |
| How much does it cost? | *duo-shao qian?* |
| Too expensive! | *tai gui-le!* |
| Too loud! | *tai chao le!* |
| Enough! | *gou le!* (go-luh) |
| Where are you going? | *qu na li?/qu nar?* |
| Is it allowed? | *ke bu keyi?* (kuh bu kuh-yee) |
| Wait a moment. | *deng yi huar* (dung yee hwar) |
| No problem. | *mei guanxi* (may gwan-shee) |
| Where are you from? | *ni cong nali lai de?* |
| I'm from (America). | *wo cong (meiguo) lai de* |
| Can you speak English? | *ni hui shuo yingyü ma?* |
| a little bit | *yi dian-dian* (yee dyen-dyen) |

I can't speak Mandarin.     *wo bu hui shuo putonghua*

Do you understand?     *ni dong ma?*

I don't understand (your language).     *wo ting bu dong*

I can't read that. (Chinese characters)     *wo kan bu dong*

## Time

| | |
|---|---|
| when? (date) | *ji hao?* |
| when? (time) | *ji dian?* |
| today | *jintian* |
| tomorrow | *mingtian* |
| day after tomorrow | *houtian* |
| yesterday | *zuotian* |
| now | *xianzai* (shyen-dzai) |
| (five) o'clock | *(wu)-dian* |
| half-past (eight) | *(ba)-dian ban* |
| (three) hours | *(san)-ge xiaoshi* (...shyow-shr) |
| half an hour | *ban-ge xiaoshi* |

## Days of the Week

Use *xingqi* (shing-chee) plus a number (Monday = 1 through Saturday = 6; for example, *xingqi wu* is Friday). Sunday is *xingqi tian*.

## Numbers

The simplest (though not always precisely grammatical) way to count is (number)-*ge*-(object); eg, 'two people' is *liang-ge ren*.

| | |
|---|---|
| ½ | *ban* |
| 1 | *yi* |
| 2 | *er* (ar) (number) |
| 2 | *liang* (counting) |
| 3 | *san* |
| 4 | *si* (sih) |
| 5 | *wu* |
| 6 | *liu* (lyoh) |
| 7 | *qi* (chee) |
| 8 | *ba* |
| 9 | *jiu* (jyoh) |
| 10 | *shi* (shr) |
| 11 | *shi yi* |
| 20 | *er shi* |
| 21 | *er shi yi* |
| 30 | *san shi* |

| 100 | *yi bai* |
|---|---|
| 200 | *liang bai* |
| 1000 | *yi qian* (chyen) |

# Uyghur

Uyghur is spoken all over Xinjiang and in parts of Kyrgyzstan and Uzbekistan. It's a Turkic language salted with words of Chinese, Mongol, Kyrghyz, Uzbek, Wakhi, Russian, Urdu, Arabic and Persian. In China, written Uyghur uses an Arabic script, although for a time children were taught a Romanised alphabet. For more words, the Lonely Planet *Central Asia phrasebook* will help. This glossary reflects the Kashgar dialect.

The letter **a** is like the 'a' in 'father', while **ä** is like the 'a' in 'hat'. The letter **o** is like the 'o' in 'go', while **ö** is pronounced by saying 'ee' but with your mouth rounded as if to say 'o' (as in the French *seul*). The letter **u** is like the 'u' in 'put', while **ü** is pronounced by saying 'ee' with your mouth rounded as if to say 'oo' (like the French *sur*). The letter combination **gh** is a guttural 'r' sound as in French or Hebrew, while **kh** sounds like the 'ch' in 'Bach'. The letter **q** is like a hard 'k', pronounced deep in the throat. Most words are accented on the last syllable. Stress is indicated here by capitals.

## Pronouns

| | |
|---|---|
| I/we | *män/biz* |
| you (sg/pl) | *siz/sizLÄR* |
| he or she/they | *u/uLÄR* |

## Possessive Form

Add -*nung* after the noun.

## Adjectives

| | |
|---|---|
| good/bad | *YAKHshi/yaMAN* |
| beautiful | *chiRAYliq or güZEL* |
| delicious | *mizLIK* |
| expensive | *khumMET* |
| left/right | *sol/ong* |
| this/that | *bu/Awu* |
| here/there | *buYER/uYER* |

## People

| | |
|---|---|
| person | *kshe* |
| man/woman | *er/aYAL* |
| father/mother | *DAda/Ana* |
| son/daughter | *oGHOL/qiz* |
| husband | *Ire* |
| wife | *aYALe* |
| elder/younger brother | *Aka/fka* |
| elder/younger sister | *Acha/SINGil* |
| friend | *dos* |
| head-man | *BASHliq* |
| foreigner | *chetelLIQ* |

## Accommodation

| | |
|---|---|
| hotel | *MIHmankhana* |
| cheap room | *erZAN yaTAQ* |
| single/double room | *bir/Iki kshLIK yaTAQ* |
| dormitory | *küp kshLIK yaTAQ* |
| bed | *karVAT* |
| key | *achKUCH* |
| public toilet | *khaLA* |

## Getting Around

| | |
|---|---|
| bus | *apTUZ* |
| bus station/stop | *apTUZ biKET* |
| ticket | *biLET* |
| bicycle | *vilSPIT* |

## Food

| | |
|---|---|
| food | *taMAQ* |
| restaurant/food stall | *ashKHAna* |
| bread | *nan* |
| bagel | *gzhde* |
| flat-bread | *akNAN* |
| fish | *biLIQ* |
| noodles | *laghMÄN* |
| fried rice & meat | *plo/poLA* |
| meat | *güsh* |
| beef | *kaLA güshE* |
| chicken | *toHO güshE* |
| mutton | *qoy güshE* |
| steamed rice | *gangPEN* |
| vegetable | *sey* |
| yoghurt | *QITik* |
| apple | *ALma* |
| fig | *enJÜ* |
| grapes | *üzÜM* |
| melon | *khoGHON* |

| | |
|---|---|
| watermelon | *TAvuz* |
| peach | *shapTUL* |
| pear | *aMUT* |

## Drink

| | |
|---|---|
| beer | *piVE* |
| tea | *chay* |
| water | *su* |
| boiled water | *khayNAQ su* |

## Some Useful Words

| | |
|---|---|
| Chinese money: yuan/kuai (*koi*) jiao/mao (*mo*) | |
| house/home | *üy* |
| family | *a'iLE* |
| hospital | *DOKtorkhana* |
| police | *sakhCHE* |
| post office | *poshtKHAna* |
| Sunday market | *YENGa baZAR* |
| shop | *duKAN* |
| lake | *kül* |
| mountain | *tagh* |
| river | *darYA* |
| guide | *yolbashCHE* |
| north | *janOP* |
| south | *shiMAL* |
| east | *shärq* |
| west | *ghärp* |

## Some Useful Phrases

| | |
|---|---|
| greeting (pol) | *äsaLAmu äLEYkum* |
| Hello/How are you? | *yakhSHImo siz?* |
| I am well/happy. | *men YAKHshi* |
| Goodbye. | *khayr khosh* |
| Thank you (very much). | *(küp) räkhMÄT* |
| Sorry/ Excuse me/ Forgive me. | *KEchurong* |
| Yes./No. | *shunDAQ/yak* |
| Maybe. | *belKIM* |
| Please. | *merheMET* |
| Where are you going? | *NÄga BARsiz?* |
| Where is (the station)? | *(biKET) khaYERde?* |
| What is the name of this place? | *buYARnung isME niME?* |

| How much does it cost? | QANche pul? |
|---|---|
| What's your name? | isMUNGuz NIme? |
| My name is (John). | MInung isMEM (jan) |
| How old are you? | QANche YASHqa KIRdunguz? |
| I am (20) years old. | (yigirME) YASHqa KIRdim |
| I (don't) understand. | chüEN (MI) dem |
| Do you have (tea)? | (chay) BARmo? |
| We do/don't. | bar/yok |
| Please give me a (beer). | (piVE) birUNG |
| I don't eat meat. | güsh yiMEY men |
| I (don't) like Kashgar. | qashQAR-ne YAKHshi KÜR(mey)men |
| I'm lost. | IZip QALdim |
| Go away! | ket! |

### Time

| What's the time? | sa'ET KANche BOLde? |
|---|---|
| It's (six) o'clock. | (ALte) BOLde |
| when?/at what time? | sa'ET KANche de? |
| at (five) o'clock | (besh) de |
| today | büGÜN |
| tomorrow | Äte |
| yesterday | TÜnegün |
| now | HAzir |
| local time | YERlik waqt |
| Beijing time | beijing waqt |
| Monday | dushemBE |
| Tuesday | seyshemBE |
| Wednesday | charshemBE |
| Thursday | peyshemBE |
| Friday | juMÄ |
| Saturday | shemBE |
| Sunday | yekshemBE |

### Numbers

| ½ | YERim |
|---|---|
| 1 | bir |
| 2 | Iki |
| 3 | üch |
| 4 | tüt |
| 5 | besh |
| 6 | alTE |
| 7 | yeTE |
| 8 | seyKIZ |
| 9 | toQUZ |
| 10 | ön |
| 20 | yigirME |
| 30 | otTUZ |
| 40 | QURuk |
| 50 | elLIK |
| 60 | atMISH |
| 70 | yetMISH |
| 80 | sekSEN |
| 90 | tokhSAN |
| 100 | yüz |
| 1000 | mung |

*(With thanks to Ablimit Ghopor)*

# Wakhi

Wakhi is the speech of the Wakhi tribe of Tajik people in Gojal and Afghanistan's Wakhan Corridor. It's very similar to the speech of other Tajiks, ie in the Tashkurgan region and Tajikistan.

### Pronouns

| I/we | uz/saak |
|---|---|
| you (sg/pl) | tu/sasht |
| he/they | yah/yasht |

### Adjectives

| very | ghafeh |
|---|---|
| good/bad | baaf/shaak |
| beautiful | khushroi |
| delicious | mazadar |
| left/right | chap/rost |
| this/that | yem/ya |
| here/there | drem/dra |

### People

| man/woman | dai/hruinan |
|---|---|
| father/mother | taat/nun |
| husband/wife | shauhar/jamat |
| brother/sister | vrut/khuy |
| son/daughter | petr/theyght |

| friend | *doost* |
|---|---|
| head-man | *arbab* |

## Accommodation

| hotel | *hoteli* |
|---|---|
| guesthouse | *mehmonkhona* |
| room | *uchaak* |
| bed | *pipr* |
| single/double room | *yi/bu khaalgeh pipr* |
| Wakhi-style | *khikwor-khun* |
| key | *weshik* |
| room | *jayi* |
| toilet | *tarkank* |

## Food

| restaurant | *shapik yiteh jai* |
|---|---|
| apple | *mur* |
| apricot | *chuan* |
| egg | *tukhmurgeh* |
| food/bread | *shapik* |
| meat | *gosht* |
| rice | *gerangeh* |
| vegetable | *ghazk* |
| whole-wheat bread | *kamishdoon/dildungi* |
| yoghurt | *pai* |

## Drink

| buttermilk | *deegh* |
|---|---|
| milk | *bursh* |
| tea | *choi* |
| water | *yupek* |

## Some Useful Words

| house | *khun* |
|---|---|
| market | *bozor* |
| shop | *dukon* |
| mountain/peak | *kho/sar* |
| river | *darya* |
| valley | *zherav* |
| hot spring | *theen kook* |
| guide | *fdek disuv nikuz* |
| north | *shumaal* |
| south | *jnu* |
| east | *mashriq* |
| west | *maghrib* |

## Some Useful Phrases

| Hello. | *asalaam aleikum* |
|---|---|
| Goodbye. | *khudar hafiz* |

| How are you? | *chiz hawli?/baaf ateya?* |
|---|---|
| I am ... | *uzum ...* |
| well | *baaf* |
| happy | *khush* |
| hungry | *merz ('mares')* |
| thirsty | *wesk* |
| Yes./No. | *yau/nei* |
| I don't know. | *dishma* |
| Please. | *mehrboni* |
| Thank you. | *shobosh* |
| Excuse me/ Sorry. | *mofsar* |
| What's your name? | *ti noongi chiz?* |
| My name is (John). | *zhu noongi (Jan)* |
| Where are you from? | *tut koom dyoren?* |
| I am from ... | *uzum ...* |
| How old are you? | *ti umri tsumar?* |
| I am (20) years old. | *uzum (wisht) tsol* |
| Do you speak English? | *torezh angrezi vizta?* |
| I (don't) understand. | *mazhe malum tei/(nahst)* |
| Where is ...? | *... kumar?* |
| How much (does it cost)? | *yem chizi tsumrer?* |
| I like (tea). | *uzesh (choiyeh) khush-tsaram* |
| I want (tea). | *uzesh (choiyeh) zokh-tsaram* |
| I do not eat meat. | *uzesh gusht nei yowem* |
| I'm lost. | *mazhe hu fdek nost* |
| Go away! | *trabarech!* |

## Time

| What time is it? | *tsumar wakhti vitk?* |
|---|---|
| When? | *tsoghdar?* |
| today | *wuthk* |
| tomorrow | *pigha* |
| yesterday | *yezi* |
| now | *niveh* |
| Monday | *dushambi* |
| Tuesday | *sishambi* |
| Wednesday | *chorshambi* |
| Thursday | *panshambi* |
| Friday | *juma* |
| Saturday | *shambi* |
| Sunday | *yekshambi* |

## Numbers

|      |                    |
|------|--------------------|
| 1    | *yiu*              |
| 2    | *bui*              |
| 3    | *trui*             |
| 4    | *tsebur*           |
| 5    | *panz*             |
| 6    | *shal*             |
| 7    | *hoob*             |
| 8    | *haat*             |
| 9    | *nau*              |
| 10   | *thas*             |
| 20   | *wist*             |
| 30   | *wista-thas*       |
| 40   | *buwist*           |
| 50   | *buwista-thas*     |
| 60   | *truwist*          |
| 70   | *truwista-thas*    |
| 80   | *tseburwist*       |
| 90   | *tseburwista-thas* |
| 100  | *saad*             |
| 1000 | *hazor*            |

*(With thanks to Mohammad Jaffar)*

# Burushashki

Burushashki is spoken in central Hunza, upper Nagar, Yasin, Ishkoman and northern Chitral. Its origins are obscure, but it may be the KKH region's oldest language. Its difficult structure makes it nearly impossible for outsiders to master; there are said to be 38 plural forms, and words change form at both ends depending on context. But simple ideas are manageable.

The vowel **u** is pronounced 'oo' as in 'moon'. Hunza and Nagar dialects are slightly different – eg a common form of 'be' is *bila* in Hunza but *dila* in Nagar. Stress is indicated here by capitals.

## Pronouns

|                      |                 |
|----------------------|-----------------|
| I/mine               | *jeh/jah*       |
| you/yours (sing)     | *um/umeh*       |
| he/his               | *in/ineh*       |
| she/hers             | *inegus/inemo*  |
| we/ours              | *mi/mi'i*       |
| you/yours (pl)       | *ma/ma'a*       |
| they/theirs          | *u/ueh*         |

## Adjectives

|              |                     |
|--------------|---------------------|
| very         | *ghafeh*            |
| good/bad     | *baaf/shaak*        |
| beautiful    | *khushroi*          |
| delicious    | *mazadar*           |
| left/right   | *GHAIpa/DOIpa*      |
| this/that    | *yem/ya*            |
| here/there   | *KOleh/Eleh*        |

## People

|                       |                     |
|-----------------------|---------------------|
| man/woman             | *hir/gus*           |
| my father/mother      | *au/Ami*            |
| your father/mother    | *gu/gumi*           |
| my son/daughter       | *ei/ai*             |
| your son/daughter     | *gui/goi*           |
| my brother/sister     | *Acho/ayAS*         |
| your brother/sister   | *GOchu/guYAS*       |
| husband/wife          | *a'uyar/a'us*       |
| head-man              | *uyum*              |
| friend                |                     |
|   for men   | *shuGUlo*           |
|   for women | *shuGUli*           |
| person from Hunza, Ganesh, etc | *hunzakut, ganeshkut, etc* |

## Accommodation

|                    |                         |
|--------------------|-------------------------|
| single/double room | *hin/alTAN SIseh KAmara* |
| key                | *chei*                  |
| room               | *kamera*                |
| toilet             | *chuKAANG*              |

## Food

|                  |                  |
|------------------|------------------|
| food             | *SHIas*          |
| apple            | *balt*           |
| apricot          | *ju*             |
| dried apricot    | *bahTERing*      |
| dry cheese       | *kurut*          |
| egg              | *tiGAN*          |
| food, bread      | *shapik*         |
| meat             | *chaap*          |
| noodle soup      | *daudo*          |
| rice             | *briw* (Nagar)   |
|                  | *bras* (Hunza)   |
| white cheese     | *burus*          |
| wholewheat bread | *phitti*         |

vegetable | *hoi*
yoghurt | *duMAnu maMU*

### Drink

buttermilk | *diltar*
grape wine | *mel*
milk | *maMU*
mulberry spirits | *arak*
tea | *chai*
milk tea | *mamu chai*
green tea | *sabaz chai*
water | *tsil*
drinking water | *minas tsil*

### Some Useful Words

channel | *gotsil*
home-place | *waTAN*
hot spring | *gahRUM bul*
house | *ha*
mountain | *chish*
river | *sinda*
valley | *har/bar*

north | *kanJOOT*
south | *jeNOOS*
east | *JILmanas*
west | *BURmanas*

### Some Useful Phrases

Hello. | *leh*
Goodbye. | *khuDA haFIZ/ khuDAyar*
How are you? | *beHAL biLA?*
I am fine. | *je shuWA ba*
Thank you. | *bakhSHISH*
Yes./No. | *aWA/beYA*
Maybe. | *MEImi*
Pardon me/Forgive me. | *maf Eti*

What's your name? | *BEHsan guik biLA?*
My name is (John). | *ja aik (jan) biLA*
Where are you from? | *oom Amilim ba?*
How old are you? | *BEHsen Umur biLA?*
I am (20) years old. | *ja (alTAR) den biLA*

Do you speak English? | *anGREZi JUchi biLA?*

What's the name of this place? | *kuteh disheh besan ik bila?*
Do you have (tea)? | *(chai) bila?*
How much does this cost? | *BEHsan koi mad biLA?*
Where is ...? | *... Amili biLA?*
I only eat vegetables. | *ja SIruf hoi SHEHchaba*
I'm lost. | *aWAlaam*
Go away! | *ni!*

### Time

What time is it? | *BEHsan KANdila?*
It is (10) o'clock. | *mu (TORimi) GHAribi*
When? | *BEHshal?*
today | *KHULtu*
tomorrow | *JImeleh*
day after tomorrow | *KHIpultu*
yesterday | *saBUR*
day before yesterday | *YARbo*
now | *mu*

### Numbers

| 1 | *han* |
| 2 | *alTO* |
| 3 | *usKO* |
| 4 | *WALto* |
| 5 | *tsunDO* |
| 6 | *miSHINdo* |
| 7 | *taLO* |
| 8 | *alTAMbo* |
| 9 | *hunCHO* |
| 10 | *TOrumo* |
| 20 | *ALtar* |
| 30 | *Altar TOrumo* |
| 40 | *alTO ALtar* |
| 50 | *alTO ALtar TOrumo* |
| 60 | *isKI ALtar* |
| 70 | *isKI ALtar TOrumo* |
| 80 | *WALti ALtar* |
| 90 | *WALto ALtar TOrumo* |
| 100 | *ta* |
| 1000 | *saas* |

*(With thanks to Latif Anwar)*

# Shina

Shina is spoken in lower Hunza and Nagar (below the KKH bridge near Minapin); Gilgit and its valleys (Naltar, Bagrot, Haramosh and the upper Gilgit River watershed); Chilas and north-east Indus Kohistan. Meanings are often expressed by tones, so only the simplest words are given here. Stress is indicated by here capitals.

## Pronouns

| | |
|---|---|
| I/we | *ma/beh* |
| you (sing/pl) | *tu/su* |
| he/she/they | *roh/reh/rih* |

## People

| | |
|---|---|
| man/woman | *manuZHO/chei* |
| father/mother | *MAlo/ma* |
| husband/wife | *muSHA/jaMA* |
| son/daughter | *pooch/di* |
| brother/sister | *zha/sa* |
| head-man/ representative | *nambarDAR* |
| friend | *somo* |
| foreigner/ outsider | *daRIneh* |

## Accommodation

| | |
|---|---|
| single room | *ek muSHAI KAmara* |
| double room | *ek du muSHO KAmara* |

## Food

| | |
|---|---|
| food | *koig* |
| apricot | *jeroti* |
| dried apricots | *faTOR* |
| egg | *haNEH* |
| food/bread | *tiki* |
| meat | *moz/mots* |
| rice | *briw* |
| salt | *paJU* |
| wholewheat bread | *chupatti/ dudurtik* |
| vegetable | *sha* |
| yoghurt | *MUtu dut* |

## Drink

| | |
|---|---|
| milk | *dut* (rhymes with 'put') |
| tea | *chai* |
| water | *wei* |

## Some Useful Words

| | |
|---|---|
| home-place | *waTAN* |
| hot spring | *TAto uts* |
| house | *goht* |
| mountain | *chish* |
| river | *sin* |
| valley | *gah* |
| left/right | *KAbo/daCHInu* |
| north | *shiMAL* |
| south | *jiNU* |
| east | *JILboik* |
| west | *BURboik* |

## Some Useful Phrases

| | |
|---|---|
| Hello. | *aLA* |
| Goodbye. | *huDA haFIZ* |
| How are you? | *je kal han?* |
| Fine. | *mishto han/mehrbani* |
| Please. | *mehrBAni teh* |
| Thank you. | *bakhSHISH* |
| Yes/No. | *aWA/neh* |
| Maybe. | *beBEY* |
| What is your name? | *tei jek nom han?* |
| My name is (John). | *mei nom (jan) han* |
| Where are you from? | *tu KONyo haNO?* |
| I am from ... | *ma ... haNOOS* |
| How old are you? | *tei UmarkaJAK han?* |
| I am (20) years old. | *mei (bi) sar han* |
| Do you speak English? | *toot anGREzi wa nah?* |
| I don't understand. | *ma (neh) paRUdus* |
| How much is it? | *jek garch han?* |
| Where is ...? | *... kon han?* |
| I like (Gilgit). | *mas (gilgit) paSANtamus* |
| I only eat vegetables. | *mas SIruf SHAkamus* |

## Time

| | |
|---|---|
| What time is it? | *je ken han?* |

| | |
|---|---|
| It's (10) o'clock | *(dai) baSHEGen* |
| When? | *gaREH?* |
| today | *aach* |
| tomorrow | *lushTEH* |
| day after tomorrow | *chiRING* |
| yesterday | *baLA* |
| day before | *iCHI* |
| yesterday | |
| now | *ten* |
| at once | *dahm* |
| Monday | *tsanDUra* |
| Tuesday | *anGAro* |
| Wednesday | *BOdo* |
| Thursday | *beRESpat* |
| Friday | *SHUkura* |
| Saturday | *shimSHER* |
| Sunday | *aDIT* |

## Numbers

| | |
|---|---|
| 1 | *ek* |
| 2 | *du* |
| 3 | *cheh* |
| 4 | *char* |
| 5 | *poe* (nasal *e*) |
| 6 | *sha* |
| 7 | *saat* |
| 8 | *aash* |
| 9 | *nau* |
| 10 | *dai* |
| 20 | *bi* |
| 30 | *bigaDAI* |
| 40 | *DUbyo* |
| 50 | *DUbiga DAI* |
| 60 | *SHAbyo* |
| 70 | *SHAbyoga DAI* |
| 80 | *CHARbyo* |
| 90 | *CHARbyoga DAI* |
| 100 | *shal* |
| 1000 | *saas* |

*(With thanks to Latif Anwar and Ali Anwar)*

# Kohistani

Kohistani is spoken in northern Swat and Indus Kohistan. It's a mish-mash of Shina, Pashto, Urdu, Persian and other languages, and varies from one village to the next. Shina or Pashto may work just as well. Stress is indicated here by capitals.

## Adjectives

| | |
|---|---|
| good | *mishTO* |
| bad | *KHAcho* |
| beautiful | *suDAcho* |
| happy | *khush* |
| expensive | *keimeTI* |
| hot/cold | *tato/shidalo* |
| left/right | *kabu/dachinu* |
| this/that | *anu/ro* |
| here/there | *adayn/al* |

## People

| | |
|---|---|
| man/woman | *maash/garyu* |
| father/mother | *aBA/ya* |
| son/daughter | *puch/dhi* |
| brother/sister | *zha/bhyun* |
| (my) friend | *(mil) doost* |

## Food & Drink

| | |
|---|---|
| bread | *gwel* |
| egg | *aNA* |
| meat | *maSU* |
| milk | *chir* |
| tea | *chai* |
| vegetable | *sabzi* |
| water | *vi/wi* |
| yoghurt | *dudi* |

## Some Useful Words

| | |
|---|---|
| high valley/pass | *dara* |
| home-place | *MIwatan* |
| mountain | *kor* |
| name | *na* |
| river | *seen* |

## Some Useful Phrases

| | |
|---|---|
| Hello. | *asalaam aleikum* |
| Goodbye. | *huDAR haWAla* |
| Good. | *suGA/mihta* |
| Thank you. | *shukria* |
| Yes/No. | *ah/ni* |

## Time

| | |
|---|---|
| today | *aaz* |
| tomorrow | *okot* |

| now | uskeh |
|---|---|
| (two) o'clock | (du) masma |

**Numbers**

| 1 | ek |
|---|---|
| 2 | du |
| 3 | cha |
| 4 | sawur |
| 5 | paz |
| 6 | sho |
| 7 | saat |
| 8 | aat |
| 9 | naan/nau |
| 10 | daash |
| 20 | bish |
| 100 | shol |
| 1000 | zir |

# Pashto

Pashto is the speech of the Pathans (Pashtuns) in eastern Afghanistan and Pakistan's North-West Frontier Province. Though there are some differences in pronunciation between the Swati and Afghan dialects (eg northerners call themselves Pakhtun, southerners Pashtun) this is still the *lingua franca* from the Indus to Kabul. Along the KKH you'll hear it, mixed with other dialects, in Besham, Batagram and Mansehra. Stress is indicated here by capitals.

**Adjectives**

| very good | (der) khey |
|---|---|
| beautiful | khesta |
| expensive/cheap | gran/arzan |

**People**

| man/woman | sarleh/khazeh |
|---|---|
| father/mother | plar/mor |
| husband/wife | khawand/khazar |
| brother/sister | ror/khor |
| friend | yar |

**Food & Drink**

| egg | ay |
|---|---|
| food | doreh/roti |
| meat | wakha |

| tea with/without milk | sur/tor chai |
|---|---|
| vegetable | sabzi |
| (cold) water | (yakha) ubuh |

**Some useful words**

| house | kur |
|---|---|
| mountain | ghar |
| name | num |
| river/stream | darya/khwar |
| valley | wadi |

**Some useful phrases**

| Hello. | asalaam aleikum |
|---|---|
| Welcome. | pakhair |
| How are you? | sa hal dey?/singa hal dey? |
| Fine. | khey ma |
| Where are you going? | chertha zey? |
| Goodbye. (when you leave) | de khuday pe aman |
| Goodbye. (when they leave) | pa makha de ha |
| Thank you. | shukhria |
| Yes/No. | au/na |

**Time**

| today | nan |
|---|---|
| tomorrow | sabah |
| yesterday | paroon |
| day after tomorrow | bel sabah |
| day before yesterday | bel paroon |
| now | os |
| later | rusto |

**Numbers**

| 1 | yau |
|---|---|
| 2 | dua |
| 3 | drei |
| 4 | salor |
| 5 | pinze |
| 6 | shpag |
| 7 | uwo |
| 8 | ata |
| 9 | haha |
| 10 | las |
| 100 | sel (sawa) |
| 1000 | zer |

LANGUAGE

# Balti

The Balti language is similar to classical Tibetan, which has four levels of speech: to/between common people, to/between honoured or revered people, colloquial, and literary. The colloquial is dominant in Baltistan. Stress is indicated here by capitals.

## Adjectives

| | |
|---|---|
| good/bad | LYAKHmo/chaang-MEN |
| beautiful | gaSHA |
| delicious | zhumBO |
| hot | tronMO (weather)/tso (thing) |
| cold | grakhMO |
| left/right | khen/trang |

## People

| | |
|---|---|
| man/woman | mi/buSTRING |
| father/mother | Ata/Ama |
| son/daughter | bu/bonGO |
| brother | kaKA (elder)/POno (younger) |
| sister | AASkeh (elder)/stringMO (younger) |
| husband/wife | aSHIpa/buSTRING |
| friend | pyokh |
| respected man | YEri PYAKHbo (your honour) |
| respected woman | Asheh (elder sister) |

## Food

| | |
|---|---|
| food/meal | zaan (something to eat: zachas) |
| eat | za |
| whole-wheat bread | kurba |
| curry | SPAQchas |
| meat | sha |
| beef | baSHA |
| mutton | raSHA |
| chicken | byaSHA |
| vegetable | TSONma |
| rice | bras |
| egg | byabJON |
| yoghurt | LOQfi onGA |

| | |
|---|---|
| tea | cha |
| water | chu |
| boiled water | SKOLfi chu |

## Some Useful Words

| | |
|---|---|
| home | nang |
| (your) village | (YIri) grong |
| toilet | chaqSA |

## Some Useful Phrases

| | |
|---|---|
| Hello. (polite) | asalaam aleikum |
| Hello. (informal) | ZHUleh |
| Hello. (in passing, or to arriving person) | shokhs/shakhsa |
| How are you? | chi hal yod? |
| Fine. | LYAKHmo yud |
| Goodbye. | huDARyi faghRING |
| Thank you/ Please. | Azhu |
| Yes/No. | YAya/men |
| What is your name? | YIri MENtakh chi in? |
| My name is (John). | ni MENtakh (jan) in |
| Where are you going? | yang gar gwen yod? |
| How much/many? | tsam? |
| Where is ...? | ... gar yod? |
| I am hungry/ill. | nga LTOKHsed/natPA yod |
| Come!/Go! | ong!/song! |
| I don't eat meat. | nga sha za MED |

## Numbers

| | |
|---|---|
| 1 | chik |
| 2 | ngis |
| 3 | sum |
| 4 | bji |
| 5 | gha |
| 6 | trook |
| 7 | dun |
| 8 | bgyad |
| 9 | rgu |
| 10 | fchu |
| 20 | ni shu |
| 30 | sum fchu |
| 40 | ni shu ngis |
| 50 | gha fchu |
| 60 | ni shu sum |
| 70 | ni shu sum na fchu |

| 80 | *ni shu bji* |
|---|---|
| 90 | *ni shu bji na fchu* |
| 100 | *bgya* |
| 1000 | *stong* |

*(With thanks to S M Abbas Kazmi)*

# Khowar

Khowar (Chitrali) is the speech not only of Chitral proper but of Ishkoman, Yasin and Ghizar on the Gilgit side of the Shandur Pass.

## Adjectives
| (very) good | *(bo) jam* |
|---|---|
| bad | *shum* |
| beautiful | *choost* |
| high | *rang* |

## People
| father/mother | *taat/naan* |
|---|---|
| brother/sister | *brar/ispisar* |
| husband/wife | *mosh/bok* |

## Food
| bread | *shapik* |
|---|---|
| meat | *pushoor* |

| water | *oogh* |
|---|---|

## Time
| today | *hanoon* |
|---|---|
| yesterday | *dosh* |
| tomorrow | *choochi* |

## Some Useful Words & Phrases
| How are you? | *tu keecha asoos?* |
|---|---|
| Very well, thanks. | *bojam, shukria* |
| Please. | *mehrbanni khori* |
| Yes./No. | *dee/no* |
| Where is (Drosh)? | *(drosh) kura sher?* |
| A little. | *kam* |
| bed | *jen* |
| mountain | *zoom* |

## Numbers
| 1 | *yi* |
|---|---|
| 2 | *ju* |
| 3 | *droi* |
| 4 | *chor* |
| 5 | *ponj* |
| 6 | *choi* |
| 7 | *sot* |
| 8 | *osht* |
| 9 | *niu* |
| 10 | *jiush* |
| 20 | *bishir* |
| 100 | shor |

LANGUAGE

# Glossary

**ahl-i-kitab** – literally 'people of the book', the collective term in the Holy Quran for Muslims, Jews and Christians
**asalam aleikum** – universal Muslim greeting, literally 'peace be with you'
**azan** – Muslim call to prayer

**baksheesh** – tip, gratuity, bribe
**burqa** – long, tent-like garment that completely hides the body shape and face, worn in public by women of conservative Muslim communities who are observing purdah

**cairn** – pile of stones marking a trail or pass
**cantonment** – military-administrative-residential district built by the British adjacent to major towns in colonial times
**chador** – lightweight woollen blanket often worn as a shawl by Pakistani men, sometimes doubling as blanket, pillow, curtain, sack etc
**chapatti** – unleavened wheat flatbread cooked in a pan
**charpoi** – simple bed of ropes knotted together on a wooden frame
**chogha** – embroidered woollen cloak with oversize sleeves, common in the NWFP and Northern Areas
**chowk** – intersection of streets
**chowkidar** – caretaker

**dhal** – over-boiled lentil soup
**dupatta** – light scarf often used by Muslim women to cover their hair while in public

**gah** – tributary stream or valley (Shina)

**hammam** – public bath-house and barber-shop
**Hui** – Chinese Muslim

**imam** – leader; (title of) one of the 12 descendants of the Prophet Mohammad who, according to orthodox Shia belief, succeeded him as temporal and spiritual leader of Muslims

**imam barga** – special meeting hall used only for the Shia festivals of Ashura and Chhelum

**insha'allah** – Arabic for 'if God wills it', almost a standard part of the future tense in Muslim countries

**jamaat khana** – Ismaili community hall, their closest equivalent to a mosque

## Abbreviations
People talk in initials along the KKH. Following are the most common abbreviations you'll hear.

**AKESP** Aga Khan Educational Services Pakistan
**AKHSP** Aga Khan Health Services Pakistan
**AKRSP** Aga Khan Rural Support Programme
**AKTC** Aga Khan Trust for Culture
**CITS** China International Travel Service
**CTS** China Travel Service
**C&W** NWFP Communication & Works Department
**FWO** Frontier Works Organisation
**GOP** Government of Pakistan
**GPO** General Post Office
**HI** Hostelling International
**IUCN** The World Conservation Union
**IYHF** International Youth Hostel Federation
**KKH** Karakoram Highway
**NAPWD** Northern Areas Public Works Department
**Natco** Northern Areas Transportation Company
**NGO** Non-Governmental Organisation
**NWFP** North-West Frontier Province
**PCO** Public Call Office
**PIA** Pakistan International Airlines
**PRC** People's Republic of China
**PSB** Public Security Bureau
**PTDC** Pakistan Tourism Development Corporation
**PTL** Pakistan Tours Ltd
**PYHA** Pakistan Youth Hostels Association
**TDCP** Tourist Development Corporation of the Punjab
**VO** Village Organisation
**WO** Women's Organisation
**WWF** World Wide Fund for Nature ■

**kacha (or kutcha)** – lesser or inferior, eg a kacha road is a jeep track; cf pakka (Urdu)

**khan** – (title of) the head of certain ex-royal families, but used more generally as a title of honour as well

**khayaban** – boulevard or avenue, eg Khayaban-i-Suhrawardy means Suhrawardy Avenue

**khwar** – tributary stream or valley (Pashto)

**kror** – 'crore', a unit of 10 million, which Pakistanis write 1,00,00,000

**lakh** – a unit of one hundred thousand, which Pakistanis write 1,00,000

**Line of Control** – the temporary administrative boundary through Kashmir, separating Pakistan and Indian administered parts following the January 1949 UN ceasefire after the first India-Pakistan war

**lungma** – tributary stream or valley (Balti)

**mir** – (title of) traditional rulers of Hunza and Nagar

**muezzin** – one who calls Muslims to prayer, traditionally from the minaret of a mosque

**muztagh** – literally 'ice mountain', a cluster of the highest peaks of the Karakoram, from which the major glaciers descend

**nala** – tributary valley or stream (Urdu)

**nan** – thick, bread rounds baked in a tandoori oven

**pakka (or pukka)** – first-rate or superior, eg a pakka road is a paved road, a pakka sahib is an excellent chap (Urdu)

**Partition** – the formal division of British India into two separate countries, India and Pakistan, on 14 August 1947

**purdah** – segregation of post-pubescent women from all men outside the immediate family in orthodox Muslim communities

**Quaid-i-Azam** – 'Great Leader', Pakistanis' honorific title for Mohammed Ali Jinnah, founder of Pakistan

**Ramadan** – Muslim month of sunrise-to-sunset fasting

**roti** – general Urdu word for 'bread'

**Sarhad** – 'frontier' in Urdu; capitalised, it refers to the NWFP

**scree** – small stones accumulated on a slope

**serai** (or sarai) – an inn for traditional caravans, now used to refer to cheap accommodation along long-distance roads

**shahrah** – road, eg Shahrah-i-Iqbal means Iqbal Rd, Shahrah-i-Resham means the Silk Road

**shalwar qamiz** (or kameez) – traditional Pakistani men's and women's clothing, consisting of a knee-length shirt worn over very loose trousers gathered at the waist

**surnai** – a squeaky horn used for traditional music all along the KKH; in Kashgar called a *sunai*

**wallah** – the person in charge or with expertise, eg a rickshaw-wallah is a rickshaw driver, a chai-wallah is one who runs a teashop

**wazir** – minister or prime minister

**ziarat** – shrine

# Index

## MAPS

## TEXT

## BOXED TEXT

## Thanks

It's amazing how many people make real additions to our editions! Of scores of correspondents, four deserve special mention: Gudrun Droop, Steve Miles, Cathy Vaughan and Pierre Willems.

Other helpful letter writers and web site respondents are Abrar Ahmed, Vaughan Andrews, Ziaullah Baig, Andreus Bamberger, Michael Barker, K Chong, Karen Collins, Janet Craze, Jim Davis, Nicole Dumolard, Juan de Gammara, Barney Garrow, John Gellert, Mary Gijsen, Rachel Gradon, Posy Greany, Catherine Griffiths-Weber, Marc Grutering, Rob Harper, Stuart Hinson, David Hodges, Makato Hosoya, Margaret Jepson, Martin Jung, Tim Katz, Eric Korpiel, F Kostbode, David Kučera, Piet Lambregts, Peter Luff, John Mackle, Hermann Maier, Nicolaus Marshall, Michael Martens, Lisa & Pat McCarthy, Neil McCarthy, James McKee, Sander Meijsen, Greg Mitchell, Gerko Oskam, Martin Rajah, Alicia Ramos, SAA Razavi, Frances Riddelle, Peter Riedel, Simon Robins, Ari Schipf, Frank Sear, Howard Sethin, Scott Sharpe, Clare Stableford, Klaus Weber, Alan Whittington, Monica & Christina Wojtaszewski, Carmen Wunn, Vern Yen, Blaž Zabukovec, Gerard Zawadzki, Richard Barwell, Jeremy Chataway, Gudrun Droop, Johanne Duhaime, Edward Genochio, John Gilchrist, Rachel Graden, George Grundy, Tim Katz, Scott Mitic, Peter Riedel, Roger Tarn, A & K Wendler, and Carmen Wunn.

# LONELY PLANET PHRASEBOOKS

**Nepali** phrasebook

**Ethiopian** Amharic phrasebook

**Latin American Spanish** phrasebook

**Ukrainian** phrasebook

**Greek** phrasebook

**Vietnamese** phrasebook

*Building bridges,*
*Breaking barriers,*
*Beyond babble-on*

*Listen for the gems*

*Speak your own words*

*Ask your own questions*

*Master of your own image*

- handy pocket-sized books
- easy to understand Pronunciation chapter
- clear and comprehensive Grammar chapter
- romanisation alongside script to allow ease of pronunciation
- script throughout so users can point to phrases
- extensive vocabulary sections, words and phrases for every situation
- full of cultural information and tips for the traveller

*'...vital for a real DIY spirit and attitude in language learning'* – Backpacker

*'the phrasebooks have good cultural backgrounders and offer solid advice for challenging situations in remote locations'* – San Francisco Examiner

*'...they are unbeatable for their coverage of the world's more obscure languages'* – The Geographical Magazine

Arabic (Egyptian)
Arabic (Moroccan)
Australia
 *Australian English, Aboriginal and Torres Strait languages*
Baltic States
 *Estonian, Latvian, Lithuanian*
Bengali
Brazilian
Burmese
Cantonese
Central Asia
Central Europe
 *Czech, French, German, Hungarian, Italian and Slovak*
Eastern Europe
 *Bulgarian, Czech, Hungarian, Polish, Romanian and Slovak*
Ethiopian (Amharic)
Fijian
French
German
Greek

Hindi/Urdu
Indonesian
Italian
Japanese
Korean
Lao
Latin American Spanish
Malay
Mandarin
Mediterranean Europe
 *Albanian, Croatian, Greek, Italian, Macedonian, Maltese, Serbian and Slovene*
Mongolian
Moroccan Arabic
Nepali
Papua New Guinea
Pilipino (Tagalog)
Quechua
Russian
Scandinavian Europe
 *Danish, Finnish, Icelandic, Norwegian and Swedish*

South-East Asia
 *Burmese, Indonesian, Khmer, Lao, Malay, Tagalog (Pilipino), Thai and Vietnamese*
Spanish (Castilian)
 *Basque, Catalan and Galician*
Sri Lanka
Swahili
Thai
Thai Hill Tribes
Tibetan
Turkish
Ukrainian
USA
 *US English, Vernacular, Native American languages and Hawaiian*
Vietnamese
Western Europe
 *Basque, Catalan, Dutch, French, German, Irish, Italian, Portuguese, Scottish Gaelic, Spanish (Castilian) and Welsh*

# LONELY PLANET TRAVEL ATLASES

Lonely Planet has long been famous for the number and quality of its guidebook maps. Now we've gone one step further and in conjunction with Steinhart Katzir Publishers produced a handy companion series: Lonely Planet travel atlases – maps of a country produced in book form.

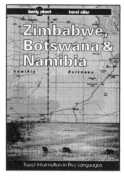

Unlike other maps, which look good but lead travellers astray, our travel atlases have been researched on the road by Lonely Planet's experienced team of writers. All details are carefully checked to ensure the atlas corresponds with the equivalent Lonely Planet guidebook.

The handy atlas format means no holes, wrinkles, torn sections or constant folding and unfolding. These atlases can survive long periods on the road, unlike cumbersome fold-out maps. The comprehensive index ensures easy reference.

- full-colour throughout
- maps researched and checked by Lonely Planet authors
- place names correspond with Lonely Planet guidebooks
  – no confusing spelling differences
- legend and travelling information in English, French, German, Japanese and Spanish
- size: 230 x 160 mm

**Available now:**
Chile & Easter Island • Egypt • India & Bangladesh • Israel & the Palestinian Territories •Jordan, Syria & Lebanon • Kenya • Laos • Portugal • South Africa, Lesotho & Swaziland • Thailand • Turkey • Vietnam • Zimbabwe, Botswana & Namibia

---

# LONELY PLANET TV SERIES & VIDEOS

Lonely Planet travel guides have been brought to life on television screens around the world. Like our guides, the programmes are based on the joy of independent travel, and look honestly at some of the most exciting, picturesque and frustrating places in the world. Each show is presented by one of three travellers from Australia, England or the USA and combines an innovative mixture of video, Super-8 film, atmospheric soundscapes and original music.

Videos of each episode – containing additional footage not shown on television – are available from good book and video shops, but the availability of individual videos varies with regional screening schedules.

**Video destinations include:** Alaska • American Rockies • Australia – The South-East • Baja California & the Copper Canyon • Brazil • Central Asia • Chile & Easter Island • Corsica, Sicily & Sardinia – The Mediterranean Islands • East Africa (Tanzania & Zanzibar) • Ecuador & the Galapagos Islands • Greenland & Iceland • Indonesia • Israel & the Sinai Desert • Jamaica • Japan • La Ruta Maya • Morocco • New York • North India • Pacific Islands (Fiji, Solomon Islands & Vanuatu) • South India • South West China • Turkey • Vietnam • West Africa • Zimbabwe, Botswana & Namibia

*The Lonely Planet TV series is produced by:*
**Pilot Productions**
The Old Studio
18 Middle Row
London W10 5AT UK

**For video availability and ordering information contact your nearest Lonely Planet office.**

*Music from the TV series is available on CD & cassette.*

# PLANET TALK

### Lonely Planet's FREE quarterly newsletter

We love hearing from you and think you'd like to hear from us.

**When...**is the right time to see reindeer in Finland?
**Where...**can you hear the best palm-wine music in Ghana?
**How...**do you get from Asunción to Areguá by steam train?
**What...**is the best way to see India?

**For the answer to these and many other questions read PLANET TALK.**

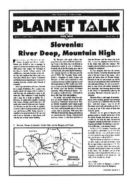

Every issue is packed with up-to-date travel news and advice including:

* a letter from Lonely Planet co-founders Tony and Maureen Wheeler
* go behind the scenes on the road with a Lonely Planet author
* feature article on an important and topical travel issue
* a selection of recent letters from travellers
* details on forthcoming Lonely Planet promotions
* complete list of Lonely Planet products

*To join our mailing list contact any Lonely Planet office.*

*Also available: Lonely Planet T-shirts. 100% heavyweight cotton.*

---

# LONELY PLANET ONLINE

### Get the latest travel information before you leave or while you're on the road

Whether you've just begun planning your next trip, or you're chasing down specific info on currency regulations or visa requirements, check out Lonely Planet Online for up-to-the minute travel information.

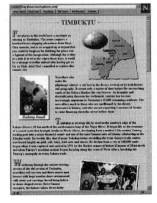

As well as travel profiles of your favourite destinations (including maps and photos), you'll find current reports from our researchers and other travellers, updates on health and visas, travel advisories, and discussion of the ecological and political issues you need to be aware of as you travel.

There's also an online travellers' forum where you can share your experience of life on the road, meet travel companions and ask other travellers for their recommendations and advice. We also have plenty of links to other online sites useful to independent travellers.

And of course we have a complete and up-to-date list of all Lonely Planet travel products including guides, phrasebooks, atlases, Journeys and videos and a simple online ordering facility if you can't find the book you want elsewhere.

### www.lonelyplanet.com
### or
### AOL keyword: lp

# LONELY PLANET JOURNEYS

JOURNEYS is a unique collection of travel writing – published by the company that understands travel better than anyone else. It is a series for anyone who has ever experienced – or dreamed of – the magical moment when they encountered a strange culture or saw a place for the first time. They are tales to read while you're planning a trip, while you're on the road or while you're in an armchair, in front of a fire.

JOURNEYS books catch the spirit of a place, illuminate a culture, recount a crazy adventure, or introduce a fascinating way of life. They always entertain, and always enrich the experience of travel.

---

## IN RAJASTHAN
### *Royina Grewal*

Indian writer Royina Grewal's travels in Rajasthan take her from tribal villages to flamboyant palaces. Along the way she encounters a multitude of characters: snake charmers, holy men, nomads, astrologers, dispossessed princes, reformed bandits . . . And as she draws out the rarely told stories of farmers' wives, militant maharanis and ambitious schoolgirls, the author skilfully charts the changing place of women in contemporary India. The result is a splendidly evocative mosaic of life in India's most colourful state.

*Royina Grewal* lives on a farm in Rajasthan, where she and her husband are working to evolve minimal-impact methods of farming. Royina has published two monographs about the need for cultural conservation and development planning. She is also the author of *Sacred Virgin*, a travel narrative about her journey along the Narmada River, which was published to wide acclaim.

---

## SHOPPING FOR BUDDHAS
### *Jeff Greenwald*

*Here in this distant, exotic land, we were compelled to raise the art of shopping to an experience that was, on the one hand, almost Zen – and, on the other hand, tinged with desperation like shopping at Macy's or Bloomingdale's during a one-day-only White Sale.*

*Shopping for Buddhas* is Jeff Greenwald's story of his obsessive search for the perfect Buddha statue. In the backstreets of Kathmandu, he discovers more than he bargained for . . . and his souvenir-hunting turns into an ironic metaphor for the clash between spiritual riches and material greed. Politics, religion and serious shopping collide in this witty account of an enlightening visit to Nepal.

*Jeff Greenwald* is also the author of *Mister Raja's Neighborhood* and *The Size of the World*. His reflections on travel, science and the global community have appeared in the *Los Angeles Times*, the *Washington Post*, *Wired* and a range of other publications. Jeff lives in Oakland, California.

# LONELY PLANET PRODUCTS

Lonely Planet is known worldwide for publishing practical, reliable and no-nonsense travel information in our guides and on our web site. The Lonely Planet list covers just about every accessible part of the world. Currently there are eight series: *travel guides*, *shoestring guides*, *walking guides*, *city guides*, *phrasebooks*, *audio packs*, *travel atlases* and *Journeys* – a unique collection of travel writing.

## EUROPE

Amsterdam • Austria • Baltic States phrasebook • Britain • Central Europe on a shoestring • Central Europe phrasebook • Czech & Slovak Republics • Denmark • Dublin • Eastern Europe on a shoestring • Eastern Europe phrasebook • Estonia, Latvia & Lithuania • Finland • France • French phrasebook • German phrasebook • Greece • Greek phrasebook • Hungary • Iceland, Greenland & the Faroe Islands • Ireland • Italian phrasebook • Italy • Mediterranean Europe on a shoestring • Mediterranean Europe phrasebook • Paris • Poland • Portugal • Portugal travel atlas • Prague • Russia, Ukraine & Belarus • Russian phrasebook • Scandinavian & Baltic Europe on a shoestring • Scandinavian Europe phrasebook • Slovenia • Spain • Spanish phrasebook • St Petersburg • Switzerland • Trekking in Spain • Ukrainian phrasebook • Vienna • Walking in Britain • Walking in Switzerland • Western Europe on a shoestring • Western Europe phrasebook

*Travel Literature:* The Olive Grove: Travels in Greece

## NORTH AMERICA

Alaska • Backpacking in Alaska • Baja California • California & Nevada • Canada • Florida • Hawaii • Honolulu • Los Angeles • Mexico • Miami • New England • New Orleans • New York City • New York, New Jersey & Pennsylvania • Pacific Northwest USA • Rocky Mountain States • San Francisco • Southwest USA • USA phrasebook • Washington, DC & the Capital Region

## CENTRAL AMERICA & THE CARIBBEAN

Bermuda • Central America on a shoestring • Costa Rica • Cuba • Eastern Caribbean • Guatemala, Belize & Yucatán: La Ruta Maya • Jamaica

## SOUTH AMERICA

Argentina, Uruguay & Paraguay • Bolivia • Brazil • Brazilian phrasebook • Buenos Aires • Chile & Easter Island • Chile & Easter Island travel atlas • Colombia • Deep South • Ecuador & the Galápagos Islands • Latin American Spanish phrasebook • Peru • Quechua phrasebook • Rio de Janeiro • South America on a shoestring • Trekking in the Patagonian Andes • Venezuela

*Travel Literature:* Full Circle: A South American Journey

## ANTARCTICA

Antarctica

## ISLANDS OF THE INDIAN OCEAN

Madagascar & Comoros • Maldives • Mauritius, Réunion & Seychelles

## AFRICA

Africa - the South • Africa on a shoestring • Arabic (Moroccan) phrasebook • Cape Town • Central Africa • East Africa • Egypt • Egypt travel atlas • Ethiopian (Amharic) phrasebook • Kenya • Kenya travel atlas • Malawi, Mozambique & Zambia • Morocco • North Africa • South Africa, Lesotho & Swaziland • South Africa, Lesotho & Swaziland travel atlas • Swahili phrasebook • Trekking in East Africa • West Africa • Zimbabwe, Botswana & Namibia • Zimbabwe, Botswana & Namibia travel atlas

*Travel Literature:* The Rainbird: A Central African Journey • Songs to an African Sunset: A Zimbabwean Story

# MAIL ORDER

Lonely Planet products are distributed worldwide. They are also available by mail order from Lonely Planet, so if you have difficulty finding a title please write to us. North American and South American residents should write to Embarcadero West, 155 Filbert St, Suite 251, Oakland CA 94607, USA; European and African residents should write to 10a Spring Place, London NW5 3BH; and residents of other countries to PO Box 617, Hawthorn, Victoria 3122, Australia.

## NORTH-EAST ASIA

Beijing • Cantonese phrasebook • China • Hong Kong • Hong Kong, Macau & Guangzhou • Japan • Japanese phrasebook • Japanese audio pack • Korea • Korean phrasebook • Mandarin phrasebook • Mongolia • Mongolian phrasebook • North-East Asia on a shoestring • Seoul • Taiwan • Tibet • Tibet phrasebook • Tokyo

*Travel Literature*: Lost Japan

## MIDDLE EAST & CENTRAL ASIA

Arab Gulf States • Arabic (Egyptian) phrasebook • Central Asia • Central Asia phrasebook • Iran • Israel & the Palestinian Territories • Israel & the Palestinian Territories travel atlas • Istanbul • Jerusalem • Jordan & Syria • Jordan, Syria & Lebanon travel atlas • Lebanon • Middle East • Turkey • Turkish phrasebook • Turkey travel atlas • Yemen

*Travel Literature:* The Gates of Damascus • Kingdom of the Film Stars: Journey into Jordan

## ALSO AVAILABLE:

Travel with Children • Traveller's Tales

## INDIAN SUBCONTINENT

Bangladesh • Bengali phrasebook • Delhi • Hindi/Urdu phrasebook • India • India & Bangladesh travel atlas • Indian Himalaya • Karakoram Highway • Nepal • Nepali phrasebook • Pakistan • Rajasthan • Sri Lanka • Sri Lanka phrasebook • Trekking in the Indian Himalaya • Trekking in the Karakoram & Hindukush • Trekking in the Nepal Himalaya

*Travel Literature:* In Rajasthan • Shopping for Buddhas

## SOUTH-EAST ASIA

Bali & Lombok • Bangkok • Burmese phrasebook • Cambodia • Ho Chi Minh City • Indonesia • Indonesian phrasebook • Indonesian audio pack • Jakarta • Java • Laos • Lao phrasebook • Laos travel atlas • Malay phrasebook • Malaysia, Singapore & Brunei • Myanmar (Burma) • Philippines • Pilipino phrasebook • Singapore • South-East Asia on a shoestring • South-East Asia phrasebook • Thailand • Thailand's Islands & Beaches • Thailand travel atlas • Thai phrasebook • Thai audio pack • Thai Hill Tribes phrasebook • Vietnam • Vietnamese phrasebook • Vietnam travel atlas

## AUSTRALIA & THE PACIFIC

Australia • Australian phrasebook • Bushwalking in Australia • Bushwalking in Papua New Guinea • Fiji • Fijian phrasebook • Islands of Australia's Great Barrier Reef • Melbourne • Micronesia • New Caledonia • New South Wales • New Zealand • Northern Territory • Outback Australia • Papua New Guinea • Papua New Guinea phrasebook • Queensland • Rarotonga & the Cook Islands • Samoa • Solomon Islands • South Australia • Sydney • Tahiti & French Polynesia • Tasmania • Tonga • Tramping in New Zealand • Vanuatu • Victoria • Western Australia

*Travel Literature:* Islands in the Clouds • Sean & David's Long Drive

# THE LONELY PLANET STORY

Lonely Planet published its first book in 1973 in response to the numerous 'How did you do it?' questions Maureen and Tony Wheeler were asked after driving, bussing, hitching, sailing and railing their way from England to Australia.

Written at a kitchen table and hand collated, trimmed and stapled, *Across Asia on the Cheap* became an instant local bestseller, inspiring thoughts of another book.

Eighteen months in South-East Asia resulted in their second guide, *South-East Asia on a shoestring*, which they put together in a backstreet Chinese hotel in Singapore in 1975. The 'yellow bible', as it quickly became known to backpackers around the world, soon became *the* guide to the region. It has sold well over half a million copies and is now in its 9th edition, still retaining its familiar yellow cover.

Today there are over 240 titles, including travel guides, walking guides, language kits & phrasebooks, travel atlases and travel literature. The company is the largest independent travel publisher in the world. Although Lonely Planet initially specialised in guides to Asia, today there are few corners of the globe that have not been covered.

The emphasis continues to be on travel for independent travellers. Tony and Maureen still travel for several months of each year and play an active part in the writing, updating and quality control of Lonely Planet's guides.

They have been joined by over 70 authors and 170 staff at our offices in Melbourne (Australia), Oakland (USA), London (UK) and Paris (France). Travellers themselves also make a valuable contribution to the guides through the feedback we receive in thousands of letters each year and on our web site.

The people at Lonely Planet strongly believe that travellers can make a positive contribution to the countries they visit, both through their appreciation of the countries' culture, wildlife and natural features, and through the money they spend. In addition, the company makes a direct contribution to the countries and regions it covers. Since 1986 a percentage of the income from each book has been donated to ventures such as famine relief in Africa; aid projects in India; agricultural projects in Central America; Greenpeace's efforts to halt French nuclear testing in the Pacific; and Amnesty International.

*'I hope we send people out with the right attitude about travel. You realise when you travel that there are so many different perspectives about the world, so we hope these books will make people more interested in what they see. Guidebooks can't really guide people. All you can do is point them in the right direction.'*

– **Tony Wheeler**

## LONELY PLANET PUBLICATIONS

**Australia**
PO Box 617, Hawthorn 3122, Victoria
tel: (03) 9819 1877  fax: (03) 9819 6459
e-mail: talk2us@lonelyplanet.com.au

**USA**
Embarcadero West, 155 Filbert St, Suite 251,
Oakland, CA 94607
tel: (510) 893 8555  TOLL FREE: 800 275-8555
fax: (510) 893 8563
e-mail: info@lonelyplanet.com

**UK**
10a Spring Place,
London NW5 3BH
tel: (0181) 742 3161  fax: (0181) 742 2772
e-mail: lonelyplanetuk@compuserve.com

**France:**
71 bis rue du Cardinal Lemoine, 75005 Paris
tel: 1 44 32 06 20  fax: 1 46 34 72 55
e-mail: 100560.415@compuserve.com

**World Wide Web: http://www.lonelyplanet.com**
or *AOL keyword: lp*